Perspectives on Mendelssohn

Perspectives on Mendelssohn
Essays in Musicology for R. Larry Todd

Edited by Anna Harwell Celenza and Katharina Uhde

This publication was funded in part by Johns Hopkins University and
Valparaiso University (USA)

First published as Anna Harwell Celenza, Katharina Uhde: *Unity in Variety.
Essays in Musicology for R. Larry Todd*
Vienna, Hollitzer Verlag, 2024
© Hollitzer Verlag, Wien 2024

Cover credit: Library of Congress, Music Division
Layout: Nikola Stevanović

Published by State University of New York Press, Albany
© 2026
All rights reserved
Printed in the United States of America

No part of this book may be used or reproduced in any manner whatsoever without written permission. No part of this book may be stored in a retrieval system or transmitted in any form or by any means including electronic, electrostatic, magnetic tape, mechanical, photocopying, recording, or otherwise without the prior permission in writing of the publisher.

Links to third-party websites are provided as a convenience and for informational purposes only. They do not constitute an endorsement or an approval of any of the products, services, or opinions of the organizzation, companies, or individuals. SUNY Press bears no responsibility for the accuracy, legality, or contents of a URL, the external website, or for that of subsequent websites.

EU GPSR Authorised Representative:
Logos Europe, 9 rue Nicolas Poussin, 17000, La Rochelle, France
contact@logoseurope.eu

For more information, contact State University of New York Press, Albany, NY
www.sunypress.edu

Library of Congress Cataloging-in-Publication Data

Names: Celenza, Anna Harwell, editor | Uhde, Katharina, editor
Title: Perspectives on Mendelssohn : essays in musicology for R. Larry Todd
/ edited by Anna Harwell Celenza and Katharina Uhde.
Description: Albany : State University of New York Press, 2026. |
Includes bibliographical references and index.
Identifiers: LCCN 2025023987 | ISBN 9798855805352 (paperback) | ISBN
9798855807080 (ebook) | 9798855805369 (PDF)
Subjects: LCSH: Mendelssohn-Bartholdy, Felix, 1809-1847--Criticism and
interpretation | Hensel, Fanny Mendelssohn, 1805-1847--Criticism and
interpretation | Music--19th century--History and criticism
Classification: LCC ML410.M5 P37 2025 | DDC 780.92/2--dc23/eng/20250520
LC record available at https://lccn.loc.gov/2025023987

ACKNOWLEDGEMENTS

We would like to express our gratitude to the wonderful contributors in this volume whose unfailing encouragement we felt throughout the process of editing this Festschrift. Our special thanks go to Michael Hüttler at Hollitzer Wissenschaftsverlag. Our gratitude also goes to our respective universities for their meaningful support: Johns Hopkins University (Anna Celenza) and Valparaiso University / LMU Munich (Katharina Uhde). Lastly, we thank R. Larry Todd who brought us all together! Larry: you have contributed greatly toward making our musicological orbit a respectful, friendly, and stimulating space. We all come from different disciplines within musicology, and in one way or another you have enriched our lives and work as a mentor, adviser, friend, colleague, pianist, co-author, and the world's finest Mendelssohnian.

Together with all the contributors assembled here, we wish you: musical fulfillment, health and happiness, and continued scholarly curiosity.

Anna Celenza and Katharina Uhde
March 16, 2024

PREFACE

This volume was created in celebration of the great Mendelssohn scholar R. Larry Todd, whose advancements in the study of nineteenth-century music have profoundly shaped musicological research for nearly four decades. Todd's scholarship is made distinctive by his meticulous engagement with archival sources, his insightful analyses of musical texts, and his nuanced understanding of historical and cultural contexts. In his books, articles, music editions, and performances, he demonstrates the benefits of interdisciplinary inquiry and paves the way for a more inclusive and multidimensional understanding of music history and performance practice.

Two of Todd's most significant contributions to music scholarship are the comprehensive biographies *Mendelssohn: A Life in Music*, named Best Biography of 2003 by the Association of American Publishers (ASCAP), and *Fanny Hensel: the Other Mendelssohn*, which received the Nicolas Slonimsky Award from ASCAP in 2011. In these compelling narratives, Todd humanizes the composers through detailed analyses of their compositions and insightful explorations of their personal lives and cultural surroundings. He offers new paths to understanding these musical siblings, and in the case of Hensel, exposes many of the challenges she faced as a composer in the nineteenth century.

Todd has strengthened the performance of Mendelssohn's works through his publication of numerous critical editions, including the oratorios, the Violin Concerto (first and second versions), and the *Lieder ohne Worte*. He has also reconstructed Mendelssohn's third Piano Concerto from the autograph drafts.

In addition to his work on the Mendelssohns, Todd has made substantial contributions to the study of music reception history, piano-related performance practices, and other Romantic composers, such as Robert and Clara Schumann. In each of these fields, he has been an exceptionally generous scholar and colleague. As the editor of the Master Musicians series for Oxford University Press and the Routledge Studies in Musical Genres, he has selflessly sought out and promoted the work of others. He has also participated in numerous successful collaborations, including the recording *Felix Mendelssohn: The Complete Works for Cello and Piano* (2013) with cellist Nancy Green, and the book coauthored with Marc Moskovitz, *Beethoven's Cello: Five Revolutionary Sonatas and Their World* (2018), which was awarded the CHOICE Outstanding Academic Title Award from the American Library Association.

Finally, a word about Todd's role as an educator. Since joining the faculty at Duke University in 1978, he has facilitated the intellectual development of numerous students and emerging scholars, many of whom are represented in the pages of this book. His teaching emphasizes the importance of critical thinking, rigorous research, and ethical considerations involved in historical scholarship. This pedagogical legacy, and the profound depth of Todd's scholarship, has ensured that his influence will continue to be felt in the academic community for years to come. For all these reasons, this book is offered as a token of appreciation from his colleagues, students, and friends.

CONTENTS

ACKNOWLEDGEMENTS	5
PREFACE	7
NOTES ON CONTRIBUTORS	13

I. THE LIFE AND WORK OF FELIX MENDELSSOHN

1 Singing without Words: Applying Mendelssohn's Aesthetics   19
    DOUGLASS SEATON

2 Mendelssohn's Fugue in E flat (R 23) and the Echo of Beethoven   31
    BENEDICT TAYLOR

3 A Brief Exploration of Mendelssohn's Cellists   39
    MARC MOSKOWITZ

4 Heart's Jewel: The "Sense" of Mendelssohn's Violin Concerto, Op. 64   49
    ROBERT WHITEHOUSE ESHBACH

5 Three Postludes to Mendelssohnian Research   61
    PETER WARD JONES

II. MENDELSSOHN RECEPTION

6 Felix Mendelssohn's English Countenance as Reflected   73
   in London Publications of His Vocal Chamber Music to ca. 1850
    JOHN MICHAEL COOPER

7 Mendelssohn and the Question of German Guilt   95
    LEON BOTSTEIN

8 To the Tomb of Genius: Heinrich, Mendelssohn,   115
   and American Musical Ambition
    MARIAN WILSON KIMBER

9 "That Mesmerizing Mendelssohn Tune":   127
   from Tin Pan Alley to the Silver Screen
    ANNA HARWELL CELENZA

III. FANNY MENDELSSOHN HENSEL

10 Chorale Transformation and Triumph in Felix Mendelssohn's   141
      Sinfonia VI and Fanny Hensel's *Das Jahr*
         CLAIRE FONTIJN

11 From Excavation to Analysis: The Lieder of Fanny Hensel   157
         MARCIA J. CITRON

12 Comprehending Heine in Fanny Hensel's "Schwanenlied"   165
         SUSAN YOUENS

13 "Other" Mendelssohns: The *Lied ohne Worte* op. 19[b] no. 2   181
         ANGELA R. MACE

IV. MENDELSSOHN'S CIRCLE

14 "The Woman for the New Era?":   189
      Johanna Kinkel's Musical Exile in London
         MONIKA HENNEMANN

15 Hearing Forward and Backward: 201
      Clara Schumann's Romance in B Minor *als Denkmal und Ruine*
         EMILY SHYR

16 Schumann Fantasies: Scene and Style in Robin Holloway's Music   213
         PHILIP RUPPRECHT

17 "My Last Hope in this Respect": The Saga of the Swedish   231
      Composer Wilhelm Bauck's Correspondence with Felix Mendelssohn
         KIRSTEN SANTOS RUTSCHMAN

18 Joseph Joachim in Oxford   239
         SUSAN WOLLENBERG

19 "I felt as if I had found a diamond": The Mozart-Enthusiast   249
      Sir William Sterndale Bennett in the Context of His
      Multifaceted Mozart Revival
         WALTER KURT KREYSZIG

20 Ferdinand Hiller and Franz Liszt: A Friendship Built   263
    at the Keyboard, Then Sundered and Never Healed
        JÜRGEN THYM and RALPH P. LOCKE

21 "Becoming" Joseph Joachim, or, "Becoming"   283
    Johannes Brahms, the Composer of Violin Concerto Op. 77 (1878)
        KATHARINA UHDE

Index   299

NOTES ON CONTRIBUTORS

Leon Botstein is President and Leon Levy Professor in the Arts and Humanities at Bard College and music director and principal conductor of the American Symphony Orchestra, founder and music director of The Orchestra Now, artistic codirector of Bard SummerScape and the Bard Music Festival, and principal guest conductor of the Jerusalem Symphony Orchestra. Botstein's scholarship focuses on the intersection of music, culture, and politics since the early 19th century. He is editor of *Musical Quarterly*.

Anna Harwell Celenza is a Professor at Johns Hopkins University, with a joint appointment in creative writing and musicology. She earned her PhD, under Larry Todd's guidance, at Duke University, with a dissertation on the early works of Niels W. Gade. Her primary research interests now involve American music, with an emphasis on jazz.

Marcia J. Citron is the Martha and Henry Malcolm Lovett Distinguished Service Professor of Musicology Emerita at Rice University. Her principal research interests concern opera and the media, gender, women composers, canon formation, and Brahms.

John Michael Cooper is Professor of Music at Southwestern University. He earned his PhD, under Larry Todd's guidance, at Duke University, with a dissertation on Mendelssohn's Italian Symphony. His most recent research activities center on Florence Price and Margaret Bonds.

Robert Whitehouse Eshbach is Associate Professor Emeritus at the University of New Hampshire, where he served as a violinist, conductor, and music historian. A colleague of R. Larry Todd's since their undergraduate days at Yale, Eshbach's principal research interests concern the music of Joachim, Brahms, Mendelssohn, and Schumann.

Claire Fontijn is the Phyllis Henderson Carey Professor of Music at Wellesley College. She earned her PhD at Duke University with a dissertation on Antonia Bembo (1640–1720). Her current research addresses the patronage of music by Barbara Strozzi (1619–77) and chamber music by Fanny Hensel.

Monika Hennemann is Professor of Music and International Dean for the College of Arts, Humanities and Social Sciences at Cardiff University. Her interdisciplinary research focuses on nineteenth-century Lieder, opera, oratorio, and their performance-practices; female composers; and on the music of Mendelssohn, Liszt and Webern.

Walter Kurt Kreyszig, a Deputy Director General of the International Biographical Centre (Cambridge, UK) and a Fellow of the American Biographical Institute (Raleigh, NC), is Professor Emeritus of Musicology at the University of Saskatchewan.

Notes On Contributors

A colleague of R. Larry Todd's since their graduate school days at Yale, Kreyszig has published widely on the Mozart family and nineteenth-century music.

Ralph P. Locke is Professor Emeritus of Music at Eastman School of Music, University of Rochester. A specialist in music and exoticism, he has also published widely in the field of nineteenth-century music and on American musical life and such composers as Aaron Copland, Virgil Thomson, and Leonard Bernstein.

Angela Mace writes on the sibling composers Fanny Mendelssohn Hensel and Felix Mendelssohn, nineteenth-century piano music and German art song, and issues of gender, society, and kinship. She earned her PhD, under Larry Todd's guidance, at Duke University, with a dissertation concerning the formation of the Mendelssohnian Style.

Marc Moskovitz is Principal Cellist of the ProMusica Chamber Orchestra of Ohio. He has also performed and toured with The Boston Pops and The Handel and Haydn Society. In addition to numerous recordings, Moskovitz is the author of several books on music, including *Beethoven's Cello*, written with Larry Todd, which earned the CHOICE Outstanding Academic Title Award.

Philip Rupprecht is Professor of Music at Duke University. Specializing in music of the twentieth and twenty-first centuries, his recent writings address the institutional politics of musical taste, concepts of narrative in operatic drama, the role of the stereotype in the formation of national traditions in music, and agency effects in instrumental music.

Kirsten Santos Rutschman is an organist and church music director in greater Philadelphia. She earned her PhD at Duke University, where she wrote a dissertation on nineteenth-century Swedish music under the supervision of R. Larry Todd.

Douglass Seaton is Warren D. Allen Professor of Music Emeritus at Florida State University. His principal research interests are in the music of Felix Mendelssohn, musical narratology, and relationships of literature and music. He has published scholarly editions of Mendelssohn's *Lobgesang* and *Elias* (Bärenreiter). His more recent work has dealt with Mendelssohn aesthetics.

Emily Shyr is a graduate student at Duke University, where she is completing a dissertation, under Larry Todd's guidance, titled "The Romantic Sublime in the Late Works of Franz Schubert." In addition to her scholarly interests, she is an accomplished oboist.

Benedict Taylor is Professor of Music at the University of Edinburgh, co-editor of *Music & Letters* and general editor of CUP's *Music in Context* series. His work focuses on the music of the late eighteenth to twentieth centuries, analysis, and philosophy.

Jürgen Thym is Professor Emeritus of Music at Eastman School of Music, University of Rochester. He has published books and articles on a range of musical figures, from Kirnberger, Schumann, and Brahms to Schoenberg and Kurt Weill.

Katharina Uhde, a specialist on 19th-century music, is Akademische Oberrätin at LMU Munich and an Associate Professor of Music at Valparaiso University, IN. She earned her PhD under Larry Todd's supervision with a dissertation on Joseph Joachim. As a violinist she has won prizes in competitions, released several CDs, and has recorded music by Joseph Joachim.

Peter Ward Jones served for four decades as the head of the Music Section of the Bodleian Library, where his responsibilities included curatorship of the Library's remarkable Mendelssohn collection. Other scholarly interests include eighteenth-century English music and the history of music publishing.

Marian Wilson Kimber is Professor of Musicology at the University of Iowa. Her publications explore issues surrounding biography, gender, compositional process, musical reception, and relationships between music and the spoken word. Her recent research examines the influence of women's organizations on American music.

Susan Wollenberg is Professor of Music Emerita at the University of Oxford and Fellow Emerita of Lady Margaret Hall. She has published widely on topics including keyboard music, the music of Schubert, social history of music in Britain, and women composers.

Susan Youens is Professor Emerita of Music at Notre Dame University. A prolific scholar, her research focuses on on German song, with a focused interest in the music of Franz Schubert and Hugo Wolf.

I. THE LIFE AND WORK OF FELIX MENDELSSOHN

1. SINGING WITHOUT WORDS: APPLYING MENDELSSOHN'S AESTHETICS

Douglass Seaton

WORDS ABOUT SONGS WITHOUT WORDS

Mendelssohn's songs without words raise—and raised already for the composer himself—issues in musical aesthetics.[1] Because the oxymoronic genre name suggests an implicit but unheard poetic text, these pieces have provoked questions about the relationship between music and words. Because they evoke a singer, they also generate ideas about speakers and listeners.

In a general sense Mendelssohn's songs without words belong to the category of the character piece, the instrumental equivalent of the lyric poem.[2] They have a different outlook, however, from those of either their Baroque predecessors or the cycles of pieces composed at about the same time by Schumann. While the aesthetic assumptions of the Baroque character piece would claim that it evokes the affect arising from or at any rate attached to its topic, in the songs without words Mendelssohn had something quite different in mind. Mendelssohn's songs without words also do not form themselves into plotted cycles *à la* Schumann. They go beyond representing characters by also foregrounding a speaking character, the fictive singer of the song.

As a matter of context, in the mid-1820s Mendelssohn wrote character pieces for the piano, published in a set of seven as *Sieben Characterstücke*, op. 7, in 1827. These pieces reflect the teenager's mastery of counterpoint rather than his proclivity for lyricism. They become character pieces because they bear titles specifying affects. In the following year, as a birthday gift for his sister Fanny, Mendelssohn wrote his first piano song, titled merely *Lied*, as continued to be the case with his later pieces in the genre. With the *Characterstücke* as the immediate predecessors of this first piece in a new style, the composer probably intended self-consciously to differentiate the lyric piano song from the instrumental character piece. The title *Lied* both indicates the vocalism of the style and implies a poetic text, even though Mendelssohn did not offer the kind of paratextual clues to the expressive content that he had provided for the character pieces of op. 7. To call a piano piece "A Song," as Mendelssohn did his second work of this type, written during his first trip to London for the daughter of an English friend and later published as the *Lied ohne Worte* op. 19 no. 4, establishes a fictive world for the music, in which there is a voice and poetry. We do not hear the singer and the text in the score, but they should be present in some way to the listener's imagination.

Schumann, in his 1835 review of Mendelssohn's second book of songs without words (op. 30), constructed a lyric persona from whom the music should be perceived to arise. He imagined himself, every reader whom he addresses, or Mendelssohn at a particular moment of inspiration:

> Who has never sat in the twilight hour at the upright piano (a grand piano seems already too aristocratic) and in the midst of improvising unconsciously begun to sing along a gentle melody? If one were able to join the cantilena to the accompaniment in the hands alone, and most of all, if one were a Mendelssohn, the most beautiful song without words would emerge therefrom. Still more easily, if one were first to compose a text and then delete the words and thus give it to the world. That would not be right, however, but a kind of deception. One would then have to propose a test of the precision of musical expression of feeling, and induce the poet whose words one suppressed to underlay a new text to the composition of his poem. If the latter instance coincided with the former one, it would be a demonstration of the reliability of musical expression....[3]

At first the persona might be any one of us, the reader of Schumann's review or the player of a song without words. Later, however, that persona takes on the figure of a fictive Mendelssohn (the Mendelssohn whom Schumann envisaged as F. Meritis). Additionally, Schumann observed that the genre of textless song raises the question of how convincingly music alone can express feeling.

Mendelssohn certainly never suggested that he imagined himself as the lyric persona for his songs without words. In discussing them, he located the persona in what might seem a rather unexpected place. In his well-known response to Marc André Souchay's attempt to identify the content of some of the songs without words Mendelssohn wrote:

> ...[Words] seem to me so ambiguous, so vague, so easily misunderstood in comparison to a piece of genuine music, which fills one's soul with a thousand better things than words.... What a piece of music that I love expresses to me are not thoughts that are too vague to be contained in words, but rather *too precise.*
>
> Thus I find in all attempts to express these thoughts something right but also in all of them something unsatisfactory, not universal, and so it seems to me with yours, too. That is not your fault, however, but rather the fault of the words, which cannot do any better. If you ask me what I was thinking with regard to it, I tell you: just the song, as it stands. And should I also have had a certain word or certain words in mind in the case of one or another of them, then I could tell them to no other person, because the word does not mean to one person what it means to another, because only the song can say the same thing to one, arouse the same feeling in him, as in another—a feeling that does not, however, express itself by means of the same words.... The word remains ambiguous, and we would still both understand the music correctly.[4]

The main and most explicit point made in this statement is well known. The composer took the position that the ideas and feelings expressed by music are stronger and more specific than those that can be stated in words. In addition to Souchay's letter, he also responded, perhaps unconsciously, to Schumann's proposed experiment. Mendelssohn argued that a right understanding of a piece of music can never be captured in words—even that to try to communicate musical meaning in words can only lead to confusion.

In English publications of the songs without words, there has been a tradition of adding suggestive titles, mostly persisting as repetitions or synonyms.[5] Most are not entirely inconsistent with the characterizations that Souchay proposed. Mendelssohn probably had in mind precisely the observation that for the first published song without words (op. 19b no. 1 MWV U 86) Souchay's response that the music expresses "resignation" is no more or less valid than a typical alternative such as "sweet remembrance." Likewise, to characterize one's response to the next song's (op. 19 no. 2, MWV U 80) emotional content as either "melancholy" (Souchay) or "regret" (popular English editions) might be equally reasonable. Mendelssohn's point is that the difference lies not in the listener's feeling, which must be precisely that of the music, but in the words chosen to describe that feeling. In such cases we can easily accept the differing verbal responses.

In other cases, however, the characterizations are so unalike that they justify Mendelssohn's objection to the entire approach. He would argue that the contrasting characterizations in the case of "lullaby" and "the brook" for op. 30 no. 5, MWA U 97, must reflect the identical feeling, although they employ very different mental images. For some listeners, "the evening star" captures a response to the same feeling in Op. 38 no. 1, MWA U 121 that Souchay describes as "boundless but unrequited love, which therefore turns into longing, pain, sadness, and despair, but always becomes peaceful again." Each listener might find another's verbal interpretation mystifyingly unhelpful, but, as Mendelssohn explains, the problem is not music's indefiniteness but rather that "the word does not mean to one person what it means to another, because only the song says the same thing to one, arouses the same feeling in him, as in another—a feeling that does not, however, express itself by means of the same words."

Mendelssohn rarely gave titles to the songs without words, heading most of them *Lied* in his manuscripts, and less often *Ein Lied ohne Worte*. On the rare occasions when he provided titles, rather than explicating the pieces' expressive content, these identify them according to sub-genres, e.g., Venetian gondola song, evening song, duet, spring song, folk song.[6] His letter to Souchay accepts that most listeners would recognize the hunting song genre. The "Funeral March" (Trauermarsch), op. 62 no. 3, MWA U 177, does not take its genre title from Mendelssohn himself, but to the extent that the name identifies a genre it is not inconsistent with his practice.[7]

More significant in Mendelssohn's aesthetic than the uselessness of words to capture music's meanings is the confidence that the feeling is immanent in the music, and the listener necessarily experiences the feeling as her or his own. That Mendelssohn granted the understanding of the work to the listener is clear in his letter to Josephine von Miller of 30 January 1833, regarding an unpublished piece that he had written out for her (MWV U 88):

> You want to know from me words to the little song in A major that I left behind with you. But how could I begin to discover such things for it? For this is exactly the main issue with such a song without words, that each person thinks of one's own words and one's own sense in it and sets it for oneself with one's own words. I have indeed done this, too, but only very disjointedly, here and there just one word on one note, then again a cluster of notes without any words, then again words with no sense—and that I may certainly not write for you in such a fashion, particularly when it properly achieves the sense. Therefore just discover the verses for yourself; I certainly know that you understand the meaning, even if you deny it or, to put it in your words, "despite all modesty," and if you should not know it, then the entire song is useless and unsuccessful. I would then promise solemnly to bring you a better one this fall, that would articulate its state of mind more clearly than this one perhaps does.[8]

Although Mendelssohn refused to supply words to the piano Lied, he believed that Fräulein von Miller must understand the music, and undoubtedly he would hope this for every listener. Further, his assurance that she understands the piece's meaning (*die Bedeutung verstehen*) leads to the corollary that the song must be unsuccessful if she does not know (*wissen*) that meaning or, in the earlier part of the discussion, its sense (*Sinn*). To succeed, the song should clearly express its state of mind (*seine Stimmung aussprechen*). Mendelssohn never says that the goal is to communicate the composer's (or anyone else's) thoughts or feelings to the listener. What he does say is that, when one hears music, the piece articulates something that the listener knows.

If the piece actually articulates something the hearer knows, then when one truly hears the music, one must fictively identify with the singer of the (wordless) song, the speaker in one's own poetic moment. Schumann's flight of fancy was not so far wrong—it is entirely consistent with Mendelssohn's aesthetic to hear Mendelssohn's songs without words by imagining them coming from oneself. Verbal responses would reflect (but necessarily distort) the listener's thought or emotion, immanent within the music.

Frieder Reininghaus astutely observed that the songs without words represent a specifically intimate and personal instance of musical experience. His insight would apply to all the songs without words: "completely individualized for the pianist alone, for a hermetically closed off, private sphere. To be sure, Mendelssohn's piano work is speechless in a conceptual sense; nevertheless, it enables [*vermag*, perhaps even in the sense of inducing] discourse."[9] The musical content belongs to the individual playing and hearing the song, either in the absence of or possibly in disregard for anyone else. The music emerges as the utterance of the individual who experiences it.

APPLICATION

Assuming such an intimate experience of a song without words, in which the listener (i.e., Schumann's twilight pianist) experiences the music as expressing her own feeling, yet acknowledging that one can never capture that content in words, how might we approach what Mendelssohn calls the piece's sense (*Sinn*)? The following case study examines the Song without Words op. 53 no. 2, MWV U 109, which Souchay characterized as "longing." English publications have titled it "The Cloud" or "The Fleecy Cloud(s)," and one modern CD release[10] calls it "Widmung" (dedication; Mendelssohn sent an autograph score to Clara Schumann). These observations consider the piece's expressive elements for player and listener but avoid translating, characterizing, or interpreting them in words. The intention here is not to identify in words the sense of the music but to foreground the ways in which one representative, modest, but meaning-charged piece manifests that sense.

Such an analysis must be phenomenological, observing the expressive materials of the music as it flows through experience. For that reason, we begin not with a schematic overview of the piece but at the beginning. To be sure, a mere blow-by-blow list of musical details also accomplishes nothing. I hope instead to observe how one might experience the features of the piece that guide one's understanding of it, or—to put it another way—how Schumann's twilight extemporization might unfold, attending to the devices that determine the sense (*Sinn*) that one knows (*weiß*) in the music.

The first five measures (Example 1) simply play through the basic chord functions in E♭, I – I6 – ii7 – V7 – I. Such a conventional progression contributes nothing unusual to a distinctive meaning. From the opening beat, however, the accompaniment rhythm, repeated-chord triplets in an allegro 3/4, requires from the pianist, and therefore establishes, persistent energy. Because the melody employs duplet rather than triplet motion, the accompaniment rhythm recedes to a rapid pulsation but is not the governing rhythmic subdivision. The melodic line unfolds (or Schumann's player in her state of reverie unfolds it) by playing with the triadic outline, deploying non-chord tones in various ways. Over the first two measures of E♭ the melody rises from G4 through B♭4 to E♭5. The spaces between the tones of the triad are filled by passing tones, chromatically through A♭4 and A♮4, then diatonically through C5 and D5. Thus the rate of melodic ascent accelerates, supported by a natural crescendo. The phrase climaxes on the downbeat of measure 3 with an appoggiatura G5, played sforzando and tenuto over the arrival of the F-minor seventh chord. At that moment the player feels the skip from her third finger on E♭ to the fifth on G, reaching both the limit of her hand and the peak of the phrase's ambitus. She feels the "overshot" effect that arises because rather than continuing scalewise from E♭5 to F5, the melody skips to the G5. The resolution of the appoggiatura then redirects the line downward, with a diminuendo to the end of the phrase. Over the ii7 harmony the melody passes through the chord tones F5 and E♭5 and the non-chord tone D5. With the arrival of V7 in measure 4 the non-chord tones occur on the strong beginning of each beat: C5 as an appoggiatura or accented passing tone to B♭4, A♮4 as a chromatic accented passing tone to A♭4 (the reverse of its first occurrence in measure 1), and still more intensely, C5 as a free non-chord tone before the return to A♭4,[11] slipping back to G4, played piano, as the third of the tonic harmony on the downbeat of measure 5.

Example 1, Mendelssohn, *Lied ohne Worte*, op. 53 no. 2, MWV U 109, mm. 1-5.

This opening phrase produces its emotive content from the integration of the conventional harmonic progression in E♭, the melody line's rhythmic independence from the rapid beat subdivisions in the accompaniment, the arched melodic contour with its dynamic support, the move from chromaticism to diatonicism to the thrill of the skip to the appoggiatura G5 at the peak and the relaxing return, along with the distinctive usage of non-chord tones, both in the pairing of successive passing tones in the upward gesture and in the emphasis on various types of dissonances on the beats in the descent. For the player, sources of the phrase's content include the necessary energy for the pulsing accompaniment, the rhythmic detachment of her right-hand line from that pulse, and the easy, natural way in which the melodic line fits under her right hand in closed positions.

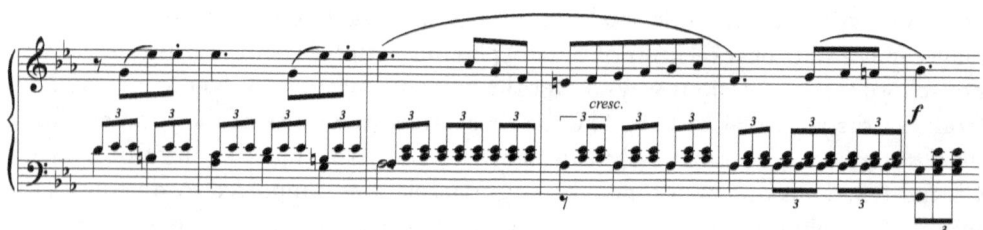

Example 2, Mendelssohn, *Lied ohne Worte*, op. 53 no. 2, MWV U 109, mm. 5b-10.

The succeeding phrase brings new effects (Example 2). The right hand begins with a leap from G4 to E♭5 and three-fold repetition of that upper note, and this melodic halting motive is repeated (as a hesitation due to indecision, in a pause for reflection, or for emphasis?) before the melody proceeds. Meanwhile, the left hand momentarily takes on a faster harmonic rhythm than its single chord per measure up to this point, using a changing-tone motion in the lowest voice that draws attention to the harmony's course from E♭ through C minor to A♭. It then settles on the subdominant and ii6/5 for two measures, then the V4/2 over the continuing A♭3 in the bass. The melody of measures 7 and 8 outlines the F minor seventh, first descending in arpeggiated motion from E♭5 to F4, then in a crescendo through a rising scalar gesture with non-chord tones on the beats, recalling the accented dissonant notes in measure 4 but in the opposite melodic and dynamic direction, so that the descending-ascending contour here inverts the arch that made up the melody of the first four measures. Although the rhythmic sensation between the hands and the comfortable hand positions are of the same sort as in the first measures, the overall expressive content both complements and contrasts with what came before.

The end of measure 9 relaunches the chromatic rise of measure 1, and the resolution to I6 continues to a repetition of the first phrase. There are only slight alterations to the music of measures 2–7 in measures 10–15, but the end of the passage brings a striking close to this first part of the piece. At measure 16 the music compresses the ii6/5 and V7 of measures 8–9. Measures 18–19 form a cadential progression through vi, IV, and ii, each intensified by a preceding applied dominant, at two beats for each unit, creating a hemiola that accelerates in relation to the 3/4 meter of the piece itself (Example 3). The harmonic acceleration is matched in the melody by a descending sequence in groupings of four eighth notes. The non-chord tones in the sequential figure, appoggiaturas, fall regularly on the first eighth note of four, i.e., in an accented position that reinforces the hemiola. The melodic descent is scalar but embellished, and the patterns lie easily under the player's fingers (4 3 2 1 4 3 2 1 . . .). At measure 20 the triplets in the accompaniment and the duplets in the melody come to a halt, and a simple, chorale-style cadence arrives on E♭ in measure 21.

Example 3, Mendelssohn, *Lied ohne Worte*, op. 53 no. 2, MWV U 109, mm. 17-21.

To some extent, this passage might seem to sum up the means that generate the expression of the entire song so far, unnamable as it is—and, it should be emphasized, unnamed here. What the player or listener feels is the composite, within a fluent pianistic idiom, of rhythmic juxtapositions, simple and strong harmonic and melodic motion, rising and falling gestures with reinforcing dynamics, and emphasis on strong-beat dissonances in the melodic line.

In the continuation these features persist, but additional impulses emerge. Beginning at the end of measure 21 the left hand takes a much more active part in presenting the leading melodic material, setting up dialogue with the right. In measures 23–29 the ruling harmony is F, the root of the ii and ultimately V/V in the overall key of E♭ (Example 4). The treatment of non-chord tones in measures 26–28 stands out. The right-hand part forms a pianistically comfortable descending sequence by thirds, in which the entire pattern begins in measure 26 as dissonant against the F minor triad: B♭5 G♭5 E♭5 D♭5. As the sequence falls, it becomes less dissonant—in measure 27 G♭5 E♭5 C5 B♭4, where the C belongs to the triad; and in measure 28 it is still less so, E♭5 C5 A♭4 G♭4, with both C and A♭ as chord tones. The minor mode takes over, with cadences in E♭ minor at measure 33 and in A♭ minor in 41. The key of E♭ minor is reestablished by a 6/4 over B♭ embellished or deferred by the iv6, and diminished sevenths on A and D lead to a return of the opening at measure 50. However vexing it might have seemed to claim—or even attempt—to characterize in words the song's first twenty measures, the next thirty measures will have both intensified the feeling and made it more complex.

Example 4, Mendelssohn, *Lied ohne Worte*, op. 53 no. 2, MWV U 109, mm. 26-29.

The opening music returns, *dolce*, leading into measure 50. Rather than recapitulate the first part of the song completely, the music skips from measure 7 to measure 16. The coda, which occupies sixteen measures, relies on only the ii (or V/V), V, and I harmonies. The three-eighth-note lead-in gestures in the bass participate in a duet with a narrow-range melody in mostly quarter notes in the top voice. The melodic activity decelerates and devolves into a repetitious E♭4 embellished by changing notes F4 and D4, except that the third statement substitutes for the F4 an unexpectedly active dotted-eighth/sixteenth-note rhythm and leap to A♭4. As the middle of the piece constituted intensification, the coda offers relaxation both harmonically and melodically.

The final tonic arrival comes in measure 73 (Example 5). At this point the piece's opening ascent returns once more, now over the persistent root-position E♭ chord. Notably, the fifth-finger G5, the characteristic dissonant appoggiatura of measure 3 and its recurrences, now comes as a chord tone. Freed from the need to resolve, it simply hangs for two measures above the decelerating pulses of the triad in the left hand. The penultimate measure produces an interesting effect, especially for the pianist, as the pedal is held down during three iterations of the E♭ triad, notated as eighth notes separated by eighth rests. At the last note of the piece the sustained G5 is superseded by E♭5, supported only by E♭2 in the bass, with the tonic triad (as well as the G5?) still kept reverberating by the pedal, under a fermata. The fictive extemporizing pianist at dusk—under no obligation to proceed to the next piece on a recital, and without an audience impatient to applaud—might decide that the fermata should extend as long as the sound is still audible, perhaps even longer.

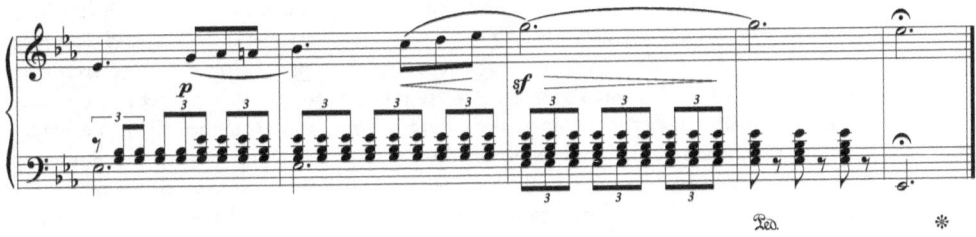

Example 5, Mendelssohn, *Lied ohne Worte*, op. 53 no. 2, MWV U 109, mm. 73-77.

Mendelssohn's *Lied* in E♭ is replete with meaningful features—i.e., *Sinnvoll*—and its emotive content, both precise and unmistakable, is exactly determined by the array of specific components in the music, unfolded in just over two minutes. The listener or player cannot help but feel the piece's sense (*Sinn*). To just the extent that the music is explicit, however, it absolutely resists translation or even paraphrase in a verbal medium. Simply hearing and paying attention to this music should make obvious the futile vagueness and inadequacy of words like "longing" or titles like "The fleecy clouds."

To be sure, Mendelssohn accepted, however ambivalently, that individual listeners would respond with words to the music's expression of feelings (i.e., the listeners' own feelings). In fact, he knew several instances of this, and even left a few of his own.[12] Yet one comes away from these settings with the sense that Mendelssohn's judgment holds up very well—the results might amount to sincere individual responses to the music, but in no sense do they suffice to identify its content.

A convinced Mendelssohnian will believe that this principle applies not only to Mendelssohn's works but to any music. One can certainly argue that we should listen to different music with different aesthetic presuppositions. Nevertheless, the composer wrote to Souchay not just about the songs without words nor about his own music. He claimed to be writing about "What *a piece of music that I love* expresses to me." What does it express? Johann Peter Lyser, who himself once attempted to write words to some of Mendelssohn's piano songs, put it best: "Mendelssohn's songs without words would more correctly be described as '*feelings for which there are no words.*'"[13] This might sound frustrating, but Mendelssohn would insist that a perceptive listener knows the sense of the music, as he put it in his letter to Josephine von Miller. As listeners we know the feeling directly as our own. We experience the song as its fictive speaker.

1. On the aesthetics of the songs without words, see Thomas Christian Schmidt, *Die ästhetischen Grundlagen der Instrumentalmusik Felix Mendelssohn Bartholdys* (Stuttgart: M & P Verlag für Wissenschaft und Forschung, 1996), 285–300. Frieder Reininghaus, "Studie zur bürgerlichen Musiksprache Mendelssohns 'Lieder ohne Worte' als historisches, ästhetisches und politisches Problem," *Die Musikforschung* 28/1 (January–March 1975): 34–51, situates the songs without words as both a key to Mendelssohn's oeuvre and a signpost for nineteenth-century music after his first collection of these pieces appeared in 1830.
2. The lineage of the songs without words was outlined briefly by Louise and Hans Tischler, "Mendelssohn's *Songs without Words*," *The Musical Quarterly* 33/1 (January 1947): 2. The character piece dates back to the Baroque, the keyboard *ordres* of Couperin representing the most prominent examples. Couperin's and Rameau's works illustrate music based on specific people, character "types" taken from the theater or other public entertainment, and even animals or mechanical devices. Schumann's *Carnaval* belongs to this tradition, since it includes real or pseudonymous characters, fictional personalities, and ball-costumed figures. For a discussion of the plotting of Schumann's *Papillons*, see Eric Frederick Jensen, "Explicating Jean Paul: Robert Schumann's Program for *Papillons*, Op. 2," *19th-Century Music* 22/2 (Fall 1998): 127–43.
3. Robert Schumann, "Felix Mendelssohn, sechs Lieder ohne Worte für das Pianoforte. Zweites Heft," *Neue Zeitschrift für Musik* 2 (23 June 1835): 202.
4. Letter to Marc-André Souchay, 15 October 1842, in Felix Mendelssohn Bartholdy, *Sämtliche Briefe* (Kassel: Bärenreiter, 2008–17), vol. 9, 74.
5. See, for example, Felix Mendelssohn Bartholdy, *Songs without Words* (Boston: F. M. Gilson [ca. 1885]); Felix Mendelssohn, *Songs without Words (Lieder ohne Worte): An Analytic Edition*, ed. Percy Goetschius, intro. by Daniel Gregory Mason (Boston: Oliver Ditson, 1906); and Felix Mendelssohn-Bartholdy, *Songs without Words for the Piano*, ed. Constantin von Sternberg (New York: G. Schirmer, 1915).
6. For original titles, see the entries in the Mendelssohn thematic catalog, Ralf Wehner, *Felix Mendelssohn Bartholdy: Thematisch-systematisches Verzeichnis der musikalischen Werke (MWV)*, Leipziger Ausgabe der Werke von Felix Mendelssohn Bartholdy, Series 13, vol. 1A (Wiesbaden: Breitkopf & Härtel, 2009).
7. So obvious, in fact, that Ignaz Moscheles transcribed it for wind band, and it was used at Mendelssohn's funeral in Leipzig on 7 November 1847. See R. Larry Todd, *Mendelssohn: A Life in Music* (Oxford: Oxford University Press, 2003), 567–68.
8. Felix Mendelssohn Bartholdy, *Sämtliche Briefe*, vol. 3, 114.
9. Reininghaus, 44. Specifically, in discussing the "Funeral march," op. 62 No. 3, MWV U 177, he remarks that although the music invokes an orchestral or wind band scoring, it is nevertheless scored for an intensely individual setting.
10. Felix Mendelssohn Bartholdy, *Songs without Words* (Selection), Péter Nagy, piano (Naxos 8.554055).
11. The C5 here, neither prepared nor resolved in conventional fashion, reflects the importance of dissonances on the beat to the expressive content of this piece. There is obviously no available conventional non-chord tone remaining in the linear motion from Bb4 through Ab4 on the way to G4. To create a dissonance here Mendelssohn had to abandon standard practices for non-chord tones in melodic writing and simply skip up to C5 and back.
12. For relevant discussions of these instances, see Christa Jost, *Mendelssohns Lieder ohne Worte* (Tutzing: Hans Schneider, 1988), esp. 19 fn38, 88–90, 127–33: R. Larry Todd, "'Gerade das Lied wie es dasteht': On Text and Meaning in Mendelssohn's *Lieder ohne Worte*," in *Musical Humanism and Its Legacy: Essays in Honor of Claude V. Palisca*, ed. Nancy Kovaleff Baker and Barbara Russano Hanning (Stuyvesant, NY: Pendragon, 1992), 367–77; John Michael Cooper, "Words without Songs? Of Texts, Titles, and Mendelssohn's *Lieder ohne Worte*," in *Musik als Text*, papers from the International Congress of the Gesellschaft für Musikforschung 1993, Freiburg im Breisgau, ed.

by Tobias Plebuch and Hermann Danuser (Kassel: Bärenreiter, 1998), 2: 341–45; R. Larry Todd, "Mendelssohn's *Lieder ohne Worte* and the Limits of Musical Expression," Chapter 10 of *Mendelssohn Perspectives*, ed. Nicole Grimes and Angela R. Mace (Farnham, Surrey: Ashgate, 2012), 197–222. For a discussion of the application of Mendelssohn's aesthetic position to vocal songs, see Douglass Seaton, "The Problem of the Lyric Persona in Mendelssohn's Songs," in *Felix Mendelssohn Bartholdy: Kongreß-Bericht 1994*, ed. Christian Martin Schmidt (Wiesbaden: Breitkopf & Härtel, 1997), 167–86.

13   Johann Peter Lyser, "Felix Mendelssohn-Bartholdy," *Wiener Musik-Zeitung* 2/154 (24 December 1842), 617–18.

2. MENDELSSOHN'S FUGUE IN E-FLAT (R 23) AND THE ECHO OF BEETHOVEN

Benedict Taylor

My starting point is a passage near the end of Felix Mendelssohn's Fugue in E-flat major, R 23, a piece written in the composer's teens but published only posthumously in 1850 as the last of the Four Pieces for String Quartet, Op. 81. From bar 118 a little phrase in the first violin, descending then ascending by step in graceful manner, briefly materialises over a long dominant pedal, echoed in canon at the interval of a fifth by the second violin at the distance of a bar (Ex. 1). In substance the melodic idea clearly grows from the preceding music, which from bar 90 develops the tail of the opening fugue subject – a falling scalic phrase – into one that falls and then rises. The imitation, however, is new to bar 118, and the idea perhaps registers most clearly for the listener at this comparatively late stage. It does not last for long, either. By bar 124 it is gone; the remainder of the piece dissolves the imitative, contrapuntal writing into quavers freely decorating fragments of the fugal opening that traverse the texture in augmentation and diminution.

Example 1, Mendelssohn, Fugue in E-flat major, Op. 81 No. 4 / R 23 (1827), bb. 118–124

The E-flat Fugue was written in 1827: the manuscript is dated 1 November, thus placing it immediately after the completion of the A minor String Quartet, Op. 13 (finished on 26 October 1827), and a little while before his next essay in the medium, the Quartet in E-flat, Op. 12, written in 1829.[1] No other composition for string quartet has come down to us from Mendelssohn in the years between 1823 and 1837, so chronologically at least, the fugue belongs to the same world as these two early quartets. On the face of it, however, they have little in common. The A minor and E-flat quartets, justly among the most celebrated of the composer's youthful productions, are truly groundbreaking pieces that not only wrestle with the musical implications of Beethoven's late quartets but take musical form and expression into new territory.[2] Whereas Op. 13 is one of the most passionate utterances Mendelssohn would ever write, the air of imperturbable calm the fugue exudes seems to hail from another planet. Hans Keller calls it "an impersonal masterpiece – the only one Mendelssohn ever wrote" – a verdict which is surprising mostly insofar as Keller singles out the piece for comment in the first place.[3]

Indeed, while Opp. 13 and 12 have garnered a modest amount of scholarly attention, the fugue has received rather fragmentary mention if at all. Often the impression conveyed by writers is that it is little more than a contrapuntal exercise, continuing the earlier efforts of the twelve fugues for string quartet from 1821, written before Mendelssohn had even reached his teens, and the fugal finale of the 1823 String Quartet (R 18), also in E-flat major and likewise unpublished by the composer.[4] Unlike the unmistakable Beethovenian orientation of the two quartets Op. 13 and 12 that chronologically surround it, commentators typically assume this piece to be a manifestation of Mendelssohn's "Bachian proclivities," in R. Larry Todd's phrase.[5] For John Horton, writing in 1946, the fugue was "probably written under the influence of Mendelssohn's growing regard for Bach's organ works" – in particular the E-flat fugue usually called "St. Anne" (BWV 552).[6] Friedhelm Krummacher likewise calls up the model of Bach, in his case pointing to the fugues in C, BWV 545 and 846, and E, BWV 878.[7] In some cases Mozart also gets a passing mention, primarily as Mendelssohn's fugal subject reproduces the opening four-note figure used by Mozart in the finale of the "Jupiter" Symphony, K. 551 – a common fugal opening motive, also used by Mendelssohn at the start of his "Reformation" Symphony (1830–2).[8] But Beethoven is rarely brought up in this context – a situation unthinkable for its companion works for quartet in this period.[9]

Mendelssohn, of course, was devoted to Bach in the late 1820s, as he remained throughout his life, and Bach's influence on his music hardly needs to be denied. Still, as we know, and Opp. 13 and 12 readily attest, he was very much under the spell of Beethoven's late music at this time, and therefore the apparent absence of this influence in R 23 makes it slightly uncharacteristic of this stage of his compositional development. Thus received, rather than a progressive stroke of daring, the fugue implicitly comes across as a mildly antiquarian exercise, a retrenchment placed alongside the innovations of Op. 13 and 12. Yet fugal techniques are a defining characteristic of Beethoven's last works, and indeed we need not spend long searching for pertinent fugal comparisons. Most apparent is the opening *Adagio ma non troppo e molto espressivo* of the String Quartet in C-sharp minor, Op. 131, and lo and behold, looking to this movement we find an idea that seems to be an earlier version of Mendelssohn's little phrase discussed above (the similarity is closest in bars 67–70, Ex. 2, where it is presented again in crotchets in canon at the fifth).[10]

Another obvious point of comparison is the *Grosse Fuge*, the original finale of the Quartet in B-flat major, Op. 130, eventually published separately as Op. 133, and again there may be a gentle hint of that work in the dissolution of Mendelssohn's quaver figuration into trills across all four parts in the passage from bars 80 to 87.[11]

Such melodic coincidences might help persuade us that Beethoven was likely a point of reference just as was Bach in Mendelssohn's writing this piece – a justifiable

Mendelssohn's Fugue in E-flat (R 23)

Example 2, Beethoven, String Quartet in C# minor, Op. 131 (1826), i, bb. 67–71

corrective, perhaps, to the limited reception of the fugue, if hardly surprising on reflexion. We know Mendelssohn was immersed in the late quartets in this period, and thus the fleeting apparition of a common turn of phrase is not to be wondered at. But this melodic similarity – inadvertent or otherwise (and we should remember that in this period Mendelssohn's musical references to Beethoven are rarely hidden but often take the form of open allusion or tribute) – might bring to mind another reference Mendelssohn made to Op. 131, this time a verbal one, contained in a letter to his friend, the Swedish composer and one-time lodger in the Mendelssohn household, Adolf Lindblad. Writing only a few months later, in February 1828, Mendelssohn reveals both his knowledge of Beethoven's opening fugal movement and some of the reasons for his professed admiration of the quartet:

> Also in the C# [minor quartet] there is a similar transition: the introduction – a fugue!! – closes very sombrely in C# major, all the voices having C#; and there enters such a sweet D major (namely the following movement) and such little ornamentation! See, this is one of my points! The relationship of all 4 or 3 or 2 or 1 movements of a sonata to the others and their parts, so that from the bare opening throughout the entire existence of such a piece one already knows the secret (for when the simple D major begins, the two notes, so my heart melts) *that* must go into the music. Help me to put it in.[12]

Mendelssohn's expression is slightly gnomic, but it may be reasonably assumed that he saw the link between the D major that forms the unexpected tonality of the *Allegro molto vivace* second movement and the prominent D natural contained in the equally unexpected real answer of the fugal subject on the subdominant degree in bar 6 of Beethoven's opening *Adagio* (Ex. 3). By drawing attention to the Neapolitan flattened second scale degree this early in the work, Beethoven obliquely prepares the listener for the distant tonal choice of the ensuing movement. D natural forms a "promissory note," in Edward T. Cone's apt characterisation.[13] And for Mendelssohn, this is surely part of the "secret in the music," which links the individual movements to each other and their parts – an example of the cyclic inter-movement relationships he had already been developing in the A minor Quartet the previous autumn, which he goes on to discuss in the following paragraph of his letter to Lindblad.

Example 3, Beethoven, String Quartet in C-sharp minor, Op. 131 (1826), i, bb. 1–8

If one of the reasons Mendelssohn gives for his love of Op. 131 lies technically speaking in its inter-movement relationships – what he singles out as his compositional principle at this time – how might this have a bearing on his own fugal movement for string quartet? Counterintuitive though it may sound, might this E-flat fugue be, or have been conceived as, part of a projected multi-movement work? In the absence of sketches for other quartet movements from this time, this might seem a decidedly unprepossessing avenue to take. The fugue clearly cannot belong with the A minor Quartet, as the tritonal disparity in key only too readily shows. Still, in the coming months Mendelssohn's thoughts were turning to the creation of the quartet in the same key, E-flat major, published as Op. 12 – a work that just like Op. 13 is highly cyclic. And looking to this quartet helps us bring out a potential "secret" locked away in the E-flat fugue.

As Op. 131 has its promissory D natural, so the Mendelssohn fugue has its own notable early harmonic anomaly, a D-flat – flat 7 – prominent in its fugal subject's upward leap in bar 3, implying an early movement towards the subdominant that is rectified by the fugal answer on the dominant (Ex. 4a). This is a common enough ploy, especially in the key of E-flat major: the first prelude in E-flat from Bach's "48" (BWV 852) features another early D-flat in its first bar, Haydn's Piano Sonata in the same key, Hob. XVI:52, plays with this same harmonic template (a version of the "Quiescenza" schema used as an opening gesture), while Beethoven's "Eroica" Symphony turns this same salient pitch enharmonically into C-sharp (perhaps the most famous of all promissory notes in the nineteenth century).[14] Mendelssohn himself had already drawn on this harmonic ploy at the start of his first essay in the quartet genre, the apprentice work of 1823. But the saliency of D-flat also calls to mind the very opening of his Op. 12 quartet (Ex. 4b). In this introduction – long compared with the closely analogous start of Beethoven's "Harp" Quartet, Op. 74, its obvious model – the immediate flattening of the seventh degree destabilises the work's E-flat major from the outset, transforming the tonic into the dominant of the subdominant.

What should we make of this coincidence? In the absence of sketches showing the gestation of Op. 12, and the fact that this quartet already possesses a slow introduction, it would be hard to claim that the 1827 fugue really belongs to this work, as a prototype introductory movement along the lines of Beethoven's Op. 131, tempting though the idea might be.[15] A "phantom cycle" is indeed an enticing

Mendelssohn's Fugue in E-flat (R 23)

Example 4a, Mendelssohn, Fugue in E-flat major, Op. 81 No. 4 / R 23, bb. 1–8

Example, 4b Mendelssohn, String Quartet in E-flat major, Op. 12 / R 25 (1829), bb. 1–4

prospect, but unlikely in this case. Just possibly when he came to write the fugue, hot on the heels of the A minor Quartet at the end of October 1827, Mendelssohn might have been considering it as a potential opening movement of a larger multi-movement cyclic work for string quartet, some of whose ideas – and the "secret" of the early D-flat – would be eventually used in what became Op. 12. But this is pure speculation. Instead, it was Mendelssohn's elder sister, Fanny Hensel, who would take up Beethoven's suggestion more fully in her own E-flat Quartet, whose opening movement – originally written in the autumn of 1829 just after receiving her brother's E-flat quartet through the post – is an *Adagio* with more than a suggestion of Op. 131 in content as well as structural placing as the opening movement of a cyclic design and not merely a slow introduction.[16]

Yet the musical affinity does suggest grounds for bringing this curious, apparently "impersonal" fugal movement more into the orbit of Mendelssohn's other works for string quartet from these years, with their Beethovenian ethos and cyclic concerns. In doing so, it offers an approach to reconsidering the musical and aesthetic backdrop against which it is heard, rescuing the fugue from the relative oblivion into which it has fallen – its implausible posthumous publication as Op. 81 alongside the two movements of the unfinished E major Quartet from 1847 (in E major and A minor, R 34 & 35) and the 1843 *Capriccio* (R 32), whose E minor tonality at least has something in common with those preceding movements, unlike the concluding E-flat fugue, dating from two decades earlier. And most practically, I would propose that R 23 makes a perfect warm up to Op. 12 in any quartet recital. Programmed as

35

a type of parergon to the more substantial E-flat quartet, the secret affinities in the music of the two would be allowed to stand side by side, in productive and teasing juxtaposition.

1 See Ralf Wehner, *Felix Mendelssohn Bartholdy: Thematisch-systematisches Verzeichnis der musikalischen Werke* (Wiesbaden: Breitkopf und Härtel, 2009); the autograph of the Fugue is housed in the Staatsbibliothek Berlin, MN 18. A scan is available online at https://digital.staatsbibliothek-berlin.de/werkansicht/?PPN=PPN856879525, accessed 1 March 2024.
2 See, for instance, my *Mendelssohn, Time and Memory: The Romantic Conception of Cyclic Form* (Cambridge: Cambridge University Press, 2011). Admittedly there are common concerns with fugal procedures between R 23 and the A minor quartet, finished five days earlier, but even here the fugal model in Op. 13 is overtly Beethovenian (the second movement openly alludes to that of Op. 95) and, by the finale, fugal technique is treated with a daring freedom as recitative is transformed into fugue and fugue into recitative (a process prefigured in the slow third movement of Mendelssohn's slightly earlier Piano Sonata in E major, Op. 6 (1826), another work indebted to Beethoven).
3 Hans Keller, "The Classical Romantics: Schumann and Mendelssohn," in H. H. Schönzeler (ed.), *Of German Music: A Symposium* (London: Oswald Wolff, 1976), 213.
4 On the purported relation with the 1823 quartet see Wulf Konold, liner notes to the Melos Quartet recording of Mendelssohn's string quartets, Deutsche Grammophon 415883-2 (1982), 9 (English translation p. 23). On Mendelssohn's contrapuntal exercises, including even earlier fugues for violin and piano, see R. Larry Todd, *Mendelssohn's Musical Education: A Study and Edition of his Exercises in Composition* (Cambridge: Cambridge University Press, 1983).
5 R. Larry Todd, *Mendelssohn: A Life in Music* (Oxford and New York: Oxford University Press, 2003), 487.
6 John Horton, *The Chamber Music of Mendelssohn (The Musial Pilgrim)* (London: Geoffrey Cumberlege / Oxford University Press, 1946), 51–2.
7 Friedhelm Krummacher, *Mendelssohn – der Komponist: Studien zur Kammermusik für Streicher* (Munich: Wilhelm Fink, 1978), 187. The latter two fugues named are from the first and second books of the *Well-Tempered Clavier* respectively.
8 Ibid. Also see Todd, "The Chamber Music of Mendelssohn," in *Nineteenth-Century Chamber Music*, ed. Stephen E. Hefling (New York: Schirmer, 1998), 185.
9 One rare exception is Misha Donat, in his notes to the recording on Decca by the Quatuor Ysaye (473-255-2, 1996), who, prefiguring my argument here, suggests Mendelssohn may have been thinking of Op. 131's opening fugue. I should also draw attention to the fact that the strength of this connection is something that can really be highlighted (or alternatively hidden) in performance: the Ysaye's recording brings it out clearly, more than most other ensembles I have heard.
10 In Beethoven's movement the phrase again grows out of the preceding music, being melodically foreshadowed in bb. 54–6 and later given again in imitation at the sixth, bb. 90–4, both times given in diminution.
11 In several places Beethoven's Op. 133 breaks down into sustained trills across one or more parts; see, for instance, bb. 229–32, 404–14, 511–32, and 688–716.
12 "Auch in dem aus cis ist so ein Ubergang, die Einleitung eine Fuge!! schliest sehr graulich in cis dur alle haben cis; und da kommts mit so einem susem d dur hinein (das andre Stuck namlich) und solch kleinen Verzierung! Siehst Du, das ist einer von meinen Puncten! Die Beziehung aller 4 oder 3 oder 2 oder 1 Stucken einer Sonate auf die andre und die Theile, so das man durch das blose Anfangen durch die ganze Existenz so eines Stuckes schon das Geheimnis wisse (denn wenn

das blose d dur anfangt, die 2 Noten, so ist mir weich um das Herz) *das* mus in die Musik. Hilf mir's hineinbringen." Felix Mendelssohn, letter to Adolf Lindblad, 19(?) February 1828, in Felix Mendelssohn Bartholdy, *Sämtliche Briefe*, ed. Helmut Loos, Wilhelm Seidel et al, 12 vols. (Kassel: Bärenreiter, 2008–17), vol. 1, 141, translation mine.

13   Edward T. Cone, "Schubert's Promissory Note: An Exercise in Musical Hermeneutics," *19th-Century Music*, 5/3 (1982): 233–41.

14   Coincidentally or otherwise, the Bach Prelude – which despite not being a fugue is strongly imitative – also contains a passage (bb. 60–1) that distantly resembles bars 118–23 of Mendelssohn's fugue. The list of works in E-flat major with a prominent early D-flat can easily be extended; see *Mendelssohn, Time and Memory*, 177.

15   The autograph score doesn't let us conclude this too strongly either. The fugue is written out on ten-stave manuscript paper, in landscape format, an unusual choice for Mendelssohn if writing a quartet, which also meant that on pages 1 and 3 he squeezed the notation from four staves onto the bottom two, the two violins and viola and cello sharing a stave.

16   The Adagio is the first of three movements of a projected piano sonata Hensel wrote in the autumn of 1829, the first two of which were later reworked as the opening movements of the string quartet in 1834. The imitative texture is especially prominent in bars 6–9 of Hensel's movement. Hensel's work is discussed more fully in my *Hensel: String Quartet in E flat (1834) (New Cambridge Music Handbooks)* (Cambridge: Cambridge University Press, 2023); on the compositional genesis see further Renate Hellwig-Unruh, "Zur Entstehung von Fanny Hensels Streichquartett in Es-Dur (1829/34)," in Beatrix Borchard and Monika Schwarz-Danuser (eds.), *Fanny Hensel geb. Mendelssohn Bartholdy: Komponieren zwischen Geselligskeitsideal und romantischer Musikästhetik* (Stuttgart: J. B. Metzler, 1999), 121–40.

3. A BRIEF EXPLORATION OF MENDELSSOHN'S CELLISTS

Marc Moskovitz

I first met Larry Todd in 2011, fittingly enough, at a performance of Mendelssohn's *Elijah* at the Duke University Chapel. Upon learning that I was a cellist – I was new to the area and was playing with the orchestra that afternoon – Larry proposed we get together to do some playing. This we were to do often, as it turned out. Before sitting down to make music, however, I invited Larry to join me for breakfast at a local Durham haunt. I wanted to discuss a possible collaboration of a different sort.

Over delicious doughnuts and coffee, I told Larry that I had, for some time, been contemplating writing a book about Beethoven's cello music. Though I regarded this a worthy undertaking, I feared committing myself to another book, particularly in light of Beethoven's well-documented and highly guarded world. Might Larry, with his insider knowledge of Beethoven's piano writing, several acclaimed monographs, and a portfolio of other writings under his belt, care to go in on the project together? I introduced him to Google Docs, where we could meet in the middle to craft a seamless document, whose every chapter would be the product of two passionate writers and lovers of Beethoven's music. Larry embraced the idea wholeheartedly and soon we were off!

I could not have found a more ideal duo partner, for Larry possessed an intense work ethic and encyclopedic knowledge of musical history. By day we played through Beethoven's sonatas and chipped away at the book as time allowed. On more than one occasion, I found myself working well into the night, only to see Larry log on and check my prose, and we always had a good electronic laugh during these midnight sessions. The act of writing typically takes place in a vacuum, but the work and play I shared with Larry during that period made the Beethoven project among my most satisfying.

When I considered my best options for this Festschrift, I thought I might string together a few words about Mendelssohn's cellists, for that was certainly common ground between myself and our man of the hour. And then I recalled that Larry had also cornered that market with his recording and Urtext edition of Mendelssohn's complete works for piano and cello! Thus, it is with deep humility that I hereby contribute a few additional words on the subject, in celebration of one of the most impressive musical thinkers whom I have had the honor – and the pleasure – of knowing.

★ ★ ★

Any consideration of Mendelssohn's cellists must begin at the composer's childhood home, in Berlin's Leipzigerstraße. As is well known, Paul Mendelssohn (1812–1874), Felix's brother, was the cellist for whom Felix wrote both his Sonatas and the *Variations concertantes*, op. 17, though far less about Paul's actual abilities at the instrument have come down to us. It is generally acknowledged that he was, at the very least, a respectable musician, and given the standards set by his precocious siblings, that is about the least we might hope for. However accomplished, Paul ultimately chose to follow in his father's footsteps, pursuing a career in banking, and a little less than two centuries later, we can only speculate as to why this was. Perhaps Paul realized the limits of his abilities, especially considering the astounding talent that surrounded him. Or maybe he simply assumed that the world of finance would provide a more secure living, a decision with which we would be hard-pressed to argue.

Whatever the case, during Felix's formative years, Paul laid down the foundations for the storied chamber music performances in the Mendelssohn home, concerts that unquestionably contributed to Felix's understanding and appreciation of what the instrument had to offer. As a twelve-year-old composing his early string symphonies, it seems logical that Felix would draw on earlier models, and the cello writing in youthful works does just that. His ventures mimic, to a lesser or greater degree, the divertimento style of the previous generation, with bass lines that function mainly as rhythmic timekeepers. Rarely do the cellos share any musical dialogue with the dominant violins.

Three years later, with his First Symphony, Op. 11, not much has changed. One might argue that the bass lines in this C minor score are less challenging still, as Mendelssohn grappled with the demands of a significantly larger orchestral palette. We might easily imagine twelve-year-old Paul occupying himself with the Op. 11's bass lines at house concerts, the challenges of which were likely commensurate with whatever else the young cellist was then studying.

In the fall of 1825, the Octet, Op. 20, appeared, and with it, the remarkable sixteen-year-old Felix left his youth behind. At thirteen, Paul might have been left behind as well, for the demands made by the Octet on both cello parts are exponentially more involved than anything his older brother had yet conceived. Sadly, no surviving records document the work's first in-home performance, so we are left to speculate about the specifics. The first reading may have occurred on or around October 17, 1825—the birthday of Mendelssohn's friend and violin teacher, Eduard Rietz (1802–1832), for whom the Octet was composed. We know that Rietz copied out the parts by hand from the manuscript – likely for this reading – and probably played the first violin part. Whether or not Paul was capable of handling either of the cello parts, at the very least a second cellist would have been on hand. It is possible that Rietz's younger brother, Julius, a budding cellist the same age as Paul and to whom we will eventually return, took part. Regardless, the room likely also included more seasoned players, given Eduard's professional connections and those of the Mendelssohn family. And as he often did in later years, Felix most certainly sat in as a violinist or violist.

It is a curious study to chart Felix's development through the cello and piano works that followed. The *Variations concertantes*, Op. 17, sprang from the year 1829, with Felix now at the ripe age of twenty and his brother Paul, now seventeen, the age when most cellists are beginning to take on sophisticated repertoire. However, beyond the sonatas of Beethoven, there was little such serious cello music available, and this fact would fuel Felix's decision to write sonatas for the instrument in the years to come. But for now, there were his Variations to learn.

Although Felix dedicated the score to his brother, the *Variations concertantes* were, in actuality, a vehicle for the pianist – and for Felix specifically – and the virtuosic nature of piano writing leaves little question that Felix already possessed the technique of a virtuoso. But as a string player, Felix also understood how to write idiomatically for the instrument, and his writing for strings from here on, whether chamber or orchestral, reveals a composer capable of crafting inspired, demanding, and effective parts for them all. The *Variations* reflect a similarly confident hand, yet beyond a few demanding passages, particularly the third variation (*Piu vivace*), the cello writing here swings far more towards the gracious and the lyrical. One can almost hear Paul asking his older brother for something more involved the next time around.

However often the Mendelssohn brothers played through the Variations during these years, certainly the greatest cellist with whom Felix ever appears to have performed the work was Robert Lindley (1776–1855). More than one journalist deemed the Englishman among the greatest, if not *the* greatest, of living cellists, as the following article, from 1824, suggests:

> As a violoncellist, Lindley perhaps can overcome greater difficulties than any performer that ever lived. ... His tone is rich, powerful, and sweet, and his upper notes are most beautiful. ... He introduces, amid most extraordinary difficulties, with a quaint yet elegant humour, popular old airs, and plays them in a style of characteristic simplicity.[1]

Bernard Romberg, among the most celebrated cellists on the continent, heard his English counterpart in London and remarked, "He is the devil," although naturally opinions differed. Fétis opined that "when he sings upon his instrument, he produces a fine tone, and possesses much tact in the management of difficulties; but his style is vulgar and the quality of his tone loses much of its intensity in his ornamental passages."[2]

Lindley's upward trajectory was swift. By the age of 16, the great Giacobbe Basevi, better known as Cervetto, was tutoring him for free, and by the age of 18 he had been appointed principal cellist of London's Italian Opera and was in demand for all the city's major concerts. And when the great double bass virtuoso, Domenico Dragonetti, joined the opera, the two became close working companions.

Mendelssohn visited England for the first time in 1829, a trip that included his now-famous visit to Fingal's Cave and featured the first London performance of his concert overture *A Midsummer Night's Dream*. In all probability, it was by way of Ignaz Moscheles, who had by this time settled in the British capital and with whom Lindley often played, that Mendelssohn made contact with the cello virtuoso, and the pair went on to perform the Variations in concert on several occasions during Mendelssohn's stay. Writing home to Berlin, Mendelssohn remarked on the allure of English women before relating that Lindley accompanied from the page rather well (!) and that his English audience repeatedly praised his music – "how beautiful" – during their performance.

While visiting Vienna in 1830, Mendelssohn crossed paths with Joseph Merk (1795–1852), among the most prominent of Austrian cellists. Merk had recently given the second performance of Beethoven's Triple Concerto, and in 1829 the cellist had received the dedication of Chopin's *Introduction et polonaise brillante*, Op. 3. Indeed, Chopin's score may have been the inspiration behind a collaboration between Merk and Mendelssohn, for during the composer's visit to the Austrian capital, the two teamed up for what Mendelssohn predicted would be a "brilliant" set of variations. While only a piano score in another's hand has come down to us – missing are both Mendelssohn's autograph and Merk's cello part – the results, little more than salon-style fare, were hardly indicative of the composer's more genuine abilities. Six years later Mendelssohn wrote to his mother from Leipzig, complaining of having to perform with Merk for "the seventh time this winter, though it is impossible for me to refuse."[3] Whether the cellist's company or his playing had worn out its welcome, no more music would spring from their mutual association.

It was in 1838, three years after moving to Leipzig, that Mendelssohn next returned to the cello and piano repertoire—or, more accurately, the piano and cello. He also now had several cellists of the Gewandhaus Orchestra at his disposal. At the time of his arrival, the cello section included Friedrich Wilhelm Grenser (1805–1859), who had joined the orchestra in 1823 and would assume the role of the orchestra's principal cellist seven years later. Grenser also figured prominently as a member of the Gewandhaus Quartet, whose longstanding first violinist was Ferdinand David, the celebrated concertmaster of the orchestra. Cellist Johann Andreas Grabau (1808–1884) joined the orchestra in 1828 and remained a member until his death. A student of Friedrich Kummer in Dresden, Grabau was also involved with a private music society led by Friedrich Wieck and thus encountered Robert and Clara Schumann. An early champion of Schumann's chamber music, it was to Grabau that Schumann later dedicated his *Fünf Stücke im Volkston,* op. 102.

Mendelssohn drew on both these cellists for his chamber music. In 1841, for instance, Grenser was invited to join the music director at his home for a morning of chamber music (trios by Beethoven and Mendelssohn). Arguably, however, Mendelssohn turned more often to Grabau. Indeed, in 1836 and 1841, Mendelssohn was joined by Ferdinand David and Grabau in performances of Beethoven's Triple Concerto, op. 56. Grabau's name is also among the first associated with Mendelssohn's B flat Sonata for Piano and Cello of 1838.

A Brief Exploration of Mendelssohn's Cellists

Mendelssohn had begun promising his brother a sonata as early as November 1837, although it was nearly a year later, in October 1838, before the completed manuscript was posted to Paul as a birthday present. When published as his Op. 45, the sonata featured no official dedication although written specifically with Paul in mind. To that end, Mendelssohn appears to have been infatuated with the instrument's lower register, and perhaps Paul's tone specifically. In the sonata's opening theme, for instance, the cello, having begun low on the G string, soon descends still lower, into the bowels of the instrument. Shortly thereafter, the cellist is asked to dispatch rapid passagework, perhaps to make up for what Felix had failed to offer his brother in his earlier Variations. Still, much of this writing is assigned to the darker registers, where it is admittedly difficult to project. Mendelssohn would correct this approach and make significant adjustments when he returned to the duo for his next – and final – cello sonata, Op. 58.

In any event, in October 1838, Mendelssohn wrote to Paul, hoping his B-flat major sonata pleased him and relating that he had recently played through the work several times with Grabau. Yet not long thereafter, in another letter, Mendelssohn confessed that Grabau was whining miserably (*"winselt kläglich"*) about the sonata. We are left to wonder if the Gewandhaus cellist was struggling with Mendelssohn's writing in his instrument's lower registers.

There is no official record of the B-flat Sonata's first performance, but in September 1839, Mendelssohn wrote his mother Lea that the work had been played on a program that also included an Op. 44 Quartets and the Octet, Op. 20, and featured the Müller brothers, a celebrated quartet that had once served the Duke of Brunswick. Although there is no record of Mendelssohn's involvement with the concert, we might assume he appeared as a violinist or violist for the Octet and as a pianist, alongside the cellist August Theodor Müller, for the Cello Sonata. In addition to his work with the quartet, August Müller (1802–1875) was among the most highly respected cello teachers of his day, numbering among his students Bernhard Cossmann, Wilhelm Fitzenhagen, and Robert Hausmann (dedicatee of Brahms's Second Cello Sonata, Op. 99, and the cellist who premiered Brahms's Double Concerto alongside Joachim).

On October 30, 1840, almost two years after corresponding with Paul about his newly composed B-flat Sonata, Mendelssohn informed his brother about yet another cello sonata and inquired when they might play it together. Intensive work on the Sonata in D major commenced only in 1842, however, and the score wouldn't be completed until the summer of the following year. Finally, in May of 1843, Felix wrote his brother that he was headed to Berlin with the cello sonata.[4]

We can only imagine Paul's delight when the pair first played through the manuscript, for the composer had this time struck the perfect balance, achieving the ideal equality of forces that Beethoven had striven for with his magisterial A Major Sonata, Op. 69 (1808). Mendelssohn's piano writing is virtuosic but never domineering, the cello writing luxurious and demandingly robust. Critically, however, it is always situated in comfortable, flattering registers, a fact Mendelssohn alluded to himself: "There is a lot of sound to be drawn from the A string and the work is in D major—certainly two major conditions for cellists."

Although Mendelssohn composed his Op. 58 with Paul in mind, nothing has come down to us about the two having played the work together. Indeed, it appears the sonata was first heard in Leipzigerstraße with Fanny at the piano and cellist Moritz Ganz, who had succeeded Bernard Romberg as the first cellist of the Berlin Hofkapelle. Mendelssohn himself premiered the work in Leipzig with Carl Franz Wittmann (1814–1860), a former student of Joseph Merk in Vienna and whose name was added to the Gewandhaus Orchestra's roster in 1836.

Wittmann remained an active member of the orchestra and the Gewandhaus Quartet for some fifteen years, during which time Mendelssohn often turned to the cellist for critical chamber music performances. These included the 1840 premiere of the composer's D minor Trio, op. 49, with violinist Ferdinand David and Mendelssohn at the keyboard. Three years later Wittmann performed the D major Sonata with Mendelssohn in a Gewandhaus concert that again included a performance of Mendelssohn's Octet. Overshadowed by the Octet performance that featured Mendelssohn on the viola, the *Signale für die musikalische Welt* reported only that the cello sonata was played "with two hearts and one pulse"[5] (*zwei Herzen und ein Schlag*).

Curiously, it was to neither Mendelssohn's brother Paul nor to Carl Wittmann that the Op. 58 was ultimately dedicated. Rather, that honor was given to a celebrated Russian count. Count Mateusz Wielhorsky (1794–1866) served his country in the War of 1812 and retired as a colonel, but music was his true passion. He excelled both as a performer and as one of Russia's most active and important impresarios, sponsoring visits to Russia by Berlioz, Liszt, and Schumann, among others. A student of Romberg, Wielhorsky developed into a cellist of impressive ability – a rare quality among the nobility – who performed alongside musical luminaries such as Liszt and Vieuxtemps. Time and again, Wielhorsky held his own among Europe's musical elite. While entertaining Clara and Robert during their 1844 visit to St. Petersburg, for instance, Clara played Mendelssohn's cello sonatas with the count and later recorded that "Playing with him is like playing with an artist."[6]

Mendelssohn's association with the count dates to at least 1841, when the pair played together at the Mendelssohn home in Berlin. Fanny, who was present, noted that the count "played like a consummate master" although *what* they played went unrecorded. Exactly why Mendelssohn subsequently dedicated his D major Sonata to Wielhorsky remains something of a mystery, though it is clear that the composer, like so many others, was impressed with the count's abilities. In September 1843, in the wake of another visit to Germany by Wielhorsky, Mendelssohn wrote the count, stating "you played the [D major Sonata] so excellently from sight that it belongs to you."[7] No doubt Wielhorky's cello also made a lasting impression. A Stradivarius of uncommon power, the instrument was later generously passed along to his countryman, Karl Davidov. And thus did Wielhorsky's name come to grace the title page of Mendelssohn's D major Sonata, Op. 58, when published by Kistner in 1843.

A Brief Exploration of Mendelssohn's Cellists

The celebrated French cellist Lisa Cristiani (1827–1853) blazed like a meteor across the continent before passing away well before her time. While still in her teens, Cristiani concertized in Paris, Rouen, and Brüssels, then obtained the Duport Stradivarius and set out on a concert tour that took her to Vienna, Linz, and Regensburg, among many other cities. She was a gifted cellist, whose playing appears to have been matched by her physical beauty and personal charm. Cristiani appeared in Leipzig in October 1845, upon Mendelssohn's recommendation, where she performed the lighter fare typical of her programs: Offenbach's *Adagio and Bolero*, a Donizetti *Romanze*, and Schubert's *Ave Maria*. In an age before female cellists were accepted upon the concert stage, Cristiani was a notable exception, performing with elegance and precision. Her appearance in Leipzig fully captured Mendelssohn's attention, no doubt among many others in the audience that evening.

Cristiani's Leipzig association with Mendelssohn was fleeting but indelible, and the fact that she inspired his *Romance sans paroles* – published posthumously as *Lied ohne Worte* – suggests the cellist made a far more lasting impression on the composer than the single passing reference in his letters would suggest. After further travels throughout Germany and northern Europe, the French virtuoso's final years were spent touring extensively throughout Russia. In Siberia, Cristiani contracted cholera and died several days later. She had not yet reached the age of thirty.

Whether or not Cristiani ever became aware of Mendelssohn's captivating *Romance*, it appears to have had one of its earliest performances in England. According to *The Musical Times*, "this melodious little piece, published after the composer's death, was first played in England – if indeed this was not its first public performance anywhere – by Signor Piatti at the Monday Popular Concert of March 30, 1868."[8] And thus we come to another of the cello giants with whom Mendelssohn was associated.

The Bergamo-born Alfredo Piatti (1822–1901) made his European debut in 1843, at a Munich concert under Liszt's direction, after which the celebrated pianist and composer presented Piatti with a magnificent Nicolas Amati cello. The following year, Piatti made his first appearance in England, the country he would come to call home: "I came to this country unknown to everybody, with no friends and no money. Some kind people advised me to go back at once; but I thought London was a rather big place and that I might find a hole for myself as others had done."[9]

Piatti found a place for himself immediately with his London debut, which took place May 31, 1844, at an Annual Grand Morning Concert. For the occasion, Piatti performed a Bach Suite – the exact Suite is not reported, though it was hailed as the first public performance of a Bach Suite in England – and a Kummer Concerto with orchestra, conducted by none other than Felix Mendelssohn. According to *The Musical Times*, the pair had met in the Regent's Park home of Moscheles, where Mendelssohn and the cellist played the former's D major Sonata.[10] Piatti and Mendelssohn were reunited three years later, during what proved the latter's last visit to the country (he would die in Leipzig following several strokes that November). According to Sir George Grove, "One of [Mendelssohn's] latest words on leaving England for the last time (in 1847) were: 'I must write a concerto for Piatti.' He had, in fact, already composed the first movement, but the M.S. seems to have been lost."[11] While no evidence of such a concerto has ever surfaced, cellists continue to lament what might have been.

I would be remiss if I failed to note, albeit briefly, Mendelssohn's association with two more of the most significant cellists of his day. In Paris, he befriended Auguste Franchomme (1808–1884), the cellist for whom Chopin wrote his Cello Sonata. Indeed, it was probably by way of the Polish-born, Paris-adopted pianist that Mendelssohn found himself in the formidable cellist's company, though we do not know if the two ever sat down together to make music.

Such was not the case with the illustrious Belgian cellist, Adrien-François Servais (1807–1866), who joined Mendelssohn for chamber music at the Leipzigerstraße home in Berlin, in January of 1844. The pair appeared again four months later in the Gewandhaus, alongside Ferdinand David, where the celebrated trio dispatched a performance of Beethoven's "Archduke" Trio, Op. 97. The remainder of the program centered around Servais's showstopping compositions, like his *Souvenir de Spa*, enabling the cellist to display his stunning technique.

In closing, I return to the Rietz family, with whom Mendelssohn was so intimately involved since childhood. Cellist Julius Rietz (1812–1877) had been a pupil of both Romberg and Moritz Ganz, and to judge by the demands of his cello music, such as his E-major Cello Concerto, Op. 16, Rietz developed into a cellist of formidable ability. He continued to play throughout his life, including performing with the likes of Ferdinand Hiller and Ferdinand David. But Rietz was eventually drawn increasingly to the worlds of composition and the baton. He followed Mendelssohn to the Düsseldorf Opera, serving as the latter's assistant, and when Mendelssohn left for Leipzig in 1835, assumed the helm of the Opera.

En route to Leipzig, Mendelssohn composed a short, nostalgic cello work for his old friend, an *Assai tranquillo* in B minor, that curiously concludes on the dominant of F sharp. Mendelssohn certainly intended to suggest that true musical closure would only be realized with their eventual reunification, and indeed Rietz went on to assist Mendelssohn at the Lower Rhine Festival of 1839. It was not until 1847, however, the year of Mendelssohn's death, that Rietz was appointed conductor and kapellmeister of the Leipzig Singakademie. Upon Mendelssohn's death, the Dane Niels Gade assumed the podium of the Gewandhaus Orchestra, but when war between Prussia and Denmark broke out a short time later, Gade returned to Copenhagen, and Rietz took over as the orchestra's chief conductor, thus once again following in his old friend's footsteps. Rietz also served as a professor at the Leipzig Conservatory, where he counted Sir Arthur Sullivan among his composition students.

Although a composer of operas, symphonies, and concertos, a gifted cellist, and an esteemed conductor, Rietz is perhaps best remembered as having edited the music of others. Julius and his brother Eduard copied parts for Mendelssohn's historic performance of Bach's *St. Matthew Passion*, so it must have been particularly gratifying for Julius to serve as editor of Bach's masterpiece for the Bach-Gesellschaft Ausgabe and later, to supervise the Breitkopf & Härtel Mendelssohn Gesamtausgabe

(1874–77). Rietz, who died the year of the Gesamtausgabe's conclusion, must have derived particular pleasure when editing the D major Cello Sonata, Op. 58, Felix Mendelssohn's crowing gift to his cello-inspired universe.

1   Anonymous, "Rise and Progress of the Violoncello," *The Quarterly Musical Magazine and Review* vol. 6 No. 23 (1824), 478.
2   *The Harmonicon: A Journal of Music* 11 vols. (1829), VII:219.
3   Felix Mendelssohn-Bartholdy, *Letters of Felix Mendelssohn Bartholdy from 1833 to 1847* (London: Longman, Green, Longman, Roberts & Green, 1864), 102, letter of 18 February 1836 from Felix Mendelssohn to his mother.
4   R. Larry Todd, *Mendelssohn: A Life in Music* (New York, NY: Oxford University Press, 2003), 455.
5   *Signale für die Musikalische Welt* No. 48 (November, 1843), 373.
6   Donald Sanders, *Experiencing Schumann: A Listener's Companion* (Lanham, MD: Rowman and Littlefield: 2016), 91.
7   Ernst Wolff, *Felix Mendelssohn Bartholdy* (Berlin: Harmonie, 1906), 159.
8   *The Musical Times* vol. 48 No. 771 (May 1907), 308.
9   *The Musical Times and Singing Class Circular* vol. 42 No. 702 (August 1901), 534.
10 *The Musical Times* vol. 32, No. 584 (October 1891), 588.
11 Sir George Grove, *A Dictionary of Music and Musicians,* 4 vols. (London: Macmillan and Co., 1984), II:285.

4. HEART'S JEWEL: THE "SENSE" OF MENDELSSOHN'S VIOLIN CONCERTO, OP. 64

Robert Whitehouse Eshbach

Joseph Joachim may never have uttered his most ubiquitously repeated observation:

> The Germans have four violin concertos. The greatest, most uncompromising is Beethoven's. The one by Brahms vies with it in seriousness. The richest, the most entrancing, was written by Max Bruch. But the most intimate, the heart's jewel, is Mendelssohn's.[1]

This dubiously genuine remark occurs nowhere in the Joachim literature. It first appeared in Heinrich Eduard Jacob's 1959 *Felix Mendelssohn und seine Zeit: Bildnis und Schicksal eines Meisters*. There, Jacob claims to have heard Joachim say it more than a half-century earlier, at his 75th birthday celebration in 1906.

Jacob's hitherto-obscure quotation has become a seemingly indispensable constituent of program notes since it entered the Internet echo chamber at the turn of the 21st century. It has at least the ring of authenticity, conveying to modern audiences the weight of Joachim's still-formidable authority. It therefore suits the rhetorical purpose of a program note *captatio benevolentiae*: to establish conditions for the audience's esteem, and to help make the work at hand seem approachable. Nevertheless, for a contemporary audience it sets forth an oddly parochial canon, constrained by nationality, number, genre, composer, and gender, and evaluated as the coin of character against traditional German standards of virtue, stereotypically arrayed from masculine to feminine: great, uncompromising, serious, rich, entrancing, intimate... the "heart's jewel." Has it always and everywhere been heard as such? How should we hear the work today?

Joseph Kerman famously wrote, "repertories are determined by performers, canons by critics."[2] As Kerman elaborated it, this statement is true by definition—yet this commingling of two somewhat specious dichotomies seems cramped.[3] Works have creators (often multiple), and they have audiences who individually and collectively hear and use them according to their own understanding and for their own purposes. As Howard S. Becker pointed out, artworks also have external support systems that are invested in promoting them and "spinning" their meanings.[4] In a very real sense, then, it "takes a village" to produce a significant work of art; the contributions to an artwork's viability, not just of performers and critics but also of many other stakeholders, are inseparably imbricated.

Repertories – and canons – are constantly in flux. The career of Felix Mendelssohn Bartholdy should, above all others, serve as an object lesson in how the reception of a composer's works can vary with time, place, circumstance, and ideology, often for reasons unrelated to the work itself. In our time, the very notion of a reified canon – a body of "timeless" or "universal" "masterpieces" – has become problematic. The issue of inclusion, of determining whose voices are heard and how they are valued, continually calls into question received means and standards of judgement. It is necessary therefore to investigate more broadly the ways in which works enter and hold their place in public discourse—how they become valuable, and even indispensable to us. Understanding this process involves examining the evolving "sense" of particular works, which we may view, in light of that word's notional provenance, as a journey.[5] (The English noun "sense" is thought to be derived from the Proto-Indo-European root "sent"—"to go, to travel, to strive after," or "to find one's way," and is related to the verb "to send.") Accordingly, this essay concerns the "sense" of the Mendelssohn Violin Concerto—not how it came to be, and not what it "is," but how it was sent into the world, and how it found its way.

BEGINNINGS

The chronicle of the Mendelssohn Violin Concerto's genesis – from its first inspiration to its simultaneous publication on 1 June 1845 by Breitkopf & Härtel (Leipzig), Ewer (London), and Ricordi (Milan) – is now authoritatively set forth and well known.[6] Mendelssohn's composition belongs to a special category which we may characterize as "friendship concerto" – concertos composed with a particular performer in mind – though in this case (as opposed to, say, Beethoven's concerto) the performer himself had considerable input as a co-creator of the work.

Despite being an artist of international reputation, the concerto's dedicatee, Ferdinand David (1810–1873) was essentially a local performer. Though the premiere was reported as far away as Paris, the brief notice was due solely to Mendelssohn's reputation—David's name was not mentioned.[7] Moreover, notwithstanding its prestige, the Leipzig Gewandhaus, where David introduced the concerto (13 March 1845), was small—in reality a large salon, accommodating only about 500 people, many of whom would presumably have been personally acquainted with the composer. David gave a second Gewandhaus performance on 23 October under Mendelssohn and played it there for a third and final time on 6 November 1851, under Julius Rietz.[8] He also conducted it twice in the Gewandhaus: on 10 October 1852 with soloist Ferdinand Laub, and again on 15 December 1853 accompanying August Pott.[9]

David was notorious for altering the works he played to suit his taste and technique.[10] His interpretation, unknown to us today, cannot therefore be considered authoritative, and though his influence on the composition itself was considerable, his subsequent impact on performance practice, repertoire- and canon-formation was negligible.

More consequential was the concerto's second performer, David's apprentice and Mendelssohn's protégé, Joseph Joachim (1831–1907). Joachim learned the concerto simultaneously with David, and performed it for the first time on 11 November 1845, under the baton of Ferdinand Hiller in the ballroom of the Hôtel de Saxe, Dresden—the third public performance outright.[11] There is evidence that Joachim's virtuosity influenced the character of the concerto's final movement and it seems plausible that Mendelssohn's esteem for the boy provided a stimulus for bringing the work's long gestation to a close.[12] Joachim's renowned rendition served as a model for generations of violinists throughout the long 19th century, and his written introduction to the work in the Joachim-Moser *Violinschule* has remained an important and influential guide to interpretation (the *Violinschule* itself was a valedictory attempt at canon formation by a performer whose critical skills were second to none).[13]

Half a year after its publication, the concerto began to receive performances outside of Saxony. Joachim's boyhood friend and sometime rival, the 17-year-old Joseph Hellmesberger, Sr. (1828–1893), introduced it in Vienna on 21 December 1845 in a critically acclaimed concert at the Gesellschaft der Musikfreunde, J. B. Schmidl conducting.[14]

Six weeks later, a review appeared in August Schmidt's *Wiener allgemeine Musik-Zeitung* by "Philokales" (Ferdinand Peter Graf Laurencin d'Armond)—not of Hellmesberger's performance, which Laurencin had attended, but of the work as set forth in its published text (available to him, as he bitterly complained, only in piano reduction).[15] The review took the form of an analysis and critique in which Laurencin attempted to provide "a deeper insight into the technical merits of [Mendelssohn's] composition... in order to be able to dwell for as long as possible on the faithful interpretation of the spiritual content peculiar to this violin concerto."[16] Influenced by Hegel's aesthetics, Laurencin describes the character and "Gefühlssituation" of the themes and their formal placement in exposition, episode, and development. The influence of E.T.A. Hoffmann also seems evident in Laurencin's review—in the nature and tone of the discourse, the inclusion of numerous musical examples, the reference to the concerto "in many moments rising to the dignity of a symphony," the opposition of inherent genius ("innewohnenden Genius") to cold, dry, calculation, and the emphasis on harmonic imagination.[17]

Laurencin's review created a context for the public reception of the concerto's second Viennese performance, a triumphant homecoming concert by the 14-year-old Joachim in the Gesellschaft der Musikfreunde on 28 February 1846, conducted by his former teacher, and Joseph Hellmesberger's father (!), Georg Hellmesberger, Sr. (1800–1873).[18] "With this choice," wrote Carl Schmidt for the *Wiener Musik-Zeitung*, "Mr. Joachim has once again brilliantly proven his reverence for classical music and his purified striving for art." Referring to "Philokales'" essay, he continues: "About the great value of this composition full of perfume and passion, in which the orchestral accompaniment asserts itself in a most felicitous, masterly manner ...—only one voice prevails ..." Schmidt's review concludes with the observation that Joachim had earned Mendelssohn's own applause with his interpretation, which, despite Joachim's passion and excessive pace (!), could thus be heard as representing the wishes of the author.[19]

After Vienna, Joachim continued his homecoming tour in Budapest, where on 26 March he gave the first Hungarian performance of the concerto in the *Nationaltheater*.[20]

ENGLAND

Mendelssohn, of course, had close ties to Great Britain and London's Philharmonic Society. There were several London performances of his concerto already during his lifetime, most notably the 29 June 1846 orchestral premiere with the Philharmonic Society Orchestra by Camillo Sivori (1815–1894).[21] The Philharmonic gave the concerto again the following 15 March with Prosper Sainton (1813–1890) as soloist. The first British audition was private, however, given a month pre-publication at the home of Mendelssohn's publisher, Edward Buxton, by the German violinist Bernhard Kreutzer, accompanied on piano by Charles Edward Horsley (1822–1876).[22] Subsequently, on 23 December 1845, "Herr Kreutzer, Director of Music to the Grand Duke of Baden," gave the work its fifth public hearing (and first public British performance), accompanied on piano by Henry J. Lincoln.[23]

Lincoln, a popular lecturer on music, had been engaged by the Western Literary and Scientific Institution to give a series of "Evenings with the Great Composers" at their rooms in Leicester Square.[24] Lincoln's programs "have a high aim," wrote the critic for the *Morning Post*. "They attempt to disseminate through all classes of society a love for music of the best masters.... Instruction and amusement go hand in hand...." The lectures were "delivered in a modest, unpretending manner," each night devoted to a single composer; "...the public is entertained with a succinct biographical sketch, an account of the particular works of the author, with a concise and not too analytic review, illustrated by selections therefrom, which are sung or played... the whole being interspersed and enlivened with a running accompaniment of anecdotes and characteristic exemplifications."[25]

In singling out composers for his attention Lincoln was, in effect, creating a canon of "masters"—a fact that did not escape the *Morning Post*'s critic: "Mr. Lincoln has already delivered lectures on Haydn and Cherubini at this institution. Last evening was devoted to Cimaroso [sic]. We can hardly understand upon what principle, or in what category, mental or musical, the name of Cimarosa should be associated with Haydn and Cherubini. [...] People who attend the whole course of these 'evenings' will be apt to clash the names of Cherubini and Cimarosa together, and opine that their greatness is parallel...."[26] Mendelssohn was the only modern "master" in his lecture series.

"These lectures are beginning to command universal attention," claimed *The Musical World*. "At each of them we have observed some of our most distinguished professors among the audience."[27] Thus, Kreutzer's "rapturously applauded"[28] performance, together with many favorable reviews of the composition, helped prepare the way for Sivori's first British performance with orchestra the following year.

The person who arguably did more than any other to promote the concerto in Great Britain was the eccentric conductor, composer, piccolo player, and musical entrepreneur, Louis-Antoine Jullien (1812–1860), known today as one of the pioneers of the "promenade" or "pops" format. From 1840 until the year before his suicide in 1860, he concertized frequently in London and on tour through England, Ireland, and Scotland. At P. T. Barnum's bidding, he gave several hundred concerts in the United States in 1853–4.[29]

A consummate showman, Jullien would sit enthroned on a crimson and gold armchair wearing a gleaming white vest and kid gloves, and have his bejeweled baton ceremoniously brought to him on a silver salver. Though often derided as a charlatan, he was nevertheless a skilled conductor known for hiring the best musicians both for his orchestra and as soloists.[30] His performances were consequently of a high technical standard. Jullien's audiences, which frequently numbered in the thousands, were a rowdy mix of the cultivated and the untutored—of those who came for edification and those who came merely for entertainment.

As the conductor of an entrepreneurial orchestra, Jullien had the insight that the highbrow could have its own popular appeal. Like Lincoln, he understood the value of devoting an evening to a single canonic composer. During the decade of the 1850s, he presented in turn "A Haydn Night, a Mozart Night, a Beethoven Night, a Weber Night," and "a Mendelssohn Night," Mendelssohn again being the only modern "master." The first half of each evening was dedicated to the composer in question; the second half to popular music: songs, waltzes, polkas, quadrilles, etc. These formulaic programs varied little from concert to concert. The Mendelssohn program often included the Symphony No. 3 in A minor, op. 56, "Scottish," the Piano Concerto No. 1 in G minor, op. 25, and the violin concerto. This strict division into "highbrow" and "lowbrow" had the effect of presenting Mendelssohn's modern works as canonic, while at the same time promoting their popularity.

Jullien first conducted the concerto in late 1849, at a "Mendelssohn Night" in London's Theatre Royal, Drury Lane (capacity 2,196), featuring Prosper Sainton as soloist.[31] *Bell's Weekly Messenger* observed:

> M. Jullien devoted the first part of his programme to a selection from the works of Mendelssohn. The step was a bold one, but was crowned with entire success, the dense mass of people listening with profound attention for at least two hours to music such as is ordinarily addressed to "select" audiences, and has been pronounced above the comprehension of the multitude. If M. Jullien perseveres in his new line of policy, this kind of music will no longer be regarded as the exclusive property of a few.[32]

Even in the "classical" section, Jullien programmed with an eye to popular taste: it was often his practice to include only one or two movements of the concerto, thus contravening Mendelssohn's explicit attempt at formal integration. In these concerts, Sainton performed the second and last, transforming the concerto into the familiar virtuoso pairing of *"Andante and Rondo."*[33]

During the 1850s, a number of renowned violinists joined Jullien's "Mendelssohn Evenings": Between December 1851 and January 1859, Jullien featured the Mendelssohn Violin Concerto at least forty times, with soloists including Camillo Sivori, Henry Weist-Hill, Viotti Collins, Heinrich Wilhelm Ernst, Prosper Sainton, Adolphe-Adrien Le Hon [Lehon], Edouard Reményi, and Henri Wieniawski. Always conscious of his exalted reputation, Joseph Joachim considered it beneath his dignity to perform with "an outright charlatan and speculator." "What connections are to remain sacred to me in life if I exploit my art in active community with a market crier?" he wrote to Clara Schumann.[34]

The young Henryk Wieniawski (1835–1880) was among the concerto's most consistent champions. As a 19-year-old, he gave its first Belgian performance (Brussels, 7 January 1855). He performed it with Julius Rietz at the Gewandhaus that September and brought it to Paris the following year (Théâtre Royal, 12 March 1856). Beginning 1 November 1858 and continuing through January 1859, Wieniawski made his first British appearances with Jullien's orchestra, playing Mendelssohn's concerto multiple times in London and on the annual tour in England in Leeds, York, Belfast, and Londonderry. The audiences were large and rowdy, and it was disapprovingly noted in the press that Wieniawski's performance featured his own cadenza (!)[35]

Jullien often advanced members of his orchestra as soloists while on tour. In 1849–50, Viotti Collins played the piece as an *Adagio and Rondo* while on tour with Jullien's orchestra, giving premiere performances in Manchester, Liverpool, Birmingham, Dublin, and Edinburgh. In December 1856 and January 1857, the young Belgian violinist Adolphe Lehon likewise gave at least eleven performances in London and on tour in Manchester, Liverpool, Edinburgh, Dublin, Birmingham, and Bath, playing the concerto's final two movements.[36]

After Jullien's final appearances in England, August Manns launched a series of "Promenade Concerts" in London's Drury Lane Theatre on the Jullien model. Wieniawski performed the Mendelssohn concerto there on the Proms' first night (26 November 1859). Though announced for the first movement only, he played the entire piece.[37]

AMERICA

Biographical notices of Sainton's pupil, Thomas Henry Weist-Hill (1828–1891), claim that he was the first to play Mendelssohn's concerto in America.[38] His reputed American premiere occurred on 13 October 1853 at Jullien's "Grand Mendelssohn Night" in Metropolitan Hall, New York.[39] By then, however, Mendelssohn's concerto was already well-known in America: there had been at least eleven performances (either partial or complete) in Boston and New York—three of them with the Philharmonic Society of New York.

In America, the concerto entered an already well-established Mendelssohn cult, founded largely upon the popularity of the composer's vocal music.[40] It was promoted by a network of musicians with close ties to Europe, and, in some cases, to Mendelssohn himself – including members of the newly founded Philharmonic Society of New York, Boston's Mendelssohn Quintette Club, and the Germania Musical Society – and also by critics like John Sullivan Dwight, who, as part of the New England Transcendentalist movement, was deeply influenced by the German *Dichter und Denker*.

The American premiere was given on 17 April 1847 in the Apollo Rooms, New York, by Michele Rapetti, with the Philharmonic Society, Ureli Corelli Hill conducting.[41] Rapetti, a Bolognese violinist and conductor, played chamber music with Sivori in 1846, when the latter toured America following his premiere performance with the Philharmonic Society of London. Rapetti also conducted the orchestra for Sivori's concerto appearances in America.[42] Rapetti and Sivori may have discussed Mendelssohn's concerto at that time.

The Philharmonic's founder, U.C. Hill was also a violinist. From 1835–7, he had traveled in Europe, taking forty-six violin lessons from Louis Spohr in Kassel, playing in the orchestra of London's Drury Lane Theatre, and assisting Felix Mendelssohn at the 1836 Lower Rhine Music Festival in Düsseldorf.[43] In 1845, Hill invited Mendelssohn to lead a music festival in New York.[44]

A famous child prodigy actor as well as violinist, the European-trained Joseph Burke ("The Irish Roscius," 1818–1902) was one of the concerto's most prominent American advocates.[45] In America since 1830, Burke was a prominent soloist, elected in 1846 to honorary membership in the Philharmonic-Symphony Society of New York (together with Mendelssohn, Spohr, Herz, and Sivori).[46] He first played the concerto in late 1848, at a private gathering of members of the Germania Musical Society.[47] Burke subsequently gave the second hearing (after Rapetti) of the concerto by the Philharmonic Society of New York in the Apollo Rooms (24 November 1849),[48] reprising his performance with the Philharmonic in Niblo's Concert Room on 28 February 1852 and 1 March 1856.[49] In 1851, Burke played the Andante movement in New York and Boston while on tour with Jenny Lind Goldschmidt, the orchestra conducted by her husband Otto Goldschmidt.[50]

In addition to Burke and Rapetti, there were numerous performances of the concerto in 1851–2 by August Fries of Boston's Mendelssohn Quintette Club, and in 1854 by Wilhelm Schultze of the Germania Musical Society. On 20 October 1855, the Dutch violinist Jean Henri (Henry) Appy, a student of Sivori, played it in the Boston Music Hall (the notices identified him as H. Appy). Appy was one of the earliest performers of Mendelssohn's concerto, having played it in Amsterdam's *Felix Meritis* on 1 December 1848.

One of the defining aspects of canonicity is that a work should serve as a model for others. As R. Larry Todd points out, Mendelssohn's concerto famously did so, influencing such composers as Schumann, Vieuxtemps, Tchaikovsky, and Sibelius. Todd also cites an intriguing example of influence: the "Grande allegro di concerto" in E Minor for double bass and string orchestra by Giovanni Bottesini (1821–1889), sometimes called "*alla Mendelssohn*." Bottesini, "the Paganini of the double bass," toured with Jullien in Great Britain and America during the 1850s, playing alongside the violinists whose repertoire he adapted and performed to great acclaim (including the Paganini *Carnival of Venice*, which violinists often used as a companion piece to the Mendelssohn concerto).[51] The similarities of Bottesini's "Grande allegro" to the first movement of Mendelssohn's concerto are striking.[52]

ENVOI

The question of whose voices are heard, and why, lies at the heart of the art-making enterprise. In a rapidly evolving cultural milieu, this concern has taken on greater urgency—yet the processes by which works come to be known and valued, and the ways in which they function within various artistic *Umwelten*, are seldom fully appreciated, or well understood.

The E Minor Concerto, as Mendelssohn and David initially conceived it, might indeed have been intended as an intimate expression of nineteenth-century Saxon domesticity – a *Herzensjuwel* – its central movement representing a kind of Bakhtinian dialogue between the public conventions of the concerto genre and the intimacy of the *Songs Without Words*, familiar to Mendelssohn's friends and throughout Leipziger salon culture.[53] As the concerto in published form began its journey, journalists attempted to assess its worth, considering its intrinsic unity, the facility of its working-out, and the felicity of its expression. By performing such a work, young violinists like Hellmesberger, Joachim, Simon, Wieniawski and others were able to transcend the stigma of Wunderkind virtuosity and establish their credibility as mature artists within the religion of art.

The presentation and significance of the piece changed radically when it crossed the English Channel, entering Britain's fiercely entrepreneurial, class-conscious culture. Often presented in altered or mutilated form – dissected and divested of its stormier moments – the work was popularized and made familiar through educational endeavors, juxtaposition with popular works and genres, and through repeated performances in "Monster Concerts" by prominent artists and their pupils. In America, the concerto enjoyed early success where the name and art of Felix Mendelssohn had already been appropriated by European-trained musicians seeking to bring "good music to a free people."[54] Finally, well into the twentieth century, composers of diverse nations were inspired to emulation by the concerto's innovations.

The often-surprising performance history of Mendelssohn's violin concerto demonstrates the value of thinking beyond the limits of a single, stratified musical tradition. Across a variety of cultures, venues, and situations, the impulse to elevate, to promote, and to overcome attention scarcity by demonstrating the concerto's stature was satisfied with courage, imagination, and great fluidity of approach. This history suggests more broadly that the vitality and pertinence of musical life depends upon discovering the ways that compositions function within the expansive ecosystem of interests and relationships that support and facilitate their evolving artistic "sense."

1. Heinrich Eduard Jacob, *Felix Mendelssohn und seine Zeit: Bildnis und Schicksal eines Meisters* (Frankfurt am Main: S. Fischer, 1959), 345–6.
2. Joseph Kerman, "A Few Canonic Variations," *Critical Inquiry* 10, no. 1 (September 1983): 112.
3. William Weber writes, in a more nuanced way, of "scholarly canons," "pedagogical canons," and "performing canons" in "The History of Musical Canon," in Nicholas Cook and Mark Everist, eds., *Rethinking Music* (Oxford: Oxford University Press, 2001), 336–55.
4. Howard S. Baker, *Art Worlds* (Berkeley: University of California Press, 2008).
5. "Sense," Online Etymology Dictionary, https://www.etymonline.com/search?q=sense/, accessed 20 December 2022.
6. See, for example, R. Larry Todd's introduction and critical commentary in the Bärenreiter complete works score (2005) and the introduction to the 2016 Breitkopf & Härtel score by Birgit Müller and Salome Reiser. See also: R. Larry Todd, "Konzert E-Moll Op. 64 für Violine und Orchester MWV O 14" in Matthias Geuting, ed., *Felix Mendelssohn Bartholdy. Interpretationen seiner Werke*, 2 vols. (Laaber: Laaber, 2016), 2:322–37.
7. *Revue et Gazette Musicale*, 12, no. 14 (6 April 1845): 112. Cited in Birgit Müller, "Introduction" Felix Mendelssohn Bartholdy, *Concerto in E minor for Violin and Orchestra, op. 64 MWV O 14* (Wiesbaden: Breitkopf & Härtel, 2018), xxvi.
8. Programs at "Concert Archive," Gewandhaus, Leipzig, https://www.gewandhausorchester.de/en/archive/, accessed 5 December 2022.
9. Ibid.
10. See Carl Reinecke, *Erlebnisse und Bekenntnisse. Autobiographie eines Gewandhauskapellmeisters*, ed. Doris Mundus, (Leipzig: Lehmstedt, 2005), 102.
11. See "Schumann, Christiani, and Lind," *Joseph Joachim–Biography and Research*, https://joseph-joachim.com/2013/07/09/schumann-cristiani-and-lind/, accessed 20 November 2022. News of the concert reached as far as Boston. *Boston Post*, 30, no. 93 (20 April 1847): 4.
12. Andreas Moser, *Joseph Joachim. Ein Lebensbild*, rev. ed. In 2 vols. (Berlin: Verlag der Deutschen Brahms-Gesellschaft, 1908, 1910), 1:58. Though, note Joachim's comment about H. W. Ernst: Joseph Joachim and Andreas Moser, *Violinschule*, 3 vols. (Berlin: Simrock, 1905), 3:231.
13. Joachim and Moser, *Violinschule*, 228–31. Joachim mentions that he was instructed and accompanied by Mendelssohn when he was sixteen years old (!).
14. *Wiener allgemeine Musik-Zeitung*, 5, no. 155 (27 December 1845): 623. The Belgian violinist Hubert Léonard performed the concerto in Berlin's *Königliches Schauspielhaus* on 2 February 1846, with members of Mendelssohn's family in attendance.
15. Philokales, "Revue," *Wiener allgemeine Musik-Zeitung*, 6, no. 15 (3 February 1846): 58. From 1841–9, the Moravian scholar Ferdinand Peter Graf Laurencin d'Armond (1819–1890) wrote criticism for August Schmidt's *Wiener allgemeine Musik-Zeitung* under the pseudonym *Philokales*. He later served as Viennese correspondent for Leipzig's *Neue Zeitschrift für Musik*, signing his articles φ.
16. "Revue," 58.
17. "I harbor a real aversion to what are called piano concertos. (Those by Mozart and Beethoven are not so much concertos as symphonies with piano obbligato.) E. T. A. Hoffmann, "Beethoven's Instrumental Music," quoted from David Charlton, ed., Martyn Clarke, trans., *E. T. A. Hoffmann's Musical Writings*: Kreisleriana, The Poet and the Composer, *Music Criticism* (Cambridge: Cambridge University Press, 1989), 101. "Only that composer penetrates truly into the secrets of harmony who is able to stir the soul of man through harmony; to him, the mathematical proportions which to the grammarian without genius are only dry arithmetical problems, are magic combinations from which he can build a world of visions." Charlton, *Hoffmann's Musical Writings*, 132.
18. In the late 1830s, Georg Hellmesberger Sr. taught a "quartet of prodigies," including Joachim, his two sons, Joseph and Georg Jr., and Adolf Simon. All four would go on to significant professional careers, though Georg Jr. died young. Simon was also one of the early performers of the

Mendelssohn concerto: after playing it in Vienna on 29 January 1847, he gave the Dutch premiere of the work on 15 March at the *Felix Meritis* Hall on Amsterdam's Keizersgracht. Another young violinist from Vienna, Adolf Pollitzer (1832–1900), like Joachim a student of Joseph Böhm, reportedly played the concerto for Mendelssohn ca. 1845, when he was 13 years old.

19 *Wiener allgemeine Musik-Zeitung*, 5, no. 28 (5 March 1846): 110.
20 *Wiener allgemeine Musik-Zeitung*, 6, no. 43 (9 April 1846): 171.
21 Sivori's success was reported in the Boston and New York press. Prior to the performance, Sivori had a pre-concert run-through with the Queen's Band at Buckingham Palace. *The Musical Times*, 37, no. 641 (1 July 1896): 453.
22 10 May 1845. Birgit Müller, "Introduction,", xxvii, n. 35. Bernhard Kreutzer (b. Düsseldorf, 1803) had been the music director and teacher of piano, guitar, violin and flute at Heidelberg University (*Anzeige der Vorlesungen der Grossherzoglich Badischen Ruprecht-Carolinischen Universität zu Heidelberg*, (Heidelberg: n. p., 1834), 19.) Though he began as a flute player, he was known as an excellent violinist, particularly as a chamber music player. He arrived in London via Rotterdam on 23 December 1842, and quickly established himself as a local performer. By 1849, he was living in Edinburgh, still styling himself "Director of Music to H. R. H. the Grand Duke of Baden." (*The Scotsman*, 32 no. 2997 (27 September 1848): 1.) About Horsley, see Charles Edward Horsley, "Reminiscences of Mendelssohn by His English Pupil" in R. Larry Todd, ed., *Mendelssohn and his World* (Princeton: Princeton University Press, 1991), 237–51.
23 Pianist, organist, and lecturer on musical subjects Henry John Lincoln (1814–1901) was music critic of the London *Daily News* from 1866–96. ("Lincoln, Henry John," *British Musical Biography*, James D. Brown and Stephen S. Stratton eds. (Birmingham: S. S. Stratton, 1897), 247.) A character description of Lincoln appears in Joseph Bennett, *Forty Years of Music, 1865–1905* (London: Methuen, 1908), 11–12.
24 The Western Literary and Scientific Institution, patronized by the king and various members of the aristocracy and high society, was a private club, established in 1825 for "the Diffusion of Useful Knowledge among Persons engaged in Commercial and Professional Pursuits." Its library and meeting hall were contained in the elegant former home and studio of Sir Joshua Reynolds. Its program included classes "for the acquisition of the Languages and the Sciences," and lectures on history, mathematics, political economy, natural and moral philosophy and, later, music. *Laws of the Western Literary and Scientific Institution*, (London: Mallkit, 1834), 5. For a full description and history of the venue, including its occupancy by Sir Joshua and later by the Western Literary and Scientific Institution see *British History Online*, https://www.british-history.ac.uk/survey-london/vols33-4/pp507-514#anchorn51, accessed 1 March 2024.
25 "Mr. Lincoln's Lectures," *The Morning Post*, no. 22,477 (17 December 1845): 5. Known for "its reputation as a record of the doings of the aristocratic and wealthy," *The Morning Post* was said to be the first London daily to publish notices of plays and concerts. ("The Growth of Journalism," *The Cambridge History of English and American Literature*, vol. 14, part 2, https://www.bartleby.com/224/0409.html, accessed 1 February 2023.)
26 "Mr. Lincoln's Lectures": 5.
27 *The Musical World*, 20, no. 52 (25 December 1845): 618.
28 "Evenings with the Great Composers," *Illustrated London News*, 7, no. 191 (27 December 1845): 411.
29 The standard work on Jullien is still Adam Carse's *The Life of Jullien: Adventurer, Showman-Conductor and Establisher of the Promenade Concerts in England* (Cambridge: W. Heffer & Sons, 1951), though see Katherine K. Preston, "'A Concentration of Talent on Our Musical Horizon': The 1853–54 American Tour by Jullien's Extraordinary Orchestra" in John Spitzer, ed., *American Orchestras in the Nineteenth Century*, (Chicago and London: University of Chicago Press, 2012), 319–47.
30 Keith Horner, "Jullien, Louis." *Grove Music Online*. 2001, https://doi-org.unh.idm.oclc.org/10.1093/gmo/9781561592630.article.14538/, accessed 4 January 2023.

31 27 November 1849. Sainton played it again with Jullien on 6 December. (*Illustrated London News*, 15, no. 401 (1 December 1849): 362; *The Morning Herald*, no. 21,084 (6 December 1849): 4.)
32 *Bell's Weekly Messenger*, no. 2,764 (1 December 1849): 381.
33 Even Joachim performed the concerto in this way in a concert in Dublin with Jenny Lind Goldschmidt, 26 September 1859. (*The Evening Freeman*, no. 508 (21 September 1859): 1.)
34 Joseph Joachim to Clara Schumann, 15 January 1857. Johannes Joachim and Andreas Moser, eds., *Briefe von und an Joseph Joachim*, 3 vols. (Berlin: Julius Bard, 1911–13), 1:400.
35 *The Era*, 21, no. 1,050 (7 November 1858): 10.
36 Adolphe-Adrien Lehon (1832[3]–1871), first prize for violin at the Brussels Conservatory, class of Wéry in 1852, also studied with Hubert Léonard (1819–180). Léonard was greatly admired by Mendelssohn and gave the first Berlin performance of Mendelssohn's concerto in the Royal *Schauspielhaus* on 2 February 1846. Léonard gave the first full performance of the concerto in Stockholm on 5 May 1859 (*Svenska Tidningen*, 103, no. 2216 (6 May 1859): 3.) Lehon later returned to Belgium, from 1861 as professor of violin at the Ghent Conservatoire. About Lehon, see Edouard G. J. Gregoir, *Les Artistes-Musiciens Belges au XVIIIme et XIXme Siècle*, (Brussels: Schott, 1885), 183; also: C[harles] Bergmans, *Le Conservatoire Royal de Musique de Gand*, (Gand: Beyer, 1901), 287.
37 *The Morning Chronicle*, no. 28,979 (28 November 1859): 5.
38 See, for example: Chitty, Alexis, and E.D. Mackerness. "Weist-Hill, Thomas Henry." *Grove Music Online*. 2001. Weist-Hill was Principal of the Guildhall School of Music from 1880 until his death.
39 (Classified Advertisement, *New York Herald*, no. 7,593 [13 October 1853]: 11.) Weist Hill performed the concerto again on the 18th, and in Boston on the 28th.
40 See Joseph A Mussulman, "Mendelssohnism in America," *The Musical Quarterly*, 53, no. 3 (July 1967): 335–46.
41 Concert program, 17 April 1847, Program ID 450, New York Philharmonic Shelby White & Leon Levy Digital Archives. https://archives.nyphil.org/index.php/artifact/c24a729b-1d1f-4512-8214-893b5d083f91-0.1, accessed 24 January 2023.
42 Frédéric Louis Ritter, *Music in America*, (New York: Scribner's Sons, 1900), 291.
43 Barbara Haws, "Ureli Corelli Hill: An American Musician's European Travels and the Creation of the New York Philharmonic," in Spitzer, ed., *American Orchestras*, 349.
44 *Felix Mendelssohn Bartholdy Sämtliche Briefe*, vol. 10, Ute Wald, ed. (Kassel: Bärenreiter, 2016), 372.
45 [Author unknown], *Biography of Master Burke, the Irish Roscius; The Wonder of the World; and The Paragon of Actors* (Philadelphia: Shakespeare Press, 1830).
46 https://nyphil.org/~/media/pdfs/about-us/history/HonoraryMembers.ashx?la=en, accessed 27 March 2023.
47 *The American Review*, 2, no. 6, New York: (December 1848): 650.
48 Concert program, 24 November 1849, Program ID 7278, New York Philharmonic Shelby White & Leon Levy Digital Archives. https://archives.nyphil.org/index.php/artifact/e82e06bd-9340-4831-9a29-85c1ea8767df-0.1, accessed 24 January 2023.
49 Concert program, 28 February 1852, Program ID 6717; Concert program, 1 March 1856, Program ID 4355, New York Philharmonic Shelby White & Leon Levy Digital Archives. https://archives.nyphil.org/index.php/artifact/e91acc45-3ae0-40c4-9972-57ed8fbd5fbd-0.1, accessed 24 January 2023.
50 Tripler Hall, New York, 30 May 1851, and Boston *Melodion*, 25 and 28 November 1851. *New York Herald*, no. 6,793 (30 May 1851): 6; *Boston Daily Atlas* 20, no. 126 (25 November 1851): 3; *Boston Post*, 39, no. 126 (26 November 1851): 3.
51 The tradition of playing a virtuoso piece alongside the Mendelssohn Concerto was established already with David, and was still alive in the 1960s when Jack Benny would perform the concerto's

first movement and follow it with Sarasate's *Zigeunerweisen* (as he did for the Boston Symphony Pension Fund on 11 February 1968).

52 R. Larry Todd, "Konzert E-Moll Op. 64 für Violine und Orchester MWV 0 14" in Matthias Geuting, ed., *Felix Mendelssohn Bartholdy* 2 vols., 2:335. See also Jaime Ramírez-Castilla, *Musical Borrowings in the Music for Double Bass by Giovanni Bottesini: A Reconsideration Beyond the Operatic Paraphrases* (PhD Diss., University of Cincinnati, 2007), 89–104.

53 See Kevin Korsyn, "Beyond Privileged Contexts: Intertextuality, Influence and Dialogue," in Nicholas Cook and Mark Everist, eds., *Rethinking Music*, 61 ff.

54 Nancy Newman, *Good Music for a Free People: The Germania Music Society in Nineteenth-Century America*, (Rochester: University of Rochester Press, 2010).

5. THREE POSTLUDES TO MENDELSSOHNIAN RESEARCH

Peter Ward Jones

In the course of writing about Felix Mendelssohn over several decades, there have inevitably been cases where subsequent reflexion or the discovery of new information has made some updating desirable. Such amendments would be too short to merit articles on their own, but this occasion seems a suitable opportunity to bring together three examples that I have accumulated in recent years. For the first two, I have endeavoured to write something that can be read independently, without a need to consult the original articles; the third, however, provides corrections and additions to the original and is designed to be used in conjunction with it.

THE PUBLICATION DATE OF MENDELSSOHN'S OPUS 1

The year of publication of Mendelssohn's Piano Quartet in C minor, opus 1, has hitherto been considered to have been 1823, a date I accepted in an article on the bibliographical problems of the work.[1] It was issued by the Berlin publisher, Adolph Martin Schlesinger, who, however, had the work engraved in Paris by his son, Maurice Schlesinger. We know from a letter of Felix's mother, Lea, to Maurice that work was about to begin in July 1823.[2] After engraving, the plates were sent to Berlin, where a few corrections were made, and the plate number 1222 added. This number correlates with other works that Schlesinger is known to have published in the latter part of 1823; so, in the absence of other evidence—it was not advertised or reviewed at the time—the assumption has been that it was put on sale that year. But new evidence has appeared in a letter of 3 February 1824, published for the first time in 2008 in vol. 1 of the collected edition of Mendelssohn's letters.[3] It is a brief note from Felix to Anton Fürst Radziwill, written on his fifteenth birthday, stating "I take the liberty, as a result of the permission graciously bestowed on me, to most obediently offer up my first published work."[4] Now Radziwill was the dedicatee of opus 1, and so it is logical to assume that Felix would have sent him the dedication copy no later than the day on which it was officially published. I would therefore suggest that opus 1 was not released to the world until 3 February 1824. This redating also makes better chronological sense of a letter that Felix's Parisian aunt, Henriette Mendelssohn, sent to Lea on 11 February, acknowledging receipt of a copy, when she added that she had already bought a copy at Maurice Schlesinger's, who we know (from a now sole surviving copy in the British Library) had printed off a few copies before he sent the plates to Berlin.

This redating throws interesting light on another event of Felix's fifteenth birthday: it was the occasion on which, if Sebastian Hensel is to be believed, Carl Friedrich

Zelter bestowed his priest-like blessing on Felix with the words "My dear son, from today you are no longer a boy, from today on you are a journeyman. I make you a journeyman in the name of Mozart, in the name of Haydn, and in the name of old Bach."[5] It has not been clear why Zelter should have chosen this moment, but we now have the perfect reason for his pronouncement: it was the publication of Felix's opus 1, which raised him to at least the junior ranks of a professional composer. This was also the day Felix first heard his opera *Die beiden Neffen* with full orchestral accompaniment, when it was rehearsed in preparation for private performances a few days later.[6] In addition, it may well be that Felix received the celebrated gift of the score of Bach's *St. Matthew Passion* from his grandmother on this birthday, rather than at Christmas 1823, as stated by Eduard Devrient in his memoir.[7] A memorable birthday, indeed!

AN ADDITIONAL THOUGHT ON MENDELSSOHN'S 1841 PERFORMANCE OF THE ST MATTHEW PASSION

In 2016, I published an extensive consideration of the sources of Mendelssohn's performances of the *St. Matthew Passion*, paying particular attention to the 1841 Leipzig performance in the Thomaskirche, about which less had been written.[8] One of the features of that performance was Mendelssohn's creation of an organ part for several numbers, employing it not as a conventional continuo instrument, but reserved for certain moments. It featured in the opening chorus "Kommt, ihr Töchter," where Mendelssohn originally had it just play the chorale melody of "O Lamm Gottes unschuldig," though he later added a sustained pedal bass note at 32-foot pitch through the opening five bars of the chorus. Did Mendelssohn know that Bach himself had used the organ to double the voices on the chorale? Mendelssohn's own score (and the published edition of 1830) had no indication of an organ part—the single unfigured bass line, which throughout the work serves the cellos and double basses, is merely marked "Continuo" or "Basso," and the vocal line of the chorale in the opening chorus is labelled "Soprano ripieno." But he may well have known the score belonging to his teacher, Carl Friedrich Zelter, director of the Singakademie, which was of the *Frühfassung*, and there the chorale stave is labelled "Organo."[9] We know that in the 1829 performances, he experimented with using various combinations of wind instruments to double the chorale line, which, in the second performance at least, he had sung by all the soloists (men and women) together with a few chorus sopranos.[10] In 1841, however, he did away with using wind instruments on the chorale, and gave it to the organ (which he also used, amongst other contributions, to double the voices in all the four-part chorales). But we don't have information as to what he did about having the chorale sung in 1841. He may possibly have adopted the same solution as in 1829—there is no indication in the sources. What he almost certainly would not have done is have the Thomaner boys sing it – the tradition of having a separate boys' choir on that line is a later nineteenth-century development.[11] We do not know if the Thomaner were involved at all, though if they were, as highly skilled singers, they would have been used to reinforce the main chorus parts, as they were accustomed to do at regular Gewandhaus choral concerts.[12] But I think there is a clue in the organ part that suggests the solution Mendelssohn adopted.

This part was prepared from Mendelssohn's drafts by his regular copyist, Eduard Henschke, but Mendelssohn subsequently decided to include the organ in further numbers, as well as making the odd amendment to the part as it stood.[13] One such amendment concerns the registration of "O Lamm Gottes unschuldig." Mendelssohn had originally asked for this to be played on "Alle 8 u 4 Fuß," i.e. presumably all the 8 and 4 foot flue stops on the Hauptwerk. But in revising the part, he added "mit Trompet u. Sesquialt[era]," thereby strengthening the sound substantially. This was clearly not a last-minute adjustment in rehearsal but planned beforehand.[14] I would suggest that Mendelssohn may have decided that, rather than have the chorale sung by the soloists (strengthened or not by chorus sopranos) as in 1829, he would have it just played by the organ—hence the alteration in the registration. Such an increase in volume would hardly have been necessary if the organ were merely there to support the voices. Indeed, it would now have tended to drown them. He may have considered that the loss of the words of the chorale was unimportant; they would presumably have been printed in the wordbook (of which no copy is traceable) as they had been in 1829, and the chorale was still to be found in Leipzig hymnbooks of the time, and so probably familiar to the audience.[15] This is clearly just a conjecture, for there is no further evidence for or against. But it would help account for Mendelssohn wanting such a prominent sound from the organ at this point, when elsewhere in the work he very much restrained its volume—even its entry after the general pause in the chorus "Sind Blitze, sind Donner" is only marked "forte," which the organist confirmed by noting "ohne Mixtur."

MENDELSSOHN'S LIBRARY

In an article of 1985, I gave an account of the books known to have been owned by the composer, based mainly on lists that Felix and his sister Fanny had drawn up in 1835 and 1844, also indicating those items that were known to still survive.[16] It dealt only with his books, not with the music he owned. Predictably, in the intervening years, further copies have turned up, including a substantial number in the hands of a descendant of the composer, as well as several previously unrecorded titles and other information. What follows is therefore an update to the original article, which is designed to be used in conjunction with it—space does not allow for the whole list to be presented in revised form, desirable as this might have been.[17] One curiosity among Mendelssohn's books is the presence in a number of volumes of a "Felix Mendelssohn Bartholdy" inscription in a hand similar to Felix's own, but not actually his; in a few cases the inscription is just "Mendelssohn Bartholdy." Some of these inscriptions are cropped at the right-hand edge, suggesting that they were added before the volumes were sent for binding.[18] Among family members, the hand most resembles that of his sister, Rebecka, and in the following list, such inscriptions have been described as "apparently" in her hand. This attribution, however, remains uncertain, as does the reason for someone other than Felix inscribing his name in the volumes.

Notes on the arrangement:
The number on the left is that of the item as given in the original article. Then follows a transcription of the title in quotation marks, just as it appears in the original lists of Felix and Fanny. The 1985 article then provided precise bibliographical identification, when possible. If there is no alteration to this, then it is not repeated here, and only additional information is supplied. Otherwise, corrected bibliographical and other details are provided. Present ownership, where known, is then added. Several items, which were completely unknown at the time of the original article, are included at the end.

Abbreviations:
FMB: Felix Mendelssohn Bartholdy
Fanny: FMB's sister, later Fanny Hensel
GB: The "Green Books" of Mendelssohn's incoming correspondence (Bodleian Library, Oxford, MSS. M.Deneke Mendelssohn, b.4, d.28–53).
Rebecka: FMB's sister, later Rebecka Dirichlet
Sämtliche Briefe: Felix Mendelssohn Bartholdy: *Sämtliche Briefe*, ed. Helmut Loos and Wilhelm Seidel, 12 vols. (Kassel, 2008–17)

5   "Schiller 1 Bd"
    Friedrich Schiller: *Sämmtliche Werke in einem Bande* (Stuttgart & Tübingen, 1834). Privately owned.
7   "Mendelssohn 5 Bde (sowie die Brockhausche Ausgabe bis jetzt geht)"
    Moses Mendelssohn: *Gesammelte Schriften*, ed. G.B.Mendelssohn. 7 vols. (Leipzig, 1843–5). All 7 vols. privately owned.
15 "Shakespeare [sic.] 1 Bd"
    William Shakspeare [sic]: *The Dramatic Works. Complete in one Volume.* (London, 1824). Berlin, Staatsbibliothek, Mendelssohn-Archiv.
18 "Aristophanes übers v. Droysen 3 Bde"
    Leipzig, Stadtgeschichtliches Museum
19 "Homer übers. v. Voss"
    Now Leipzig, Stadtgeschichtliches Museum,
21 "Pickwick 1 Bd"
    Charles Dickens: *The Posthumous Papers of the Pickwick Club* (London, 1837). A gift from his mother, Lea, at Easter, 1842. Offered for sale, Bernard Halliday, Leicester, Catalogue 163 (1933), no. 235.
22 "Nickleby 1 Bd"
    Gift of Charles Horsley *ca.* Oct. 1841 – cf. FMB's letter, 2 Nov. 1841 (*Sämtliche Briefe*, no. 3319) and Horsley's, 24 Dec. 1841 (GB XIV, 149).

| 23 | "Humphrey clock 3 Bde" |

Gift of Charles Horsley, brought to Berlin by William Sterndale Bennett in Feb. 1842 – cf. FMB's letter to Horsley, 5 Mar. 1842 (*Sämtliche Briefe*, no. 3456).

| 25 | "Gil Blas 4 Bde" |

A.R. Le Sage: *Histoire de Gil Blas de Santillane*. (Paris, 1811). Berlin, Staatsbibliothek, Mendelssohn-Archiv.

| 26 | "Bocaccio Decameron 1 Bd" |

"'Edizione seconda," which includes the original 1820 titlepage of the first edition as well as one dated 1827. Now Leipzig, Stadtgeschichtliches Museum.

| 27 | "Bocaccio Decameron 4 Bde" |

Giovanni Boccaccio: *Il Decameron*. 4 vols. (Firenze, 1832). Privately owned.

| 28 | "Cervantes novelas 4 Bde" |

Miguel de Cervantes Saavedra: *Novelas exemplares*. 4 vols. Vols. 1, 2 and 4 published: Gotha, 1805, 1806, 1814; vol. 3 published: Chemnitz, 1809. Vols. 1 and 2 have the inscription "F. Mendelssohn Bartholdy" in Fanny's hand; vol. 4 is inscribed "Felix Mendelssohn Bartholdy," apparently in Rebecka's hand. Privately owned.

| 29 | "D Quixote 6 Bde" |

Miguel de Cervantes Saavedra: *El ingenioso hidalgo Don Quixote de la Mancha*. 6 vols. (Berlin, 1804). Inscribed "Felix Mendelssohn Bartholdy," apparently in Rebecka's hand. Privately owned.

| 34 | "Herschel die Lehre der Astronomie 1 Bd" |

Privately owned.

| 38 | "Uhland Gedichte 1 Bd" |

Ludwig Uhland: *Gedichte*. Neueste Auflage (Stuttgart & Tübingen, 1841). Privately owned.

| 57 | "Lessing Nathan 1 Bd" |

Gotthold Ephraim Lessing: *Nathan der Weise*. Fünfte verbesserte Auflage (Berlin, 1815). Oxford, Lady Margaret Hall Library (donated by FMB's grandson, Paul Benecke, 1942).

| 69 | "Andersen Bazar 1 Bd" |

Hans Christian Andersen: *Eines Dichters Bazar*, transl. W.C. Christiani, (H.C. Andersen's sämmtliche Werke, Theil 1–3) (Braunschweig, 1843). 3 vols. in 1. Leipzig, Stadtgeschichtliches Museum.

| 75 | "Majorca v. Laurens 1 Bd" |

Privately owned.

| 76 | "Granada v. Jennings 1 Bd" |

A birthday present from his sisters Fanny and Rebecka, 1835 – cf. Fanny's letter to FMB, 16 Jan. 1835 (GB IV, 6), printed in *The Letters of Fanny Hensel to Felix Mendelssohn*, ed. Marcia J. Citron ([Stuyvesant, NY], 1987), pp. 485–7.

| 80 | "W. Scott Life v. Lockhart 7 Bde" |

Gift of Anne Joanna Alexander (inscribed 1837–8). Privately owned.

86 "W. Scott Old Mortality 1 Bd"
Walter Scott: *Old Mortality*. The correction of the press by Dr. Flügel. In three volumes. (Waverley novels, vol. 14–16) (Pest, Leipsic and London, 1831). 3 vols. in 1. Privately owned.

87 "W. Scott Rob Roy 1 Bd"
Walter Scott: *Rob Roy*. The correction of the press by Dr. Flügel. In three volumes. (Waverley novels, vol. 10–12) (Pest, Leipsic and London, 1831). 3 vols. in 1. Privately owned.

89 "W. Scott Heart of M. L. (4 Theile) in 2 Bänden"
Walter Scott: *The Heart of Mid-Lothian*. The correction of the press by Dr. Flügel. In four volumes. (Waverley novels, vol. 17–20) (Pest, Leipsic and London, 1832). 4 vols. in 2. Privately owned.

90 "W. Scott Guy Mannering 1 Bd"
Walter Scott: *Guy Mannering; or, The Astrologer*. The correction of the press by Dr. Flügel. In three volumes. (Waverley novels, vol. 4–6) (Pest, Leipsic and London, 1831). 3 vols. in 1. Privately owned.

91 "W. Scott Montrose 1 Bd"
Walter Scott: *A Legend of Montrose*. The correction of the press by Dr. Flügel. In two volumes. (Waverley novels, vol. 23–24) (Pest, Leipsic and London, 1832). 2 vols. in 1. Privately owned.

93 "W. Scott Black Dwarf 1 Bd"
Walter Scott: *The Black Dwarf*. The correction of the press by Dr. Flügel. In one volume. (Waverley novels, vol. 13) (Pest, Leipsic and London, 1831). Privately owned.

94 "W. Scott Castle Dangerous 1 Bd"
Walter Scott: *Castle Dangerous*. The correction of the press by Dr. Flügel. In two volumes. (Waverley novels, vol. 28–29) (Pest, Leipsic and London, 1832). 2 vols. in 1. Privately owned.

95 "W. Scott Robert of Paris 1 Bd"
Walter Scott: *Count Robert of Paris*. The correction of the press by Dr. Flügel. In three volumes. (Waverley novels, vol. 25–27) (Pest, Leipsic and London, 1832). 3 vols. in 1. Privately owned.

96 "W. Scott Waverley 1 Bd"
Walter Scott: *Waverley; or, 'Tis Sixty Years Since*. The correction of the press by Dr. Flügel. In three volumes. (Waverley novels, vol. 1–3) (Pest, Leipsic and London, 1831). 3 vols. in 1. Privately owned.

98 "Spanische Dramen übers. v. Dohrn 3 Bde"
Spanische Dramen übersetzt von C.A. Dohrn. 4 vols. (Berlin, 1841–44). All 4 vols. privately owned.

113 "Terentius 1 Bd 8[0]"
Terentius: *Comoediae*. Ed. F.G. Reinhardt (Lipsiae, 1827). Inscribed "Felix Mendelssohn Bartholdy," apparently in Rebecka's hand. With a few pencil annotations in FMB's hand. Privately owned.

116 "Odysee. 2 Bde"
With annotations by Felix and Carl MB. Now Leipzig, Stadtgeschichtliches Museum.

118 "Phaedrus 1 Bd"
Inscribed "Felix Mendelssohn Bartholdy," apparently in Rebecka's hand. Now Leipzig, Stadtgeschichtliches Museum

124 "Ovid 2 Bde"
Although there is a privately owned copy of Johann Heinrich Voss: *Verwandlungen nach Publius Ovidius Naso*. 2 vols. (Berlin, 1798), with the inscription "Mendelssohn Bartholdy" in an unidentified hand in both volumes, it is probably not to be identified with this item, since works in translation are usually identified as such in the list by FMB.

125 "Eutrop 1 Bd"
Eutropius: *Breviarium historiae Romanae*, ed. Hendrik Verheijk (Norimbergae, 1800). Inscribed "Felix Mendelssohn Bartholdy," apparently in Rebecka's hand. Leipzig, Stadtgeschichtliches Museum.

135 "Die Orgel v. Seydel 2 Bde"
1843 edition offered for sale by Quaritch, London, 2009.

139 "Eros u. Psyche v. Clodius 1 Bd"
With presentation inscription from the publisher, J.B.Hirschfeld, 7 Mar. 1842. Privately owned.

144 "Devrient Herr Baron"
Gift of the author – cf. Devrient's letter to FMB, 28 Jan. 1843 (GB XVII, 55) and FMB's reply of 14 Feb, 1843 (*Sämtliche Briefe*, no. 3813).

149 "Lanjuinais Leben"
This item is wrongly identified in the original article. The correct description is: Victor Lanjuinais: *Notice historique sur J.-D. Lanjuinais* (Paris, 1832). Presumably a gift from the author or his brother (Paul Eugène Lanjuinais) while FMB was in Paris in 1832 – cf. FMB letter to his family, 28 Feb. 1832 (*Sämtliche Briefe*, no. 508). Privately owned.

151 "Jacoby 4 Fragen"
Gift of FMB's brother, Paul – cf. Paul's letter, 2 Mar. 1843 (GB XIII, 101) and FMB's reply, 4 Mar. 1843 (*Sämtliche Briefe*, no. 3045).

163 "Berlin eine Wochenschrift (Geschenk von Gans)"
With a presentation inscription from Eduard Gans. Now Berlin, Staatsbibliothek, Mendelssohn-Archiv.

169 "Sophocles übers. v. Donner 1 Bd"
Sophokles [übersetzt] von J.J.C. Donner, 2 vols., 2. verbesserte Auflage (Heidelberg, 1842). Vol. 1 only, with annotations by FMB. Leipzig, Mendelssohn-Haus.

178 "Über Paulus v. Mosewius"
Actually published in 1837 – cf. *Sämtliche Briefe*, commentary to no. 1831. Gift of the author – cf. his letter to FMB, 16 Dec. 1837 (GB VI, 157).

195 "Lothar v. Kinkel"
Gift of the author – cf. Kinkel's letter to FMB, 27 June 1843 (GB XVII, 302/3) and FMB's reply, 31 July 1843 (*Sämtliche Briefe*, no. 4042).
199 "Schachspiel v. Thon"
FMB had the 1840 edition (apparently published towards the end of 1839) – cf. his letter to Hermann Franck, 1 Jan. 1840 (*Sämtliche Briefe*, no. 2570).
205 "Beschreibg. [der] Westminster Abbey"
An Historical Description of Westminster Abbey, its Monuments and Curiosities (London, 1827). Inscribed "Felix Mendelssohn Bartholdy," apparently in Rebecka's hand. Privately owned.
210 "Catalog der Rembrandtschen Rad[ier]ungen (by an Amateur)"
Vienna, Gesellschaft der Musikfreunde.
229 "Die Musik für Kirche u. Schule v. Alberti"
Gift of the author – cf. his letter to FMB, 22 Nov. 1843 (GB XVIII, 203) and FMB's reply, 12 Dec. 1843 (*Sämtliche Briefe*, no. 4168).
252 "Kreuser Die Overstolzen"
Probably returned to the author–cf. commentary to FMB's letter to E.H.W. Verkenius, 17 Aug. 1835 (*Sämtliche Briefe*, no. 1203).
270 "Kurze und faßliche Darstellung der Pestalozzischen Methode"
Now Leipzig, Stadtgeschichtliches Museum.

Additions:
Dante Alighieri: *Göttliche Komödie*. Translated by K.L. Kannegießer. 4., sehr veränderte Auflage. 3 vols. in 1. (Leipzig, 1843). Leipzig, Stadtgeschichtliches Museum.
Homer: *Odyssea. Tomus I: Rhapsodia I–XII*, Nova editio stereotypa (Lipsiae, 1839). Leipzig, Mendelssohn-Haus.
Louis Reybaud: *Jérome Paturot à la recherche d'une position sociale* (Paris, 1846). Inscribed "Dem verehrten Freunde F. Mendelssohn Bartholdy am 3 Februar 1847 von Ignaz u. Charlotte Moscheles." Privately owned.
Alfred Tennyson: *Poems*. 2nd ed. 2 vols. (London, 1843). Vol. 2 only, inscribed "Felix Mendelssohn from an English friend." Privately owned.
M.A. Thiers: *Histoire de la Révolution Française*, 2nd ed. 10 vols. (Bruxelles, 1828–9). Vol. 4 only. Leipzig, Stadtgeschichtliches Museum.
The Traveller's Guide to Scotland, and its Islands. 6th ed. 2 vols. (Edinburgh, 1814). Vol. 2 only. FMB's copy according to family tradition. Privately owned.
D.G. Türk: *Anweisung zum Generalbassspielen* (Halle & Leipzig, 1800). A 12th birthday present in 1821 from Johann Ludwig Casper. Berlin Staatsbibliothek, Musikabteilung.
The following three volumes may also have belonged to FMB, or at least passed through his hands:
J.J. Barthelemy: *Voyage du jeune Anacarsis en Grece*. 7 vols. (Paris, 1810). Inscribed "Mendelssohn Bartholdy" in vols. 2–7, apparently in Rebecka's hand. Privately owned.

Jean Paul: *Die unsichtbare Loge: Ein Lebensbeschreibung* Erster Theil. Zweite, verbesserte Auflage (Berlin, 1822). Inscribed "Mendelssohn Bartholdy," apparently in Rebecka's hand. Privately owned.

[Karl Spazier]: *Anti-Phädon, oder Prüfung einiger Hauptbeweise für die Einfachheit und Unsterblichkeit der menschlichen Seele: In Briefen* (Leipzig, 1785). With a six-line quotation from Moses Mendelssohn on a preliminary leaf. Privately owned.

1   "Mendelssohn's Opus 1: Bibliographical Problems of the C minor Piano Quartet," in *Sundry Sorts of Music Books: Essays on the British Library Collections: Presented to O.W. Neighbour on his 70th Birthday*, ed. Chris Banks, Arthur Searle & Malcolm Turner (London, 1993), 264–73.
2   Ibid., 267.
3   Felix Mendelssohn Bartholdy, *Sämtliche Briefe*, ed. Helmut Loos and Wilhelm Seidel, 12 vols. (Kassel, 2008–17), vol. 1, no. 35, 112.
4   "nehme ich mir die Freiheit, in Folge der mir gnädigst ertheilten Erlaubniß, die erste Arbeit, die ich publicire, gehorsamst darzubringen."
5   "Mein lieber Sohn, von heut ab bist Du kein Junge mehr, von heute an bist Du Gesell. Ich mache Dich zum Gesellen in Namen Mozart's, im Namen Haydn's und im Namen des alten Bach;" Sebastian Hensel, *Die Familie Mendelssohn, 1729–1847: nach Briefen und Tagebüchern*, 2nd ed., 2 vols. (Berlin, 1880), vol. 1, 139.
6   Larry Todd, *Mendelssohn: A Life in Music* (Oxford, 2003), 124.
7   Peter Ward Jones, "Mendelssohn's Performances of the 'Matthäus-Passion': Considerations of the Documentary Evidence," *Music & Letters*, 97 (2016): 409–64; at 411.
8   See note 7.
9   Berlin, Staatsbibliothek, SA 4658, which derives from a mid-18th century copy by J.C. Farlau (Staatsbibliothek Am, B 6–7), where the word "Organo" appears above the start of the chorale itself.
10 Ibid., 430.
11 A separate boys' chorus was being used at Leipzig by the late-1850s for, by then, annual performances of the Passion in the Thomaskirche, conducted by Julius Rietz. According to John Barnett, who was a student at Leipzig between 1857 and 1860 and heard two performances of the work: "One thing struck me greatly, on account of the fine combination of tone produced. This occurs in the opening chorus. The boys who sing the chorale, while elaborate counterpoint is in progress, stand apart in the gallery of the church, and their voices seem to soar above the rest of the chorus like a celestial choir joining in with those who are on the earth below." (John Francis Barnett: *Musical Reminiscences and Impressions* (London, 1906), 110–11). Who the boys were is unknown, but rather than the skilled Thomaner, they may have been boys from a charity school who sang at the Paulinerkirche (cf. Anselm Hartinger, *"Alte Neuigkeiten": Bach-Aufführungen und Leipziger Musikleben im Zeitalter Mendelssohns, Schumanns und Hauptmanns* (Wiesbaden, 2014), 615). The first use of a boys' chorus at the Berlin Singakademie's performances, appears to have been in 1902 (Gottfried Eberle, *250 Jahre Sing-Akademie zu Berlin* (Berlin, 1991), 177). In England it first occurred in William Sterndale Bennett's Bach Society performances, certainly at the 1862 one (*Musical World*, 40 (1862): 342–43) if not at the earlier ones of 1854 and 1858.
12 Anselm Hartinger, *"Alte Neuigkeiten"*, 533–36.
13 Bodleian Library, Oxford, MS. M. Deneke Mendelssohn b.9, fols. 153–56.
14 The part also has pencil markings, which were evidently made by the organist at the rehearsal.
15 As for example in the *Gesangbuch zum gottesdienstlichen Gebrauche in den Stadtkirchen xu Leipzig* (Leipzig, 1844). I thank Prof. Daniel Melamed for this reference.

16 Peter Ward Jones, "The Library of Felix Mendelssohn Bartholdy," in *Festschrift Rudolf Elvers zum 60. Geburtstag*, ed. E. Herttrich and H. Schneider (Tutzing, 1985), 289–328.
17 Thanks for valuable assistance are due to Dr. Ralf Wehner (Leipziger Mendelssohn Ausgabe), Dr. Roland Schmidt-Hensel (Staatsbibliothek, Berlin), and a direct family descendent of the composer.
18 In addition to those noted in the list below, the following items in the original article also have inscriptions in the same hand: 17, 106, 107, 114, 140 and 276.

II. MENDELSSOHN RECEPTION

6. FELIX MENDELSSOHN'S ENGLISH COUNTENANCE AS REFLECTED IN LONDON PUBLICATIONS OF HIS VOCAL CHAMBER MUSIC TO CA. 1850[1]

John Michael Cooper

One of the most celebrated episodes in Felix Mendelssohn Bartholdy's life is his third audience with the Prince Consort Albert during his seventh trip to England (9 July 1842)—an audience in Buckingham Palace that began with just the composer and the Prince Consort but was eventually joined by Queen Victoria, the Prince and Princess of Gotha, and the Duchess of Kent (the German-born mother of Victoria).[2] Although most commentators focus on either Mendelssohn's dedication of the English editions of his "Scottish" Symphony to the Queen, Her Majesty's decision to sing a song by Fanny from Felix's Op. 8 (*Italien*, H-U 157), or his embarrassment at having to admit that *Italien* had been composed by his older sister, even though it was published under his own name, a closer examination of this audience raises three other questions worthy of consideration:

- What edition was used for this reading of Mendelssohn's and Hensel's songs?
- In what language did Victoria and Albert sing these songs—and, for that matter, converse with the composer?
- What does the selection of songs presented in this royal audience tell us about the nature of the processes by which Mendelssohn's British contemporaries transferred and assimilated his German song persona into their own culture—what they emphasized or created, and what they downplayed or ignored altogether?[3]

Considering the publications of Mendelssohn's vocal chamber music in England that formed the context for this oft-discussed royal reading of his and his older sister's songs, and those that followed in its wake—offers some answers to these questions. It also illuminates important trends in the emergence of a distinctively English artistic persona for Mendelssohn, sheds light on the surprisingly high level of authority of many English versions of his songs, and reveals that one of his well-known German vocal duets, *Wie kann ich froh und lustig sein*, is not German at all, but rather a translation of a poem by Scots poet Robert Burns (1759–96).

I

The emergence of Mendelssohn's British song persona falls into three stages that roughly parallel the growth of his fame in Britain and reveal that this fame coincided with the gradual emergence of a distinctively British Mendelssohnian song persona.[4] During the first stage (1829–ca. 1836), he was viewed and treated as a talented and promising, but not necessarily commercially viable, performer/composer, and English publications of vocal-chamber repertoire consisted entirely of individual solo songs published in albums or larger collections of such works by other composers who were, for the most part, better established on the English market (see Table 1).

Most of these songs were retrospective publications of works which had been published in the German lands at least two years prior to the English editions. Because there was no question of copyright issues,[5] the works could be printed at minimal expense. The only exceptions are *Charlotte to Werther* (MWV K 48, based on Goethe), which was actually composed in English and offered by Mendelssohn to an English publisher without also being published in the German lands; and the *Frühlingslied* (Leise zieht durch mein Gemüt, MWV K 71 / Op. 19[a], no. 5), which was published in the original German rather than English translation and was printed in England in the same year as the original German publication. Both songs were extracted from collections that at the time were not published in their entirety in England.

After a two-year hiatus in vocal-chamber publications of Mendelssohn's music in 1837–38, then, a different and, in one sense, more authentically English Mendelssohn began to emerge at the turn of the 1840s.

As shown in Table 2, the earliest publications in this second stage were the two Romances on texts by Byron (MWV K 76 and K 85), which had been composed in 1833–34 on Byron's original texts and published in German translation in 1836/37;[6] these were released in their original (English) form in 1839 in a bilingual edition (with English texts beneath the German) by Wessel & Co. as Nos. 138 and 139 in the firm's well-established series *Auswahl deutscher Lieder / Series of German Song*. Around the same time, Ewer and Co. introduced Mendelssohn into the convivial realm of the English glee in Book 8 of the well-known series published under the collective title *Orpheus*. The song in question "Ah! Tell Me Not" is an anonymous English translation of one of the Heine partsongs that had been published as part of his Op. 41 in Germany in 1838 (MWV SD 18). Additionally, in June 1841 Mendelssohn sold Ewer & Co. the rights to "The Garland," his setting of "By Celia's Arbour All the Night" (MWV K 44, based on Ode XVIII of Thomas Moore's *Odes of Anacreon*, 1800). The latter publication may have been prompted by the apparently considerable commercial success of a publication issued by Wessel & Stapleton in October or November 1840: *Six German Songs by Fleming, Voss & Grillparzer, composed for Voice and Piano by Felix Mendelssohn Bartholdy*, a collection that was culled from Mendelssohn's Op. 8 and Op. 9 song collections (which had been published in Germany in 1827 and 1830) and was bilingual, with English translations presented above rather than below the German texts. These translations were prepared by Clara de Chatelain (1807–1876), who published under her maiden name, "Miss de Pontigny."

The songs in these last two publications are noteworthy in several regards. "The Garland" is the first song that Mendelssohn sold to an English publisher almost immediately after composing it on an English-language text. By contrast, the pieces

Table 1, Vocal Chamber Music Attributed to Mendelssohn and Published in English Editions, 1829–36

Year	MWV[1]	Engl. Title (Text Incipit) / translator	Engl. Collection Title (Publisher)[2]	German Title (Text Incipit) / Collection	Year of Ger. Edn.
1829	K 31	Song of the Pilgrim (The griefs, the cares that rend thee) / Wm. Ball	Apollo's Gift, or The Musical Souvenir for 1830 (Chappell, Clementi, & Co.)	Pilgerspruch (Laß dich nur nichts nicht dauern) / Op. 8, no. 5	1827
1830	K 48	Charlotte to Werther (All Moveless in Her Dark Bright Eye) / F. W. Collard	Apollo's Gift, or The Musical Souvenir for 1831 (Chappell, Clementi, & Co.)	Charlotte & Werther (Lang ist's her)	[1850][3]
1832	K 51	The Confiding Heart (Amid the limes the Zephyrs play) / William Ball	The Musical Gem: A Souvenir for 1833 (Mori & Lavenu)	Frühlingsglaube (Die linden Lüfte sind erwacht) / Op. 9, no. 8	1830
1832	K 54	Oh! Father, Let Me Fly to Thee (Lord! Amid this gloom and sorrow) / William Ball	The Musical Gem: A Souvenir for 1833 (Mori & Lavenu)	Entsagung (Herr, zu dir will ich mich retten) / Op. 9, no. 11	1830
1833	K 71	Gruß (Leise zieht durch mein Gemüt) / N/A[4]	Original Compositions in Prose and Verse, to Which Is Added Some Vocal and Instrumental Music (Edmund Lloyd)	Gruß / Frühlingslied (Leise zieht durch mein Gemüt) / Op. 19[a], no. 5	1833
1833	K 17	Maid of the Valley (Maid of the Valley, oh! Listen the cry) / W. E. Attfield	The Musical Gem: A Souvenir for 1834 (Mori & Lavenu)	Frühlingslied (Jetzt kommt der Frühling) / Op. 8, no. 6	1827
1833	K 39	Is It True? (Is it true? Whilst afar, where Pleasure's train) / Walter Thornton	The Musical Gem: A Souvenir for 1834 (Mori & Lavenu)	Frage (Ist es wahr?) / Op. 9, no. 1	1830
1834	K 52	O Lovely Spring (Ye Birds, for whom the soft dews swell!) / Walter Thornton	The Musical Gem: A Souvenir for 1835 (Mori & Lavenu)	Im Frühling (Ihr frühlingstrunknen Blumen) / Op. 9, no. 4	1830
1834	K 31	Sacred Song (Lord, when we bend before thy throne) / anon.	Sacred Minstrelsy: A Collection of Sacred Music (J. W. Parker)	Pilgerspruch (Lass dich nur nichts nicht dauern) / Op. 8, no. 5	1827
1836	K 56	A Spring Song (To the birds' glad songs I listen) / anon.	The Musical Library, vol. 3 (Charles Knight & Co.)	Frühlingslied (In dem Walde süße Töne)	1833
1836	K 42	Romance. Expectation (The lady's fair hand a swift falcon bore) / anon.	The Musical Library, vol. 3 (Charles Knight & Co.)	Wartend (Sie trug einen Falken auf ihrer Hand) / Op. 9, no. 3	1830

1 Wehner, Ralf. *Felix Mendelssohn Bartholdy: Thematisch-systematisches Verzeichnis der musikalischen Werke (MWV)*. Wiesbaden: Breitkopf & Härtel, 2009.
2 All publishers based in London.
3 First published in Germany in 1850, with new text by Hoffmann von Fallersleben, as Seemanns Scheidelied (Lang ist's her).
4 Title and words given in German only.

Table 2, Mendelssohn's Vocal Chamber Music Published in English editions, 1839-41

Year	MWV / H-U[1]	Engl. Title (Text Incipit if different) / translator or author	Engl. Collection or Series Title (Publisher)[2]	German Title (Text Incipit) / Collection or Publisher <Translator>	Year of Ger. Edn.
1839	F 4	*Ah! Tell Me Not* (Ah! tell me not that jealous fear betrays a weak suspicious mind) / anon. [Buxton?]	Orpheus, Book 8, no. 55 (J. J. Ewer & Co.)	*Entflieh mit mir* (Entflieh mit mir und sei mein Weib) / Op. 41, no. 2	1838
1839	K 76	*Romance No. 1* (There be none of beauty's daughters) / Byron	Series of German Songs / Auswahl deutscher Lieder, no. 138 (Wessel & Co.)	*Romanze [Nr. 1]*. (Keine von der Erde Schönen) / *Zwei Gesänge von Lord Byron*, in *Album Musical*[3] <Klingemann>	1836/1837
1839	K 85	*Romance No. 2* (Sun of the Sleepless) / Byron	Series of German Songs / Auswahl deutscher Lieder, no. 139 (Wessel & Co.)	*Romanze [Nr. 2]*. (Schlafloser Augen) / *Zwei Gesänge von Lord Byron*, in *Album Musical*[4]	1836/1837
1841	K 44	*The Garland* (By Celia's arbour all the night) / Thomas Moore	N/A (J. J. Ewer & Co.)	*Der Blumenkranz* (An Celias Baum in stiller Nacht) / anon.	1841
1841	F 14	*The First Day of Spring* (Come balmy breezes come) / anon. [Buxton?]	Orpheus, Book 10, no. 62 (J. J. Ewer & Co.)	*Frühlingsanfang* (O sanfter, süßer Hauch) / Op. 48, no. 1	1840
1841	MWV K 31	Let naught that's earthly pain thee / "Miss de Pontigny"[5]	*Six German Songs by Fleming, Voss & Grillparzer*. Series of German Songs / Auswahl deutscher Lieder, no. 239 (Wessel & Co.)	*Pilgerspruch* (Lass dich nur nichts nicht dauern), Op. 8, no. 5	1827
	MWV K 51	*Spring Is Returning* / "Miss de Pontigny"	*Six German Songs by Fleming, Voss & Grillparzer*. Series of German Songs / Auswahl deutscher Lieder, no. 240 (Wessel & Co.)	*Frühlingsglaube* (Die linden Lüfte sind erwacht) / Op. 9, no. 8	1830
	H-U 157	*Fairer the Meads Are Growing* / "Miss de Pontigny"	*Six German Songs by Fleming, Voss & Grillparzer*. Series of German Songs / Auswahl deutscher Lieder, no. 241 (Wessel & Co.)	*Italien* (Schöner und schöner schmückt sich der Plan) / Mendelssohn's Op. 8, no. 3	1827

	MWV K 35	*The Tender Greeting.* *Spanish Romance* (One kiss, one tender greeting) / "Miss de Pontigny"	*Six German Songs by Fleming, Voss & Grillparzer.* Series of German Songs / *Auswahl deutscher Lieder,* no. 242 (Wessel & Co.)	*Romanze* (Einmal aus seinen Blicken) / Op. 8, no. 10	1827
	MWV K 36	*O Come to the Greenwood* / "Miss de Pontigny"	*Six German Songs by Fleming, Voss & Grillparzer* . Series of German Songs / *Auswahl deutscher Lieder,* no. 243 (Wessel & Co.)	*Im Grünen* (Willkommen im Grünen) / Op. 8, no. 11	1827
	MWV K 37	*There Is a Reaper* / "Miss de Pontigny"	*Six German Songs by Fleming, Voss & Grillparzer.* Series of German Songs / *Auswahl deutscher Lieder,* no. 244 (Wessel & Co.)	*Erntelied* (Es ist ein Schnitter) / Op. 8, no. 4	1827

1   Hellwig-Unruh, Renate. *Fanny Hensel geb. Mendelssohn Bartholdy: Thematisches Verzeichnis der Kompositionen*. Adliswil: Ed. Kunzelmann, 2000.
2   All publishers based in London.
3   Composed in English, 1833.
4   Composed in English, 1834.
5   Pseud. Clara de Chatelain, née Clara Du Mazet de Pontigny (1807-1876).

in Wessel & Stapleton's *Six German Songs* were retrospective translations of works composed and published only in Germany (and thus not protected by copyright in Britain) in 1827 and 1830. This widely circulated collection appears to have established Mendelssohn's commercial viability in the English song market once and for all. Indeed, so well-received was Wessel's publication of de Chatelain's translation of Hensel's "Italien" that it was selected as Mendelssohn's [sic] sole contribution to the prestigious *Prince of Wales's Album*, released by Wessel & Stapleton in early 1842 to celebrate the baptism of the future King Edward VII.[7]

Those circumstances, interesting enough in themselves, also have a larger suggestion—for they make it probable that this was the volume used in Mendelssohn's royal audience—and the fact that the Wessel & Stapleton volume presented the English text above the German raises the possibility that Her Majesty sang the songs in the language of the country whose sovereign she was. Moreover, the Ewer and Wessel publications of 1840–41 launched a veritable bidding war between those two firms as they sought to tap into Mendelssohn's rapidly growing fame in England and establish a secure presence for him in the realm of vocal chamber music in Britain (see Table 3). In the summer of 1842—around the time of the audience with the Queen and Prince Consort—Mendelssohn opened a new chapter in the creation of his English song persona by discussing with Wessel the publication of English editions/translations of some of his new songs contemporaneous with the German editions, and on 24 November he offered that firm the English copyright to what would eventually

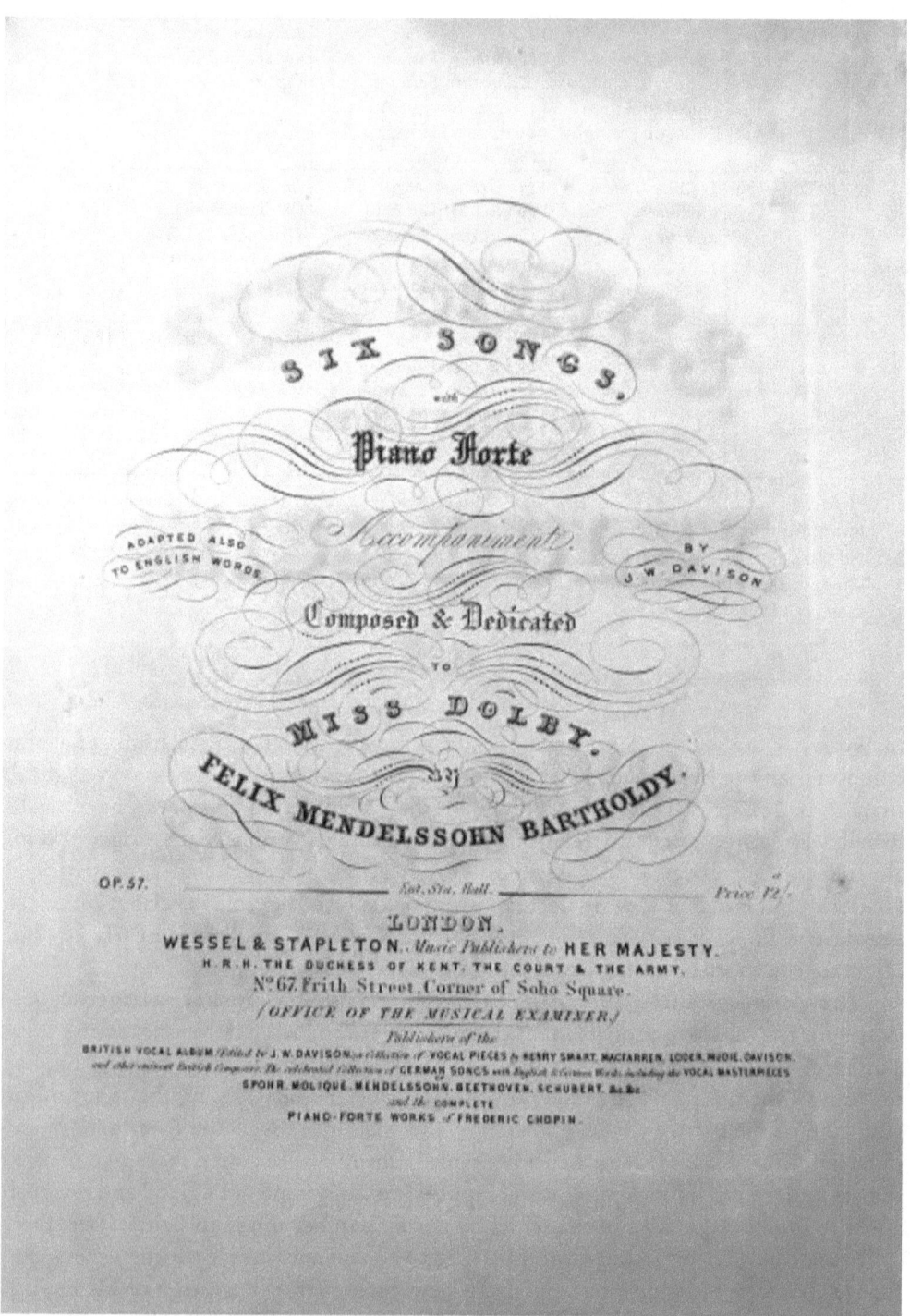

Figure 1, Title Page of Wessel Edition of Mendelssohn Op. 57 (MWV SD 26)

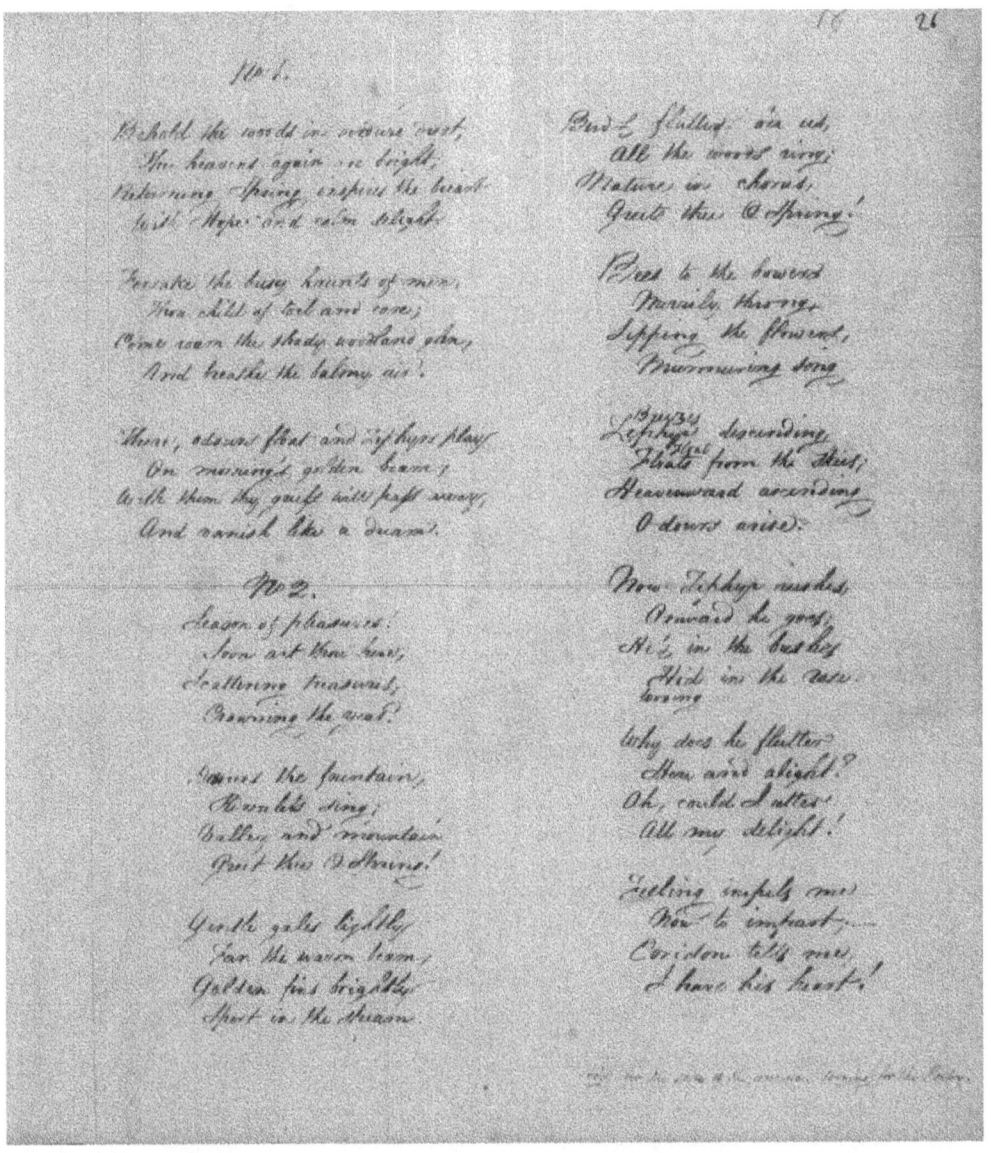

Figure 2, Bartholomew's Draft Translations for Mendelssohn's Op. 59 Partsongs (Bodleian Library, Oxford, GB 18- 26)

be released as his Op. 57 songs (MWV SD 26, 1843).[8] The translator for this edition was James William Davison (1813–85), eventual chief music critic of the *Times*. The opus was published in England and Germany—but in March 1843 Mendelssohn had offered Ewer the rights to an English translation of his new partsongs for mixed voices (SD 27/ Op. 59).[9]

He submitted those works to Buxton at Ewer & Co. on 29 June 1843 with the

Table 3, Ewer *contra* Wessel, 1842-47

Year	Ewer & Co.	Wessel & Co.	Notes
1842	*My Bark Is Bounding to the Gale* = *Wasserfahrt* (Ich stand gelehnet an den Mast), MWV J 3. Heine, trans. Bartholomew.	[Hensel], *Fairer the Meads Are Growing* = *Italien* (Schöner und schöner schmuckt sich der Plan), H-U 157. Grillparzer, trans. "Miss de Pontigny. In *The Prince of Wales's Album*, no. 14.	Wessel announced as "received for review" in *The Musical World* 17 (3 Feb. 1842): 39
	The Recompence (Jovial hearts love a glass of wine) = *Ersatz für Unbestand* (Lieblich mundet der Becher Wein), MWV G 25. Rückert, trans. anon. [Buxton?].		
1843	*Six Vocal Quartetts for Two Trebles, Tenor & Bass (to Be Sung without Accompaniment)* = *Sechs vierstimmige Lieder für Sopran, Alt, Tenor und Bass im Freien zu singen*, Vol. 3. MWV SD 27 / Op. 59. Various authors, trans. Bartholomew.	*How Can I Light and Joyous Be?* = *Volkslied* (Wie kann ich froh und lustig sein?), MWV J 1. Kaufmann, trans. F. W. Rosier.	
	Home, Far Away! = *Volkslied* (Wie kann ich froh und lustig sein?), MWV J 1. *The Siren: A Collection of Vocal Duets*, no. 10. Kaufmann, trans. W. Bartholomew.		
	Evening Song (Oh, when on my couch reclining) = *Abendlied* (Wenn ich auf dem Lager liege), MWV J 2. *The Siren: A Collection of Vocal Duets*, no. 11. Heine, trans. anon.	*Lord Byron's Ballads, composed for Voice and Piano by Felix Mendelssohn-Bartholdy*. Contains "There Be None of Beauty's Daughters" (MWV K 76), "Sun of the Sleepless" (MWV K 85), and "How Can I Light and Joyous Be?" (Kaufmann, trans. F. W. Rosier). Series of German Songs, Nos. 138-40.	
	Swiss Spring Song (Spring cometh hither) = *Frühlingslied* (Jetzt kommt der Frühling), MWV K 17 (Op. 8/6).		
	Lord! Have Mercy = *Responses to the Commandments* (Zum Abendsegen), MWV B 27. Orpheus, Book 12. Trans. anon.		
1844	*Six Vocal Quartetts for Male Voices (to Be Sung without Accompaniment)* = *Sechs Lieder für vierstimmigen Männerchor*, MWV SD 22 (Op. 50). Various authors, trans. Bartholomew.	*Six Songs with Piano Forte Accompaniment, . . . Composed and Dedicated to Miss Dolby*, MWV SD 26 (Op. 57). Various authors, trans. J. W. Davison.	
	Six Two-Part Songs for Female Voices with Acompaniments of the Piano-Forte = *Sechs Lieder für zwei Singstimmen und Klavier*, MWV SD 30 (Op. 63). Various authors, trans. anon.		No. 5 of Ewer Op. 63 is originally by Walter Scott and composed in English (O wert thou in the cauld blast). In German edn (Leipzig: F. Kistner) trans. F. Freiligrath as "O sähe ich auf der Heide dort."

1845	*Eleven Songs . . . in Two Books* = *Zwölf Gesänge*, MWV SD 2 (Op. 8). Various authors, trans. Bartholomew. Nos. 2 and 3 comp. by Fanny Hensel. No. 12 of German publication is a duet and is omitted from the Ewer edn.	*On Deck, Beside the Mast I Stand* = *Wasserfahrt* (Ich stand gelehnet an den Mast), MWV J 3. Heine, trans. "Miss de Pontigny."	
	Twelve Songs . . . in Two Books = *Zwölf Gesänge*, MWV SD 3 (Op. 9). Various authors, trans. Bartholomew. Nos. 7, 10, and 12 comp. by Fanny Hensel.	*Six Lieder for Voice and Piano* = *Sechs Lieder*, MWV SD 20 (Op. 47). Series of German Song, nos. 265-70. Various authors, trans. "Miss de Pontigny"	
	Six Songs with Piano-Forte Accompaniment = *Sechs Gesänge mit Begleitung des Pianoforte*, MWV SD 16 (Op. 19[a]). Various authors, trans. Bartholomew.	*On Songs [sic] Bright Pinion* = *Abendlied* (Auf Flügeln des Gesanges), MWV K 86 (Op. 34/2). Series of German Song, no. 252. Heine, trans. "Miss de Pontigny."	
	Savoyard Song (With my mandoline [sic]) = *Pagenlied* (Wenn die Sonne lieblich schiene), MWV K 75. Gems of German Song, Book 14, no. 5. Eichendorff, trans. Bartholomew.	*All thro' the woods* = *Sonntagslied* (Ringsum erschallt in Wald und Flur), MWV K 84 (Op. 34/5). Series of German Song, no. 253. Klingemann, trans. "Miss de Pontigny."	
	Six Songs with Piano-Forte Accoompaniment = *Sechs Gesänge mit Begleitung des Pianoforte*, MWV SD 13 (Op. 34). Various authors, trans. Bartholomew.	*'Tis Night* ('Tis night, the dry leaves are rustling) = *Reiselied* (Der Herbstwind rüttelt die Bäume), MWV K 90 (Op. 34/6). Series of German Song, no. 254. Heine, trans. "Miss de Pontigny."	
1846	*Six Songs with Piano-Forte Accompaniment* = *Sechs Gesänge mit Begleitung des Pianoforte*, MWV SD 20 (Op. 47). Various authors, trans. Bartholomew.		
	The Mountain Burgh (Above the haunts) = *Das Waldschloß* (Wo noch kein Wandrer gegangen), MWV K 87. Gems of German Song, book 16, no. 8. Eichendorff, trans. [?] Bartholomew.		
	I Hear a Small Bird Calling = *Im Frühling* (Ich hör ein Vöglein locken), MWV 107. Böttger, trans. Bartholomew.		
1847	*Sun of the Sleepless*, MWV K 85. Gems of German Song, book 18, no. 2. Byron.		
	Six Songs with Accompaniments for the Piano-Forte = *Sechs Gesänge mit Begleitung des Pianoforte*, MWV SD 35 (Op. 71). Various authors, trans. Bartholomew.		

Table 4, Comparison of text and translations of *Pilgerspruch* (MWV K 31 / Op. 8, no. 5)

Pilgerspruch (Fleming) (as composed by Mendelssohn)	Prose translation	Trans. William Ball[1] (1829)	Trans. anon. [J. W. Parker] (1834)[2]	Trans. "Miss de Pontigny" (pseud. Clara de Chatelain) (1841)[3]	Trans. William Bartholomew (1845)[4]
Laß dich nur nichts nicht dauern Mit Trauern, Sei stille! Wie Gott es fügt, So sei vergnügt Mein Wille.	But do let anything sustain your grief, Be still! As God ordains it, May my will be content in it.	The griefs, the cares that rend thee, Restraining, Disdaining, Be still my wayward Soul, and cease, ah! Cease thay vain complaining.	Lord, when we bend before thy throne, And our confessions pour, Teach us to feel the sins we own, And shun what we deplore!	Let nought that's earthly pain thee, Restrain thee, and ever, to bow thy will God's law to fill, endeavor.	Let nothing cloud thy gladness with sadness; denials thou must abide. Thou'rt purified by trials.
Was willst du heute sorgen Auf morgen? Der Eine steht allem für; Der gibt auch dir das Deine.	Why do you want to worry today about tomorrow? The one and only God Stands for all; He also gives you what is yours.	Tho' gath'ring shades enfold thee, Tomorrow thoul't borrow From never-failing Heav'ly Love A balm for all thy sorrow.	Our contrite spirit pitying see, True penitence impart, And let a healing ray from thee Shed hope upon the heart.	O think not that with sorrow tomorrow may blight thee! From God thy due there shall accrue to right thee.	What fills thy heart with sorrow? Tomorrow? Thou'rt guided; Heav'n cares for thee, thy wants will be provided.
Sei nur in allem Handel Ohn Wandel, Steh feste! Was Gott beschleußt, Das ist und heißt das Beste.	But in all your dealings Do not stray, Stand fast! Whatever God decides, That is the best and is for the best.	To Nature's Friend and Father Still flying, Relying On Him for whatsoe'er is best, with faith and hope undying.	When we disclose our wants in prayer, May we our wills resign, And not a thought our bosom share That is not wholly thine.	Let truth in all thy dealings and feelings be purest! 'Tis God's behest must be the best and surest.	Serve God, obey, revere Him, and fear Him: Stand fast, man! What He decrees must be, and is the best plan.

1 *Apollo's Gift, or, The Musical Souvenir for MDCCCXXX* (London: Chappell, 1829).
2 *Sacred Minstrelsy: A Collection of Sacred Music*, Vol. 1, pp. 172–73 (London: J. W. Parker, 1834).
3 *Six German Songs by Fleming, Voss & Grillparzer, Wessel & Co.'s Series of German Songs, no. 239* (London: Wessel & Stapleton, [1841].
4 *Eleven Songs. The English Words Written and Adapted by W. Bartholomew Esqre. The Music by Felix Mendelssohn Bartholdy. In Two Books.* (London: J. J. Ewer & Co., [1845]).

explicit request that he be allowed to vet the translation before they were engraved.[10] On 18 July the principal house translator of Ewer & Co., William Bartholomew (1793–1867), with whom Mendelssohn had already collaborated on the incidental music to *Antigone* (Op. 55 / MWV M 12), sent the requested translations.

As we shall see, after a protracted exchange of letters hammering out how the translation should be handled, the edition was issued simultaneously by Breitkopf & Härtel in Germany and Ewer & Co. in England later in the fall of 1843.

By 1844, then, both Ewer and Wessel were vying for exclusive rights to Mendelssohn's new and recent vocal chamber music and publishing these works in collections devoted exclusively to Mendelssohn—much different than the situation that obtained with the individual pieces published between 1829 and 1836. The flashpoint in this bidding war was the collection of solo songs that had been released by Breitkopf & Härtel in 1839 as Mendelssohn's Op. 47 (MWV SD 20), which had been published in Germany only and thus was not under copyright in England. Both Wessel and Ewer seized the opportunity to publish it. Bartholomew, working for Buxton at Ewer & Co., wrote to Mendelssohn on 16 March 1844, that he had "written words to your Opera 8. 9. 19. 34. 47 + 50,"[11] and Ewer's edition of Bartholomew's translations of Opp. 8, 9, 19, and 34, as well as the "Pagenlied" (MWV K 75)[12] all came out in 1845. In the spring or early summer of 1845, Wessel, watching his rival's progress in this venture, released new English editions / translations of three songs from Op. 34 (Leipzig: Breitkopf & Härtel, 1837),[13] reminded Mendelssohn that he had offered them "3 new Duets" and various unspecified "new Songs and other works,"[14] and in September 1845[15] beat Ewer to the punch and released the first English edition of Mendelssohn's most recent set of old songs, Op. 47 (once again in a translation by Clara de Chatelain).[16] Buxton and Ewer finally released their own edition of that opus in the spring of 1846[17] – with the result that there are two competing English editions of Mendelssohn's Opus 47 songs.

As Peter Ward Jones has documented, Ewer eventually won out, in what emerges as the third stage in the English reception of Mendelssohn's vocal chamber music.[18] Although Wessel re-issued a number of previously published songs during the final few years of the composer's life, only Ewer managed to release new vocal chamber music. Although the principal contributions in these final two years—the C-minor Piano Trio (MWV Q 33 / Op. 66), the Op. 69 motets (MWV SD 37), and of course *Elijah* (MWV A 25 / Op. 70)—dwarf the vocal chamber music, between the spring of 1846 and the spring of 1848 Ewer released Bartholomew's translation of three (possibly four) individual songs[19] as well as Mendelssohn's final authorized opus (Op. 71) (it actually came out several months after the composer's death on 4 November 1847).[20]

Ewer's monopoly also extended for some time thereafter: they released the Op. 75 and Op. 76 partsongs (MWV SD 38 and 43) in 1849, the Op. 84 songs (MWV SD 45) in 1850, the Op. 86 songs (MWV SD 47) in 1850/51, the Op. 88 partsongs (SD 49) in 1850/51, the Op. 99 songs (SD 50) in 1852, and the Op. 100 partsongs (SD 51) in 1852. All these editions used translations by William Bartholomew. These posthumous publications also included the first complete issues of the partsong volumes originally published as opp. 41 and 48.[21]

II

If this convoluted set of edition-histories demonstrates that the quantity and authority of English publications of Mendelssohn's vocal chamber music released during his lifetime is greater than has previously been recognized, it also illuminates several issues and themes that shaped the emergence and cultivation of Mendelssohn's English song persona. The first of these issues—which was naturally exacerbated by copyright law of the day—is simply that of control: control of language, text, translation, the interpretation of textual themes, and of course control of diction. A comparison of the various translations of Mendelssohn's "Pilgerspruch" (MWV K 31 / Op. 8, no. 5), the first song released in Britain, illustrates this issue.

"Pilgerspruch" came out in four English versions during Mendelssohn's lifetime. As shown in Table 4, the quality and character of the translations vary widely. The first of these translations, prepared by William Ball, has some authority because Ball had provided the English translation of *St. Paul* (MWV A 14 / Op. 36); but the second translation (published in J. W. Parker's *Sacred Minstrelsy*, 1834) is more remarkable, for it bears little resemblance to either Fleming's original or Mendelssohn's setting: the English words do not fit Mendelssohn's melody in any sense. By contrast, Clara de Chatelain's and William Bartholomew's translations (1841 and 1845) both retain the essential textual themes of Fleming's poem and are reasonably well-fitted to Mendelssohn's music. Nonetheless, they also reveal substantial difficulties. In the first stanza of de Chatelain's version, the original textual theme of acceptance is replaced by one of guilt and repentance; at this same point Bartholomew turns instead to tribulation. De Chatelain's translation of the second strophe is reasonably true, but in that strophe Bartholomew abandons the unassuming language of the poem. His stilted "Thou'rt guided; Heav'n cares for thee, thy wants will be provided" makes no effort to preserve the connotations of humility that normally attend the concept of pilgrimage.

More faithful translations resulted when Mendelssohn himself was involved in the process. As noted above, by the time Mendelssohn offered his op. 59 partsongs to Ewer, he had collaborated with Bartholomew on the English translation of the incidental music to *Antigone*. Bartholomew knew well that in Mendelssohn's aesthetics of translation it was more important to convey the general "sense" or "idea" of the text in terms that the target audience could identify with than to translate the text literally.[22] This awareness clearly underlies the cover letter Bartholomew and Buxton sent to Mendelssohn on 18 July 1843, as well as the translations. The letter also makes clear that Goethe's "Frühzeitiger Frühling" and Eichendorff's "Jagdlied" (no. 6) were the most difficult texts to translate—an idea that was corroborated by Buxton and by Mendelssohn himself. Bartholomew wrote:

> ...In the accompanying [v]ersions[23] of your 4part songs I have endeavoured to render the *ideas*: and I hope you [wil]l credit me for the intention if I have

failed in the execution.
No[.] 6 is an exception: fo[r n]either Mr. Buxton (who is more than half a German) nor a German friend of his, can render the [illegible] of its ideas clear to me. "O Lieb O Liebe, so lass mich los."—Is this addressed to Love, o[r] a Mistress who is endeavoring to detain, him—or whoever the speaker may be? This vagueness [wi]ll not do for our unimaginative English. I therefore have taken the liberty of departing fr[om i]t, & writing a free version, or imitation of a Hunting Song which will I think be better understo[od] here. I do not need the music, because it will stand as you have given it. At the sa[me] time I beg you will [?]fully criticise, and point out any thing you object to, and may wish me to al[ter,] and I will <u>endeavour</u> to meet your wishes. I am expecting to hear from you about the "Lied" version [I] last sent you: —if you dislike it, say so: and yet I know not what I can substitute for it—yet I will, again & again....[24]

To this, Buxton—who spoke good German and was able to correspond with the composer in German[25]—appended his own note supporting Bartholomew:

...I canno[t] for the life of me give Bartholomew a clear idea what the Jagdlied means & consequently he cannot write up to it. If you don't like what he has written please to tell us what the poem really does mean. I have shewn it to 2 or 3 of my friends, but they are as stupid as I am in the matter.[26]

To this Mendelssohn replied with admirable grace, wit, and detail on 31 July[27]:

...Many thanks for yesterday's letter with the translation of the 6 songs. I like it very very much & have only a few trifling objections to make, none to any of them as a whole, but only to some details. Your despair about Eichendorffs [sic] poetry has made me laugh very much; it is a very odd thing, and meant to be so, & would sound still more wild if translated litteraly [sic]; I think your version a very good one, & as a whole it corresponds with the German meaning perfectly; although I miss some details "O Lieb o Liebe" &c. (which by the bye is *not* addressed to a lady) for which I am not sorry at all, as it sings the better, & is much easier understood & is indeed much more the thing than a more litteral [sic] translation would be. My objections (for you see I am the eternal objector) are:
(1) In no. 2, the last two stanza's [sic] and more particularly the last, and more particularly the last two lines, & most particularly the Corydon in them. – Pray don't let us have Corydon, or any such name in it! I could never reconcile it to my feelings, if Corydon, or Phyllis, or Damon came in at the end. I would even wish that neither: "he" nor "she" was mentioned, & that it was something of love which the Tenor & Bass could say as well, as the Soprano & Alto. So it is in the German although it does not seem so, & although it is rather a difficult

passage, of which a litteral [sic] translation would not do at all. There are some more objections I have in that song. "Now Zephyr rushes onward he goes" there I should prefer something more litteral [sic], because it is one of the greatest beauties of the poem. The "mächtiger" "more powerful" ought to be expressed if possible as well as the "doch er verliert" "but it vanishes"; this contrast is so beautifully expressive of Spring time. Then I would wish in the beginning of the last but one Stanza to have the German expression "zum Busen kehrt er zurück" it returns to the bosom – at least the *returning*, because it is this word that gave me the idea of coming back to the first subject, & it does therefore well with the music. And then it is so fine in the poetry to follow the Zephyr (or what wind it may be) on its way: beginning first "more powerfully", "vanishing" then directly in the bushes, & returning at last to the bosom or the feeling of the poet! But before all, pray kill Corydon, because I detest him amazingly....

Bartholomew replied:

Your objections are most excellent; and they enhance my admiration of your genius in sense as well as sound. No. 2 now stands thus. –

6. Breezes descending Float from the skies	7. One [t?]hither rushes Lightly it flies! Tis in the bushes Fading in sighs.	8. Now hither winging Tis in my breast! Muses: all singing say I am blest!	9. Yesterday sisters Who should appear? Wafted on Zephyrs <u>Beauty</u> come here!

"Beauty" is the only equivalent I can find for "Liebchen" which Goethe meant, as I suppose, to imply *Spring*, or, under the rose as we term it, not only Spring, but the Spring of Love. – We could not say "Sweetheart" – "the dear one" [inserted: "the dearest"] might have done; but not for your music. I thought of "Cupid" but Mr Buxton said it was likely to be objected to by you. He said "Sweet Spring" – did not sing well – and was too definite – so upon quiet reflection I put *Beauty*; which may be considered as Spring, for she is Beauty's self embodied in the youth of Nature's charms. If also Goethe meant a more definite person "a lover" *Beauty* still will do. – I am this minute to show you how highly I respect *all* your suggestions; and how greatly I desire to please you. ...

Now "the hunting song" – I rendered it as the sense was given to me, *feather bunches* (in the hats of the hunters) – (When I was at Chateau [illegible] the young men of the present prince used with him to start at day dawn dressed fantastically with *feathers* in their hats – chapeaux-caps-two.) But it now is – "Now farther and farther / they lowed along / the woodlands and vallies [sic] / Reecho their song! *Like gales o'er the heather / they sportively stray / Hearts bounding together / while steeds bound away!*/" at the conclusion, on the word "reecho" – at B in the bass, I have taken the liberty to alter a crotchet to a quaver thus ♪♪♩♪ – re-e-cho-their this is answered by the octave a bar or so after in the Tenor I think (for I am writing from a recollection). The imitation by sound and sense thus becomes more pointed, besides which the word sings better thus noted on the open Ó....[28]

After this protracted and detailed exchange, the Op. 59 partsongs finally were released simultaneously in November 1843 by Breitkopf & Härtel and Ewer & Co.[29] We may assume that Mendelssohn was satisfied with the collaboration, for as we have seen, after 1844 he entrusted Ewer with no fewer than three separate *opera* of new vocal chamber music, to say nothing of other major projects such as *Die erste Walpurgisnacht* (MWV D 3 / Op. 60), the *Midsummer Night's Dream* incidental music (MWV M 13 / Op. 61), and of course *Elijah*.

III

The Op. 59 translations also illuminate another issue that is commonly overlooked in Mendelssohn's vocal chamber music—namely, that the British construction of Mendelssohn as composer of vocal chamber music was quite selective, far more so than the German one during his lifetime. And this issue entails a paradox, for if quantities of publication, translation, and edition (i.e., bibliographic bulk) are any indication, then Fanny Hensel, not Felix Mendelssohn, was the most celebrated "English" Mendelssohn song composer in the 1830s and 1840s. The "Pilgerspruch" sung by Queen Victoria was Felix's most-published song during his lifetime, with four separate English translations and editions with four different English publishers between 1829 and 1845; this was closely followed by "Frühlingsglaube," which was published in three editions and translations with different publishers between 1830 and 1845. By contrast, there were at least six separate English issues of Hensel's "Italien," all attributed to Felix and most translated by Clara de Chatelain. In view of that song's popularity, it seems telling that "Italien" was the first song that Queen Victoria sang for the composer. And that choice is hardly surprising, for Fanny's song consistently garnered euphoric reviews in the British press—as for example in *The Musical World* of 30 September 1841. There, Fanny's song—attributed to Felix—is described as "[a] melody once heard never to be unremembered; one that will haunt you in your sleeping and in your waking, like an undying conscience; ... a world in sixteen bars."[30]

This reception commingled with mistaken identity is itself a symptom of a broader and deeper issue; for in their initial nonchalance about Mendelssohn's secular vocal music and later cultivation of a small and specific set of works that they found particularly suited to the needs and tastes of their world, the English musical public effectively constructed a distinctively English Mendelssohn song persona. The "Pilgerspruch" is a song of piety; "Frühlingsglaube" a song of springtime as metaphor for the awakening of new feelings of love and joy. And most of the seventeen additional songs that were published in competing translations as part of the rivalry between Ewer and Wessel have to do with these same themes. Noticeably lacking among the songs most popular in England are the serious songs whose subjects deal with death or other overtly sad topics of loss and/or mourning. While German-language consumers of Mendelssohnian song knew Mendelssohn was a thematically diverse and multifaceted voice that musically cultivated the rich irony and probing spiritual questions prominently associated with German romanticism, for Britain's musical public he was a voice associated first and foremost with piety, then with amorous, happy springtime, and then with sentimental love tinged with melancholy. The British song-composing Mendelssohn is a highly selective construction whose one-dimensionality would have been barely recognizable to the German-speakers who enjoyed a more holistic view of his song output.

But perhaps the most fascinating insight to be gained from the bibliographic and translational issues touched on above is the ascendancy of a Mendelssohn with pronounced British stripes. In 1843 Wessel & Co. elected to re-publish the Byron Romances they had first published in 1839, and in 1846 Ewer, consolidating its command as the leading publisher of Mendelssohn's vocal chamber music in the U.K., published those works anew, now with the English texts above the German ones. Similarly, the late 1840s and early 1850s saw the ascent of Mendelssohn's setting of the Irish poet Thomas Moore's "The Garland" (MWV K 44) from a warmly but not overly enthusiastic reception after its release in 1841[31] into a work that became an absolutely ubiquitous staple of British musical life—not only with many documented concert performances, but also through numerous transcriptions and arrangements as well as pirated editions.[32]

Perhaps most compellingly, so complete was the fusion of Mendelssohn's cultural identity with that of authentically British poets by the late 1840s that the original authorship of "How Can I Light and Joyous Be" was obliterated. This vocal duet was initially published in Germany only and without opus number (Berlin: A.M. Schlesinger, [1836/37]), and in England it was released in 1843 by both Wessel & Co. and Ewer & Co.

But although (as shown in Table 3) the title page of Wessel's edition includes it in a volume of "Lord Byron's Ballads" and specifies that "How Can I Light and Joyous Be" is "Translated and Adapted" by F. W. Rosier, the title at the head of the score for that song identifies it as a "Volkslied von P. Kaufmann," while the contemporaneous Ewer edition uses a new translation by Bartholomew that closely follows the original German text. Both of these editions overlook an issue that has until now also been overlooked by Mendelssohn scholarship:[33] the fact that "Wie kann ich froh und lustig sein" (MWV J 1) is neither by Byron nor the German poet Philipp Kaufmann (1802–46). Rather, it is an abridged translation of the 1788 poem "My Bonnie Lad That's Far Awa" (O how can I be blythe and glad) by the Scot Robert Burns (see Table 5).

Exactly how and when Mendelssohn came into contact with Kaufmann's translation of Burns's poem is unclear, since the latter's collected translations of the Scot's poetry first appeared in book form in 1839, some three years after Mendelssohn's duet.[34] But perhaps it is not too great an exaggeration to interpret this poetic confusion as an indication that by the last five years of Mendelssohn's life, his English collaborators construed him (in his selectively constructed early Victorian persona) as so much an adopted native son of their land, or so convincingly British, that they unknowingly overlooked genuinely British (in this case Scots) elements in his music and construed them as his own Britishness.

Table 5, Comparison of text and translations of *Wie kann ich froh und lustig sein?*

Kaufmann / FMB	Burns[1]	Rosier (1843)
Wie kann ich froh und lustig sein? \ Wie kann ich gehn mit Band und Strauss? \ Wenn der herzge Junge, der mir so lieb, \ Ist über die Berge weit hinaus!	O how can I be blythe and glad, \ Or how can I gang brisk and braw, \ When the bonie lad that I lo'e best \ Is o'er the hills and far awa!	How can I light and joyous be? \ Or deck thy band with posy gay? \ When the youth who is so dear to me \ Is over the mountain far away \ . . .
's ist nicht der frostge Winterwind, \ 's ist nicht der Schnee und Sturm und Graus, \ Doch immer kommen mir Traenen ins Aug, \ Denk ich an ihn, der weit hinaus.	It's no the frosty winter wind, \ It's no the driving drift and snaw; \ But aye the tear comes in my e'e, \ To think on him that's far awa.	'Tis not the frost in winter drear, \ Causes my heart this fond dismay, \ Or dims my eyelid with one falling tear, \ But only he, who's far away . . .
Der lange Winter ist vorbei, \ Der Frühling putzt die Birken aus, \ \ Es grünt und blüht und lacht der Mai, \ Dann kehrt er heim, der weit hinaus!	O weary Winter soon will pass, \ And Spring will cleed the birken shaw; \ And my young babie will be born, \ And he'll be hame that's far awa.	The dull cold winter's past and o'er, \ And soon will laughing flow'ry May, \ \ To my fond heart the youth restore \ Who's over the mountain far away!

1 Strophes 3 and 4 of Burns's poem were not set by Mendelssohn: "My father pat me frae his door, My friends they hae disown'd me a'; But I hae ane will tak my part, The bonie lad that's far awa. A pair o' glooves he bought to me, And silken snoods he gae me twa; And I will wear them for his sake, The bonie lad that's far awa. awa."

Figure 3, Title Page of Felix Mendelssohn Bartholdy [and Fanny Hensel], Six German Songs by Fleming, Voss & Grillparzer (London- Wessel & Co., [1840/1841])

* * *

Returning to the questions with which we opened this inquiry: by the time of Mendelssohn's audience with Victoria and Albert in July 1842, all the songs that came up in that performance had been published in English translations by Wessel & Stapleton. While it is true that everyone present at the audience (the composer, Her Majesty, the Prince Consort, the Crown Prince of Gotha, and the Duchess of Kent) spoke German, and that after a previous audience Mendelssohn had commented to his mother that the Queen spoke good German,[35] Victoria's own private journals were written in English, not German. What is more, the title page to the 1841 publication of *Six German Songs by Fleming, Voss & Grillparzer* also identifies Wessel & Co. as "importers and publishers of foreign music, by special appointment, to H[er] R[oyal] H[ighness] the Duchess of Kent," who was the mother of Victoria and a member of the group that day. And this audience took place in Buckingham Palace and with Victoria and Albert, the personification of the English monarchy and of Britain itself.

Under these circumstances, it would have been only natural—indeed, culturally and politically fitting—for Wessel's *Six German Songs* to have been among the editions Mendelssohn found lying on Her Majesty's piano that day, and for Victoria and Albert to have sung Mendelssohn's and Hensel's songs in de Chatelain's English translations.

Finally, the edition-history of Felix's songs and Fanny's "Italien" suggests that the songs the Queen and Prince Consort selected were much more than just personal choices. On the contrary, they were reflections of the emergent construction of a British Mendelssohnian song persona. The English assimilation of Mendelssohn did more than just put different translations of his songs into competition with each other and the original German; it also unknowingly pitted the real Felix Mendelssohn against a pseudo-Felix Mendelssohn (i.e., Fanny), whose work had been tacitly included alongside his own. Perhaps the nature of this carefully wrought British Mendelssohn, and the contradictions that crucially inform it, are the most important insights to be gained from that oft-discussed royal audience in the summer of 1842.

---

1   Earlier versions of this paper were given at the invitation of Prof Mark McKnight (University of North Texas) and Prof. Monika Hennemann (Cardiff University), whom I thank for their support of this inquiry.

2   See Felix Mendelssohn Bartholdy, Letter to Lea Mendelssohn Bartholdy of 9 July 1842. Translated from *Felix Mendelssohn Bartholdy: Sämtliche Briefe, Band 8: März 1841 bis August 1842*, ed. Susanne Tomkovič, Christoph Koop, and Sebastian Smideler (Kassel: Bärenreiter, 2013), 452–56 at 453–54 (Letter 3591).

3   Several important ways in which nineteenth-century copyright law differed from its latter-day counterparts must be remembered in addressing these questions. First, copyright protections were applied on a country-by-country basis; i.e., a work published in in only one country was essentially in the public domain in other countries. Second, as a practical matter copyright protections were strongest when publication occurred in multiple countries on the same day. And perhaps most

bafflingly for the modern observer, when nineteenth-century composers sold a work for publication, they effectively relinquished the copyright, which now belonged to the publisher rather than the composer. This meant that once a work was published, the issuing publisher could further sell the rights to that composition and arrangements of it to other publishers, without necessarily having to involve the composer at all. Even this was not necessary, however, if the work had been published in only one country. Thus, when Mendelssohn published his Opus 8 songs [MWV SD 2] in the German lands but only there, they became fair game for English and French publishers to publish in their own countries in any translations or other adaptations that the publishers wished.

4   The most compact account of this rise to fame (as traced in Mendelssohn's relations with his English publishers) is Peter Ward Jones, "Mendelssohn and His English Publishers," in *Mendelssohn Studies*, ed. R. Larry Todd (Cambridge: Cambridge University Press, 1992), 240–55. See also Colin Timothy Eatock, *Mendelssohn and Victorian England* (Farnham: Ashgate, 2009); R. Larry Todd, *Mendelssohn: A Life in Music* (Oxford: Oxford University Press, 2003); and Clive Brown, *A Portrait of Mendelssohn* (New Haven: Yale University Press, 2003), especially 325–427.

5   The composition and publication history of *Charlotte to Werther* remains obscure. Significant is that the autograph (now lost), dated 25 November 1829, contained only an English text by F. W. Collard with the incipit "All moveless in her dark bright eye," and that the surviving manuscript copy by Mendelssohn's close friend Carl Klingemann bears both an English text beginning "Far from the moveless dark bright eye" and Klingemann's German translation "Lang ist es her, dass Du von mir den schweren Abschied nahmst." The first of these three texts is the one published in *Apollo's Gift, or the Musical Souvenir for 1831* (London: Chappell, 1830), 36–37. Today the song is generally known only in a posthumous contrafactum as *Seemanns Scheidelied* (Es freut sich Alles weit und breit) by Hoffmann von Fallersleben (Berlin, 1850). See Ralf Wehner, *Felix Mendelssohn Bartholdy: Thematisch-systematisches Verzeichnis der musikalischen Werke (MWV): Studien-Ausgabe* (Wiesbaden: Breitkopf & Härtel, 2009), 145.

6   On the two Byron Romances, see Monika Hennemann, "Mendelssohn and Byron: Two Songs Almost without Words," *Mendelssohn-Studien* 10 (1997): 131–56.

7   See Peter Horton, "The British Vocal Album and the Struggle for National Music," in *Music and Performance Culture in Nineteenth-Century Britain*, ed. Bennett Zon (Farnham: Ashgate, 2016), 195–220 at 199.

8   Letter from Mendelssohn (Leipzig) to Stapleton, 24 November 1942 (in *Felix Mendelssohn Bartholdy: Sämtliche Briefe* [hereinafter, FMB SB], Band 9: September 1842 bis Dezember 1843, ed. Helmut Loos, Wilhelm Seidel, Stefan Münnich, Lucian Schiwietz, Uta Wald, and Ingrid Jach, [Kassel: Bärenreiter, 2015], 105 (letter 3687).

9   FMB SB 9: 234–35 at 234 (letter 3860). Buxton accepted Mendelssohn's offer on 31 March (GB 17: 169).

10 Letter from Mendelssohn (Leipzig) to Buxton at Ewer & Co. (London), 29 June 1843 (*FMB SB* 9: 332–33 at 332).

11 GB 19: 157.

12 "The Savoyard's Song." Bartholomew is not credited as the translator in this first edition, but when Ewer released its edition of *Mendelssohn's Songs with English and German Words*, the English translations credited to Bartholomew, the "Pagenlied" was included along with Bartholomew's other translations.

13 Reviewed in *The Musical World* 24, no. 24 (June 12, 1845): 299. These were "On Song's Bright Pinion" (No. 253; = Op. 34/2), "All thro' the wood" (No. 254 = Op. 34/5), and "'Tis night" (No. 255; = Op. 34/6), all translated by Clara de Chatelain.

14 Wessel (London) to Mendelssohn (Leipzig), 28 May 1845 (GB 21: 194).

15 Advertised in *MW* (091845): 456

16 *Six Lieder for Voice and Piano*, Auswahl deutscher Lieder / Series of German Song, nos. 265–70 (London: Wessel & Stapleton, 1845).

17 Mendelssohn, *Six Songs with Piano-Forte Accompaniment, The English Words by W. Bartholomew Esqure....* Op. 47 (London: Ewer & Co., [1846]). On 14 April 1846 Buxton was able to report that he had [quote] "now completed an uniform edition of your songs up to op. 47 with Germ. & Englished words..." (GB 23: 208).
18 Ward Jones, "Mendelssohn and His English Publishers," 250–55.
19 *The Mountain Burgh* (= *Das Waldschloß* / *Wo noch kein Wandrer gegangen*, MWV K 87); *I Hear a Small Bird Calling* (= *Im Frühling* / *Ich hör ein Vöglein locken*, MWV 107; *Romance No. 2. Sun of the Sleepless* (MWV K 85). I have been unable to trace an exemplar of the first of the two Byron Romances (*There Be None of Beauty's Daughters*) from this set of 1846 Ewer publications, but because *Sun of the Sleepless* is identified as "Romance No. 2" we may surmise that it was in fact released.
20 Op. 71 advertised in *MW* 23/13 (25 March 1848): 208.
21 Of Op. 41 (MWV SD 18), only no. 2 (*Entflieh mit mir und sei mein Weib*, MWV F 4) was published during Mendelssohn's lifetime, as "Ah! tell me not" in Book 8 of the *Orpheus* series in November 1839. Of Op. 48 (MWV SD 21), no. 1 (*Frühlingsahnung*, MWV F 14) had been published separately in Book 10 of the *Orpheus* series in 1841 and was republished together with nos. 2-3 of that opus in 1851/52, but nos. 2-6 did not appear together until Ewer's publication of Book 29 of the *Orpheus* series in April 1856.
22 See my "'For You See I Am the Eternal Objector': On Performing Mendelssohn's Music in Translation," in *Mendelssohn in Performance*, ed. Siegwart Reichwald (Bloomington: Indiana University Press, 2008), 207–248.
23 Some characters fall into a fold in the page on the reproduction and are not visible. These are indicated here by brackets.
24 GB 18: 26.
25 See Ward Jones, "Mendelssohn and His English Pubishers," *passim*.
26 GB 18: 26.
27 But see also his description of these issues to his younger sister, Rebecka Dirichlet dated 10 August 1843 (*FMB SB 9*: 360-62 [letter 4047]). "...Das Lied von Eichendorff [Op. 59/6, F 22] 'Das schwankende Gipfel schiesst goldener Strahl, tief unter den Gipfeln das neblige Thal; fern hallt es vom Schlosse, das Waldhorn ruft, es wiehern die Rosse, in die Luft, in die Luft, in die Luft, etc.' wollten sie nebst den übrigen in's Englische übersetzen, aber sie haben mir geschrieben, sie hätten eine neues Gedicht unterlegt, den das Deutsche verstände kein Engländer; aber auch einige dortige Deutsche seien gefragt worden, die verständen es aber auch nicht! ..."
28 Letter from Bartholomew to Mendelssohn, 23 August 1843 (Bodleian Library, Oxford, GB 18: 67). Bartholomew also addresses the other specific and comparatively small points Mendelssohn had raised.
29 Glowing review in the Leipzig *Allgemeine Musikalische Zeitung* 44, no. 45 (1 November 1844): col. 788–91.
30 *MW* 16, no. 288 (30 September 1841): 217.
31 *MW* 16, no. 286 (16 September 1841): 187
32 On the eventual popularity of "The Garland" in public performance in Britain, see Melissa Evelyn Givens, "The Wings of Song Stilled: The Rise and Decline of Felix Mendelssohn's *Lieder* in London, 1829–1915" (D.M.A. diss., University of Houston, 2012), *passim*.
33 See, for example, Wehner, *Thematisch-systematisches Verzeichnis der musikalischen Werke (MWV)*, 121; further, Todd, *Life in Music*, 335.
34 One possibility is that Mendelssohn knew F. W. Jähns's setting of the same poem, which is also a duet using Kaufmann's poetry and was also published in Berlin in 1836 (by Cranz, not A.M. Schlesinger) – but this explanation is not entirely satisfactory, since Mendelssohn and Schlesinger identify only Kaufmann as the source of the text while Jähns and Cranz clearly state that the text is Kaufmann's translation of poetry by Burns.
35 Letter from Felix Mendelssohn (London) to Lea Mendelssohn (Berlin), 21 and 28 June 1842 (*FMB SB* 8: 434–37):

7. MENDELSSOHN AND THE QUESTION OF GERMAN GUILT

Leon Botstein

On 13 June 1933, the young Nicolas Nabokov (an aspiring composer and nephew of Vladimir) and his wife had breakfast in Paris with the diplomat, connoisseur, journalist, and incomparable diarist, Harry Graf Kessler. Nabokov had just arrived from Berlin. An ardent anti-Nazi, Kessler had fled Germany earlier in the year. Kessler recounted in his diary how agitated Nabokov was about the rapid Nazification of cultural life throughout Germany, particularly in music. The news Nabokov brought led Kessler to quip that "the dead have it worse than the living." Paul Hindemith and Kurt Weill, after all, still had options. But not Felix Mendelssohn.

Mendelssohn's music was "now forbidden in Germany," Nabokov informed Kessler. Musicians who sought to defy this order put themselves at risk. One could no longer even use Mendelssohn's music alongside performances of Shakespeare's *A Midsummer Night's Dream*. Kessler found this a "hardly believable story." It appeared that "the height of absurdity has become possible in this unlucky Nazi Germany." Kessler chose a facile but ironic distortion of the closing lines of Goethe's *Faust* Part II to express his conclusion: not "the inscrutable" but rather "the unimaginable" had become reality in his own lifetime.[1]

That Kessler—who was born just two years before the Franco-Prussian War and the creation of a modern Imperial Germany—identified the banning of Mendelssohn as evidence of the metaphorical Rubicon he once assumed the Nazis would not dare to cross is itself remarkable. It suggests that Kessler, like many others, was taken by surprise not merely by the rapid seizure of power but by the aggressive implementation of Nazi cultural policies, especially anti-Semitism. The banning of Mendelssohn was clear evidence that Hitler was not about to be tamed by less radically nationalist and conservative traditions. Kessler's reaction also highlights the exceptional resilience of Mendelssohn's presence in a widely shared construct of what constituted "Germanness" and German culture in Wilhelmine Germany and the Weimar Republic.

No doubt, the predominant character of German national self-image and sentiment—that which represented the uniquely German spirit—in Kessler's lifetime, in terms of music, derived from Richard Wagner, not Mendelssohn. In Heinrich Mann's 1918 novel *Der Untertan*, a scathing indictment of Wilhelmine Germany, Wagner's influence on culture and values plays a significant role. Wagner's astounding popularity was a tribute to his mesmerizing, sensuous music that narrated myths as a German spiritual heritage, securing their place as modern national symbols. Wagner communicated a chauvinist philosophy of history in whose framework an idealized construct of German attributes took center stage, in an intoxicating, accessible and enveloping "total work of art," the music drama.

Furthermore, Wagner, had been not only a composer of astounding originality but a theorist and gifted essayist. He altered the normative criteria by which music as an art came to be judged well beyond Germany during the second half of the nineteenth century.[2] Music was understood as a progressive artform that advanced alongside social and political history. It had evolved, therefore, into a modern narrative art, akin to the realist novel; its nineteenth-century history developed from the premise that what had been prescient about Beethoven's revolutionary genius was the drama in his music. Mendelssohn misunderstood Beethoven, Wagner argued, and promoted a stylistic retreat from Beethoven's transformation of instrumental music into an explicit experience of the dramatic. Mendelssohn pursued a sterile, imitative, regressive, abstract formalism, masked by a romantic sentimentalism that denied the objective tide of history.

Motivated by envy of Mendelssohn's wealth, fame, and precocity, Wagner, between 1850 and his death in 1883, used Mendelssohn (along with Meyerbeer) as his *locus classicus* for a critique of established musical practices and inherited forms, such as quartets and symphonies. Wagner codified, integrated, and disseminated a persuasive racialist theory of artistic inspiration and creativity, in which genuine art was construed as the exclusive province of historically and geographically rooted races, those seemingly "pure." Since Jews were the primary and most visible minority in the world of German culture, Wagner formulated a new justification within German-speaking Europe's long-standing tradition of anti-Semitism, one that could counter the rapid acculturation and assimilation of Jews after their gradual emancipation between the end of the eighteenth century and the fall of Napoleon.

Wagner's depiction of the Jew as rootless parasite and devious imitator of the culture of others rapidly became a dominant image in nineteenth-century populist and nationalist anti-Semitism. Wagner claimed that Jews were incapable of genuine creativity and emotional spontaneity. They were skilled mimics and imitators, calculators, speculators, and crafty capitalists who manipulated modern commerce and journalism to undermine nativist roots and a collective spiritual coherence in culture and politics. Jews favored an alienated individualism and a deracinated conformist cosmopolitanism and materialism that thrived on an aesthetic of mere theatricality and superficiality.

Nevertheless, Mendelssohn's public prominence between the turn of the century and 1933 remained intact. It was linked to a proud multigenerational national commitment to civic and domestic amateurism, in church, school, and home. Mendelssohn benefited equally from the vibrancy of public concert life (and radio broadcasts), which boasted a crowded field of professional vocal and instrumental recitals, and performances of orchestral and choral music. Until 1933, Mendelssohn was a key component of the core concert repertoire. Furthermore, a conservative and explicitly anti-Wagnerian tradition of contemporary "German" composition of music loyal to Mendelssohn's example flourished prior to the Nazi seizure of power. This made it imperative, therefore, for the Nazis to terminate Mendelssohn as quickly and effectively as possible.

He was not easy to erase. When the Nazis banished Mendelssohn and criminalized the presence of his music in public and private culture, they were aware that they were targeting the most significant German composer of Protestant sacred music since J. S. Bach.[3] Mendelssohn's music had served the dissemination of faith through communal church life. He was also the composer of beloved secular songs, choral music, solo piano music, and chamber music. Mendelssohn appealed to listeners, with orchestral works and oratorios that were alluringly transparent, yet complex and refined, and that combined a learned tradition with a romantic sensibility.

An unbroken allegiance to classicism within German culture sustained Mendelssohn's continuing legacy. Artist biographies were popular within the German reading public.[4] Mendelssohn was known to have been a loyal subject and a political conservative. He even served the Prussian Court. He wrote alluring and elegant music that was immediately popular and, as composer and conductor, met the rapidly growing demand among musically literate contemporaries for sophisticated music for listening and playing in the era before the watershed revolutions of 1848.

The prominence music assumed in the everyday life of the urban middle class in the decades immediately after Mendelssohn's death was, to a great extent, due to the ways in which Mendelssohn successfully adapted classical practices to give voice to romantic expressiveness. He sparked a distinctive German trajectory of musical culture that sought a synthesis of classical and romantic aesthetic ideals; Mendelssohn looked to Beethoven not as a harbinger of the future in which the music drama would prevail, but as a model of how the norms of classicism could be adapted to the subjectivity and intensity of romantic tastes. He became a favorite of Goethe in the poet's later years, and he inspired the music of Robert Schumann, Niels W. Gade, Ferdinand Hiller, Max Bruch, Carl Reinecke, Johannes Brahms, and Max Reger.

This tradition of composition enjoyed a renewal after 1918 (in the works of Adolf Busch, for example) when twentieth-century musical modernism embraced neoclassicism and sought to distance itself from lush sonorities, late-romantic harmonic practices, and a Wagnerian ideal of music that linked music to theatricality and narration and prose, rather than to poetry and intimate expression. Kessler's curiosity about Hindemith and Weill stemmed not only from their quite divergent political predicaments under Nazi rule but also from the fact that both composers shared Mendelssohn's ambition to reach a broad public and, in Hindemith's case, sustain Germany's proud heritage of active amateurism in many genres of music. In this respect, as German composers, they were more the heirs of Mendelssohn than Wagner.

Schumann (who harbored his own strong anti-Semitic prejudices) characterized memorably the quality in Mendelssohn that would protect his posthumous stature, not only as a beloved and respected composer but as a characteristically German composer. He did so, ironically, by contrasting Mendelssohn with Meyerbeer. In a notorious comparison from the late 1830s of Mendelssohn's oratorio *Paulus* and Meyerbeer's grand opera *Les Huguenots*, Schumann credited Mendelssohn with writing music that avoided the "defects" of contemporary life and resisted pandering to the philistine tastes that assured immediate fame. Mendelssohn was an idealist who affirmed a "glorious future" for normative criteria of musical beauty and pointed the way, through art, to human "happiness," and not, as in the case of Meyerbeer, to "evil."[5]

Among the ironies of history is that Schumann's public (and Mendelssohn's largely private) aversion to Meyerbeer's music would be appropriated and distorted by Wagner in his nationalist and racist ideology. Wagner was intent to displace Mendelssohn in a manner that could justify anointing himself as the "prophet" of the future and central to German culture. He blamed Mendelssohn for the defects in Schumann's music from his later years. Nevertheless, the association of Mendelssohn with an aesthetics of human happiness, linking the good and the beautiful in the sense of Friedrich Schiller's 1794 *Letters on the Aesthetic Education of Man*, continued to thrive throughout the nineteenth and early twentieth century. At the same time, in part because of its popularity in *bourgeois* circles, Mendelssohn's music became a target of sharp and sarcastic philosophic criticism, especially from the pens of Friedrich Nietzsche and Ludwig Wittgenstein.

A striking example of the persistence of Schumann's praise of Mendelssohn as exemplary of an ideal musical aesthetic of hope and happiness—one that linked a classical construct of beauty and a shared cultural practice with ethical integrity and moral goodness that could proudly claim to be uniquely German—was Mendelssohn's visibility and prominence in the proceedings of the first official gathering of the newly constituted all-German association of choral societies: *Das erste deutsche Sängerbundesfest*, a festival that took place in Dresden between 22 and 25 July 1865.[6] Civic voluntary choral societies, primarily male choral ensembles, had flourished throughout German-speaking Europe since the 1820s and served as centers of liberal and national political agitation in the 1840s.

The Dresden conclave took place in a specially-constructed hall, graced with towers and a historicist façade. The festival, a continuous stream of concerts and parades, attracted thousands of participants and listeners from the German states, the Habsburg Empire, and even America. Forty banners decorated the hall. Eighteen were dedicated to geography, depicting rivers and regions. Thirteen represented concepts, such as "fortitude" and "harmony," and genres such as vocal music and the heroic song. One banner represented "Germania" and two others legendary figures from the distant past: Walther von der Vogelweide and Hans Sachs. Only two poets had banners dedicated to them: Ludwig Uhland and Theodor Körner. Four composers were commemorated with banners: Mozart, Beethoven, Weber, and Mendelssohn.

Each banner was accompanied by an explanatory text that was reprinted in the official book issued to memorialize the festival. Mendelssohn's citation read as follows:

> Felix Mendelssohn-Bartholdy—born in Hamburg on 3 February 1809, died in Leipzig on 4 November 1847, grandson of the philosopher Moses Mendelssohn, from a highly talented family and raised in fortunate circum-

stances—showed his great talent for music, both as virtuoso and composer, astonishingly early. Under the excellent guidance of teachers both at home and abroad, he dedicated himself to the art of music exclusively, and acquired universal admiration on his many long and wide-ranging travels. Striving for a permanent sphere of activity, he and Karl Immermann founded a theater in Dusseldorf that reflected the ideals of both; sadly, it failed, owing to real material obstacles. Repeatedly called abroad to lead the increasing number of large music festivals, he eventually moved to Leipzig in 1835 to assume the leadership of the subscription concerts of the Gewandhaus. Here Mendelssohn realized his greatest accomplishments. Supported by the many and important musical forces of this city of muses, he lent this venerable and famous cultural institution new splendor. After a short pause of his activities there, during which he assumed the position of general director of church music in Berlin, he resumed his place of leadership in Leipzig. The conservatory there is his creation, and he fully dedicated himself to it. His brilliant and highly original overture to Shakespeare's *A Midsummer Night's Dream*, which first brought his name to wide prominence, was followed by many poetic compositions in sound (*Tondichtungen*) that, without exception, demonstrate the magnificent talent and idealism of this sophisticated composer. His mastery was widely acknowledged already in 1835 [sic] when the oratorio *Paulus* was performed in Düsseldorf. Among his large number of works, his songs have reached the widest circles, and have become indispensable in the world of German song. He never suffered that hidden pain of life experienced by most great souls; consequently, his muse preserved the serene smile of those who are blessed—the bliss of inner calm which finds such amiable and graceful expression in Mendelssohn-Bartholdy's works. Our image shows the master with an expression of that happiness, holding a score in one hand, and in the other, a baton.[7]

What stands out, apart from Mendelssohn's privileged place, was the emphasis placed on the composer's civic contribution, his role as a conductor, and the breadth of the audience he reached. The mention of his grandfather revealed no particular awkwardness concerning his heritage and lingering status as a Jew. The citing of *Paulus* underscored Mendelssohn's prominence as a Christian (albeit a Protestant) and the place of faith in his musical output. The only other Mendelssohn work specifically mentioned was the one whose banishment startled Kessler in 1933—the incidental music to Shakespeare.

Explicit in the 1865 Dresden encomium was the idea that Mendelssohn's "bliss of inner calm" characterized beauty in music, a beauty ("the serene smile") that was graceful and amiable, and conducive to happiness in others and the larger community, particularly the protagonists of German musical culture who were present.

Mendelssohn and Weber were selected as recent German composers and exponents of Romanticism who merited a place alongside the uncontested giants of Viennese Classicism, Mozart, and Beethoven. The significance of this choice is underscored by the fact that, by 1865, the tensions that emerged during the 1850s between Liszt and Wagner on the one hand, and the circle around Joseph Joachim, Robert and Clara Schumann, and Johannes Brahms on the other, had already become public. Meyerbeer had died in 1864, and in the 1860s Wagner was making his mark. Four years after the Dresden festival Wagner felt secure enough to confirm the widely held suspicion that he was the author, under a pseudonym, of a notorious 1850 anti-Semitic essay, *Das Judenthum in der Musik*, by issuing a second revised version. Nonetheless, Mendelssohn's failure to project a tortured romantic personality was not yet seen as damaging him either as a composer or as the representative of a German cultural ideal. To German nationalists still committed to liberalism, Mendelssohn was a national cultural icon, despite his Jewish ancestry. His musical aesthetic of tranquility inspired *eudaimonia*, whose spread was then considered essential to civic wellbeing.

This dimension within the collective German national cultural self-image persisted into the twentieth century, despite being overwhelmed by the spread of Wagnerism and, subsequently, the post-Wagnerian success of composers such as Richard Strauss, Hans Pfitzner, and even Gustav Mahler. Mendelssohn's place as an alternative to Wagner as a national symbol in German musical culture would be sustained, in the twentieth century, by Brahms, who admired Mendelssohn. Neither Brahms's nor Mendelssohn's stature would suffer as the consequence of the notoriety accorded early twentieth-century German modernists, including Ferruccio Busoni, Arnold Schoenberg, Franz Schreker, and Alexander Zemlinsky. By the decade before the outbreak of World War I, nationalist pride in German musical culture included Brahms and Wagner. Furthermore, Wagner's efforts to discredit Mendelssohn had never obscured the audible influence Mendelssohn's music had exerted on Wagner. And suggestions of Mendelssohn kept appearing in the music of subsequent generations of prominent German composers (all ardent nationalists), particularly Max Bruch, Strauss, and Max Reger, and above all, Brahms. A wistful nostalgia for Mendelssohn's virtues—the accessible lyricism, transparency, lightness, intimacy, and a calm eloquent expressiveness in his music, all suggestive of optimism and happiness, and an integral link between the goodness (understood in terms of Protestant Christianity) and beauty—never entirely disappeared from the way German musicality and its contribution to a national self-image were framed, especially among the educated middle classes who continued to pursue vocal and instrumental amateurism.

★ ★ ★

By the time the Nazis came to power in 1933, Mendelssohn still posed a challenge to those who had followed Wagner's lead in trying to rid German culture of Jewish influence. The Nazis could only exclude Mendelssohn on the narrow logic of racial anti-Semitism. As Kessler intuited, anti-Semitism was sufficient to persecute living Jews. As a justification for excising Mendelssohn out of an inherited German cultural heritage, the Nazis would have liked to make the case, as Wagner had done, that Mendelssohn was an example of the deleterious effects of Jewish aesthetics on authentic German cultural virtues. Wagner had succeeded in making his music of the future the dominant marker of German culture. A "healthy" art in classical and concert music appropriate to the Aryan purity favored by the Nazis was evocative of Wagner in sound and rhetoric. However, Mendelssohn was not entirely displaced by Wagner's triumph as far as audiences in post–World War I Germany were concerned. The Nazis recognized that Mendelssohn's music did not fit the Wagnerian Nazi historical and cultural argument that Jews were promoters of values and practices that threatened the health and survival of all things truly German. If anything, Mendelssohn's music was evocative of a shared moral certainty at risk in modernity—one communicated through music, derived from religion, and linked to a pleasing commonsense beauty suggestive of a normative ethics unaffected by Nietzsche's transvaluation of good and evil.

The intertwining of conventional ethics and aesthetics in Mendelssohn's music undermined the Nazis' use of anti-Semitism as central to their ideological crusade regarding German culture. Inspired by Wagner, Naziism adopted the juxtaposition of "healthy" and exemplary human communities—those with presumed authenticity owing to organic historic roots located in land and language—against a cosmopolitan society in which ephemeral pluralism, eclecticism, and alienation and materialism thrived. A Judaized cosmopolitanism merited condemnation as artificial and corrosive; it held together only through greed and self-interest and promoted degeneracy. "Degeneracy" was particularly a danger to twentieth-century culture, which according to Nazi apologists had entered an age of "decadence" and decline that made Germany particularly vulnerable to influences capable of undermining the character of a presumed authentic and traditional national community.[8]

The modernist art, architecture, music, theater, and dance that flourished in the interwar years of the Weimar Republic were symptoms of what the Nazis identified as decadence and degeneracy, whose root cause was Jewish influence, the same enemy Wagner had identified in 1850. Their distinctive "racial" characteristics were alluring, permitting Jews to exert a pernicious influence within German society, exploiting the vulnerability of the historical moment (decadence) and reducing the chance and opportunity for society to be reborn by spreading degeneracy.

Within Nazi propaganda, neither "degeneracy" nor "decadence" were ever consistently defined; they functioned as convenient and flexible weapons of condemnation and censorship. Nonetheless, by condemning anti-traditional qualities in artistic form and content that celebrated innovation and explicitly disrupted time-honored practices seen as securing cohesion in the national community, particularly in musical life, the Nazis abandoned Wagner's overarching commitment to art as historically progressive. Wagner himself, at the turn of the century, was widely held responsible for promoting decadence.[9] The Nazis appropriated the categories of degeneracy and decadence derived from the reactionary ultra-nationalist cultural criticism that became widespread between 1890 and the early 1920s.[10] But they could not easily be applied to Mendelssohn's music.

However, the varied surfaces of musical modernism of the 1920s made the charge of being decadently subversive of a German nativist cultural chauvinism seem plausible. The Nazis readily deployed decadence and degeneracy to validate essentialist and determinist notions of race and Aryan distinctiveness and superiority. Although the Nazis sought to connect degeneracy to a pervasive Jewish influence, the proponents they targeted did not necessarily turn out to be themselves Jewish (consider, for example, in music, Alban Berg, Anton Webern, J. M. Hauer, Hans Erich Apostel, Ernst Krenek, and the entire world of jazz). The new music the Nazis deemed rootless, artificial, abstract, immoral, i.e., "degenerate" and cosmopolitan was frequently inspired by political radicalism (in the cases of Weill, Eisler, and Krenek). It dispensed with the uses of tonality and continuity in form (Schoenberg and Webern). Modernism, especially on the operatic stage, often directly challenged conventional moral pieties and their attendant hypocrisies (e.g., Hindemith's one-act operas of the 1920s, *Neues vom Tage*, *Mörder Hoffnung der Frauen*, *Sancta Susanna*, and *Das Nusch-Nuschi*; Berg's 1925 *Wozzeck*, and Max Brand's 1929 *Maschinist Hopkins*). By 1933, the dichotomy between a "healthy" musical aesthetic and its modernist opposite had become seductively comprehensible within the musical public.

What was ironic in this constructed divide (one not lost on Kessler and many anti-Nazis) was that Mendelssohn's music—and the music of twentieth-century composers influenced by him such as Walter Brauenfels—was, as the 1865 celebration made clear, free of "degeneracy," political radicalism, or immorality (far more than Wagner). Mendelssohn had long been a standard bearer for a common-sense ideal of the timeless qualities of beauty and moderation in music. His music was even free of atheism. Mendelssohn expressed piety in music in ways comparable to Bruckner (a favorite of Hitler's). The banishment of Mendelssohn in 1933 did not resonate with appeals to combat "degeneracy" through state censorship; it could only be justified by the composer's racial identity at birth as a Jew that no baptism nor profession of faith could offset. It was easy to stop performances and broadcasts and commission "replacements" for Mendelssohn's most well-known works (e.g. from Carl Orff); but throughout the Third Reich it remained implausible to decry Mendelssohn's music as "unhealthy" to a national community with a multi-generational habit of affection for it.

What made the task of the Nazis somewhat easier was a history of a visible and sustained criticism of Mendelssohn that rapidly gained traction after 1848. In the 1850s, Mendelssohn's music was attacked as superficial and sentimental, not only by Wagner but by critics such as Wilhelm Heinrich Riehl. It was said to lack originality, profundity, and emotional depth.[11] Even Meyerbeer, who avoided personal contact but respected Mendelssohn (he even attended Fanny Mendelssohn's funeral), expressed little admiration for Mendelssohn's craft. He found, for example, the melodic invention of *Elijah* strikingly deficient.[12] Later in the century, George Bernard Shaw railed famously against the prevailing English taste for Mendelssohn, encouraged by Victoria and Albert, and held the currency of his music responsible for the worst in the public's allegiance to smug bourgeois sentimental conventions of beauty and form. Likewise, in France, the entry in the 1875 edition of F. J. Fetis's famed *Biographie universelle des musiciens* was comparably condescending. Mendelssohn's output, except for the Octet, the *Midsummer Night's Dream* Overture, and the first movement of the Third Symphony, were dismissed as little more than elegant and charming (if also tiresome) and bereft of deeper spiritual significance.[13]

This strain in criticism, however, was not entirely persuasive to Germany's large community of middle-class amateurs and concert goers; it was, after all, equally an attack on them. Furthermore, by the turn of the century the musical public had simultaneously fallen under Wagner's spell in the theater and retained an attachment to Mendelssohn in church and home. The Nazis may have silenced Mendelssohn between 1933 and 1945 but not the memory of his music nor his contribution to a conceit about the superior musicality of German culture. Writing after what would be the last public performance, on 11 March 1935, of a work by Mendelssohn in Nazi Germany, the critic of the *Berlin Börsen-Zeitung* remarked on the applause for Mendelssohn's "once so beloved and frequently performed violin concerto."[14]

Consequently, after the unconditional surrender and defeat of the Nazis in 1945, Mendelssohn emerged as a promising vehicle in the process of de-Nazification and re-education toward a new ideal of national identity. Mendelssohn's residual popularity was a valuable resource in reconstructing a "good" German national cultural heritage rooted in Weimar classicism, particularly Goethe and Schiller. The foregrounding of Mendelssohn in public musical culture could lend meaning to otherwise routine and hollow postwar acts of contrition and reparation. Indeed, shortly after the war's end there was a rush to perform Mendelssohn.[15]

Heine also retained a comparable following within the reading public and presented a parallel opportunity in literature. These two early nineteenth-century contemporaries, both born Jewish and converts with an idiosyncratic attachment to their Jewish heritage, were brought back into public view in the service of creating a postwar German culture free of the taint of the Third Reich.

The damage done by Wagner, subsequent anti-Mendelssohn criticism, and finally by the Nazis still presented a challenge. Anti-Semitic stereotypes about the lack of creativity among Jews in the arts and their skill at imitation remained widespread. These premises remained unexposed, hidden, and uncontested in any serious and sustained public manner after 1945. Mendelssohn's postwar resurrection in public concert life through performances of a few signature works became therefore a purely symbolic reckoning that was easy and convenient.

The hollow character of the postwar effort to undo the legacy of Nazi cultural policy and ideology was apparent in the 1947 Leipzig celebration of the centenary of Mendelssohn's death. The events included concerts and an unveiling of a bust of the composer in front of the Gewandhaus to compensate for a prominent statue that had been torn down in 1936. Wilhelm Furtwängler, among Germany's most celebrated cultural figures and its most admired conductor, spoke. Furtwängler, who rose to international fame in the early 1920s, had remained, by choice, a visible figure in the musical and cultural life of Nazi Germany. Not an anti-Semite himself, he had, early in the Nazi era, between 1933 and 1935, sought to compromise and accommodate the new regime's cultural policies without entirely capitulating. In the end, Furtwängler fell in line, even though he held out longer than anyone else. The last public performance of Mendelssohn in Nazi Germany (the Violin Concerto) took place in 1935 with his orchestra, the Berlin Philharmonic but without Furtwängler on the podium. Furtwängler last conducted Mendelssohn – selections from the *Midsummer Night's Dream* music – the previous season, on 12 February 1934.[16]

Furtwängler's collaboration may have been reluctant, but he did lend the Nazi regime his international stature as a conductor. Despite misgivings and many efforts to help individual Jewish colleagues, he believed that by remaining in Nazi Germany as a public figure he could protect the "good" German cultural heritage from being distorted and destroyed. The extensive debate about his motives and behavior since his death in 1954 has neither fully explained nor exonerated Furtwängler's complicity. By 1947, with a highly visible and controversial denazification hearing process behind him, Furtwängler had returned to public life with renewed popularity.

Furtwängler's public statements about Mendelssohn, made just two years after the Nazi defeat and in the context of the postwar effort to reconstruct German cultural life, were astonishing. He revealed no reconsideration of the claims and terms of Nazi cultural ideology.[17] Mendelssohn, he argued, did not merit the status of exemplar of the German spirit or a great composer he had been accorded in 1865. Mendelssohn was merely "of particular, if limited significance" as a composer in "the course of German Romantic music." At best, Mendelssohn was the most "fertile" example of a historic "symbiosis" of "German-ness" and "Jewish-ness." The racist framework of Nazi rhetoric and its ideological antecedents survived Germany's defeat intact; Furtwängler merely turned it upside down.

For Furtwängler, Mendelssohn exhibited the presumed creative deficit of being Jewish. To underscore this, Furtwängler validated his claim that Mendelssohn was not among the greatest of German composers by citing, explicitly, a musical authority who was also Jewish. He quoted his Berlin colleague from pre-Nazi times, the great violinist Carl Flesch, who had been forced to flee Germany and died in 1944 in exile. Flesch was quoted as saying that Mendelssohn had been merely a "leading" composer "in the second rank," with "but few" works of "originality and spontaneity." Having marshalled racial essentialism in support of this familiar axiom of anti-Semitism, Furtwängler went on to declare that among Mendelssohn's contemporaries, Schumann had been the far greater composer, an oft-repeated judgment in nineteenth-century anti-Mendelssohn criticism that Nazi propaganda had sought to reinforce. Furtwängler concluded his condescending judgment of Mendelssohn's works by conceding the virtue of "naturalness" in the music. For Furtwängler, however, Mendelssohn's main contribution was his "synthesis" of tradition in German music between Bach and Beethoven.

Furtwängler's main point of revisionism was that in Germany there had been a "synthesis" between two distinct populations, Jews and Germans. Mendelssohn had been exemplary of a German-Jewish symbiosis. Furtwängler placed him alongside Joseph Joachim, Heinrich Schenker, and Gustav Mahler as evidence of the possibility, past and present, to be both a Jew and a German. The achievements of these distinguished musicians—all born Jews—he concluded, "testify that we Germans have every reason to see ourselves as a great and noble people. How tragic that this has to be emphasized today."

Furtwängler seemed oblivious to the fact that Felix had been converted as a child. What, therefore, was "Jewish" about a composer who became a devoted member of the Protestant community, and who married the daughter of a Protestant minister? What then warranted a comparison between Mendelssohn and the others? Merely that they were lumped together by an anti-Semitic theory popularized by the Nazis? In 1947, Furtwängler employed concepts that were at the heart of the perverse logic behind the humiliation and slaughter of European Jewry. Furtwängler reused the racialist categories and thinking of Wagner and the Nazis; he failed to reconsider the premises or validity of the aesthetic criteria and judgments that resulted from the adherence to essentialist notions of racial differences between Germans and Jews. The anti-Semitism inherent in the devaluation of Mendelssohn as a composer and the consequent exclusive attribution of profundity and greatness to "Aryan" German composers were expressed without any embarrassment. Indeed, Furtwängler's most celebrated and visible act of defiance against Nazi cultural policies was his defense, in 1934, of Hindemith, an individual unquestionably "Aryan." Furtwängler witnessed but tacitly endorsed the Nazi expulsion of composers of Jewish origin such as Franz Schreker, who was dismissed in 1933 as professor of composition at the Prussian Academy.

To make matters worse, the examples Furtwängler cited in 1947 were odd choices. Heinrich Schenker had been a Jew who hailed from Galicia in Austro-Hungary. He was a theorist and editor whose career was centered in Vienna. He was brilliant and idiosyncratic. Schenker was an outspoken German cultural chauvinist, a fierce critic of Mahler, a powerful advocate of Brahms, as well as a loyal and observant member of the Viennese Jewish community. His theories about musical structure and form and his validation of the compositional practices of Viennese classicism as normative impressed and influenced Furtwängler. But Schenker was only peripherally a composer.

Joseph Joachim was no more "German" than Schenker. Born a Jew in the Hungarian part of the Habsburg Monarchy, he composed, but relatively little, despite the encouragement of Brahms, his closest friend. In contrast to Schenker, much of Joachim's meager output is worthy of a place in the active repertoire. His major distinction, however, was as a virtuoso violinist, quartet leader, and teacher. Furtwängler justified his choice of Joachim (a convert like Mendelssohn) by appealing, perversely, to the authority of "no less a man than Wagner." Furtwängler appeared not to know anything about Joachim's own attitude to his Jewish origins or their presence in his music. The posthumous betrayal of Joachim's reputation by the musicologist Hans Joachim Moser (1889–1967), the son of Joachim's biographer Andreas

Moser, who served in the Nazi Propaganda Ministry and, like Furtwängler, went on, albeit for longer, to enjoy a stellar postwar career—left no impression. The postwar imperative to rethink the causes and consequences of the Nazi regime and form a cultural construct of German national identity bereft of race thinking was entirely lost on Furtwängler.

The appeal to the example of Mahler underscores best Furtwängler's obtuseness and his intellectual resistance. Mahler, like Schenker and Joachim, was born and raised in the Habsburg Monarchy, in the Czech lands of Bohemia and Moravia. Joachim's career may have flourished largely in what subsequently became Imperial Germany, but Mahler's did not, apart from six years in the 1890s when he was based in Hamburg. Mahler made his mark in Budapest, Vienna, and New York. He never considered himself truly "German" and never felt accepted as a "German," in stark contrast to his closest rival as composer and conductor, Richard Strauss. Like Joachim and Schenker, Mahler's musical roots were eclectic and encompassed Mendelssohn. Mahler drew from sources more outside than within the frame of what became, when he was ten years old, the political entity of Imperial Germany. As a composer Mahler did not limit his sources to the literary and folk traditions of German-speaking communities; he eschewed musical nationalisms. The German sources closest to Mahler (e.g., *Das Knaben Wunderhorn*, Achim von Arnim and Clemens Brentano's collection published between 1805 and 1808) mirrored a German cultural national ethos similar to Mendelssohn's. Mahler evinced no sympathy for the triumph of nationalism during the second half of the nineteenth century, a nationalism that fueled a populist anti-Semitism that dominated the stark political realities Mahler faced during his career and which compelled him, among other things, to convert as an adult.

None of Furtwängler's three historical examples, either as Germans or Jews, were actually remotely comparable to Mendelssohn as representative figures of public influence and authority in Germany. None of them left, as Mendelssohn did, a lasting impact in three major German cities: Düsseldorf, Berlin (where Joachim did leave a mark), and Leipzig. Mahler had an impact on Vienna when it was the capital of a multinational empire. Mahler would posthumously attain an astonishing degree of worldwide fame, rivaling Mendelssohn. But in 1947, his achievement, range, and influence as a composer seemed hardly a match for Mendelssohn. What made Furtwängler's reference to Mahler all the stranger was the fact that he had never been a Mahler advocate. He conducted his music only four or five times before 1933. *The Songs of the Wayfarer* and the *Kindertotenlieder* were the two works he performed in the postwar era.[18] As Furtwängler observed in 1939 and 1940, in private notes entered into his personal pocket calendar, Mahler was exemplary of a composer who merely "reproduced" the "content of past music" in a "monumental" and "diluted" manner; his music was an "inflation" of the past that mirrored the "poverty of the times."[19]

Furtwängler did not attempt to restore Mendelssohn in 1947 to his historic and central place within a German cultural tradition. Such a restoration was neither imaginable nor justified for Furtwängler. Mendelssohn continued to be seen through the lens of anti-Semitism, as an artist lacking creativity in precisely the terms employed by Wagner. Implicit in Furtwängler's argument was the premise of a uniquely Aryan German, non-rational, spontaneous, and spiritual capacity for profound philosophical inspiration in music. The characterization of Mendelssohn's aesthetics as naïve and derivative grew out of the anti-Semitic arguments the Nazis adopted from Wagner. Furtwängler adhered to the idea the Nazis promoted: that modernity was a decadent age. This helps explain why the defeat in 1945 left the inherited Nazi discourse intact for Furtwängler and his 1947 Leipzig audience. The ethics of reason, the classical ideals of restraint, and an affirmative universalism that embraced individualism—all audible in Mendelssohn—were juxtaposed as non-German against a uniquely German aesthetics of heroic grandeur, resistance, community solidarity, and metaphysical speculation audible in Wagner and Bruckner.

Germany surrendered in political and military terms, leaving intact the antimodernist, post-Wagnerian rhetoric of Hans Pfitzner, an ardent Nazi. These flourished, undamaged, in postwar musical culture. Pfitzner had been, for Furtwängler an exception from the mediocrity and sterility caused by the decadence of modernity. Furtwängler valued Pfitzner even above Strauss. And Furtwängler's thoughts about spirituality, authenticity, and inspiration in music, as well as his own compositions, all evoked Pfitzner's music and his writings on the aesthetics of music.[20]

The acceptance of Wagnerian premises blinded Furtwängler to considering other German Jews who might have fit, in 1947, his argument of a German-Jewish symbiosis, such as Schoenberg, Schreker, Zemlinsky, Weill, even perhaps Ferdinand Hiller and Jacques Offenbach, and certainly Meyerbeer, not to speak of his many contemporaries who became exiles and victims under Nazi rule, e.g., Ernst Toch, who had been singled out during the Nazi era as a modernist. Last but not least, Furtwängler's suggestion of a constructive historical German-Jewish "symbiosis," from both the vantage point of German history and the history of European Jewry, was rhetorical and self-serving. Whether the dynamic between Jews in Germany and non-Jewish Germans since the mid eighteenth century – the era of Moses Mendelssohn – could be termed a "symbiosis" (disputed by Gershom Scholem and described rather as a one-sided unrequited love affair with German culture) or a "dialogue," neither form of supposed contact was based on equality. The connections remained asymmetrical, and thus neither term could properly describe a mutually respectful, beneficial, or honorable history. Furtwängler's use of it was an evasion of any candid analysis of modern German history before the Holocaust.[21]

Was Furtwängler's tone-deafness to the lingering appeal and contextual awkwardness of the substance of Nazi aesthetics an unconscious and perverse reaction against the hypocrisies within the postwar outpourings of disbelief, regret, and denial among his German contemporaries to the horrors of the Nazi era? Or was Furtwängler's commitment to criteria of aesthetic worth and musical value—his allegiance to normative concepts of originality and spontaneity and distaste for modernism—just evidence of how deeply inscribed a tradition of philosophical ideas about history, race, and aesthetics were in the language and thought of Furtwängler's generation? Perhaps Furtwängler tried to suppress any sense of guilt and circumvent any admission of his own culpability by defending the devaluation of Mendelssohn as a composer. But the 1947 speech commemorating Mendelssohn's death revealed the obstacles to rehabilitating Mendelssohn the composer in the mid twentieth century, and to restoring his enormous body of work to the active concert repertoire.[22]

As Larry Todd has argued, the sustained postwar effort to reverse the posthumous devaluation of Mendelssohn's music was not trivial.[23] An outpouring of scholarship, performance, and recording in Germany and the United States aimed at rehabilitating Mendelssohn's music occurred for half a century. It culminated in 2003 with the publication of Todd's magisterial and definitive biography, itself the result of decades of pathbreaking scholarship. Then came the 2017 publication of Mendelssohn's voluminous and compelling correspondence in twelve volumes. Still underway is the systematic preparation of a complete and comprehensive "Leipzig" critical edition of his music. Apart from that "official" enterprise, new editions of the major works, from Carus (a "Stuttgart Mendelssohn Edition") and other publishers have come out. These have facilitated the recording and performance of everything from the early string symphonies to the later choral music and chamber music. In his biography, Todd elegantly articulates a lingering Mendelssohn reception problem, despite these efforts. The prejudices that date back to the mid-nineteenth century and culminated in Nazi cultural policy still block renewed appreciation of and affection for most of Mendelssohn's music apart from the few works that have remained consistently in the repertoire.

We seem unable to shake off the shackles of late nineteenth-century thought. We resist a philosophical aesthetics of musical beauty that links reason, the good, and the accessible. We resist affirmation through music, and the seemingly naïve effort to inspire through music a sense of a shared human community. The failure to reverse the prominence of Wagnerian ideas within Germany and beyond is the result of a well-earned skepticism about progress, an attachment to complexity in criticism, the allure of irony, and the suspicion of optimism. Charles Rosen's account of Mendelssohn in his 1995 *The Romantic Generation* is a case in point. Furthermore, between 1945 and the mid-1970s, avant-garde musical modernism shunned Romanticism, in part on account of its link to official fascist aesthetics. But high modernism failed to capture an audience. The musical past that supplanted Romanticism from the era of Mendelssohn and Wagner was premodern "early" music, from medieval to eighteenth-century Classicism. In the later twentieth century came a Mahler revival, followed by audience enthusiasm for Shostakovich, Strauss, and Sibelius. Wagner's prominence never waned. But the past that occupied the foreground in concert life during the second half of the twentieth century did not include Mendelssohn.

To return to postwar Germany. Insight with respect to the postwar reception and reputation of Mendelssohn can be found in the ideas and analysis of Karl Jaspers, published in 1947, and those of Jaspers' distinguished disciple, the philosopher Hannah Arendt, in subsequent decades. In his influential book *Die Schuldfrage* (translated as *The Question of German Guilt*), Jaspers sought to differentiate types of guilt and responsibility for the success of the Nazis and the carnage and catastrophe that their rise to power and the twelve-year regime caused. Though he probed dimensions of the legal understanding of guilt that demanded prosecution in war crime trials, Jaspers was most concerned with assertions of "moral" guilt that might be applied to those who "tolerated" the regime and those who gave it "support and cooperation." Beyond that, Jaspers explored "metaphysical guilt," the culpability of those who were "guilty of standing by inactively when the crimes were committed."[24]

Germany needed to go beyond the legal process exemplified by the Nuremberg Trials and the application of legal standards for genocide and crimes against humanity. Only by addressing the moral and metaphysical dimensions of guilt could the German nation elude the "collectivist type of thought and appraisal" that would merely reverse the use of racial stereotypes and the language of prejudice to condemn a whole nation to inferiority.[25] Jaspers addressed precisely the lack of public discourse and introspection that facilitated the continuity in habits of mind and uses of language that he had observed after the war's end and that informed Furtwängler's 1947 appraisal of Mendelssohn.

There was, as Jaspers suspected, little sustained exploration of the moral and metaphysical dimensions of guilt and responsibility among surviving musicians in Germany and Austria who had been active in the Nazi era. Between 1950 and 1968, the pretense of denazification and the reconsideration and revision of the German past had all but disappeared in West Germany, and also in the German Democratic Republic (whose record in these matters was perhaps marginally better). Prominent adherents of Nazism, from enthusiastic collaborators to those who tolerated the regime (and benefitted from the exclusion of Jews after 1933), not to mention more passive bystanders (including members of the audience), all returned to the public space for music. Among the professional performers most prominent (but rarely transparent about their past) were Karl Böhm, Clemens Krauss, Herbert von Karajan, Elisabeth Schwarzkopf, Carl Orff, Werner Egk, Walter Gieseking, members of leading orchestras, notably in Berlin and Vienna, and leading German musicologists. Foremost among immediate postwar luminaries who collaborated were Richard Strauss and Furtwängler himself. Nothing remotely resembling Jaspers's call for a "purification of the soul" or an "inner purification" (rather than mere public confession and contrition, rare as those sentiments were), essential preconditions of any future political liberty in Germany for Jaspers, could be witnessed.

Within the sphere of musical culture there was little interest, fueled by philosophical introspection or emotional remorse, to discuss reparations, or explore truths yet unspoken to gain some genuine shared sense of humility. Jaspers wished to inspire a "seriousness and resolution" that might transcend a reflexive return to a reawakened normalcy that he termed the "gaiety" of life. In musical tastes, the Wagnerian—including murky efforts at profundity—prevailed, as in Furtwängler's Third Symphony, which was left incomplete at his death. The "Indian summer" of music from Strauss's last years, from 1945 to 1949, was more intimate and reserved than that of earlier periods; it was glorious and touching in communicating loss and resignation, but it was also marked by a nostalgia that deftly shielded any responsibility for the brutality and horror.

The same lack of "seriousness and resolution" could be found in the music of younger composers who looked to radical modernism, those who gathered at the Darmstadt Summer Course that began in 1946 and participated in the postwar Donaueschingen festivals of contemporary music. They distanced themselves from musical practices favored by the Nazi regime, from the scale and the surfaces resembling those of late Romanticism. They pioneered in fragmentation and embraced harsh and brutal sonorities that sounded modern but did not always shed the monumental grandiosity of Wagner and his followers. The postwar compositions of Karlheinz Stockhausen and Bernd Alois Zimmerman are two examples. Modernism was an effective but also convenient means by which to express anger rather than recognition or remorse.

In music, the far-reaching "inner purification" Jaspers sought for postwar Germany needed to engage the past more directly and to reinvent it rather than avoid and reject it. That strategy, in addition to giving voice to anguish and anger, also suggested moral recognition; it was most eloquently audible before 1968 in the music of Karl Amadeus Hartmann and Walter Braunfels, and in the postwar music of exiles such as Toch, Egon Wellesz and even Hindemith. Lightness, clarity in expressiveness, comprehensibility, and an affectionate nobility, qualities pioneered by Mendelssohn, would take longer to reappear.

In this sense, a confrontation with the question of guilt did not take place within music. It remained restricted to the question of how to mask the culpability for those individuals whose collaboration most resembled those who were liable to legal prosecution. The most penetrating analysis of the dilemma described by Jaspers in 1947 came, not surprisingly, from Theodor Adorno and Max Horkheimer, both exiles.[26] Through their writings, they sought to answer Jaspers's challenge that genuine freedom and happiness for the German nation would only come gradually as individuals throughout the nation confronted their incapacity for "perfection," embraced humility, were active on behalf of the truth, and acknowledged the inevitable "melancholy background" from which, ultimately, the "amiable magic" of life would be rekindled. Unfortunately, Adorno's own partisanship for the Second Viennese School and conception of Beethoven blinded him from considering Mendelssohn as a potential alternative model within the history of German culture. Critical theory, however, did little to offset the silence, denial, and hollow official gestures merely suggestive of the need to reverse the Nazi criteria and record of censorship that prevailed in Germany before 1968.[27]

Mendelssohn may have been partially restored to the postwar repertoire. But a sustained interrogation of how music, even radical experimental modernism, might be understood and function, and how the practices of high art traditions of classical and concert music intersected with the success of Nazism, did not occur. The questions of why classical musical culture flourished alongside radical evil and survived essentially intact out of the rubble of total war were never adequately answered.

Mendelssohn was intent in producing music that would foster a human community defined by a spiritual universalism rooted in the "Sermon on the Mount" and in the ethics of Judaism as articulated by his grandfather. Music, as public artform, possessed the imperative to foster harmony and genuine tolerance in the face of divisions and differences. Mendelssohn's ideal of beauty remained rooted in the forms of classicism he cherished, not only in literature (the work of the late Goethe) and in Beethoven, but also in the painting, architecture, and sculpture of his Nazarene German-Roman contemporaries, in Jean-Auguste-Dominique Ingres, Karl Friedrich Schinkel, Friedrich Wilhelm Schadow, Bertel Thorwaldsen, and his brother-in-law, Wilhelm Hensel, for whom Raphael remained the ideal. Music needed to affirm values that resisted the strident and divisive nationalism that troubled Mendelssohn in the mid-1840s and persuaded him to reject the Nibelungen saga as a possible subject for an opera.

That no substantial revision of the narrative of the history of music, in which Wagner was validated as normative by criteria of aesthetic judgment readily appropriated within Nazi ideology, took place after 1945 suggests the utility of Hannah Arendt's provocative notion of the "banality of evil." Arendt, between 1947 and 1963, took up Jaspers's framework for German guilt and sought to illuminate why the horror of the Nazi era lost its radical character as evil, sufficiently so to make passivity and the levels of collaboration described by Jaspers seem uneventful if not respectable. Did music play a role in blunting the recognition and revulsion that ought to have led to active resistance?[28] Arendt remains a useful starting point in explaining the virtually seamless continuity, modernism and technological progress notwithstanding, in musical culture between the Nazi era and the proximate postwar world.

Did music help reconfigure and mask the radical character of Nazism, its barbarism, sadism, and cruelty, and permit brutality to be accepted as unremarkable and normal? Did aesthetic means help divest collaboration and consent of the appearance of wrongdoing? Did high culture become an acceptable façade that excused moral and ethical failure? Aesthetic values and canons of beauty were severed from the plausible link to ethics, a link that had remained consistently audible in Mendelssohn. But the Wagnerian, which displaced Mendelssohn and Meyerbeer's aesthetic with a persuasive camouflage of realist illusionism, managed to inoculate the mass of humanity against responding with resistance and rejection to the unprecedented cruelty and violence delivered on an industrial and technologically advanced scale. The aspiration for the cultivation of aesthetic taste and judgment had been justified in the eighteenth century as a path to a high standard of ethics and morals. This conceit framed Mendelssohn's aspirations as a musician. Its plausibility was shattered in the Nazi era. The postwar challenge was how to continue the traditions of literature and music in a manner that would not again facilitate the appearance of radical evil as normal and ordinary.

From the vantage point of the second decade of the twenty-first century, all may not be lost. In the aftermath of the fall of the Berlin Wall, the resurgence of populist right-wing politics, and a weakened European Union after Brexit, revisiting Mendelssohn and his music, aesthetics, and ambitions for musical culture, seems appropriate. A sympathetic relationship now prevails between contemporary classical music and the massive and diverse world of popular music. The compulsion to reject categorically the sound world of the nineteenth century has passed. The overwhelming accessibility of video and audio recordings, the contemporary antimodernist sensibility in terms of melody, harmony, and rhythm, and a widespread desire to find through musical culture a community in real space and time augur well for a renewed appreciation of Mendelssohn. Larry Todd's portrait of the composer and his wise understanding of the greatness of Mendelssohn's music within many genres provide us a starting point. There is every reason that a lasting renewal in the reception of Mendelssohn can gain momentum well before 2047, the 200th anniversary of the composer's death.

1 Harry Graf Kessler, *Das Tagebuch*, vol. 9: *1926–1937*, ed. Sabine Gruber and Ulrich Ott (Stuttgart: Cotta, 2010), 584.
2 For the place of music and the influence of Wagner in German national and communal self-identification at the end of the Hohenzollern monarchy and in the early 1920s, see Thomas Mann's 1918 *Reflections of a Nonpolitical Man*, trans. Walter D. Morris (New York: New York Review Books, 2021), esp. 22–28, 59–69, and 336–54.
3 Mendelssohn was performed during the Third Reich, until 1941, within the framework of the Jüdischer Kulturbund, an arts organization of Jews supported by the Nazi regime.
4 See Leo Lowenthal, "German Popular Biographies: Culture's Bargain Counter," in *The Critical Spirit: Essays in Honor of Herbert Marcuse*, ed. Barrington Moore Jr. and Kurt H. Wolff (Boston: Beacon Press, 1967), 267–87.
5 Robert Schumann, "Meyerbeer and Mendelssohn," in *On Music and Musicians* (New York: McGraw-Hill, 1964), 193–99.
6 *Das erste deutsche Sängerbundesfest in Dresden* (Dresden: B. Friedel, 1865), 78.
7 Karl Leberecht Immermann (1796–1840) was a novelist, poet, and playwright. He worked with Mendelssohn in Düsseldorf in the 1830s. See R. Larry Todd, *Mendelssohn: A Life in Music* (Oxford and New York: Oxford University Press, 2003), 250–51 and esp. 297–300 on their collaboration and its collapse. *Paulus* was premiered in 1836, not 1835 as the citation claimed.
8 The currency of the idea of historical cycles and the notion that the present moment, i.e., the early twentieth century after World War I, was an era of decline in the West owed much to Oswald Spengler's book, *Decline of the West*, which appeared between 1918 and 1922. The assertion that the historical moment was one of decadence functioned as a justifying framework for the embrace of movements that promised spiritual regeneration and rebirth such as Naziism.
9 See, for example Chapter 5 in Max Nordau, *Degeneration* (New York: Appleton and Company, 1895),171-213
10 See Fritz Stern's classic, *The Politics of Cultural Despair: A Study in the Rise of Germanic Ideology* (Berkeley: University of California Press, 1961). The Nazis organized in 1938 a "Degenerate Music" exhibition in Düsseldorf. See Olaf Peters and Steven Lindberg, "Fear and Propaganda: National Socialism and the Concept of Degenerate Art," *Social Research* 83, no. 1 (2016): 39–66.
11 W. H. Riehl, *Musikalische Charakterköpfe: Ein kunstgeschichtliches Skizzenbuch*, 2 vols. (Stuttgart and Augsburg: Cotta, 1857), 1:110–16.
12 Giacomo Meyerbeer, *Briefwechsel und Tagebücher*, vol. 4: *1846–1849*, ed. Heinz Becker and Gudrun Becker (Berlin: De Gruyter, 1985), 322; and Todd, *Mendelssohn: A Life in Music*, 547.

13 F. J. Fetis, *Biographie universelle des musiciens*, vol. 6 (Paris: 1875; repr. Brussels: Culture et Civilisation, 1972), 77–84.
14 Quoted in Fred K. Prieberg, *Kraftprobe: Wilhelm Furtwängler im Dritten Reich* (Wiesbaden: F. A.Brockhaus, 1986), 164.
15 Toby Thacker, *Music after Hitler 1945–1955* (Aldershot: Ashgate 2007), 75–76. On the perfunctory attempt at "re-education" with respect to the Berlin Philharmonic, see Abby Anderton, "It was never a Nazi Orchestra": The American Re-education of the Berlin Philharmonic," *Music and Politics* 7, no. 1 (2013). https://quod.lib.umich.edu/m/mp/9460447.0007.103/--it-was-never-a-nazi-orchestra-the-american-re-education?rgn=main;view=fulltext, accessed 1 March 2024.
16 Prieberg, *Kraftprobe: Wilhelm Furtwängler im Dritten Reich*, 162–63.
17 Ronald Taylor, ed., *Furtwängler on Music: Essays and Addresses*, trans. R. Taylor (London and New York: Routledge, 2016), 59–61.
18 John Ardoin, *The Furtwängler Record* (Portland, OR: Amadeus Press, 1994), 261.
19 Wilhelm Furtwängler, *Aufzeichnungen: 1924–1954* (Wiesbaden: F. A. Brockhaus, 1980), 186, 207, 209.
20 Ibid., 207, 231–32.
21 See Robert S. Wistrich, "The German-Jewish Symbiosis in Central Europe," in *European Judaism: A Journal for the New Europe* 23, no. 1 (Spring 1990): 20–30.
22 Mendelssohn's place in the repertoire of Furtwängler, whose first major concert, ironically, was a performance of *Elijah*, is slight before 1934 (the exception being performances of the *Hebrides* Overture, the only work Wagner held in high regard). Mendelssohn then disappears and reappears after the conductor's postwar return to the podium from 1947 on; he concentrated on three well-known works, the *Hebrides*, the *A Midsummer Night's Dream* Overture, and the Violin Concerto. The only exception was at the 1947 Mendelssohn festival in Leipzig at which the conductor gave his address: https://furtwangler.fr/en/concert-list/?wpv_view_count=166&wpvsaison=0&wpvorchestre=0&wpv_post_search=mendelssohn&wpv_paged=6, accessed 1 March 2024.
23 Todd, *Mendelssohn: A Life in Music*, xx–xxviii
24 Karl Jaspers, *The Question of German Guilt*, trans. E. B. Ashton, with a new introduction by Joseph W. Koterski (New York: Fordham University Press, 2000).
25 See Anson Rabinbach, *In the Shadow of Catastrophe: German Intellectuals Between Apocalypse and Enlightenment* (Berkeley: University of California Press, 1997).
26 See Theodor W. Adorno and Max Horkheimer, *Dialectic of Enlightenment*, trans. John Cumming (New York: Continuum, 2000).
27 For a recent analysis of the immediate postwar era and efforts, particularly by the U.S., to reconstruct culture and education in Germany, see Maxim H. Botstein, "Democracy and the University: America and the Reconstruction of German Higher Education, 1945–1966" (PhD diss., Harvard University, 2023), 24–76.
28 Hannah Arendt, *Eichmann in Jerusalem: A Report on the Banality of Evil,* rev. and enlarged ed. (New York: Penguin, 1977).

8. TO THE TOMB OF GENIUS: HEINRICH, MENDELSSOHN, AND AMERICAN MUSICAL AMBITION

MARIAN WILSON KIMBER

The death of Felix Mendelssohn in 1847 at the age of thirty-eight was considered an international tragedy. The composer's untimely demise inspired poetic tributes, and concerts of his music honored his memory.[1] In New York City, six musical organizations combined to present a "Mendelssohn Solemnity" on February 5, 1848, with a program that featured selections from *St. Paul*, *Elijah*, and *Lobgesang*, as well as the Recordare from Mozart's Requiem and the funeral march from Beethoven's *Eroica*.[2] Held at the Castle Garden, the event was one of the largest concerts ever before held in the city, attended by as many as ten thousand people. The *Courier & Enquirer* reported that "even the staircases were crowded with a dense mass of human beings."[3] Audience members, many of whom had been attracted to the event because of the free tickets, were noisier than was considered appropriate for the occasion's memorial character and had to be reminded through hissing not to clap between numbers. Although the performance appeared to be under-rehearsed, and the *Mirror* reported that concertgoers were reluctant to donate to the evening's expenses in the boxes provided, it was nonetheless considered a success.[4] The Solemnity was hailed, not for furthering the reputation of Mendelssohn, but as an American achievement: the *Albion* nationalistically declared that it would be long remembered "in the Musical History of America, which cannot be paralleled in any country in Europe."[5]

Yet not everyone was pleased with the concert. The Bohemian-American composer Anthony Philip Heinrich penned a letter to the *New York Herald* critiquing the Solemnity's lack of any newly-composed piece in honor of Mendelssohn and promoting his own symphonic work, *To the Tomb of Genius*, and other compositions inspired by the composer's death:

> Mr. Editor:—Permit me, through the medium of your paper, with "tears in my eyes," to inquire how it came to pass that none of the great master spirits, who originated and conducted the Mendelssohn solemnity, at Castle Garden, produced not a single effusion of their own, to evince their *real* musical condolence, springing spontaneously from the heart, in an original requiem to the memory of the illustrious departed composer? Almost immediately after the demise of Mendelssohn was known, I published an impromptu, "the Laurel and Cypress," indicating, at the same time, that I had also ready in manuscript, (among many printed obituary works,) "The Musician's Requiem," and "The Tomb of Genius," both in honor of the manes of Mendelssohn, my lamented friend.[6]

That Heinrich claimed Mendelssohn as his friend and knew other leading figures of his day has played an important role in validating his historical place in the scholarship on American music. This essay reexamines the evidence for a relationship between the eccentric Heinrich and the renowned Mendelssohn in order to illuminate both composers' cultural positions in American musical life. Heinrich's desire to memorialize Mendelssohn in music was inspired by the German composer's renown in the United States, which began to take shape in the 1840s and continued to grow throughout the nineteenth century.[7] While Heinrich is best known for numerous nationalistic compositions celebrating the American landscape and Native Americans, the works that he composed dedicated to Mendelssohn and other highly-regarded figures demonstrate both his Romantic proclivity toward ritualistically memorializing the dead and his ongoing pursuit of professional validation in his chosen country through creating European connections.[8]

Heinrich's large circle of acquaintances is frequently cited as evidence of his international prominence. His relationship with Mendelssohn is mentioned several times in William Upton's seminal biography of 1939; the introduction by Oscar Sonneck states, "It is extremely unlikely, in fact, that there was anyone in private life in America at that time . . . whose acquaintance with representative people (particularly in his own field of music, both in Europe and America) was broader . . ."[9] The article about Heinrich in *Grove Music Online* echoes Sonneck, calling the "scope of his personal contacts . . . astonishing." Authors J. Bunker Clark and David Barron make special note of Heinrich's reputation among his better-known contemporaries: "Unlike most American composers of the period, Heinrich's reputation extended beyond the U.S.A. He was acquainted with Mendelssohn, and Marschner praised his compositions."[10] In his 2004 book on American "mavericks," Michael Broyles hypothesizes that Heinrich's encounter with Mendelssohn and his nature-inspired compositions such as the *Hebrides* Overture might have instigated the former composer's turn toward large-scale orchestral works influenced by the American landscape.[11] The continual repetition of Mendelssohn and other well-known names has functioned to validate Heinrich's historical position. Upton summarizes: "wherever we have found Heinrich so far, whether in music or social relations, it has always been with the highest type of cultured people . . . . If a man is known by the company he keeps—and then is not only acquainted with but dearly loved by the choicest spirits of his time, he needs no further guarantee of respectability."[12]

Yet, what is the evidence for the relationship between Heinrich and Mendelssohn? The meeting between the two composers is supposed to have taken place during Mendelssohn's first trip to London in 1829. Heinrich worked as a violinist in the Drury Lane orchestra off and on between 1826 and 1831, and so he may have been in the orchestra that Mendelssohn heard when he attended the theater. Heinrich stated that Mendelssohn came to dine with him in his lodgings.[13] But the evidence for such a meeting is at best extremely slim. Heinrich's statement comes from almost thirty years later; it is found in an 1857 letter to the Berlin scientist Alexander von Humboldt. Humboldt's brief reply indicates that Heinrich had used their mutual acquaintance with Mendelssohn to initiate a request for assistance in making musical contacts in Berlin, something that the eighty-eight-year old scientist was unable to do. Heinrich's friendship with Mendelssohn is also occasionally mentioned in the contemporary press, most often in his own letters to the papers, but occasionally in articles by others. The author of an unidentified press clipping in Heinrich's scrapbooks at the Library of Congress wrote: "What degree of merit his works possess, we do not know. Some of them, however, received the praise of Mendelssohn, with whom Mr. Heinrich used to correspond."[14]

Heinrich's scrapbooks, which contain letters from Heinrich Marschner and Thomas Moore, contain nothing in Mendelssohn's hand. Furthermore, no letters from Heinrich exist in the Bodleian Library's "Green Books" in which Mendelssohn meticulously preserved his incoming correspondence. The Green Books consist of twenty-seven volumes, containing over six thousand letters in all; the earliest date from the 1820s. The wide range of correspondents, who consist of family, friends, professional acquaintances, and strangers, suggests a comprehensive compilation, not a careful selection. It is surprising that in a collection of this size and scope, no letter from Heinrich is preserved. Bodleian librarian and Mendelssohn scholar Peter Ward Jones located the name "Heinrich" in the diaries in which Mendelssohn recorded his appointments, though it appears on May 2 during his 1833 trip to London, not the one from 1829;[15] Heinrich had returned to England the previous month. But this tantalizing clue unfortunately does not confirm that the Heinrich in question was, in fact, "Anthony Philip." Mendelssohn was a prolific letter writer himself, and his correspondence is scattered worldwide, so one cannot presume to have had access to all of his letters from the period following the reported 1829 meeting or a later 1833 one. Nonetheless, there appears to be no known letter, published or unpublished, that mentions Heinrich. For scholars of American music, Heinrich's association with Mendelssohn and other famous persons has been a recognized part of his professional history.[16] But if Heinrich did indeed meet Mendelssohn, it seems that the interchange was of no significance to the latter composer.

Around 1832, Heinrich dedicated two piano works to Mendelssohn: *La Promenade du Diable* and *The Rübezahl Dance on the Schneekoppe*.[17] Both compositions evoke the supernatural; perhaps Heinrich encountered the overture to *A Midsummer Night's Dream* in London, as he was still in Europe when the New York Philharmonic first performed it in 1830. However, neither work seems stylistically related to any of the Mendelssohn works that Heinrich might have known. The former work is a tarantella hurtling on in Heinrich's characteristic fantasia-like style in order to suggest a devil's dance, and the latter piece refers to the capricious spirit of a mountain on the border of Heinrich's Czech homeland.[18] The title page of *The Rübezahl Dance* mentions both Mendelssohn and Viennese pianist Karl Maria von Blocket, indicating that Heinrich had selected not one, but two European pianists to whom to dedicate his latest piano composition; he dedicated *The First Labour of Hercules* to Franz Liszt around the same time. Perhaps Heinrich heard Mendelssohn, an up-and-coming young pianist, when he performed Weber's *Konzertstück* or Beethoven's *Emperor* Concerto in 1829—but the misspelling of Mendelssohn's name on the title pages of both of the dedicated works may indicate that his knowledge of the German composer was distant rather than first-hand.[19]

Heinrich called *The Laurel and the Cypress* for piano a "petit impromptu," that was "suggested by pleasing recollections of the Departed Felix Mendelssohn Bartholdy." The cypress served as a funereal symbol since Roman times;[20] yet the piece's triple meter and regular phrase structure evoke a slow dance. In addition to the impromptu, there is one other piano solo by Heinrich loosely related to Mendelssohn, a *Song without Words*, dedicated to Jenny Lind and published in 1850. It is likely that both of the two piano works were influenced by Mendelssohn's *Lieder ohne Worte*, which Heinrich may have first encountered in England.[21] Both compositions are brief, have slow tempos and largely homophonic textures with expressive melodies in the right hand. Both are constructed with a modified ternary form; in the *Song without Words*, the opening music returns in the minor mode. Other than texture and general mood, however, any specific stylistic features demonstrating Heinrich's indebtedness to Mendelssohn's music are difficult to locate. Both pieces feature Heinrich's characteristic ornamentation of melodies, particularly the *Song without Words*, which also indulges in a somewhat stream-of-consciousness approach to its Italianate melody that is typical of the composer's style.

Heinrich's orchestral homage to Mendelssohn, *To the Tomb of Genius*, bears no resemblance to any of Mendelssohn's orchestral music. Like many other of Heinrich's symphonic works, it is a massive piece scored for full orchestra with organ and piano, and a large brass section, including ophicleides.[22] As seen in Figure 1, the piece is in seven continuous sections, many of which have a slow, perhaps funereal, tempo; the work's centerpiece, an *Allegro ma non tanto*, makes up approximately a third of the piece. In both form and content, the *Tomb of Genius* resembles Heinrich's *Bohemia's Funeral Honors to Josef Jungman* for piano, which dates from around the same time, and his symphony, *To the Spirit of Beethoven*, composed a few years earlier.[23] These two works feature multiple attacca sections constructed to depict, programmatically, crowds gathering for ceremonial events: Jungman's funeral and the unveiling of the Beethoven monument at Bonn, respectively. However, the sections of *To the Tomb of Genius* contain no specific titles or obvious program that could account for the work's unusual formal structure. Heinrich advertised the piece as a "Sinfonia Sacra," and although he marked "fuga" in measure 157, there are only two fugal entrances; the "fugue" is more of a fleeting notion than an actuality. Heinrich wrote the words "Anfang" and "Commencement" over measure 94 and provided an orchestral *Cadenza dolorosa*, suggesting that he may have had some extra-musical content in mind. Although most of the piece is in B-flat major, the opening Adagio is permeated with turns to the minor mode to create the sepulchral atmosphere.

Thus, there is little musical evidence in Heinrich's output for anything more than a passing encounter with Mendelssohn's style. However, within the manuscript of *To the Tomb of Genius* is one final shred of evidence that hints at interchange with Mendelssohn. Between pages 53 and 54 is a torn half sheet containing the first verse

Measures	Tempo	Meter	Key
1–98	**Adagio**	4/4	B-flat major
	94–98 "Anfang" / "Commencement"		
99–122	**Andantino**	6/8	B-flat major
123–144	**Andante Largo**	3/4	B-flat major
145–435	**Allegro ma non tanto**		
	157 "Fuga"		
	221		C major
	309		F major
	428		B-flat major
436–441	**Andante**	2/4	B-flat major
442–455	**Adagio. Cadenza dolorosa**	2/4	B-flat major
456–585*	**Allegro**	2/4	B-flat major

*550–573 missing from manuscript

Figure 1, Overview of Anthony Philip Heinrich, *To the Tomb of Genius*

of *Ewige Nähe* by Munich poet Agnes von Calatin. This text was set to music by Calatin's close friend, Josephine Lang, whom Mendelssohn met in 1830 and whose Lieder he championed. We might hypothesize that Mendelssohn shared this poem with Heinrich if he did meet him in 1833, although Lang's song was not published until five years later. In addition, the quotation marks around the verse's final line and the substitution of the word "verbannt" for "verband," suggests that Heinrich did not get the text from Mendelssohn or from Lang's setting, but instead from Marie König's, published in Dresden in 1851 with these changes. Perhaps Heinrich encountered König's song during his 1857 trip to nearby Prague.[24] Whether the poetic verse's insertion into *The Tomb of Genius* is related to the work itself is not clear. Its appearance in the score may have been an entirely random occurrence, or it may suggest Heinrich's personal identification with Mendelssohn due to their shared vocation for composition: "Seit ein gleiches hohes Streben / Herz mit Herz so eng verband."[25]

Heinrich's dedication of his compositions to Mendelssohn should not be considered musical homage, but is better understood within the larger context of his tributes to as many as twenty ruling monarchs and multiple European cultural celebrities, not only Lind, but also Henry Bishop, Charles Dickens, Fanny Essler, Niccolò Paganini, and others. Although an extreme example, Heinrich's obsession with linking his works to others falls within the period's dedicatory practices explored by

Emily Green; his dedications to royalty recalled the customs of eighteenth-century patronage and those for artistic figures reflected the nineteenth-century shift towards Romanticism and capitalism.[26] Heinrich's commentary surrounding his dedications demonstrates that they were intended to fulfill many of the functions Green outlines: to enhance the composer's status and "authority as an author," to demonstrate "sociability" and a "personal relationship with the dedicatee," and, most importantly, to "contribute to a composer's celebrity and brand name."[27] Heinrich, whose previous residence in a Southern log cabin inspired the moniker "The Beethoven of Kentucky," served as a one-man publicity campaign for himself and his compositions. He used both his dedications and his personal correspondence to get powerful individuals to notice his music, and he made sure that both his efforts and any response he might receive were duly noted in the press. The composer obviously believed that he could gain cultural capital from even less-than-ideal interchanges with famous individuals. He published his letters from Moore and Marschner, despite their both containing politely-worded but fundamentally critical suggestions as to how he might improve his compositions. Moore explained that his music's unpopularity came from a "harmonic science" beyond the capacity of amateur musicians and counseled Heinrich to curtail the "perpetual variety of your modulations," which "disturb too much the flow of the melody."[28] Twenty years later Marschner acknowledged that Heinrich's compositions "offer the performers too great difficulties, and . . . require of the human voice too extensive a compass."[29] Given that Heinrich was willing to publish such criticism simply to show that notable figures had acknowledged his compositions, it is likely that if he had received a letter from Mendelssohn, even a critical or merely ambiguously polite one, he would have had no qualms about publishing it.

Heinrich's contemporaries recognized his marketing strategies. In 1851, after complaining in print about a bad review of *General Taylor's Funeral March* and producing a positive testimonial in the form of his letter from Marschner, Heinrich suffered a scathingly sarcastic response from the editor of *Saroni's Musical Times*:

> But cannot so perfect a composer occasionally write a piece that is worthless? Mozart and Beethoven have been guilty of something of the kind . . . and is Anthony Philip Heinrich the only mortal who is infallible? But true, neither of the above composers had a testimonial from Mr. Marschner, wherewith to blind the judgment of the people. Neither of them had dedicated voluminous works to all the potentates of the earth . . . . All this remained for Mr. Heinrich to accomplish. Wonder how many of the *favored* Princes, Dukes, Kings, Emperors, &c. &c., have favored him with an answer? Perhaps Mr. Heinrich will inform us on the subject; it will prove interesting to our readers.[30]

Saroni later suggested, in spite of Heinrich's subsequent protests, that the letter from Marschner had actually been solicited on his behalf by a "very amiable lady" and that Heinrich had had to pick up the letter "at that lady's house."[31] Saroni, at least, was publicly willing to discount Heinrich's self-reported affiliations with nineteenth-century celebrities. Even Heinrich's biographer Upton, ever sympathetic to his subject, admitted, "There is no question that Heinrich was his whole life a decided opportunist, attempting to take advantage of every possible chance to advance his professional interests. But so simple and sincere was he in it all that we are never inclined to take it amiss. In fact, we share whole-heartedly in his regret that so seldom was there any tangible result from all this effort."[32]

Heinrich's tributes to Mendelssohn following his death were not his first compositions honoring departed luminaries, but were among ca. twenty pieces listed with his advertised "obituary works" (seen in Figure 2), dedicated to prominent individuals who had recently died.[33] Given that Heinrich knew some of the departed subjects personally, many are American; some compositions honored friends and colleagues, while many others were inscribed to well-known artistic or political figures. Several additional compositions have texts, titles, or programmatic content related to death. The obituary works include piano pieces, solo songs, and choral anthems, all genres in which Heinrich typically composed. Although *To the Tomb of Genius* is the only extant orchestral piece of this type, Heinrich also composed symphonic works named for Friedrich Schiller and, as mentioned previously, Beethoven.[34] The career of the person who served as the inspiration for the work may have had some influence on Heinrich's choice of genre. Presidents Harrison and Taylor were commemorated by patriotic funeral marches, while close friends inspired choral anthems. The death of Daniel Schlesinger resulted in the composition of *An Elegiac Impromptu Fantasia*, an appropriate tribute to a virtuoso pianist.[35]

Figure 2, Anthony Philip Heinrich's death-related works
Compositions specifically identified by the composer as "obituary works" are indicated by an asterisk. Dates have been taken primarily from Heinrich's works list in *Grove Music Online*.

Date	Composition	Subject(s)
1820/51	*How Sleep the Brave* (song, also STB)	"Heroes who fell at Tippecanoe And The River Raisin"
1820/22	*Ode to the Memory of Commodore O.H. Perry* (song, also violin, flute, piano)	Oliver Hazard Perry (1785–1819), naval hero, War of 1812
1820	*Columbia's Plaint* (song)	George Washington and his contemporaries
1823	*Canone funerale* (piano)[1]	
1825	*Epitaph on Joan Buff* (5vv, piano)[1]	Mrs. Martha Osborne (d. 1825), friend of Heinrich
1832/36/54	**Death of a Christian / Des Christen Tod* (SSTBB, piano/organ); variant is *Death of a Christian* (SATBB, piano/organ)	
1832	**Funeral Anthem* (SSTBB, piano/organ)	Isaac Thom (of Kentucky) and William H. Eliot, (of Massachusetts), patrons of Heinrich
c. 1835	**The Amaranth* (piano)	
1840	**An Elegiac Impromptu Fantasia* (piano), alternate title is *Fantasia Dolorosa*	Daniel Schlesinger (1799–1839), pianist

1840?	*The Stranger's Requiem (duet, not extant)	Schlesinger
1841	*The Maiden's Dirge (piano)	Lucretia Maria Davidson (1808–1825) and Margaret Miller Davidson (1823–1838), poets
1841	*The President's Funeral March (piano/organ)[1]	President William Henry Harrison (1773–1841)
c. 1842	Funeral Anthem (SATBB, organ; incomplete)	
1842	The Loved One's Grave (song)	
1846	*Elegiac quintetto vocale (SATBB, piano/organ)	Leopold Herwig (1810–1845), violinist
1847	*Funeral Anthem (SATBB, chorus, organ); variant is Coro funerale (SATBB, chorus, semi-chorus, organ, orchestra)	J. G. L. Libby (d. 1847), Boston merchant and friend of Heinrich
1847	***The Laurel and the Cypress (piano)**	**Felix Mendelssohn Bartholdy (1809–1847)**
1847?	***To the Tomb of Genius; Sinfonia Sacra (symphony)**	**Mendelssohn**
1847?	***The Musician's Requiem (not extant)**	**Mendelssohn**
1847	*Bohemia's Funeral Honors to Josef Jungmann (piano)	Josef Jungmann (1773–1847), Czech literary figure
1848	*The Soul Released From Feeble Clay (song)	Thomas Cooke (1782–1848), English composer and music director, Drury Lane Theatre
1849	*The Cypress, an Obituary Ode (song)[2]	Karl XIV Johan (1818–1844), King of Sweden
1849	*The Moan of the Forest, or The Cherokee's Lament (Toccata Indiana) (piano)	
1849	The Festival of the Dead and the Cries of the Souls (piano)[1]	
1849?	*Denmark's Funeral Honors to Thorwaldsen (piano, not extant)	Bertel Thorwaldsen (1768–1848), Danish sculptor
1850?	*An Elegiac Song (song)	[Alexander] Hamilton C[oates] Browne (1830–1850), artist
1850	*General Taylor's Funeral March (piano); other variants are Marcia funerale (brass band, perc.) and Marcia funebre for the Heroes in Battle Slain (brass band, perc.)	President Zachary Taylor (1784–1850)
1852–3	*That Awful Day Will Surely Come, an Obituary Solo Song (song)	John Howard Payne (1791–1852), actor, dramatist, editor, diplomat
18??	Du bist gestorben, Elegie (song)	
18??	An Elegy for the Organ[2]	
18??	*Sweden's Plaint (not extant, possibly The Cypress)	

1 J. Bunker Clark pointed out the musical similarities between *Canone Funerale, Epitaph on Joan Buff, The President's Funeral March*, and *The Festival of the Dead and the Cries of the Souls* in *The Dawning of American Keyboard Music* (New York: Greenwood Press, 1988), 358.

2 *The Cypress* and *An Elegy for the Organ* are both variants of *Ode to the Memory of Commodore O. H. Perry*.

Although it was customary for funeral marches to be composed for important political figures, Heinrich's outpouring of musical memorials seems, like his persistent dedications, to be extremely opportunistic.[36] Several of the choral works have the word "funeral" in the title, even though it is unlikely that Heinrich could have produced these pieces in time for performances at actual funerals. However, they might have been programmed at memorial concerts such as the Mendelssohn Solemnity. Obituary works would have appeared well within the customary mourning period, during which grieving loved ones would be willing to purchase a copy of Heinrich's composition as a way of honoring the memory of the recently deceased. Heinrich's scrapbooks in the Library of Congress frequently include notices of forthcoming publications pasted directly alongside the related obituaries. It would almost seem that the composer was a musical ambulance-chaser, using the deaths of various individuals to draw attention to his music. Indeed, Heinrich's complaint about the Mendelssohn Solemnity closes with his self-identification as a composer for the dead, "who can venture to assert that he alone, has done more in memory of the dead, than the whole bunch of these fanciful musicians put together."[37] Perhaps in the 1840s Heinrich discovered that, unlike the living, those who had passed on could not ignore or reject his musical tributes.[38]

Lest it appear that Heinrich's motives were only opportunistic, it must be granted that he was deeply saddened by the deaths of his friends, particularly that of violinist Leopold Herwig.[39] Furthermore, Heinrich's outpouring of mourning works, morbid to twenty-first-century sensibilities, is actually characteristic of nineteenth-century American bereavement customs in which highly public social rituals served to preserve the memory of the departed through visible symbols created in various art forms.[40] Heinrich's obituary works are the musical equivalents of such artifacts of mourning: jewelry that featured the deceased's name or image, or was woven from his or her hair,[41] or prints of graveyard scenes with tombstones designed to be filled in with the deceased's name.[42] His musical tributes stem from the same artistic impetus as posthumous mourning portraits[43] of dead loved ones preserved in art works or in later daguerreotypes, matted with black frames.[44] (For example, portraits of Mendelssohn on his deathbed were drawn by Wilhelm Hensel, Eduard Bendemann, and Julius Hübner.[45]) Heinrich's choice of texts reflects what Ann Douglas has dubbed "consolation literature" which included "obituary poems and memoirs, mourner's manuals, prayer guide-books, hymns, and books about heaven."[46] The sentimental texts of hundreds of parlor songs, in which bereaved male lovers linger over young women's tombs next to weeping willows or cypress trees, can also be considered part of this consolation literature.[47] America's memorialization of the dead found its ultimate symbol in the rural cemetery movement;[48] cemeteries such as Boston's Mount Auburn provided lush, pastoral settings which became major tourist attractions, inspiring guidebooks and verse.[49] In light of the fixation with death found in American culture in the mid-nineteenth century, Heinrich's obituary works are perhaps not as morbid as they might at first seem.

Heinrich's Mendelssohn tributes were thus a paradigmatic Romantic expression of grief and death, as well as a characteristically opportunistic maneuver on the part of the struggling composer, rather than a personal memorial to someone he had known well. His Mendelssohn-inspired works were but one example of the various expressions of emotion in America at the more famous composer's premature death. Nonetheless, the seemingly mythic meeting of the two composers—the rugged individualist and the epitome of a Germanic tradition—has frequently been cited as evidence that an American original had received international recognition, despite one musicologist acknowledging that Heinrich was one of a "few nationalistic, chauvinistic odd balls... prophets without honor in their own country."[50]

Heinrich's composition of *To the Tomb of Genius* reflects the growing regard for Mendelssohn by American musicians and their audiences; whether or not Heinrich actually met Mendelssohn, he clearly understood that to perform Mendelssohn's music in the United States was considered a national achievement and that to demonstrate recognition by European musicians would only increase his value as an American musician. In 1848, Heinrich advertised that he planned to program *To the Tomb of Genius* on an upcoming "Farewell Concert," an event he hoped would be "original, meritorious, and *national*."[51] A press clipping in his scrapbooks describing *The Laurel and the Cypress* is even more characteristic of the way Heinrich viewed his relationship to Europe. The piece dedicated to Mendelssohn is part of "that library of original music, composed by Heinrich in the forests of Kentucky, and amid the hum of New York, and which he will carry to Europe, to be produced there, to be appreciated, and to come back to us and be recognized and welcomed as our own."[52] By linking his music to Mendelssohn and the Old World, Heinrich hoped to receive recognition in the new. Heinrich's highly public aspiration to establish a cultural position like that of the revered European composer and its continual retelling in the musicological scholarship can both be interpreted, like the Solemnity that motivated him, as symbols of an American struggle for musical legitimacy.

---

1 *The Musical World* printed four poems on Mendelssohn's death in 1847–8.
2 These were the Philharmonic Society, the Sacred Music Society, Liederkranz, Concordia, Euterpean, and the American Musical Institute. Vera Brodsky Lawrence, *Strong on Music: The New York Music Scene in the Days of George Templeton Strong. Volume 1: Resonances, 1836–1850* (Chicago: University of Chicago Press, 1988), 498.
3 *Courier & Enquirer*, 8 February 1848, quoted in Lawrence, 499.
4 In his diary, George Templeton Strong reported that the ensemble came close to breaking down. Lawrence, 499–500.
5 "Concert," *The Albion* 7, no. 7 (12 February 1848): 83.
6 "Theatrical and Musical," *New York Herald*, 9 February 1848. "The Musician's Requiem" is not extant.
7 Joseph A. Mussulman, "Mendelssohnism in America," *Musical Quarterly* 53, no. 3 (July 1967): 335–40.
8 See Denise Von Glahn, *Sounds of Place: Music and the American Cultural Landscape* (Boston: Northeastern University Press, 2003), 17–35; Michael Pisani, *Imagining Native America in Music* (New

Haven, CT: Yale University Press, 2005), 106–10; William Gibbons, "The Musical Audubon: Ornithology and Nationalism in the Symphonies of Anthony Philip Heinrich," *Journal of the Society for American Music* 3, no. 4 (November 2009): 465–491; and Douglas W. Shadle, *Orchestrating the Nation: the Nineteenth-Century American Symphonic Enterprise* (New York: Oxford University Press, 2016), 35–55.

9   Oscar Sonneck, Preface to William Upton, *Anthony Philip Heinrich, a Nineteenth-Century Composer in America* (New York: Columbia University Press, 1939), xii.
10 J. Bunker Clark and David Barron, "Heinrich, Anthony Philip," *Grove Music Online*, http://www.oxfordmusiconline, accessed 20 August 2022. The newer article by Barron and Douglas Shadle in the *Grove Dictionary of American Music* (2013) calls Heinrich's circle of contacts "astonishing" yet identifies the circle as being outside of music.
11 Michael Broyles, *Mavericks and Other Traditions in American Music* (New Haven: Yale University Press, 2004), 57.
12 Upton, *Anthony Philip Heinrich*, 85.
13 Mendelssohn dining with Heinrich is again recounted in Viola Shaula Valerio, "A Journey through Heinrich's Personal Archive and the American and European Influences in his Music," in *The Western Minstrel: Voyages through the Life and Music of Anthony Philip Heinrich*, ed. Peter J. F. Herbert (Wallington: The Dvořák Society, 2020), 32.
14 In Anthony Philip Heinrich, Scrapbooks, Library of Congress [microfilm], 1112, and quoted in Upton, *Anthony Philip Heinrich*, 217.
15 Personal correspondence, 2009.
16 As a "bit player" surrounded by the famous, Heinrich has been called "a cross between Zelig and Forrest Gump" in Michael Beckerman, "Introduction: Song Birds on the Shelf," in *The Western Minstrel*, viii.
17 Published in modern editions in Anthony Philip Heinrich, *Piano Music*, vol. 1, ed. Andrew Stiller (Philadelphia: Kallisti Press, 1995).
18 Stiller, Preface to Heinrich, *Piano Music*, vol. 1, 3.
19 Heinrich was not happy with these works' engraving, so the misspelling may have been an engraver's error. Stiller, Preface, 3.
20 John W. Draper, *The Funeral Elegy and the Rise of English Romanticism* (New York: New York University, 1929), 336.
21 Mendelssohn's *Songs without Words* were all issued by American publishers Oliver Ditson and G. B. Russell before 1870. British editions of *Songs without Words* had an inauspicious beginning; op. 19 sold only 114 copies in four years. See Peter Ward Jones, "Mendelssohn and His English Publishers," in *Mendelssohn Studies*, ed. R. Larry Todd (Cambridge: Cambridge University Press, 1992), 242–4.
22 The first page of the autograph is reproduced in *The Western Minstrel*, 54.
23 Shadle, *Orchestrating the Nation*, 50–1.
24 I am deeply grateful to Sharon Krebs for identifying the connection to König's publication.
25 Lines 1–4 of *Ew'ge Nähe* is translated by Sharon and Harald Krebs, in *Josephine Lang: Her Life and Songs* (Oxford: Oxford University Press, 2007), 47:
    Heller ward mein inn'res Leben,   My inner life became more radiant,
    Schöner, seit ich dich erkannt,   More beautiful since I met you,
    Seit ein gleiches hohes Streben   Since the same exalted striving
    Herz mit Herz so eng verband.   So closely united our hearts.
26 Emily H. Green, *Dedicating Music, 1785–1850* (Rochester, NY: University of Rochester Press, 2019), 4.
27 Ibid., 34.
28 Thomas Moore, 1 September 1929, quoted in Upton, *Anthony Philip Heinrich*, 103. Mendelssohn might have commented, as he did to Leipzig Conservatory students, "I call that modulation ungentlemanlike." Quoted in Clive Brown, ed., *A Portrait of Mendelssohn* (New Haven: Yale University Press, 2003), 288.

29 Heinrich Marschner, 10 May 1849, translated in Upton, *Anthony Philip Heinrich*, 215.
30 "Offended Dignity no. 2," *Saroni's Musical Times* 3, no. 7 (10 May 1851): 73.
31 *Saroni's Musical Times* 3, no. 9 (24 May 1851): 92.
32 Upton, *Anthony Philip Heinrich*, 109.
33 Not all of these compositions are extent, and some are variants of the same work.
34 Shadle, *Orchestrating the Nation*, 38–40.
35 *Du bist gestorben* and *An Elegy for Organ* are in manuscript; Heinrich might have designated beneficiaries upon publication.
36 See Vera Brodsky Lawrence, *Music for Patriots, Politicians and Presidents: Harmonies and Discords of the First Hundred Years* (New York: Macmillan, 1975) and Sterling E. Murray, "Weeping and Mourning: Funeral Dirges in Honor of General Washington," *Journal of the American Musicological Society* 31 (1978): 282–308.
37 "Theatrical and Musical."
38 For example, Mrs. Coutts rejected Heinrich's dedication of "The Minstrel's Musical Compliments to Mrs. Coutts, a Fancy Contillon [sic]: Vivat Britain's Fair!," 29 October 1826, Scrapbooks, 1015, quoted by J. Bunker Clark in *The Dawning of American Keyboard Music* (New York: Greenwood, 1988), 349.
39 Scrapbooks, 476.
40 Barbara Todd Hillerman, "Chrysalis of Gloom: Nineteenth-Century American Mourning Costume," in *A Time to Mourn: Expressions of Grief in Nineteenth Century America*, ed. Martha V. Pike and Janice Gray Armstrong (Stony Brook, NY: The Museums at Stony Brook, 1980), 99.
41 Lawrence Taylor, "Symbolic Death: An Anthropological View of Mourning Ritual in the Nineteenth Century," in *A Time to Mourn*, 46.
42 Pike and Armstrong, eds., *A Time to Mourn*, 67–8.
43 Phoebe Lloyd, "Posthumous Mourning Portraiture," in *A Time to Mourn*, 85.
44 Floyd and Marion Rinhart, "Rediscovery: an American Way of Death," *Art in America* 55, no. 5 (1967): 80.
45 R. Larry Todd, *Mendelssohn: A Life in Music* (New York: Oxford University Press, 2003), 567.
46 Ann Douglas, *The Feminization of American Culture* (New York: Alfred A. Knopf, 1977; reprint ed., New York: Doubleday, 1988), 201.
47 Nicholas E. Tawa, *Sweet Songs for Gentle Americans: The Parlor Song in America, 1790–1860* (Bowling Green, OH: Bowling Green University Popular Press, 1980), 134; see also Colin B. and Jo B. Atkinson, "Changing Attitudes to Death: Nineteenth-Century Parlour Songs as Consolation Literature," *Canadian Review of American Studies* 23 (1993): 79–100.
48 David Charles Sloane, *The Last Great Necessity: Cemeteries in American History* (Baltimore: John Hopkins University Press, 1991), 93.
49 Blanche Linden-Ward, "Strange but Genteel Pleasure Grounds: Tourist and Leisure Uses of Nineteenth-Century Rural Cemeteries," in *Cemeteries and Gravemarkers: Voices of American Culture*, ed. Richard E. Meyer (Ann Arbor: University of Michigan Press, 1989), 309.
50 Irving Lowens, *Music in America and American Music* (Brooklyn: Institute for Studies in American Music, 1978), 12.
51 Scrapbooks, 645. Italics added. The program of Heinrich's eventual concert in 1853 (see *The Western Minstrel*, 68) did not contain *To the Tomb of Genius*. Heinrich was perhaps displeased when the Philharmonic Society programmed Niels Gade's "Grand Symphony dedicated to Mendelssohn" the following season. Howard Shanet, ed., *Early Histories of the New York Philharmonic* (New York: Da Capo Press, 1979), 103.
52 "Musical" [undated clipping], Scrapbooks, 644.

9. "THAT MESMERIZING MENDELSSOHN TUNE": FROM TIN PAN ALLEY TO THE SILVER SCREEN

Anna Harwell Celenza

In celebration of Felix Mendelssohn's 200th birthday, R. Larry Todd published an article in 2009 titled "Mache mir ein wenig Lärm vor" ("Give me a little shout out") in the Berlin newspaper *Welt am Sonntag*. The central purpose of the article was to give an overview of Mendelssohn's "changeable and unpredictable" reception, at home and abroad, during his lifetime and after death. In this engaging narrative, Todd highlighted Mendelssohn's countless accomplishments. He reflected on the composer's colleagues, and his detractors, too. In one passage, Todd discussed Mendelssohn's reception in America. In 1845, after the premiere of Mendelssohn's first oratorio *Paulus*, "Ureli Corelli Hill, music director of the newly founded New York Philharmonic, invited the composer to America. Hill promised to assemble a huge 750-person orchestra and choir, which would perform the composer's works in a large music festival meant to rival those being organized in Germany and England." Tempting as Hill's offer must have seemed, Mendelssohn turned him down. As Todd explained, "He felt exhausted, and announced privately that traveling across the Atlantic was as impossible for him as going to the moon."[1]

Nonetheless, Mendelssohn eventually enjoyed a warm reception in America, if not in person while alive, then in spirit after death. As Todd briefly noted, "Mendelssohn's music was very popular in twentieth-century mass culture." In addition to "the ubiquitous 'Wedding March'" from *A Midsummer Night's Dream*, Mendelssohn's *Lied ohne Worte*, op. 62, no. 6 ("Spring Song") hit the top of the charts in 1910, after Irving Berlin interpolated it into "That Mesmerizing Mendelssohn Tune" (aka The Mendelssohn Rag), his first bestselling song.[2]

In the spirit of continuing the story where Todd left off, I dedicate this essay to an exploration of Felix Mendelssohn's "Spring Song" in early-twentieth-century American popular culture. As I quickly discovered upon embarking on this topic, Berlin's so-called "Mendelssohn Rag" was just the tip of the iceberg. From Tin Pan Alley and Vaudeville to Broadway and the Silver Screen, Mendelssohn's music mesmerized American listeners during the first three decades of the twentieth century. Like many an immigrant who arrived in New York City at the turn of the century, Mendelssohn's "Spring Song" assimilated into its new surroundings and quickly became a vital ingredient in the melting pot of American musical culture.

Before we do a deep dive into Berlin's take on Mendelssohn's tune, however, we should note that he was not the first American composer to reimagine "Spring Song." That honor appears to go to Egbert Van Alstyne (1878–1951), a Chicago native who toured the United States as a vaudeville musician before moving to New York in

1900 to work as a song plugger for Tin Pan Alley publishers. In 1901, Van Alstyne published "Darkies' Spring Song," an instrumental work conceived during his time as a vaudeville musician. Originally composed for dance orchestra, "Darkies' Spring Song" is a syncopated rag built on the lilting melody of Mendelssohn's original. The work proved so popular on the vaudeville circuit that Will Rossiter, a Chicago publisher specializing in popular music, had it arranged for piano by Lewis Reiterman.[3] "Darkies' Spring Song" contains no lyrics, but the title alone references a regretful tradition in American popular music—blackface minstrelsy. Minstrel songs were a staple in vaudeville acts. Beginning in the 1890s, a similar type of blackface song, set to ragtime rhythms, began to appear in Tin Pan Alley catalogues. Known by the offensive term "coon songs," these works were promoted as harmless novelty songs. We know better than to believe that. But as offensive as the blackface tradition appears to us now, it played an influential role in the development of American musical culture. And Mendelssohn's "Spring Song," like several other classical tunes that were parodied at the turn of the century, served as a popular sonic device in blackface vaudeville performances.[4] How this came about is an interesting topic that deserves a more in-depth discussion than I can offer here. But to make a long story short, white Tin Pan Alley composers originally parodied Mendelssohn's music—including his "Spring Song"—because Mendelssohn's music featured prominently in African American culture during the second half of the nineteenth century.

Studies concerning Mendelssohn's early reception in the United States have been largely informed by Joseph A. Mussulman's 1967 study "Mendelssohnism in America."[5] When Mussulman wrote his account of Mendelssohn's popularity in the United States, he focused on the reactions of white musicians and audiences. His primary sources were the reviews and biographical essays that appeared in white newspapers and magazines. There was no consideration of Mendelssohn reception in the African American press, which I have discovered was substantial. Indeed, one of the earliest references to Mendelssohn in the Black press dates from 1854, when Frederick Douglass included a brief article praising the composer in the August 4 issue of *Frederick Douglass' Paper*, a Rochester-based weekly centered on antislavery efforts and other social reform causes. "Few men so distinguished have been so simple, so cordial, so considerate," notes the author. "No portrait extant does him justice," nor can capture "the many characteristics and humors of the poet; his earnest seriousness—his childlike truthfulness—his clear, cultivated intellect—his impulsive vivacity.[...]" Mendelssohn is praised for his pure spirit. "In him, there was no settled sentiment, no affected heartiness." Mendelssohn is described as "no sayer of deep things, no searcher for witty ones." Instead, he is portrayed as a man "of pure, sincere intelligence—bright, eager and happy, even when most imaginative."[6] Douglass's inclusion of Mendelssohn as a figure of social reform was in response to the antisemitic assessments of the composer that had been flowing from the pen of Richard Wagner and his acolytes across the Atlantic. In fact, other contributors to *Frederick Douglass' Paper* discussed the rise of anti-Semitism in Europe in tandem with the racial prejudice African Americans were experiencing in the United States.[7]

Douglass's interest in Mendelssohn was not uncommon. A perusal of African American newspapers in the 1880s and 90s reveals dozens of references to Black Mendelssohn societies, choral groups, and schools of music across the country. Equally prominent are notices of performances of the composer's music, in particular his "Spring Song," which had become a staple in concerts of classical music by Black performers.[8] Mendelssohn and his music served as symbols of social uplift and respectability in African American communities during the late nineteenth century. And it was the popularity of Mendelssohn's music among Black audiences that made it the perfect fodder for blackface songs written to ridicule African Americans in the decade that followed. This was the backdrop to "That Mesmerizing Mendelssohn Tune" published by Irving Berlin in 1909, the centennial of Mendelssohn's birth.

Interest in Mendelssohn's music increased among the public in 1909, and this was reflected in discussions in the national press about the Mendelssohn centennial. For example, music critic Henry T. Fick noted in *The Nation* the positive effects of the anniversary year: "The universal interest in the Mendelssohn centenary indicates that the public is eager to return to the land where flows the milk and honey of melody."[9] And in *Putnam's Magazine*, Daniel Gregory Mason predicted that interest in Mendelssohn's music would "surely be rehabilitated, provided the sensationalism, subjectivity and enthusiasm for realistic suggestion [...] cease to crowd out our natural love for what is objective in conception, restrained in expression and elegant in style."[10] Unfortunately for Mason, "sensationalism" *did* "crowd out" the more serious attempts to honor Mendelssohn's music in 1909. A prime example involved Gertrude Hoffman, a statuesque dancer who garnered national acclaim by performing in "the briefest feminine costume on record since the fig leaf became passé."[11] Hoffman spent most of the 1908/1909 vaudeville season touring the country in a musical revue called *The Mimic World*, in which she performed her two most famous dances, "A Vision of Salome" to music by Richard Strauss, and "Mendelssohn's Spring Song," which she danced barefoot in a sheer Grecian toga.[12] Hoffman's interpretations of the classical repertoire "made her name ring from coast to coast."[13] And when *The Mimic World* returned to New York in July 1909 for a series of performances at the Paradise Roof Garden (on the northwest corner of Seventh Avenue and 42nd Street), the antivice activist Anthony Comstock was ready. Comstock and his evangelical followers filed a formal complaint with the police about Hoffman's risqué performances, and on 23 July she was arrested for public indecency. But her banishment didn't last long; she was released from jail the following day when a judge dismissed the charges. Hoffman's arrest made the front page of the *New York Times*,[14] and for the next three months, *The Mimic World* enjoyed sold out performances, proving the adage that there is no such thing as bad publicity.

Berlin no doubt took notice of the attention Hoffman's dance brought to Strauss's *Salome* and Mendelssohn's "Spring Song." Both tunes had become titillating topics, and Berlin decided to strike while the iron was hot. "That Mesmerizing Mendelssohn Tune" was published on 22 December 1909, and according to the earliest advertisements, the sheet music went on sale nationwide on 5 February 1910 for

15 cents a copy.¹⁵ "That Mesmerizing Mendelssohn Tune" was composed for the vaudeville stage, and like "Darkies' Spring Song" it was meant to evoke America's minstrel heritage. As Jeffrey Magee has noted, the song "features the dropped 'g' diction and other language (like 'gwine') common to black-dialect song."¹⁶ This is clearly displayed in the song's opening lines:

> Honey, listen to that dreamy tune they're playin',
> Won't you tell me how on earth you keep from swayin'?
> Umm! Umm! Oh, that Mendelssohn Spring Song tune,
> If you ever loved me show me now or never.
> Lord, I wish they'd play that music on forever.
> Umm! Umm! Oh, that Mendelssohn tune.

The earliest recordings of "That Mesmerizing Mendelssohn Tune" accentuate the song's minstrel characteristics. On 12 February 1910, the noted blackface performers Arthur Collins and Byron Harlan recorded the tune for Victor Records.¹⁷ Their performance accentuates the Black dialect of the original lyrics and interpolates a short dialogue that highlights even further the negative stereotypes associated with minstrelsy.

> — Mmm, Mmm, Sam, I certainly am inspired ovah dat meddlesome music.
> — What kinda music you say?
> — Meddlesome.
> — No, not "meddlesome."
> — Well, den, what is it?
> — Why, Men-dels-sohn.
> — What did I say?
> — Why, you said "med-dle-some".
> — Did I say dat? Why, how phantasmagorious!¹⁸

Al Jolson also recorded "That Mesmerizing Mendelssohn Tune" in 1910, but no known copies of the recording still exist.¹⁹ The most important performer of "That Mesmerizing Mendelssohn Tune," however, was the woman who premiered it on Broadway—a popular vaudeville singer named Grace Tyson, who also appears to have served as the model for the sheet music's cover illustration (see Figure 1).

The original sheet music shows the image of a young white woman, with enormous eyes and clasped hands, looking dramatically towards the heavens as she stands in a field of spring flowers. This illustration has perplexed contemporary scholars, who have noted that the image of a white women on the cover conflicts with the Black dialect used in the lyrics.²⁰ But to contemporary audiences, the mix of image and dialect would have served as a clear reference to Grace Tyson, whose performances were regularly described as being "full of ginger, rag-time music and fun."²¹ As a review in the *Kalamazoo Gazette*, her hometown paper, noted as early as 1900, "Miss Tyson was most pleasing in her coon songs and the cakewalk."²² Indeed, one of her most popular routines involved her appearing on stage as a "comely soubrette", and then transforming into a "coon shouter" by contorting her face, movements, and singing style. Tyson's great "talent" was her ability to evoke Black caricatures without the use of blackface makeup. As a journalist for the *The Evening World's Home Magazine* noted: "She has the faculty of contorting her countenance so as to be unrecognizable even to her own mother, but, unlike many of the grimacers, she does not sacrifice her daintiness."[23] Like the woman on the cover of "That Mesmerizing Mendelssohn Tune," Tyson had large, bulging eyes, which she used to great effect in her performances of "coon songs." Her eyes were so important to her, that she took out an insurance policy on them for $15,000.[24] Tyson's eyes also earned her a coveted role in the cast of *The Mimic World*, which is where Berlin probably first saw her perform. While Gertrude Hoffman danced barefoot to Mendelssohn's "Spring Song," Tyson performed a comedy number called "Eyes, Eyes, Eyes."

It was likely that performance that led to Tyson being cast in the *Ziegfeld Follies* of 1910. The show ran for eighty-eight performances in New York, from 20 June through 3 September 1910. Tyson appeared in a comedy skit called "In the Music Publisher's Office," which included her distinctive rendition of "That Mesmerizing Mendelssohn Tune." The performance "won frequent encores" from audiences and "helped elevate Tyson's status...to that of a true star."[25]

The popularity of "That Mesmerizing Mendelssohn Tune" was not limited to white audiences. In 1910, the song was also added to the programs of Black vaudeville shows. As the African American newspaper *The Freeman* noted on 25 June, "Maud Campbell, 'The baby doll,' has set Mobile [Alabama] wild with 'That Mesmerizing Mendelssohn Tune.'"[26] And in December, the *Washington Bee* reported that the "Down in Dixie Minstrels" entertained listeners at the Howard Theatre with their own rendition of the "Mendelssohn Rag."[27] The popularity of the song continued for several years. In 1910, Berlin wrote a duet called "Spring Song Melody" for the well-known songwriters Ernest R. Ball (1878–1927) and Gus Edwards (1879–1945). The song was never published, but it was performed on various occasions, at least once at a Friars Club dinner. The song describes the abuse of Mendelssohn's "Spring Song" by Tin Pan Alley composers. According to the chorus:

> Poor old "Spring Song" melody,
> Everyone has stolen thee.
> Everyone who writes a song
> Puts you where you don't belong.
> You've been in almost every key,
> Poor old "Spring Song" melody,
> Every song you seem to be.
> Seems to me that everyone
> Picks on poor old Mendelssohn
> And his poor old "Spring Song" melody.[28]

In one version of this song, as Ball sings each line of the chorus, Edwards responds with a line from a song that lifted the melody from Mendelssohn's "Spring Song." These include Berlin's own "That Mesmerizing Mendelssohn Tune," "I Wish I Had

My Old Girl Back Again" (by Paul Wallace and Ballard McDonald),[29] "Ev'ry Little Movement" (by Karl Hoschna and Otto Harbach),[30] "The Arab's Dream" (by Edwin F. Kendall and Joseph Snyder),[31] and "I Wish I Had A Girl" (by Grace Le Boy and Gus Kahn).[32] Most of these songs quickly faded from view, but in April 1912, "That Mesmerizing Mendelssohn Tune" was still entertaining passengers on board the Titanic before it struck an iceberg and sank in the Atlantic.[33]

Berlin attributed the success of the song, and many others he composed, to what he called his "9 Rules for writing a popular song."

First — The melody must musically be within the range of the *average voice* of the average public singer.[...]
Second — The title, which must be simple and easily remembered, must be "*planted*" effectively in the song. It must be emphasized, accented again and again, throughout verses and chorus.[...]
Third — A popular song should be *sexless*, that is, the ideas and the wording must be of a kind that can be logically voiced by either a male or a female singer. Strive for the happy medium in thought and words so that both sexes will want to buy and sing it.
Fourth — The song should contain *heart interest*, even if it is a comic song. [...]
Fifth — The song must be *original* in idea, words, and music. Success is not achieved, as so many songwriters mistakenly believe, by trying to imitate the general idea of the great song hit of the moment.
Sixth — Your lyric must have to do with ideas, emotions, or objects known to everyone. Stick to nature—not nature in a visionary, abstract way but nature as demonstrated in homely, concrete, everyday manifestations.
Seventh — The lyric must be euphonious—written in easily singable words and phrases in which there are many open vowels.
Eighth — Your song must be perfectly *simple*.[...]
Ninth — The song writer must look upon his work as a *business*.[34]

When asked why he chose Mendelssohn's music as the model for his first big hit, Berlin responded: "I had always loved Mendelssohn and his 'Spring Song,' and simply wanted to work it into a rag tune."[35] The success of "That Mesmerizing Mendelssohn Tune" led to additional "Mendelssohn" songs penned by Berlin. For example, in September 1910 he incorporated the characteristic half-tone steps from Mendelssohn's "Spring Song" into his own "Stop! Stop! Stop! (Come Over and Love Me Some More)." The lyrics of this tune weren't written in Black dialect. Instead, they reference the amorous effect that Mendelssohn's mesmerizing tune can have on white listeners. This same effect is witnessed in another Berlin song from 1910—"Herman, Let's Dance That Beautiful Waltz." In verse two, "Miss Lena Kraussmeyer, with hair red as fire," references the aphrodisiacal power "That Mesmerizing Mendelssohn Tune" can have on a woman, no matter her race:

> I heard that a coon who heard Mendelssohn's tune,
> Kissed the first man she saw, if it's true;
> That very same feeling I feel on me stealing
> And Herman I'm looking at you.[36]

A decade later, Berlin distanced Mendelssohn's "Spring Song" even further from Black references. This time, he added the tune to a production number for the *Ziegfeld Follies* of 1919. The act was built around a series of famous melodies from classical music, each representing a verse in his newly composed song, "A Pretty Girl is like a Melody." Berlin described how the act came together:

> There were five of these melodies, each representing a girl. I wrote a special lyric for each classic so [John] Steel [a classically trained tenor] could sing it. I then found it necessary to have some kind of springboard for these old classics. The result was "A Pretty Girl is Like a Melody." It is interesting to note that the last thing I thought of was this song. In other words, I had no idea it would be anything more than a "special material" song.[37]

Decades later, a Ziegfeld dancer named Doris Eaton who had performed in the show published her recollection of the scene.

> The curtain parted on an empty, dark stage. As the music started, the spotlight picked up John Steel walking slowly to center stage from the backdrop. John had a beautiful, clear tenor voice, and he sang the verse and chorus of the Berlin song. Then as each girl appeared—one at a time—the music switched to refrains of well-known classical compositions, such as Mendelssohn's "Song of Spring" and Offenbach's "Barcarolle." With each "haunting refrain," the spotlight picked up a showgirl, dressed to match the mood of the music. She walked toward John, flirted a bit, and continued past him, fading into the darkness of the stage, while he sang the humorous lyrics of love found and love lost to one of those classic melodies. After all five girls had appeared, John sang "A Pretty Girl is Like a Melody," as the five beauties surrounded him.[...][38]

When "A Pretty Girl is Like a Melody" was published in 1919, only the first two verses and chorus were included in the sheet music. For many years, it was believed that the lyrics to "Spring Song" and the other classical melodies in this production number had been permanently lost. But thanks to the diligent archival work of Jeffrey Magee, the original lyrics were recently recovered, enabling us to get a full sense of how Mendelssohn's "Spring Song" was transformed, once again, in the hands of Irving Berlin. For audiences attending the *Ziegfeld Follies* in 1919, Mendelssohn's melody served as a humorous expression of the unrequited love experienced by a theatrical tenor. The lyrics below were sung to the opening melody of Mendelssohn's "Spring Song."

> Once, I met a girlie at the close of spring;
> I began to woo her, and she answered "yes" that summer;

> But, when I went off to buy the wedding ring, She
> left me flat and ran off with the drummer.[39]

Although Berlin milked Mendelssohn's "Spring Song" for all it was worth in the decade after 1910, he still wasn't finished with the tune. In 1924, he composed a song called "Tell Her in the Springtime" (1924), which referenced Mendelssohn's "Spring Song" a final time, on this occasion as a reflection of young love.

> Tell her in the springtime,
> In May or June;
> Tell her in the springtime,
> The best time to spoon,
> When ev'rything begins blossoming,
> You'll hear Mendelssohn's "Spring Song" tune.
> When the moon is shining,
> You speak of her charms;
> Then is when she's pining
> To rest in your arms.
> Don't worry so—
> She won't answer no,
> If you play Romeo in the spring.[40]

In this final example of Berlin's use of Mendelssohn's "Spring Song," all references to minstrelsy, ragtime, and comedy are gone. Instead, we hear a love ballad fit for a Victorian parlor. Berlin wrote this song for his *Music Box Revue of 1924*, which opened on 1 December and ran for 184 performances.[41] Like many tunes performed in Broadway revues, "Tell Her in the Springtime" contained a musical interlude that featured a short dance routine. In this case, an orchestral arrangement of Mendelssohn's "Spring Song" served as the backdrop for a solo by Ula Sharon (1905–1993), a classically trained dancer who later founded the Kansas City Dance Theatre.[42]

Berlin's treatment of Mendelssohn's "Spring Song" in the *Music Box Revue* restored the tune to its original highbrow "classical" realm in 1924. This year also witnessed the premiere of George Gershwin's *Rhapsody in Blue*, a work commissioned by Paul Whiteman for his Experiment in Modern Music concert on February 12—Lincoln's birthday. The concert date was no coincidence. Gershwin's composition was promoted as "the Emancipation Proclamation of jazz."[43] As a lighthearted response to *Rhapsody in Blue*, Duke Ellington composed a work for piano titled *Rhapsody Jr.* that liberated classical music—namely Mendelssohn's "Spring Song"—from the concert hall.[44] This early work, with its ninth and augmented chords, whole-tone melodies, and parallel triads, was the first of Ellington's many experiments with music from the classical realm.[45]

Before concluding this essay, I will turn briefly to the use of Mendelssohn's "Spring Song" in film. In 1910, Carl Laemmle, who later founded Universal Studios, produced a short film titled "Mendelssohn's Spring Song." Featuring Charles Arling as Felix Mendelssohn, the film offered a fictional account of the composition's origin.

"That Mesmerizing Mendelssohn Tune"

The film opens in early spring with Mendelssohn setting off on a stroll in the Austrian Tyrol. As he makes his way through the scenic countryside, he encounters an array of characters who inspire various strains of his famous "Spring Song." A hunter blowing his horn furnishes the opening notes. A mother comforting her crying child inspires the second strain. Next, he encounters some sleepy laborers followed by a group of peasant girls singing in a cabbage patch. When one of the peasant girls gets into a quarrel with an older woman, Mendelssohn humorously prolongs the dispute to his own benefit. The final lines of music come to him when he encounters a pair of lovers making music. The man plays a violin while the young woman sings. Taking the violin from the man, Mendelssohn continues his walk, playing music as he goes. Eventually he arrives at a beer garden, where he completes the piece surrounded by the many followers he has picked up along the way.[46]

Laemmle's film was screened in vaudeville theaters the same year Berlin's "That Mesmerizing Mendelssohn Tune" hit the top of the charts. Although the film makes no references to minstrelsy, its comedic effects were praised in the press. For example, A reviewer for *The Moving Picture World* described the characters who inspire Mendelssohn as "quite commonplace" and "more humorous than they would be otherwise." In addition to the music, which would have been performed live by a keyboard player or small chamber orchestra, the reviewer noted that "the variety of facial expression[s] is remarkable."[47]

When I began my research for this essay, I assumed that Mendelssohn's "Spring Song" would appear often in the cue sheets of photoplay music that began to be distributed with silent films around 1910. But after reviewing the collections of several companies (e.g. Sam Fox Music, Academic Music, Cameo Thematic Music Co., and Erno Rapée's *Motion Picture Moods*), I realized that although Mendelssohn's music appeared often on photoplay cue sheets, the tunes most often parodied in Tin Pan Alley songs—"Spring Song" and the "Wedding March" from *A Midsummer Night's Dream*—were rarely included in silent film music collections. Instead, the most popular Mendelssohn excerpts performed with silent films came from *Ruy Blas, Fingal's Cave, Athalia, The First Walpurgis Night*, The Overture to *A Midsummer Night's Dream*, and "Rondo Capriccio."

Finally, I would be remiss if I did not mention Cyrus "Cy" Young's animated short film "Mendelssohn's Spring Song," which appeared in 1931.[48] Young created the film while studying at the Art Students League in New York, and his seven-minute masterpiece features an odd array of colorful cartoon creatures who frolic and play to the rhythm of Mendelssohn's music. When Walt Disney saw the cartoon, he was so impressed by its quality and innovation that he eventually hired Young to lead Disney's department of special effects animation. In the years that followed, Young's "Spring Song" served as a model for Disney's *Silly Symphonies* series, and it set the bar for future feature-length animated music films like *Fantasia*.

So, let's follow Todd's advice from 2009 and give Mendelssohn a little shout out for his mesmerizing tune. From Tin Pan Alley and Vaudeville to Broadway and the Silver Screen, his "Spring Song" added flavor, both bitter and sweet, to the melting pot of American musical culture.

Figure 1, Cover of Sheet Music for "That Mesmerizing Mendelssohn Tune" by Irving Berlin (New York: Ted Snyder, 1909). The Lester S. Levy Sheet Music Collection, Johns Hopkins Sheridan Libraries & University Museums.

"That Mesmerizing Mendelssohn Tune"

1. R. Larry Todd, "Mache mir ein wenig Lärm vor," *Welt am Sonntag* (1 February 2009). An acquaintance of Mendelssohn's noted that he declined the invitation to America in 1845, see Bayard Taylor, *Views A-Foot; or, Europe Seen with Knapsack and Staff* (New York: George P. Putnam & Co, 1855), 168–71.
2. Irving Berlin, "That Mesmerizing Mendelssohn Tune," (a "Mendelssohn Rag") was published by the Ted Snyder Co. on 22 December 1909. Todd notes that this may have been in honor of the Mendelssohn centennial.
3. Egbert Van Alstyne, "Darkies' Spring Song," (Chicago: Will Rossiter, 1901). A PDF of the complete work is accessible through the website of the University of Wisconsin-Madison's Library https://search.library.wisc.edu/digital/A3BAVCK3ZPWDI38B
4. According to Doron K. Antrim, "The Top Ten Tunes of the Last Fifty Years: A Thumb Nail History of Popular American Music," *Metronome* 50/1 (January 1934): 31, "In 1909 Berlin began tampering with that tantalizing tempo [found in ragtime] in That Mesmerizing Mendelssohn Tune, giving one of the first performances in jazzing the classics."
5. Joseph A. Mussulman, "Mendelssohnism in America," *The Musical Quarterly* 53/3 (July 1967): 335–346.
6. "Mendelssohn," *Frederick Douglass' Paper* (4 August 1854): 1.
7. For example, see "Communications. Heads of the Colored People. No. 4. The Sexton," *Frederick Douglass' Paper* (16 July 1852); "Letter from William G. Allen, *Frederick Douglass' Paper* (30 July 1852).
8. A simple search of the term "Mendelssohn" in the databases *African American Newspapers: The Nineteenth Century* and *African American Newspapers: 1827-1998* identifies over 100 nineteenth-century reviews and articles referencing Mendelssohn and his music.
9. Henry T. Finck, "Mendelssohn and Strauss," *Nation* 88 (4 February 1909): 129–33.
10. Daniel Gregory Mason, "Two Musical Centenaries: Mendelssohn and Chopin in 1909," *Putnam's Magazine* V (1909): 656.
11. David S. Shields, "Gertrude Hoffman," an entry in the on-line exhibition *Broadway Photographs* https://broadway.library.sc.edu/content/gertrude-hoffman.html
12. For an excellent biography of Hoffman see Sunny Stalter-Pace, *Imitation Artist: Gertrude Hoffmann's Life in Vaudeville and Dance* (Northwestern University Press, 2020). Hoffman was not the first to dance to Mendelssohn's "Spring Song." Loie Fuller, Isadora Duncan, Maud Allan, and Ruth St. Denis also performed to the piece between 1900 and 1910.
13. "Amusements," *The Purdue Exponent*, XX/148 (17 March 1909): 3. Larry Hamberlin, *Tin Pan Opera: Operatic Novelty Songs in the Ragtime Era* (Oxford: Oxford University Press, 2011), 130, 276, explains, Hoffman's performances to these two pieces were combined in "Salome," a song in Black dialect that quotes Mendelssohn's "Spring Song" in the chorus. "Salome was composed by British songwriters Orlando Powell and John P. Harrington and published in 1909 by Remick in New York.
14. "Arrest Gertrude Hoffman," *New York Times* (24 July 1909): 1.
15. Advertisement for "That Mesmerizing Mendelssohn Tune" in *The Evening Star* (Washington, DC) (4 February 1910): 8.
16. Jeffrey Magee, *Irving Berlin's American Musical Theater* (Oxford: Oxford University Press, 2012), 26.
17. *Discography of American Historical Recordings*, s.v. "Victor matrix B-8625. That mesmerizing Mendelssohn tune / Collins and Harlan," accessed 15 March 2023. https://adp.library.ucsb.edu/index.php/matrix/detail/200008714/B-8625-That_mesmerizing_Mendelssohn_tune.
18. *Discography of American Historical Recordings*, s.v. "Victor matrix B-8625. That mesmerizing Mendelssohn tune / Collins and Harlan," accessed 15 March 2023. https://adp.library.ucsb.edu/index.php/matrix/detail/200008714/B-8625-That_mesmerizing_Mendelssohn_tune.
19. "Lost Recording List" compiled by the Library of Congress https://www.loc.gov/programs/national-recording-preservation-board/about-this-program/donations/lost-recording-list/, accessed 1 March 2024.

20 See for example the Blog post by Lodewijk Muns, "That Mesmerizing Mendelssohn Tune," dated 17 January 2021. https://lodewijkmuns.nl/2021/01/17/mendelssohn-tune/
21 *The Kalamazoo Gazette* (10 February 1900). Cited from the Kalamazoo Public Library's on-line exhibition "Grace Tyson (1881-1942): Actress, Comedian, Vaudeville Star" https://www.kpl.gov/local-history/kalamazoo-history/women/tyson-grace-2/, accessed 1 March 2024.
22 Ibid.
23 *The Evening World's Home Magazine* (25 June 1903). Cited from the Kalamazoo Public Library's on-line exhibition "Grace Tyson (1881-1942): Actress, Comedian, Vaudeville Star" https://www.kpl.gov/local-history/kalamazoo-history/women/tyson-grace-2/, accessed 1 March 2024.
24 David Soren, "Arthur McWatters and Grace Tyson: Singing Vaudeville Comedians," University of Arizona Library, American Vaudeville Museum https://vaudeville.sites.arizona.edu/2023/03/28/arthur-mcwatters-and-grace-tyson-singing-vaudeville-comedians-by-david-soren/, accessed 1 March 2024.
25 "Grace Tyson (1881–1942): Actress, Comedian, Vaudeville Star" https://www.kpl.gov/local-history/kalamazoo-history/women/tyson-grace-2/, accessed 1 March 2024.
26 "Lagman's Theater, Mobile Ala.," *The Freeman* (Indianapolis, IN) (June 25, 1910): 6.
27 "The Week in Society," *Washington Bee* (December 31, 1910): 5.
28 Robert Kimball and Linda Emmet, eds., *The Complete Lyrics of Irving Berlin* (New York: Knopf, 2001), 14.
29 Published by Jos. W. Stern in 1909.
30 Published in 1910 by M. Witmark & Sons.
31 Published in 1910 by Seminary Music Co.
32 Published in 1907 by Thompson Music Co.
33 Ronny S. Schiff, ed., *Mel Bay presents the Titanic songbook: music as heard on the fateful voyage--April 1912: a collection by Ian Whitcomb* (Pacific, MO: Mel Bay Publications, 1997).
34 Frank Ward O'Malley, "Irving Berlin Gives Nine Rules for Writing Popular Songs," *American Magazine* 90 (October 1920): 242.
35 Cited from Michael Freedland, *Irving Berlin* (New York: Stein and Day, 1974), 30; Philip Furia, *Irving Berlin: A Life in Song* (New York: Schirmer Books, 1998), 36.
36 Irving Berlin, "Stop! Stop! Stop! (Come Over and Love Me Some More)" (New York: Ted Snyder Co., 1910).
37 Cited from Magee, *Irving Berlin's American Musical Theater*, 85.
38 Ibid., 85–86.
39 Ibid., 93.
40 Robert Kimball and Linda Emmet, eds., *The Complete Lyrics of Irving Berlin*, 211.
41 Ibid.
42 The Ula Sharon Robinson Bergfeldt papers are housed in the State Historical Society of Missouri. https://collections.shsmo.org/manuscripts/kansas-city/k1223
43 Maurice Peress, *Dvořák to Duke Ellington: A Conductor Rediscovers America's Music and Its African-American Roots* (Oxford: Oxford University Press, 2004), 84.
44 Mark Tucker, *Ellington: The Early Years* (Champagne-Urbana, IL: University of Illinois Press, 1991), 199.
45 Other notable examples include his *Symphony in Black* (1935), *Black, Brown, and Beige* (1943), *The Peer Gynt Suite* and *Nutcracker Suite* (both 1960).
46 "Mendelssohn's Spring Song" was released on 27 October 1910 by the Independent Moving Pictures Co. of America. The film was produced and directed by Carl Laemmle, who would go on to found Universal films two years later. The film's synopsis is supplied by the International Movie Database (IMDb). https://www.imdb.com/title/tt0449315/?ref_=ttpl_ov, accessed 1 March 2024.
47 *The Moving Picture World* (12 November 1910).
48 Cy Young "Mendelssohn's Spring Song – A Jingles Cartoon," Fairmount Pictures, 1931. A restored version of the film is available on YouTube https://www.youtube.com/watch?v=tuslNKB4Ixg, accessed 1 March 2024.

III. FANNY MENDELSSOHN HENSEL

10. CHORALE TRANSFORMATION AND TRIUMPH IN FELIX MENDELSSOHN'S *SINFONIA VI* AND FANNY HENSEL'S *DAS JAHR*[1]

CLAIRE FONTIJN

The music of the Bach family played an integral role in the development of composers Felix Mendelssohn (1809–47) and Fanny Mendelssohn Hensel (1805–47). Their father Abraham Mendelssohn (1776–1836) collected works by Johann Sebastian Bach (1685–1750) but, more importantly, the siblings inherited their artistic proclivities from their mother Lea Salomon Mendelssohn (1777–1842), their maternal grandmother Bella Itzig Salomon (1749–1824), and their three great-aunts: Fanny Itzig von Arnstein (1758–1818), Cäcilie Itzig von Eskeles (1760–1836), and keyboardist Sara Itzig Levy (1761–1854). Levy in particular helped to further the careers in Berlin of Bach sons Wilhelm Friedemann (1710–84), Carl Philipp Emanuel (1714–88), and Johann Christoph Friedrich (1732–95) through subscribing to their publications, and collecting and performing their music.[2] Levy thrived in the late-eighteenth-century tolerant climate for the Jewish population of Berlin, a climate partially influenced by Moses Mendelssohn (1729–86), the Enlightenment thinker and paternal grandfather of Mendelssohn and Hensel.[3] Policies instituted by the Prussian kings Frederick II (1712–86) and Frederick William III (1770–1840) led to the Edict of Emancipation for the Jews in 1812.[4] As promising a development as this might have seemed, the Edict held within it the expectation that Jewish families would convert to Christianity. In order to create a safe environment with optimal access to education, Abraham and Lea had their four children baptized and converted to Protestantism on March 21, 1816.[5]

As children, Mendelssohn and Hensel enjoyed a comparable education and established a means of communication through music and correspondence that would endure throughout their short lifetimes; such intellectual games continued into adulthood and resulted in their many compositions employing a new genre: *Lieder ohne Worte* or *Lieder für das Pianoforte*.[6] The musical allusions that they used in their pieces, both explicit and cryptic, testify to an extraordinary fabric of associations. Christopher A. Reynolds noted that, in their correspondence, "Fanny Mendelssohn writes Felix that she has cited one of his works in one of hers."[7] In the third movement of her piano trio, "Lied," Hensel quoted the melody from Obadiah's air at the outset of *Elijah*. This explicit citation is easily discernable and provides one example of what Reynolds denoted. However, in her *Lieder für das Pianoforte*, Opus 8, no. 3, titled "Lied (Lenau)," Hensel implies a reference to a poem by Nikolaus Lenau, but this reference remains cryptic since the poem has not yet been identified.[8]

To both composers, chorales represented a body of allusions full of religious and spiritual meaning. By espousing the music of Johann Sebastian Bach, Mendelssohn and Hensel acknowledged their family's role in the stewardship of the repertory and deepened their connections to German culture via a Lutheran present. They were bolstered by the musical and religious foundations—as Jews converted to Protestantism—that they had inherited, respectively, from the Bachs and their own family. Both composers exploited the chorale as fertile material for composition, a staple of their musical instruction from Carl Friedrich Zelter (1758–1832). Among the voluminous exchange of letters between Hensel and Mendelssohn, she wrote on his 27th birthday (February 3, 1836) of a chorale from the first movement of Cantata BWV 139:

> Dear Felix…Do you know a Cantata by Bach in E major that [Franz] Hauser has: *Wohl dem, der sich auf seinen Gott recht kindlich verlassen*? It is the old chorale of the blind hurdy-gurdy man on the new Promenade. In case you don't know it, I'll have the first chorus copied out and sent as a belated birthday present. I find it absolutely beautiful; it is so much a reflection of the [quietude] one experiences here.[9]

This is just one example of many in which Mendelssohn and Hensel wax poetic about Johann Sebastian Bach's music, which they were in a continual process of discovering. In the two examples selected for examination in this study, both composers—Mendelssohn early in his career, Hensel later in hers—employed the chorale in novel ways.

Mendelssohn adapted a chorale tune in one of his childhood compositions for string symphony from the 1821–22 period: *Sinfonia VI*. Hensel incorporated three chorale tunes into the movements of *Das Jahr*, the piano cycle that she gave as a Christmas present in 1841 to her husband, Prussian court painter and poet Wilhelm Hensel.[10] Because they have not received much scholarly attention until relatively recently it is noteworthy that both *Sinfonia VI* and *Das Jahr* remained unpublished during the lifetimes of both composers.[11] Mendelssohn's adaptation of the chorale tune "Befiehl du deine Wege" provides a backdrop against which to consider the chorales found in Hensel's piano cycle, which were intended to underscore the highpoints of the liturgical year—Christmas ("December") and Easter ("March")—as well as the New Year ("Postlude").[12]

On which sources did Mendelssohn and Hensel rely for the transmission of the chorale tunes that they used in these compositions? Given their residence in Berlin and their family's close acquaintance with the circle of Carl Philipp Emanuel Bach, it seems likely that they knew his collection of Johann Sebastian Bach's chorales for keyboard.[13] Mendelssohn provided a clue to one source when he wrote "aus Fischers Choralbuch" as a subtitle to his chorale variations on "Wie gross ist des Allmächt'gen Güte," which, like *Sinfonia VI*, was composed when he was an adolescent.[14] The composer wrote an acronym into his score, asking for divine assistance: "L.e.g.G." ("Laß es gelingen, Gott"), recalling Johann Sebastian Bach's "S.D.G." ("Soli Deo Gloria").

AN ALLUSION TO ONE OF J.S. BACH'S FAVORITE CHORALE TUNES IN MENDELSSOHN'S *SINFONIA VI*

In the second of the three movements of *Sinfonia VI* for string symphony, the Menuetto–Trio I–Trio II complex, Mendelssohn alluded in Trio II to a chorale tune based on a secular melody originally devised by Hans Leo Hassler and published in his 1601 *Lustgarten*.[15] This melody is known by a number of textual incipits including, among others, "Befiehl du deine Wege," "O Haupt voll Blut und Wunden," and "Herzlich tut mir verlangen." Ex. 1 shows the two opening phrases of the chorale "Befiehl du deine Wege," in a four-part setting—BWV 270 as transmitted in the book of J.S. Bach chorales for organ collected by C.P.E. Bach[16]—that is based on the sixth and final movement of Cantata BWV 161, "Komm, du süße Todesstunde."

Example 1, J.S. Bach, Chorale "Befiehl du deine Wege" (BWV 270), mm. 1–4

The melody is found throughout the *St. Matthew Passion*, fitting a variety of texts—including "Befiehl du deine Wege" and "O Haupt voll Blut und Wunden."[17]

In Mendelssohn's reference to his own cantata *O Haupt voll Blut und Wunden*, composed some ten years after writing *Sinfonia VI*, he revealed that it was the modally ambiguous aspect of the generative chorale tune that fascinated him: "I am very happy with this piece—no one will be able to discern whether it will be in C minor or E-flat [major]."[18] By all appearances, he had already enjoyed a similar pleasure in the possibilities for tonal ambiguity when adapting the chorale tune in *Sinfonia VI*, composed when was about 12. As Wulf Konold has noted, Mendelssohn regularly took unusual harmonic turns in the Menuetto-Trio I-Trio II complex.[19] The illustration presented below shows a page from the composing score, which contains important information about the genesis of Trio II.[20]

At the end of the first system and start of the second, the first violins seem set to play the "Befiehl du deine Wege" tune, but it comes minus its *e-flat¹*, which would otherwise have sounded as the last note in the first violins on the first system. Following the first phrase of the truncated "Befiehl du deine Wege," four intercalated measures of a fragment of the music from the Menuetto appear in the second system. For the re-entry of the first phrase of the chorale, now in a homophonic chordal texture, the composer originally wished to have a *fortissimo* dynamic, but later crossed out the second letter *f* to yield a *forte* in all four parts. Moreover, accents appear over the notes

Figure 1, Mendelssohn Bartholdy, Sinfonia VI, Trio II, Autograph. *D-B, Mus. Ms. autogr. F. Mendelssohn Bartholdy 3*, page 188

of the first violins and below the notes of the cellos and basses. It is as if Mendelssohn temporarily forgot his new version of the tune, for he later cancelled the harmonized $e\text{-}flat^1$ in all four parts with an "X." The third system presents the second phrase of the chorale tune (corresponding to Ex. 1, mm. 3–4). Instead of the descent found in the Bach chorale, Mendelssohn made the phrase ascend to move up to a B-flat-major cadence. It is only here on the third system that he marks *fortissimo*. This astonishing effect shifts the tune up one octave and inverts its original direction. Hereby he transformed the chorale tune in a playful way, joyfully bursting its boundaries. Mendelssohn's new twist of the second phrase turns it into a moment of triumph moving a^2-b-$flat^2$-c^3-d^3 in the first violins as they move up toward the cadence, instead of down via a minor-third progression. Trio II builds to a climax as the first violins ring out at top volume d^3, the major third of B-flat, the Menuetto's home key. Indeed, one might speculate that the composer recalled his fun at having taken this "wrong turn" as a boy, when later he would write to his sister Rebecka about the ambiguity of the key of the chorale found in his cantata O Haupt voll Blut und Wunden.

R. Larry Todd has interpreted such moments in the music of Mendelssohn as instances of "sacred music, real and imaginary," and this concept helps to understand what the composer may have intended here.[21] With the insertion of a phrase that seems to allude to sacred chorales in an otherwise secular piece, Mendelssohn complicated our understanding of the symphony and its status as non-referential, or absolute, music. His adaptation of the chorale tune corresponds to the period when his parents were preparing for their conversion, joining their children whom they had had baptized earlier.[22] Is it be possible that, with the new guise of the chorale melody, Mendelssohn Bartholdy was in some way referring to their conversion?[23] Or might he have done this to amuse his sisters and his teacher Zelter? The chorale tune's associations with the *St. Matthew Passion* are noteworthy, given that his grandmother Bella Salomon would soon give him the score of the work, which he had long awaited from Zelter.[24] Both Mendelssohn and Hensel were familiar with the *St. Matthew Passion*, having joined the Berlin Singakademie in 1820, when Zelter held rehearsals of portions of the work.[25]

Mendelssohn's ingenious play with the multivalent chorale tune sometimes named "Befiehl du deine Wege" also suggests his awareness of the clever acrostic of vertically-positioned words (in boldface below) found at the beginning of each of the 12 stanzas of the poem written by Paul Gerhardt (1607–76):[26]

1. **Befiehl** du deine Wege...
2. **Dem Herren** mußt du trauen...
3. **Dein** ewge Treu und Gnade...
4. **Weg** hast du allerwegen...
5. **Und** ob gleich alle Teufel...
6. **Hoff**, o du arme Seele...
7. **Auf**, auf, gib deinem Schmerze...
8. **Ihn**, ihn laß tun und walten...
9. **Er** wird zwar eine Weile...
10. **Wird's** aber sich befinden...
11. **Wohl** dir, du Kind der Treue...
12. **Mach End**, o Herr, mach Ende...

The resulting acrostic reads: "befiehl dem Herren dein Weg und hoff auf ihn, er wird's wohl machen,"[27] which Gerhardt derived from the penitential Psalm 37, verse five, found in Luther's Bible. The composer's musical game seems to mirror the poet's, reinforcing faith's triumph over the darkness of fear and profound difficulty, and recalling Mendelssohn's religious acronym, "L.e.g.G." for "Laß es gelingen, Gott."

THE "CHRIST IST ERSTANDEN" CHORALE IN HENSEL'S "MARCH" IN DAS JAHR

Mendelssohn's transformation of the chorale tune bears comparison with the way in which Hensel would incorporate the ancient Easter chorale "Christ ist erstanden" into her evocation of the month of "March" in *Das Jahr*. Hensel styled the programmatic *Charakterstück* "März" as a "Präludium und Choral." The prelude spans mm. 1–28, and the chorale setting completes the movement in mm. 29–97. To evoke Easter in "March," Hensel chose "Christ ist erstanden,"[28] an older and much less familiar tune than "Christ lag in Todesbanden," the chorale that Johann Sebastian Bach so magnificently elaborated in the chorale cantata by the same name (BWV 4). "Christ ist erstanden" was harmonized in D minor in Bach's chorale setting from the *Orgel-Büchlein*, BWV 276, whose four phrases are shown in Example 2:

Example 2, J.S. Bach, Chorale "Christ ist erstanden" (BWV 276), mm. 1–10

Hensel chose to set the chorale first in the key of C-sharp minor. She identified the chorale's textual incipit between the staves and marked the tempo as "Andante" in the presentation of the harmonized chorale tune, mm. 29–37 (Ex. 3).

Example 3, Fanny Hensel, "März" from Das Jahr, mm. 29–39

A second presentation of the entire chorale melody one octave higher begins in m. 38 in the final measures of Example 3. The middle registers feature filigreed figuration throughout mm. 38–51. In mm. 51–55, Hensel provided an exciting build-up to her third, "triumphant" presentation of the melody (Ex. 4).

With the rubric "sempre cresc. e ritard.," Hensel signaled the momentum needed for the presentation of the chorale in C-sharp major, the parallel key, mm. 54–55. The arrival of the chorale tune in m. 56 in the major mode is marked "Allegro moderato ma con fuoco," while under the bass staff, Hensel indicated "marcato il Basso" at a *forte* dynamic. Here at m. 56, Hensel devised a counterpoint of two bold melodies: the higher countermelody begins with E octaves in the right hand while the simultaneous chorale melody sounds in C-sharp major, with doubled octaves, in the left.

Example 4, Fanny Hensel, "März" from Das Jahr, mm. 52–62

The procedure that Hensel used for "Christ ist erstanden" recalls Mendelssohn's similarly triumphant setting of "Befiehl du deine Wege." However, unlike Mendelssohn's experimental approach to the insertion of the transformed chorale, Hensel made her programmatic intentions explicit in *Das Jahr*. She inserted yet another level of meaning into the score with the epigrams appearing under the name of each month.[29] The epigram for "March" is a question posed by Faust in the chapter, "Night," from Goethe's *Faust* I, lines 744–45: "Has the time come, deep bells, when you make known the Easter holiday's first holy hour?" ("Verkündiget ihr dumpfen Glocken schon des Osterfestes erste Feyerstunde?"). In the final section of "February," a C-sharp pedal in octaves tolls those "deep bells" on the very tonic in which "March" will be grounded (Ex. 5):

Example 5, Fanny Hensel, "Februar" from Das Jahr, mm. 157–68

The epigram not only contributes to Hensel's programmatic intention with her piano cycle, but it also holds multivalent meaning that enriches an understanding of her decision to choose this ancient chorale tune.

It is helpful to see the context in which Goethe cited "Christ ist erstanden" in *Faust*. A Choir of Angels sings before Faust poses three questions, the second of which Hensel cited for the "March" epigram (Table 1):

Table 1, Johann Wolfgang von Goethe, *Faust*, lines 737–748

(Glockenklang und Chorgesang.)	(Chime of bells and choral song.)
<u>Chor Der Engel</u> Christ ist erstanden! Freude dem Sterblichen, Den die verderblichen, Schleichenden, erblichen 740 Mängel umwanden.	<u>Choir of Angels</u>: Christ is arisen! Hail the meek-spirited Whom the ill-merited, Creeping, inherited Faults held in prison.
<u>Faust</u> Welch tiefes Summern, welch ein heller Ton Zieht mit Gewalt das Glas von meinem Munde? **Verkündiget ihr dumpfen Glocken schon** **Des Osterfestes erste Feyerstunde?** 745 Ihr Chöre, singt ihr schon des tröstlichen Gesang, Der einst, um Grabes Nacht, von Engelslippen klang, Gewißheit einem neuen Bunde?	<u>Faust</u>: What deeply humming strokes, what brilliant tone Draws from my pipes the crystal bowl with power? **Has the time come, deep bells, when you make known** **The Easter holiday's first holy hour?** Is this already, choirs, the sweet consoling hymn That was first sung around his tomb by cherubim, Confirming the new covenant?[30]

If we interpret Hensel's C-sharp-major rendition of "Christ ist erstanden" in the same triumphalist terms as those used to understand Mendelssohn's new ascending phrase in Trio II, the allusion she makes to this part of *Faust* complicates an understanding of the triumph of the Lutheran faith. In his next monologue, Faust expresses his skepticism of faith, "Why would you, heaven's tones, compel me gently to rise from my dust? Resound where tenderhearted people dwell: Although I hear the message, I lack all faith or trust; and faith's favorite child is miracle" (lines 762–66).[31] Heinrich Heine, a fellow Jew by birth, famously referred to *Faust* as "the secular Bible of the Germans," which is of interest when considering the meaning of Hensel's quotation.[32]

After Hensel gave the work to her husband as a Christmas gift in 1841—her composing manuscript[33]—she made a fair copy in which he drew illustrations for each month to accompany the music and the poetry.[34] Wilhelm Hensel's drawing of Faust and Mephistopheles from the 1820s shows the widespread popularity of Goethe's ubiquitous work.[35] His illustration for "March" features an angel tolling the bells at once mentioned by Faust and sounded by Hensel.[36] *Das Jahr* resulted in a notable *Gesamtkunstwerk* produced by Fanny and Wilhelm Hensel, serving as a testament to the composer's assimilation into her artistic and religious environment.

CONCLUSION

The two instances of chorale transformation by Felix Mendelssohn and Fanny Hensel examined in this essay have brought into focus a question. What kind of triumph do they represent? I posit that, with both transformations, the siblings had similar goals. On one hand, they wished to reinforce the Bach legacy that they had inherited and, on the other, to stamp that legacy with the mark of their own Protestant faith. In some ways, as Jews converted to Protestantism, they were even more zealous than people who had been born into that faith.

John Edward Toews has written eloquently about the philosophical, ethical, and religious matters pertaining to Mendelssohn[37] as well as to Hensel.[38] With regard to the religious upbringing of Fanny Hensel in particular, Toews explained that "'confessional' identities were ... quite confused, and often secretive and hidden, with Mendelssohn's family during her childhood."[39] By extension, this remark applies equally to Felix Mendelssohn. This "confused" religious identity can be traced back at least to the six children of the siblings' paternal grandparents Moses Mendelssohn and Fromet Gugenheim: two (Joseph and Recha) remained Jewish, two (Henriette and Brendel [Dorothea]) became Catholic, and two, including the siblings' father Abraham and his brother Nathan, became Protestant. Following Abraham and Lea's conversion to Protestantism in October 1822, they dared not write the christianizing "Bartholdy" after the Mendelssohn family name until after the death in 1825 of Lea's mother, Bella Salomon, who was an orthodox Jew.[40]

Both Mendelssohn and Hensel saw allusions to, and quotations of, Johann Sebastian Bach's sacred music as a link not only to their Protestant upbringing but also to the musical legacy established, as we have seen, by their maternal grandmother, great-aunts, and their mother and father. The combination of faith and music brought about something even more powerful than either in isolation. As Toews explains:

> For Fanny and Felix Mendelssohn and the younger generation with which they identified, the tradition of Protestant sacred music, especially as embodied in the great passions and cantatas of the elder Bach, was not merely a priceless aesthetic legacy echoing a past world of metaphysical security and rational order, but contained as a kind of prophetic essence the foundations of a new national ethical consciousness.[41]

The chorale embodied a shared vocabulary that brought those of the faith together: "The integration of the Bach chorale into the structures of modern classical and romantic forms was an embodiment of the historical project that had formed them [Hensel and Mendelssohn] in the 1820s."[42] The chorale itself was charged with meaning. While both composers incorporated chorales into multiple works,[43] they invested them with special intensity and importance in the two instances examined here. There was some tension around the chorale in their household, because "Mendelssohn's father felt that 'no liberties ought ever to be taken with a chorale,' because it was so bound to its liturgical function."[44] Obviously, neither of his composer children heeded this injunction, but this quotation does reveal Abraham Mendelssohn's attitude toward organized religion.

In the chapter of *Becoming Historical* in which Toews focuses on Mendelssohn in particular, he underscores the symbolic importance of the chorale, which was just as true for Hensel as it was for Mendelssohn:

> [Mendelssohn's] interest [was] in articulating the fulfillment of the personal religious quest within the forms of religious community, musically expressed in the chorale. The chorale became a musical symbol for the communal functions of his religious faith and ethical principles, pointing to the hidden, essential truth within the historical forms of the traditional ecclesiastical service. In Bach's compositions Mendelssohn found a model for the elevation of such historical forms to the universality of art. In fact, he would not concede that Bach's passions and cantatas could be reduced to their liturgical function, and thus subordinate to the specific ecclesiastical needs of their time. The *St. Matthew Passion*, he insisted, was an "autonomous piece of music" designed for religious "edification" (*Erbauung*).[45]

Toews made an important point that, for Hensel, "the Protestant tradition was intrinsically connected to the universal, edifying ethos she found in the Bach tradition."[46]

The triumph portrayed by the chorale transformations examined here exceeds mere quotation: the modifications that the two Mendelssohn siblings made to their chorales were tailored to their musically creative inclinations. They invested the chorales with potent musical meaning through the creative changes that they made to them: Mendelssohn with his new tune alluding to "Befiehl du deine Wege," and Hensel with her presentation of the solemn "Christ ist erstanden" in the parallel major key at the full dynamic and registral extremes of "März."

---

1   This essay represents an abbreviated and revised version in English of my "Bach-Rezeption und Lutherischer Choral in der Musik von Fanny Hensel und Felix Mendelssohn Bartholdy," 255–77 in "'*Zu groß, zu unerreichbar*'—*Bach-Rezeption im Zeitalter Mendelssohns und Schumanns*, ed. Anselm Hartinger, Christoph Wolff and Peter Wollny (Wiesbaden, Leipzig, and Paris: Breitkopf & Härtel, 2007). Stephanie Wollny translated my original essay into German for that volume. I am grateful to Professor Todd for his input on the original essay, and I dedicate the present one to him. Thanks, too, to Dr. Eva Kuhn for assistance with translations from the German, and to Deborah Banketa, Wellesley College Class of 2024, for assistance with the musical examples.

2   See Peter Wollny, "Anmerkungen zur Bach-Pflege im Umfeld Sara Levys," 39–49 in "'*Zu groß, zu unerreichbar*'," in which the names of Eskeles and Levy appear among those in Berlin subscribing to music published by J.C.F. Bach (39, 48). See, too, Christoph Wolff, "Sara Levy's Musical Salon and Her Bach Collection," 39–51 in *Sara Levy's World: Gender, Judaism, and the Bach Tradition in Enlightenment Berlin*, ed. Rebecca Cypess and Nancy Sinkoff (Rochester: University of Rochester Press, 2018), 40, 42.

3   Britta L. Behm, *Moses Mendelssohn und die Transformation der jüdischen Erziehung in Berlin—Eine bildungsgeschichtliche Analyse zur jüdischen Aufklärung im 18. Jahrhundert* (Münster, New York, Munich, and Berlin: Waxmann, 2002), 250–68.

4   Emily D. Bilski and Emily Braun, "The Romance of Emancipation," 22–37 in *Jewish Women and Their Salons: The Power of Conversation*. Exhibition Catalogue (New Haven and London: Yale University Press, 2005), 31.
5   R. Larry Todd, *Mendelssohn: A Life in Music* (New York: Oxford University Press, 2003), 33.
6   R. Larry Todd, *Oxford Music Online*, s.v. "Mendelssohn, Felix," explains that "the idea of creating songlike piano pieces may have originated in a game Fanny and Felix played, in which they apparently added texts to piano pieces."
7   Christopher A. Reynolds, *Motives for Allusion* (Cambridge: Harvard University Press, 2003), xi.
8   Renate Hellwig-Unruh, *Fanny Hensel geb. Mendelssohn Bartholdy—Thematisches Verzeichnis der Kompositionen* (Adliswil: Kunzelmann, 2000), 354: H-U 461.
9   "Lieber Felix…Kennst Du eine Cantate v. Bach aus e dur, die Hauser hat: Wohl dem, der sich auf seinen Gott recht kindlich verlassen? Es ist der alte Choral des blinden Leiermannes, von der neuen Promenade. Kennst Dus nicht, so lasse ich den ersten Chor abschreiben u. schicke ihr Dir nachträglich zum Geburtstag, ich finde ihn wunderschön, er ist so einer von den St[illen] im Lande." The letter is reproduced in German in Eva Weissweiler, ed. *Fanny und Felix Mendelssohn: Briefwechsel* (Berlin: Propyläen Verlag, 1997), 213–14, 453; and in English and German in Marcia Citron, ed. and trans. *The Letters of Fanny Hensel to Felix Mendelssohn* (n.p.: Pendragon Press, 1987), 197–98, 507.
10 Her dedication reads as follows: "Dem Mann, der schon manches Jahr daher;/So lang ich ihm verbunden war,/Zum steten Festtag mir verkürzt,/Mit Poesie das Leben gewürzt,/Ihm sey gereicht, dem Ersten, Tüchtigen,/Das spielende Bild des Jahres, des flüchtigen" ("To the man who has, for as long as I have been with him, entertained me on this feast day and enriched my life with poetry; may this playing picture of the fleeting year be given to him, the first, the most excellent man"). Cited in Christian Thorau, "Entgrenzung der Notation—der musikalische Zyklus und seine Reinschrift," VIII–IX, XV–XVI in *Fanny Hensel, Das Jahr—Illustrierte Reinschrift mit Zeichnungen von Wilhelm Hensel*. Epilogues by Beatrix Borchard, Ayako Suga-Maack, and Christian Thorau (Kassel: Furore Verlag, 2000). For an illustrated biography handsomely laying out Wilhelm Hensel's career, see Cécile Lowenthal-Hensel and Jutta Arnold, *Wilhelm Hensel, Maler und Porträtist 1794–1861—Ein Beitrag zur Kulturgeschichte des 19. Jahrhunderts* (Berlin: Mann, 2004).
11 Hellmuth Christian Wolff published the first edition of the twelve "youthful symphonies" of Mendelssohn in 1972. In the Preface to Wolff's edition of *Sinfonia VI* he placed it among the "first seven symphonies … to be understood as study works," *Leipziger Mendelssohn-Ausgabe* I/1 (Leipzig: Deutscher Verlag für Musik, and Wiesbaden: Breitkopf und Härtel, 1972). In a preamble to his complementary article about the symphonies, Wolff noted the long delay from manuscript to edition, examining the problematic reception history for Mendelssohn's work in general: "Zur Erstausgabe von Mendelssohns Jugendsinfonien," *Deutsches Jahrbuch der Musikwissenschaft* 12 (1967): 96–115, at 96–97. Liana Gavrila Serbescu, Barbara Heller, and Ayako Suga-Maack published the first edition of Hensel's *Das Jahr: 12 Charakterstücke fur das Forte-Piano* and revised it after the discovery of the *Reinschrift* (fair copy) (Kassel: Furore Verlag, 1989, rev. 1998). See Barbara Gabler's Preface to the second edition, V–VI.
12 This essay focuses exclusively on the Easter chorale "Christ ist erstanden."
13 Source "F1" in the *Kritischer Bericht* for the *Neue Bach Ausgabe*, hereafter *NBA*, Serie III, Band 2.2, 42: "Johann Sebastian Bachs vierstimmige Choralgesänge, gedruckt bei Breitkopf in vier Bänden, Leipzig, 1784–1787." These chorale settings correspond to BWV 253–438.
14 See William A. Little, ed., *Felix Mendelssohn Bartholdy Complete Organ Works*. 5 vols. V: Supplement: Selected Juvenilia (London and Sevenoaks: Novello, 1990), ix, 35. For more about the *Choralbuch* of Michael Gotthardt Fischer, see my "Bach-Rezeption und Lutherischer Choral," 258, notes 14–15.
15 *Lustgarten Neuer Teutscher Gesäng* (Nürnberg: Paul Kauffmann, 1601).
16 The *NBA* title is "Choräle der Sammlung C.P.E. Bach nach dem Druck von 1784–1787," Serie III, Band 2.2, 160–61 (also see note 13).

17 In the *St. Matthew Passion*, BWV 244, the chorale melody appears five times: in movements 15, 17, 44, 54, and 62. Although in this essay I have not specifically discussed Mendelssohn's 1829 revival of the *St. Matthew Passion* in Berlin, I hope to have shown the important stewardship of Johann Sebastian Bach's music among the female members of his family. For a critical understanding of the mythos surrounding the revival, see Ellen Exner, "Rethinking 1829," 37–57 in *Rethinking Bach*, ed. Bettina Varwig (New York: Oxford University Press, 2021), particularly 50–51.

18 A quote from Mendelssohn Bartholdy's August 22, 1830 letter to his sister Rebecka, cited by R. Larry Todd, ed., Preface to *Felix Mendelssohn Bartholdy, O Haupt voll Blut und Wunden*. Collegium Musicum: Yale University, Second Series, Volume IX (Madison, WI: A-R Editions, 1981): "Ich freue mich auf das Stück von welchem niemand Wissen wird, ob es in c moll oder in es geht" (viii, xiv). Todd also noted here an unfinished set of chorale variations on the tune from the period 1844–45, testifying to the composer's preoccupation with it throughout his career. Todd proposed a connection of these variations to Mendelssohn's concert in the Thomaskirche on August 6, 1840; see R. Larry Todd, "New Light on Mendelssohn's *Freie Phantasie* (1840)," 205–18 in *Literary and Musical Notes: A Festschrift for Wm. A. Little*, ed. Geoffrey C. Orth (Bern, Berlin, Frankfurt am Main, New York, Paris, and Vienna: Peter Lang, 1995), 206.

19 Although the Trio II in which the chorale appears is itself in the dominant key area, B-flat major, Konold remarked on the unusual choice of B major for the Trio I that precedes it: "ungewöhnlich ist die Tonart des ersten Trios," 18 in "Mendelssohns Jugendsymphonien. Eine analytische Studie," *Archiv für Musikwissenschaft* 46 (1989): 1–41 and 161–83.

20 D-B, *Mus. Ms. Autogr. F. Mendelssohn Bartholdy* 3, 188.

21 R. Larry Todd, "On Mendelssohn's Sacred Music, Real and Imaginary," 167–88 in Peter Mercer-Taylor, ed., *The Cambridge Companion to Mendelssohn* (Cambridge: Cambridge University Press, 2004). See, too, Douglass Seaton, "Symphony and Overture," 91–111 in Mercer-Taylor, ed. *The Cambridge Companion*: "In the second trio comes the unexpected effect of a chorale-like (but apparently original) melody," 95. Mendelssohn's procedure in Trio II is described as "Reminiszenz im Choralhaften" in Armin Koch, *Choräle und Choralhaftes im Werk von Felix Mendelssohn Bartholdy* (Göttingen: Vandenhoeck & Ruprecht, 2003), 112–17.

22 Todd, "On Mendelssohn's Sacred Music," 168: "In October 1822, Felix's parents were baptized in a clandestine ceremony in Frankfurt, and from this time date the earliest surviving family letters with signatures that incorporate the name Bartholdy."

23 Koch considers the same speculation in *Choräle und Choralhaftes*, 117.

24 Todd, *Mendelssohn*, 122. The date on which he received it was Christmas 1823. See, too, Celia Applegate, *Bach in Berlin—Nation and Culture in Mendelssohn's Revival of the* St. Matthew Passion (Ithaca, NY: Cornell University Press, 2014), "Bach Among the Mendelssohns," 13–18, and note 17 above.

25 See Andreas Glöckner, "Zelter und Mendelssohn – Zur 'Wiederentdeckung' der Matthäus-Passion im Jahre 1829," *Bach Jahrbuch* 90 (2004): 133–55 at 141.

26 Paul Gerhardt, *Geistliche Lieder* (Stuttgart: Reclam, 1991), 52–55. Gerhardt also wrote the poem for "O Haupt voll Blut und Wunden."

27 "Commit your way to the Lord; trust in him, and he will act."

28 Mendelssohn's chorale tune dates from 1601, whereas the tune associated with Hensel's "Christ ist erstanden" appears at least as early as 1533, in the print *Geistliche lieder auffs new gebessert zu Wittemberg. M. Mart. Luth. XXXiii*. Konrad Ameln, ed. Druckschriften-Faksimiles XXXV (Kassel, Basel, and London: Bärenreiter, 1983), folios 93–94r.

29 For the sources of the poetry that Hensel used in the epigrams, see Marian Wilson Kimber, "Fanny Hensel's Seasons of Life: Poetic Epigrams, Vignettes, and Meaning in *Das Jahr*," *Journal of Musicological Research* 27 (2008): 359–95 at 394–95.

30 Goethe's *Faust*, Translated and with an Introduction by Walter Kaufmann (New York: Anchor Books, 1961; 1990), lines 737–48.

31 Goethe's <u>Faust</u>, lines 762–66: "Was sucht ihr, mächtig und gelind,/Ihr Himmelstöne, mich am Staube?/Klingt dort umher, wo weiche Menschen sind!/Die Botschaft hör ich wohl, allein mir fehlt der Glaube/Das Wunder ist des Glaubens liebstes Kind."
32 Helen Mustard, trans., "The Romantic School," 1–127 in *Heinrich Heine, The Romantic School and Other Essays* (New York: Continuum, 1985), 40–41.
33 Staatsbibliothek zu Berlin, Preußischer Kulturbesitz, Mendelssohn Archiv, Ms. 47.
34 Staatsbibliothek zu Berlin, Preußischer Kulturbesitz, Mendelssohn Archiv, Ms. 155. On the discovery of the *Reinschrift*, see Beatrix Borchard, "I think I've got it," Epilogue to *Fanny Hensel, Das Jahr*.
35 D-B, MA Hensel Album 3, Number 58. The image is reproduced in my "Bach-Rezeption und Lutherischer Choral," 268. It is also found in *Wilhelm Hensel (1794–1861) Porträtist und Maler—Werke und Dokumente. Ausstellung zum 200. Geburtstag* (Wiesbaden: Reichert, 1994), 21.
36 The image is reproduced in my "Bach-Rezeption und Lutherischer Choral," Illustration 2, 267.
37 John Edward Toews, *Becoming Historical—Cultural Reformation and Public Memory in Early Nineteenth-Century Berlin* (Cambridge: Cambridge University Press, 2004), Chapter 4, "The Generation of Ethical Community from the Spirit of Music: Mendelssohn's Musical Constructions of Historical Identity," 207–78.
38 John E. Toews, "Memory and Gender in the Remaking of Fanny Mendelssohn's Musical Identity: The Chorale in 'Das Jahr'," *The Musical Quarterly* 77/4 (1993): 727–48.
39 Ibid., 730.
40 Angela Mace Christian, *Oxford Music Online*, s.v. "Hensel, Fanny Cäcilie," and Toews, "Memory and Gender," 729–30.
41 Toews, "Memory and Gender," 736.
42 Ibid., 743.
43 Because Mendelssohn's oeuvre is so much bigger than Hensel's, therefore he used chorales more frequently—enough to inspire Armin Koch to devote an entire book to the subject.
44 Toews, *Becoming Historical*, 220.
45 Ibid., 224.
46 Toews, "Memory and Gender," 729.

11. FROM EXCAVATION TO ANALYSIS: THE LIEDER OF FANNY HENSEL

Marcia J. Citron

I first met Larry Todd in a chance encounter. We were standing next to each other in a registration line at the 1980 Annual Meeting of the American Musicological Society, and we started to chat. After the usual pleasantries, we discovered our mutual interest in the Mendelssohns. He invited me to talk about Hensel's letters to Felix, a project I was working on, at the forthcoming International Conference on Schumann and Mendelssohn he was co-organizing with Jon Finson.[1] Thus began a special relationship with a great Mendelssohnian, and equally great Henselite, that has lasted to this day.

At the time, I was also doing research on Hensel's Lieder and aiming for a foundational article on the topic.[2] This involved digging into the manuscripts and fair copies of her songs at the Mendelssohn Archiv (MA) at the Staatsbibliothek Preussischer Kulturbesitz (SPB) in West Berlin, the main repository of her Lieder. In the present essay, I'd like to trace major moments in the research arc of Hensel's Lieder from that era of excavation to the present period of rich musical analysis: an extraordinary change that marks Hensel's acceptance into the canon of composers whose works invite close reading. This last stage is represented by Stephen Rodgers's brilliant essay collection of 2021, *The Songs of Fanny Hensel*,[3] discussed in the final section of my study. In between we look at key moments in the forty-year span: the publication of Annette Maurer's *Thematisches Verzeichnis der klavierbegleiteten Sololieder Fanny Hensels*, from 1997;[4] and the appearance of websites devoted to female composers and their music. Limited space precludes a more thorough study of important moments, be they music editions, recordings, conferences, publications, or websites.

EXCAVATION

I learned of Hensel's songs when writing an article on female composers of Lieder for the groundbreaking anthology, *Women Making Music*, edited by Jane Bowers and Judith Tick.[5] Hensel's music and milieu fascinated me, and I decided to research her more fully. After an exploratory trip in 1979, I visited the MA for a few months in 1980 to study her Lieder. Rudolf Elvers, the head of the archive, had published articles listing the call numbers of collections containing her pieces, although not individual titles of Lieder. As the MA lacked a card catalog, at least not for its Hensel holdings, the article was key to locating her music, and I was able to examine it *in situ*. But doing serious research required copies of the music to work with at home.

In pre-internet days, this typically meant photocopies or microfilms. Most libraries, US and international, granted access as a matter of course, viewing their holdings as vital resources in the promotion of scholarship. Apparently, the MA was not one of them. Elvers denied permission for photocopies or microfilms, and no reason was given. The only way I could duplicate the music was by notating each Lied by hand, in pencil. Given the large number, probably over 200 of her 249 Lieder, notating all would be impossible in my time frame. In addition, the method is conducive to errors. But I started notating and hoped for the best given tired eyes and the pressure to work quickly. It's hard not to infer that the denial of permission not only impeded my project but was intended to discourage it altogether. This contrasted with other Hensel repositories—the Bodleian in Oxford, the Goethe-Museum in Düsseldorf, and the Heinrich-Heine Institute in the same city—where the librarians and curators not only allowed photocopies but went out of their way to be helpful.[6]

Approximately forty Lieder were notated during the Berlin visit, and it wasn't easy to choose which ones to copy. For an introductory study, it seemed wise to cover the range of her work in terms of chronology, language, style, and text, and I notated a wide variety of types. Still, thorny questions arose. There were many early Lieder. Should they be considered juvenilia and passed over? What about the relatively small number but striking presence of Lieder in English, Italian, and French: should they be ignored because there are so few? Should the Lieder in strophic form, by far the most prevalent, be given the most attention? Should Lieder on Goethe's texts hold pride of place because she set him more than any other poet, and he recognized her talent and was a family friend? In the end, I aimed for balance in the pieces to copy and the issues to stress in the article, which appeared in 1983.

This was far from a smooth excavation. Today, when Hensel's manuscripts are readily available at the SPK website and elsewhere (more below), it's hard to grasp what it means when sources are inaccessible. It begs the question, why did Elvers deny permission? One answer is suggested in a 1986 piece on Hensel in *The Christian Science Monitor*, where Elvers characterizes female researchers of Hensel as "piano-playing girls" and the composer as "nothing; [s]he was just a wife." He's looking for the "right man for the job" of basic source study of her music; "qualified musicologists are not interested."[7] I also wonder if he was saving the material for himself. In recent years, I've had a further thought, that Cold War politics may have played a role. In divided Berlin there was tremendous competition between the Deutsche Staatsbibliothek in the East and the SPK in the West. As a result, Elvers may have been obsessively possessive towards "his" holdings in the MA. I came from a friendly country, but releasing materials apparently went against the grain.[8] In any event, my being a young female scholar from the US doing research on a female Mendelssohn didn't work in my favor. The good news is that the article was completed, accepted, and published, and it helped lay the groundwork for a growing interest in Hensel's Lieder.

THEMATIC CATALOG

In 1997, Annette Maurer published a thematic catalog of Hensel's Lieder with the German firm Furore, a press founded in 1986 devoted exclusively to the music of women. By the time of Maurer's volume, Furore had issued several unpublished Hensel works, among them the score and parts to her *Oratorium, Ouverture,* and *Lobgesang,* all from 1831. We are indebted to them for these editions—to date, over 150 unpublished Hensel works have been issued[9]—and for the *Thematic Catalog*, a not inexpensive venture.

Maurer's volume is an invaluable resource. In one place, and for the first time, it codifies what Hensel composed in the genre and offers the basic facts behind her 249 Lieder, most of them unpublished. These include date of composition; location and call number of autographs, copies, and fair copies; published editions through 1997 (if any); poets; and other information on the genesis, provenance, sources, and dissemination of the piece. Most importantly, it provides the notated incipit of each piece, its key, and the total number of bars.

An interesting feature is that Maurer's list is arranged alphabetically by song title, or first line if title is missing. In the Appendix she presents a chronological list of titles by year. Maurer doesn't explain why the main list is alphabetical, but apparently, she envisioned a user who was targeting a particular song and wanted to look up its history and location. That would suggest a performer, less so a scholar. As a musicologist, I had imagined that the main list would be chronological, as in many a thematic catalog. But I reminded myself that Hensel's complete output had not been arranged chronologically at that point.[10] Moreover, Maurer's volume is devoted to a specific genre, and the decision to list the pieces according to its traditions—i.e., according to the song's title or text—was probably a good one.

Additional lists contribute to the comprehensive treatment, allowing users to search from a variety of perspectives. One offers the locations of sources; another gives the titles of the published Lieder, including modern editions; and yet another lists the poets Hensel used, with song titles appended. Individual entries in the central list also show Maurer's thoroughness. For the Lied "Hausgarten," for example, no. 121 alphabetically, Maurer provides three paragraphs of supplementary information on the genesis of the Lied, including quotations from family correspondence and Hensel's diary.[11]

WEBSITES

The website "Hensel Songs Online" was started by British tenor Tim Parker-Langston in 2021.[12] It offers many features, including a list of all Hensel's songs and notated scores of each that are free to download. While imperfect and a work in progress, the site is an invaluable resource for research and performance.

The scores are arranged chronologically by year and H-U number and begin with the title and date of composition. The poet's name follows. Next comes one or more notated versions of the Lied, with the original-key version marked with an asterisk. All were produced by Parker-Langston and appear to have been generated by notation programs like Finale. For the sake of completeness, this could have been a place to cite commercially published editions, although it would bump into Parker-Langston's purpose of offering free downloadable music and create much more work for its organizer. Elsewhere on the site, however, under "Shop," a multi-volume edition of unpublished Hensel Lieder, edited by Parker-Langston, is available for purchase.

The last item of the score entry is possibly the most valuable: a link to the autograph source on the website of the Staatsbibliothek.[13] A click takes you to the Sammelband containing the song, and you scroll down the contents to find it. Fortunately, one can manipulate the buttons on the SPK's site to adjust the size of the image. If the autograph is in another location—the manuscript of "Aglaë" (1828), for example, resides in the Goethe-Museum in Düsseldorf—it is usually noted in the entry. Omissions occur, however. For "Bergeslust" (H-U 466), Hensel's last song (and composition), well-known for at least that reason, the site says "Autograph lost," whereas the Bodleian houses the autograph and a handwritten copy.[14]

Many of the songs present comments by Parker-Langston about Hensel's life and general musical activity, which he states are drawn from Todd's biography of the composer.[15] He also offers personal recommendations for many songs. The wording is casual, not scholarly, and may contain errors.

The site also has a category of "Recordings," a very important component. Its first section mentions a recent recording of Parker-Langston and others that emphasizes overlooked pieces. The link takes you to "Shop" to buy it. The second part has audio previews on Spotify of a hundred songs, in no particular order, performed by various artists. The quality is uneven, but among the best are the twenty-five or so sung by tenor Parker-Langston and the twenty by baritone Tobias Berndt. I would suggest that the "Scores" listings indicate if a Lied appears in "Recordings."

A relatively new offering on Henselsongsonline is #Hensel, a space that invites performers to share their performances of unrecorded Hensel songs on YouTube. A marvelous feature, especially since the hashtag also appears in the main entry for the song, it shows the power of the internet and social media to foster what Parker-Langston calls "a global collaborative effort" and bring Hensel's Lieder to the fore.

Another useful website is "Women's Song Forum," established in 2020. It boasts a broad scope and is devoted to all aspects of women in song and all manner of song, emphasizing ignored figures and repertoire.[16] A few blogs ("Publications") appear each month, and although Hensel is no longer unknown, some address her Lieder. In January 2022, for instance, Stephen Rodgers posted a piece called "200-Year Wait for a Fanny Hensel Performance," a plea for quality performances that includes a video from a recital.[17] Not coincidentally, Rodgers has been a guiding force behind the site.

ANALYSIS[18]

Rodgers has also led the way in the analysis of Hensel's Lieder. A music theorist (and fine tenor), Rodgers published five articles on her songs between 2011 and 2020. His energy and passion resulted in the editorship of a landmark collection, *The Songs of Fanny Hensel* (2021), which marks a new stage in Hensel scholarship. Instead of the more typical topics in Hensel research—editions, biography, and the gendered context—*Songs* focuses on the music and shows that her Lieder are worthy of serious study. Nearly every author recognizes the quality and originality of Hensel's Lieder and the ways in which they broaden our understanding of the genre. Contributors come from musicology as well as music theory, with diverse areas of interest. There are scholars of Hensel (Susan Wollenberg, R. Larry Todd), Lieder (Susan Youens, Harald Krebs, Jürgen Thym), Romantic aesthetics (Scott Burnham, Amanda Lalonde), and musico-poetic relations (Jennifer Ronyak, Yonatin Malin). The relationship between music and text is a major theme and helps to unify the volume.

The twelve chapters are divided into five parts, and I'll discuss representative chapters. Part I, "Nature and Travel," opens with Lalonde's "The Wilderness at Home: Woods-Romanticism in Fanny Hensel's Eichendorff Songs."[19] Lalonde zeroes in on the trope of *Waldromantik* in an exploration of four Lieder based on Eichendorff's poems. She notes the poet's references to sound and the way Hensel avoids direct imitation of nature by "center[ing] her settings on the texts' moments of sonic revelation, responding to and extending the role of music in *Waldromantik* literature."[20] Lalonde makes another perceptive observation when she connects Hensel's performing space—the *Gartensaal*, with its juxtaposition of wildness and domesticity—to the way the songs "sometimes emphasize how the real performers and domestic performance environment are part of the narrative of the song.… In performance, in other words, these lieder cloud the domesticity of the genre."[21] The rich texture of the essay, interweaving music theory, poetics, performance, narrative, and biography, sets the tone for the collection.

Two chapters comprise Part II, "Settings of English Verse." Ronyak's essay, "Women's Private Cosmopolitanism in Literary Translation and Song: Fanny Hensel's *Drei Lieder nach Heinrich Heine von Mary Alexander*,"[22] explores gender through the lens of cosmopolitanism and what it means for Hensel's settings of English texts that are translations of Heine's German originals. This chapter more than any other engages with women's social context. Mary Alexander, a family friend who lived in London, was Scottish. Like many Germans at the time, Hensel was fascinated by Scottish culture; she also wanted to learn English. For Ronyak, the cultural exchange represents a study in cosmopolitanism related to Hensel's class and involves a rejection of the provincialism of the local sphere. Such insights raise further questions: Did many women act as amateur translators? Was Alexander unique? And was Hensel unique in setting poems translated into another language by a woman?

Part III, "Tonal Ingenuity," includes Rodgers's revelatory piece, "Plagal Cadences in Fanny Hensel's Songs."²³ His thesis is that "most plagal cadences [in the nineteenth century] come *after* authentic cadences; they are post-cadential ... [Hensel] elevates the plagal cadence from its conventional status as a 'cadence confirmer' to that of a 'cadence maker,' casting it not in a supporting role but in a starring role."²⁴ This is an important observation, "yet another reason why Fanny Hensel's once-marginalized songs deserve a central place in discussions about the aesthetics of nineteenth-century music."²⁵ The main argument involves readings of three songs that together display her three strategies to bring about plagal closure. In conclusion, Rodgers gives possible reasons for Hensel's practice: her immersion in Bach's music; and her "novel handling of closure more generally" that often avoids, defers, or undermines finality.²⁶ This compelling study helps us understand what makes Hensel's Lieder "tick," and why Rodgers is considered a pre-eminent voice on Hensel's Lieder.

Part IV is devoted to "Responses to Poetic Form" and offers Malin's stimulating study, "Modulating Couplets in Fanny Hensel's Songs."²⁷ The structure of the couplet is the starting point as Malin explores its effect on music and expression. Because of Hensel's fluid tonal practices and frequent use of folk poetry, her music is suitable for this kind of inquiry. Malin analyzes several songs and makes some remarkable points. One relates to a comparison of Schumann's and Hensel's settings of Eichendorff's "Ich kann wohl manchmal singen." He notes how Hensel emphasizes "das bedeudet" (that means), stressing the very act of interpretation, while Schumann does not. More generally, Malin calls for greater sensitivity to poetic structure in Lieder analysis. He observes at the end that Hensel's music might serve as a model for analysis of Lieder in terms of couplet structure. "[This] may lead us, now, to hear other songs, [by other composers], in new ways."²⁸

Finally, I'm pleased to turn to Todd's contribution. "Fanny Hensel's *Lieder (ohne Worte)* and the Boundaries of Song: The Curious Case of the *Lied* in D-flat major, Op. 8, No.3,"²⁹ appears in Part V, "Beyond Hensel/Beyond Song," and forms a fitting close to the volume. Genre is key to the study, which showcases Todd's thorough familiarity with the life and music of Hensel and Mendelssohn. He provides a detailed account of the term "song without words" and its place in the siblings' music. The work in question, Hensel's piano piece Op. 8 No. 3, behaves in some ways like a "song without words," and "Lied" is curiously affixed in the first edition. Interestingly, she was working on Lieder set to Lenau's poetry when the piece may have been written (1846), and we know that texts were removed from other Hensel piano works. But there is no documentary evidence to settle the generic ambiguity, and so Op. 8 No. 3 remains a curiosity.

★ ★ ★

In the bigger picture, the journey from excavation to analysis of Hensel's Lieder that I have traced could be considered a passage from darkness to light, from pessimism to optimism. The fraught politics, the possessiveness, and the machismo of the early years gave way to a new political reality, new opportunities for exploration, and new methods of research that have changed the landscape for Hensel scholarship. As manifested in Rodgers's *Songs*, Hensel's Lieder now receive the sort of sophisticated treatment they deserve. We can only look forward to future work.

1. My talk appears in a volume culled from the conference, which occurred in spring 1982: Marcia J. Citron, "Fanny Hensel's Letters to Felix Mendelssohn in the Green-Books Collection at Oxford," 99–108, in *Mendelssohn and Schumann: Essays on Their Music and Its Context*, ed. Jon W. Finson and R. Larry Todd (Durham, NC: Duke University Press, 1984).
2. Marcia J. Citron, "The Lieder of Fanny Mendelssohn Hensel," *The Musical Quarterly* 69 (1983): 570–94.
3. Stephen Rodgers, ed., *The Songs of Fanny Hensel* (New York: Oxford University Press, 2021).
4. Annette Maurer, *Thematisches Verzeichnis der klavierbegleiteten Sololieder Fanny Hensels* (Kassel: Furore, 1997).
5. Marcia J. Citron, "Women and the Lied, 1775–1850," *Women Making Music: The Western Art Tradition, 1150-1950*, ed. Jane Bowers and Judith Tick (Urbana: University of Illinois Press, 1986), 224–48.
6. The point is elaborated in the recent documentary "Fanny: The Other Mendelssohn," directed by Sheila Hayman (London: Mercury Studios, 2023). See also Marcia J. Citron, "A Bicentennial Reflection: Twenty-Five Years with Fanny Hensel," *Nineteenth-Century Music Review*, 4/2 (2007): 8–10.
7. In Christopher Swan, "The Other Mendelssohn," *The Christian Science Monitor* (27 March 1986): 17.
8. Others were also denied Hensel's music. Swan mentions that the Portland String Quartet was denied access to her String Quartet in 1985, and a follow-up request by C. F. Peters didn't fare any better (Swan, "The Other Mendelssohn," 17). Even German scholars had trouble accessing manuscripts. Feminist musicologist Eva Weisweiler was denied consistent permission by the SPK to see documents related to the Schumanns unless she worked with scholar Wolfgang Boetticher (who, by the way, was a Nazi musicologist who co-authored the infamous *Lexikon der Juden in der Musik*). Only when she appealed to the Mayor of West Berlin, Richard von Weiszäcker, was the decision overturned. Email communication of Weisweiler to the author, 2 June 2005.
9. https://furore-verlag.de/en/verlagschronik/, accessed 3 July 2023.
10. A chronological thematic catalog of Hensel's entire oeuvre appears a few years later: Renate Hellwig-Unruh, *Fanny Hensel, geboren Mendelssohn Bartholdy: Thematisches Verzeichnis der Kompositionen* (Adliswil: Kunzelmann, 2000). Since its publication, Hensel's pieces are often designated with H or H-U numbers.
11. Maurer, *Thematisches Verzeichnis*, 110–11. The souces of the quotes are given: Citron, *Letters of Fanny Hensel to Felix Mendelssohn* (Stuyvesant, New York: 1987), 602; Tagebücher 1834–43, Abschrift von Eva Roemer, MA Ms. 103; and two portions of a family letter in the Bodleian Library, MS MDM c. 34, No. 22.
12. https://henselsongsonline.org, accessed 10 December 2023.
13. The general link is https://digital.staatsbibliothek-berlin.de/ (accessed 1 March 2024) and then refining the search to Hensel and work.
14. Maurer, *Thematisches Verzeichnis*, 20.
15. R. Larry Todd, *Fanny Hensel: The Other Mendelssohn* (New York: Oxford University Press, 2010).
16. https://www.womensongforum.org/, accessed 4 July 2023.
17. https://www.womensongforum.org/2022/01/15/200-year-wait-for-a-fanny-hensel-performance/, accessed 1 March 2024.

18 This section is based on my review of Rodgers' *The Songs of Fanny Hensel*, in *Music and Letters* 102/4 (November 2021): 837-40.
19 Lalonde, "The Wilderness at Home," 15–34 in Rodgers, *Songs*.
20 Lalonde, "The Wilderness at Home," 21.
21 Lalonde, "The Wilderness at Home," 26.
22 Ronyak, "Cosmopolitanism," 77–92 in Rodgers, *Songs*.
23 Rodgers, "Plagal Cadences," 129–45 in Rodgers, *Songs*.
24 Rodgers, "Plagal Cadences," 129.
25 Rodgers, "Plagal Cadences," 142.
26 Rodgers, "Plagal Cadences," 142.
27 Malin, "Modulating Couplets," 171–91 in Rodgers, *Songs*.
28 Malin, "Modulating Couplets," 189.
29 Todd, "Op. 8, No. 3," 217–38 in Rodgers, *Songs*.

12. COMPREHENDING HEINE IN FANNY HENSEL'S "SCHWANENLIED"

Susan Youens

Twenty-five years ago, when I was drowning in 5,000 or so of the 8,000-plus compositions based on poetry by Heinrich Heine, I adopted a kitten from Pet Refuge, an animal rescue organization in Indiana. (I am quite sure you did not expect the sentence to end that way.) The kitten had been fostered from birth by an elderly European couple, the woman originally from Poland, the man from Germany. A few weeks later, they were given the customary task of making a home visit to whoever had adopted one of their charges to make sure that the animal had gone to a good home and was being cared for properly. When the couple arrived, they saw my dining room table groaning under stacks of Heine songs and masses of books on him. At the sight, the woman's face lit up, and she exclaimed, "Oh, I love Heine's poetry! It's so simple and true," upon which she recited "Sie liebten sich Beide" from memory. I had just been wrestling that very morning with the complexities of that same poem and with the utter marvels that are Clara Schumann's two versions of it. The incident made me reflect anew on the precise nature of Heine's poetic enterprise, especially his use of non-grandiloquent vocabulary and folk-like stanza forms—Graham Johnson calls him "king of the quatrain"—to create multi-level complexity. Someone not clued-in to look for the ironic resonances, the paradoxes Heine loves so much, the masks and hidden agendas, *can* enjoy a seemingly sentimental surface; nineteenth-century composers who were not reading closely enough whipped up one sugary musical confection after another with which to surround Heine's words. In a particularly ironic instance of misprision, Adolf Bartels, a virulently anti-Semitic literary critic in the last years of the century, wrote diatribe after diatribe against Heine, but semi-praised "Du bist wie eine Blume" as one of the few "sincere and lovely" poems this "Jewish manipulator ever wrote;" even here, he couldn't resist taking a swipe at Heine's "oriental-sentimental" vein.[1] Sincerity, I can assure you, is not the purpose of that work.[2]

After my lengthy immersion in Heine settings, I came to the conclusion that the century's women composers understood him more than most—his cloaked messages and multiple associations, his deconstruction of society's ills, his profound sadness enveloped in wit and word-play, his nuanced manipulation of language—and were able to transform that depth of understanding into astute compositional decisions, born of their unique harmonic/tonal/melodic resources; Clara Schumann, Marie Hinrichs, Fanny Hensel, Josephine Lang, and others. Both Fanny Hensel and Clara Schumann knew Heine personally and disliked him, or at least distrusted him in any capacity that was not poetic. Fanny had discovered the *Buch der Lieder* hot off the press in 1827 and knew of him in Berlin even earlier through Rahel von Varnhagen and Eduard Gans, as Larry Todd has detailed.³ Fanny would surely have been pleased at Heine's characterization of her brother as a "musical miracle" and a "second Mozart," but she took a great dislike to Heine the man. Writing to Karl Klingemann in 1829, she confided that

> Heine is here, and I do not like him at all, he is so affected. If he would let himself go, he would of all eccentric men be the most amiable; or if in good earnest, he would keep a tight hand over himself, gravity also would become him, for he is grave too. But he gives himself sentimental airs, is affectedly affected, talks incessantly of himself, and all the while, he looks at you to see whether you look at him.⁴

She was an astute observer: there are few sharper portraits of Heine in company than this. On a trip to Paris in 1835, the Hensels took pains to avoid the poet, by then a self-exile in the City of Light.

But she was also an astute admirer of his verse, or at least, *some* of his verse; she set six poems from the *Buch der Lieder* in 1827-28 and was enraptured by the *Reisebilder* in 1829: "They contain delightful things; and though for ten times you may be inclined to despise him, the eleventh time you cannot help confessing that he is a poet, a true poet! How he manages the words! What a feeling he has for nature, such as only a real poet has!"⁵ Heine's borrowings (always selective) from Wilhelm Müller, the distillation of means that so suited her own approach to song composition, the *Stimmungsbrechungen* that she could, and did turn into harmonic surprises at song's end. These were all factors in the creation of twenty-six Heine settings by Hensel. One of them, "Gleich Merlin" of 1836, may have been the result of Heine's gift of the text upon a chance encounter in Boulogne the previous year.⁶ And yet, ambivalence remained a marked aspect of her attraction to Heine's verse. She liked him best on those occasions when he abandoned what she calls his "ironic conceit" (this in the context of her praise in February 1834 for Felix's *Drei Volkslieder*, nos. 2, 3, and 4 of *Sechs Lieder*, Op. 41)⁷ and she availed herself of quite a few opportunities in her music to contradict, undercut, even replace, what she found objectionable in his poetry. Larry Todd points to several revealing examples, one in her setting of "Warum sind denn die Rosen so blaß?," where she replaced "Warum steigt denn aus dem Balsamkraut / *hervor ein Leichenduft*?" with "Warum denn aus dem Balsamkraut / *verwelkter Blütenduft*?" Wilted flowers are less malodorous and less horrifying than corpses, albeit still evocative of death. For her setting of "Ach, die Augen sind es wieder," she eliminated the entire final stanza ("Von den weißen, schönen Armen / fest und liebevoll umschlossen, / lieg ich jetzt an ihrem Herzen, / dumpfen Sinnes und unverdrossen"), thus doing away with the shockingly bitter ending in which sensuality becomes a desert and love poetry something else altogether.⁸ She also changed Heine's ending in her setting of "Wenn der Frühling kommt," in which the poet at the close rejects stars, flowers, and the like: "No matter how much you like such stuff, / to make a world they're just not enough" ("Wie sehr das Zeug auch gefällt, / So macht's doch noch lang keine Welt").[9] Hensel substitutes her own lines: "Sind alles nur tändelnder Scherz / Und meine Welt ist dein liebendes Herz." Composers are entitled to emendations in service of their music, but there is still something more than a trifle ironic about the substitution of actual sentimentality for Heine's condemnatory words directed at other poets' sentimentality.

Hensel had company in her dislike of Heine's distinctive brand of bile-and-gall. More than seventy writers busied themselves with critiques of this startling original young man between 1821 and 1831. In 1823, Friedrich de La Motte-Fouqué wrote a poem "An H. Heine. Am 21. Mai 1823" for the Cologne journal *Agrippina* that begins as follows:

Du lieber, Herzblutender Sänger,	You dear, bleeding-heart poet,
Dein Lied versteh' ich ja wohl!	I understand your poem quite well!
Doch singe so wirr nicht länger!	But don't sing so wildly any longer!
So zürnend nicht und hohl!	No more so angry and hollow!
Hohl wie die Geister um Mitternacht!	Hollow like the spirits at midnight!
Wie im Walde der Wind so wirr!	When the wind in the forest is so wild!
Und zürnend, wie in Gewitterpracht	And raging, like the dazzling roar of
Der Blitze blendend Geschwirr!	lightning in the thunderstorm's splendor!
. . . .	. . . .
Du, dem die Kraft in den Liedern schäumt,	You, whose strength foams in the songs,
Dem zuckt auf der Lippe der Schmerz,—	Whose pain twitches on his lips—
Du hast schon einmal so Schlimmes geträumt,—	You've had just such a bad dream before—
O hüte dein liebes Herz!	Guard your dear heart!
(stanzas 1-2 and 6 of 7)[10]	

One notes the blizzard of exclamation marks. "If you play with snakes, they will creep after you into the grave . . . your God loves your loving heart and says, 'I forgive you,'" the salvation-minded Fouqué insists near the end. If Heine saw this screed, I would like to think that he chuckled. Another critic, an anonymous woman whose subject was periodical literature in 1825 Leipzig, declared that his "schneidende, hohnlachende Ironie läßt kein Gefühl rein anklingen und austönen" (the cutting, hollow laughter of irony allows no feeling to sound forth and then die away in purity), that he "stürmt in wilden Contrasten, mit epigrammatischem Sarkasmus, durch die lyrischen Weisen hin" (rages in wild contrasts, with epigrammatic sarcasm, throughout his lyrical songs). But she enjoyed his wittily capricious portrait of the devil in *Die Heimkehr* XXXV, "Ich rief den Teufel und er kam," so clearly there were exceptions to her opprobrium.[11] Elsewhere, Adolf Peters first points to Heine's wit and then slams his contemporary for not knowing the limits of decency, for exercising a spitefulness ("Boshaftigkeit") that reminded the critic unpleasantly of Voltaire (others might take that as a compliment), for playing in a "heillos und frevelhaft" (unholy and wicked) manner with the purest and most elevated feelings.[12] Heine was forever being accused of impurity. But it is fascinating to note that much of the criticism directed his way, including some of the harshest, is often mixed with praise. In like fashion, Fanny's dislike of his manner in society and his use of irony in his writings was paired with her recognition, enthusiastically expressed, that he was a true poet.

Hensel's "Schwanenlied," Op. 1, no. 1, is a setting of Heine's *Lyrical Intermezzo*, no. 59.[13]

Es fällt ein Stern herunter	A star is tumbling down
Aus seiner funkelnden Höh!	from its glittering height!
Das ist der Stern der Liebe,	It is the star of love
Den ich dort fallen seh.	I see falling there.
Es fallen vom Apfelbaume	From apple trees are falling
Der Blüten und Blätter viel!	many blossoms and leaves!
Es kommen die neckenden Lüfte	The merry breezes gather
Und treiben damit ihr Spiel.	and whirl them around in play.
Es singt der Schwan im Weiher,	The swan on the lake is singing
Und rudert auf und ab,	as it glides to and fro,
Und immer leiser singend,	and singing ever more softly,
Taucht er ins Flutengrab.	plunges to its watery grave.
Es ist so still und dunkel!	It is so quiet and dark!
Verweht ist Blatt und Blüt,	Gone are leaf and flower,
Der Stern ist knisternd zerstoben,	the star has fizzled and gone,
Verklungen das Schwanenlied.	the swan song is no more.

As with most of the great poems by Heine, this one has been interpreted in several different ways. More sentimentally inclined readers have, especially in Heine's own century, read his poetry as autobiographical, telling tales of unhappy love for his uncle Salomon Heine's daughters, Amalie and Therese. The fine pianist Eugene Asti and the soprano Susan Gritton, in their Hyperion recording of Hensel's songs, describe "Schwanenlied" as being "about a love that has gone unnoticed," and I would guess that my kitten-fostering Polish friend might read the poem the same way. (Gritton's and Asti's performance is, however, beautiful.)[14] And yet, Heine brings in too many other signifiers, too many other poetic processes, for us to be content with this summation as all there is, despite the attraction of poignance drawn from life. Laura Hofrichter sees "Es fällt ein Stern herunter" as a series of commonplace images reduced to their absolute essentials until in the last stanza, the poem itself seems to participate in the dissolution it records.[15] Klaus Briegleb sees the poem as a cryptogram for four fundamental motifs that recur throughout in Heine's *Buch der*

Lieder: love, freedom ("free as the wind"), poetry, and death, each allotted a single stanza.[16] Michael Perraudin states that "'This poet's feeling' is represented by the absence of the star, the blossom, and the swan song," a reading which succumbs to the old equation of a poem with its poet's life and feelings, rather than with the stuff of language and the making of poetry, but does take note of the emphasis on serial losses.[17] These readings have their virtues, but I prefer Anthony Phelan's perceptive analysis as a starting point for a discussion of how Fanny Hensel turned the poem into *her* music.

As Phelan observes, there is a pattern of repetition—and Hensel too will depend on a repeated pattern, albeit more cloaked than Heine's—that sustains the whole structure by means of a series of impersonal verbs, "Es fällt," "Es fallen," "Es kommen," "Es singt," "Es ist."[18] It is impossible to render this literally into English without being unbearably awkward—"It sings, the swan as it circles," or some such—, but the effect in German is striking, immediately available to eye and ear. At first, the shooting star seems a random phenomenon that the persona observes, but it is quickly particularized as "the star of love," that is, as a poetic metaphor and a commonplace one at that. The same process seems to be underway at the start of stanza two, but the transformation into a metaphor does not happen. Instead, the observation that leaves fall is amplified by the arrival of the merry breezes, another force of Nature and one that animates the leaves in mid-air even as they go to their impending dissolution. In stanza three, however, the singing swan is already a myth, already a signifier of a poet's final, most beautiful utterance as he/she is dying. Ever since the grieving Cygnus of Greek myth mourned in plangent songs for his dead friend Phaethon and was transformed into a swan, swan songs are the last creations of dying artists, the emblem and assurance of their immortality. By now, we realize yet again, as is so often the case with Heine, that this is a poem about the stuff of poetry, a requiem for moribund language and outworn images (but with a twist that is itself common to swan songs).

In the final stanza, the order of the metaphorical elements is changed as they each become first generic, then dead and gone: "Blatt und Blüt," "leaf and blossom" as archetype instead of belonging to an apple tree; a fizzled star, its light extinguished before it vanishes; and finally, not the swan—it has already gone under the water as its song is dying away—but the swan *song*. Each metaphor leads only to isolation, exhaustion, dissolution, and disappearance.[19] Both poet and poem expire ("The song and the death are one," says Phelan)[20]...except for the Heine-esque paradox in its aftermath. If this is the emptying-out of metaphor in the realm of literature, it is also a poetic lament that affixes shooting stars, blossom time, and singing swans onto the page forever and allows the likes of Fanny Hensel to revivify them for the sake of her music. That is precisely the bet taken by the many creators of swan songs, that as they hymn swan-poet and song alike, they fashion their own immortality. In Horace's ode, "Non usitata nec tenui ferar," the poet is transformed into a swan while singing that very song,[21] and in another country, another era, Yeats wrote a fanciful will in "The Tower," in which he bequeaths to "upstanding men" the pride "of the hour /

When the swan must fix his eye / Upon a fading gleam, / Float out upon a long / Last reach of glittering stream / And there sing his last song."[22] From Virgil to Spenser, from Hölderlin to Mallarmé, many poets have availed themselves of a myth already in circulation in the third century B.C.[23]

"Schwanenlied" is born of the Hensels' travels in Italy in 1839-1840, including a visit en route to their Italian destination at the Bavarian palace of Neuschwanstein near Hohenschwangau, a nineteenth-century castle built by Maximilian II and his son Ludwig II on the ruins of a medieval fortress. At a nearby Alpine lake, Fanny Hensel took note of swans that resembled, in her lovely phrase, "floating stars on the dark green water." Larry Todd wonders whether she remembered this experience when she composed her "Schwanenlied" some months later.[24] On that journey, the couple explored Venice, including excursions on gondolas, and their travels culminated in expeditions southward to Naples, the Sorrento coast, Paestum southeast of Naples and more. Gondoliers and their songs were part and parcel of her mostly enchanted journey, despite occasional bouts of bad weather that she describes in one instance as "schlechtissimo" (my new favorite word).[25]

But even without that personal experience, Hensel would have known barcarolles bursting out of the woodwork in late eighteenth- and nineteenth-century music. Charles Burney was already reporting in 1773 that "the songs of the Gondoleri, or Watermen . . . are so celebrated that every musical collector of taste in Europe is furnished with them."[26] By Fanny's day, the conventions of barcarolle composition were well-known: the use of minor mode, a sweet and simple melody (that is part of Hermann Mendel's definition of the genre in 1880),[27] and 6/8 meter were the most commonplace. As barcarolles found their way into opera and song, the ubiquity of love as the subject par excellence of barcarolles was often mingled with thoughts of death, as with Rossini's well-educated gondolier in Act III of *Otello* who sings Dante's famous words about bygone happiness being the bitterest sorrow, "Nessun maggior dolore," as a barcarolle. Schubert's "Auf dem Wasser zu singen" is also a swan-song, with its invocation of gliding "wie Schwäne," "like swans," its poet Ludwig von Stolberg dwelling on a metaphor familiar from Horace, Virgil, Plato, Ovid, Petrarch, Yeats, Hölderlin, and scores of other poets.[28] On first hearing, Hensel's Lied seems to adhere to every one of the standard descriptors for "music to be sung on the water," from the G minor tonality and the entrancing melody in 6/8 meter to the gentle motion of the arpeggiated waves in the piano, lapping upwards, turning downward at the end of each harmony. But judgments of "simplicity" are soon replaced by recognition of profundity when one realizes the subtlety with which the composer manipulates her traditional materials.

Hensel's decision to shape this song as two musical strophes for four stanzas of verse tells us that the swan song is already sounding throughout the initial two verses, although it has not yet been named as such in the text; upon repetition of this same music (with some variations), its identity as a swan song is made explicit. Hensel stitches together her barcarolle-swan song in part by means of a traditional musical emblem of death in music, a pattern almost as pedigreed as the metaphors

Heine condemns to death: the *lamento* descending tetrachord both in its diatonic and chromatic guises and the ascending chromatic tetrachord. Chromatic scales, wrote the Thuringian theorist-astronomer-composer Sethus Calvisius (1556-1615) in 1592, are most apt "wann man eine traurig Music machen will" (when one wishes to make sad music),[29] and thereafter we find chromatic scales couched within the interval of a fourth in thousands of compositions.[30] The descending forms of this figure are familiar from Monteverdi's "Lamento della Ninfa," from Purcell's lament "When I am laid in earth" at the end of *Dido and Aeneas*, and many other examples, including Schubert's instrumental self-elegies in the *Quartettsatz* in C minor and the G-flat major Impromptu for piano, Op. 90, no. 3. The rising chromatic scale (the *passus duriusculus*, or "harsh steps, harsh passage") resounds throughout the Act 2 finale of *Don Giovanni* and dominates Schubert's "Gruppe aus dem Tartarus," not to mention all the instances in Bach's cantatas, such as the ascending chromatic tetrachords at the words "Hat dir dein Sünd' vergeben" in the chorus "Nun lob', mein' Seel', den Herren" from Cantata BWV 28 (*Gottlob! nun geht das Jahr zu Ende*). Horror at impending death is its signification in many such famous instances, and is so again here, but in very distinctive guise. Unlike the earlier manifestations as Furies and denizens of hell in Gluck, Mozart, and elsewhere, in which rising chromaticism clouds the key and is overtly powerful, here, the terror and tension are cloaked in a context of wistfulness, resignation, beauty.[31]

In Hensel's song, the figure is first hinted incompletely, almost imperceptibly, and then appears in the following forms, the same four for each of the two musical stanzas:

1) its descending diatonic form in mm. 5-8 and again in mm. 31-34, temporarily halted in place; when the B-flat third pitch is repeated four times over two measures;
2) a complete adumbration of its rising chromatic form in mm. 11-14 and again in mm. 38-41;
3) an incomplete descending version in the bass of mm. 16-18 and mm. 43-45, on the downbeats and mid-measure points;
4) A complete descending version in the implied inner voice of the left hand, off the main beats, in mm. 21-23 and mm. 48-50.

None of these versions are the same, and they are each separated from one another by at least a measure or two in the piano. Nor do these tetrachords fall at the same place in the phrase: the first ushers in the second phrase in each musical stanza and underlays most of it; the second begins in the last half of the third phrase and bridges the gap between the third and fourth phrases; the third begins right before the end of the fourth phrase and carries over into the beginning of the fifth phrase; and the last one is couched within the elongated repetition of the last two lines of the text. Hensel is being too subtle to place this poem over a ground bass that would call attention to strict patterning from the outset, a pattern in which the bass formula and the harmonies are the same each time, and the challenge is in fashioning melodic embroidery above and around the serial repetitions. Instead, here each version of the lamento gesture has its own configuration while stemming from the same familiar historical pattern, just as the falling star, falling blossoms, diving swan, and dying-away song are like, yet varied manifestations of death. The initial bass motion in the song happens in mm. 3-4 beneath the word "herunter," the first hint that in this world, everything falls, everything goes under to its destruction. That motion takes us away from the tonic G pitch in the bass for the first time and consists of just the pitches G F E-flat, flowing by before we can register the fragment as, possibly, a truncated hint of a tetrachord (Ex. 1).

Example 1, Fanny Hensel, "Schwanenlied," Op. 1, no. 1, mm. 3-4. Reproduced from *Fanny Hensel, Lieder Op. 1. Op, 7 für Singstimme und Klavier* (Boosey & Hawkes/Bote & Bock, n.d.)

It is also typical of Hensel in that, while G minor is established both by the arpeggiated G minor triads in the piano and the vocal line, the lowered seventh degree and minor dominant triad in m. 3 give the first phrase a modal tinge; if the F-sharp leading tone reappears in mm. 4-5 both in the piano and the singer's part, we are nonetheless already inducted into this composer's customary tonal fluidity. Alternation between the raised and natural versions of the seventh pitch of the G minor scale are rife thereafter.

As we go from one manifestation to the next, we become increasingly aware of their signification. Beginning with the bar in the piano that carries us from the first phrase to the second, from lines 1-2 to lines 3-4 of the poem, Hensel gives us the diatonic version of the lamento tetrachord in mm. 5-8, complete this time although paused in place by repetition of the third pitch B-flat (D beneath the dominant chord of a half-cadence / C / B-flat sustained through two bars of I and V in a brief emphasis on E-flat major / and finally, A as V of D minor/major); we note the semitone between B-flat and A as the bottom half of the tetrachord, with the quasi-Phrygian progression from E-flat to D minor—the dominant key in minor mode (Ex. 2).

The turn to the heightened submediant harmony E-flat where we expect G minor beautifully underscores, especially with its change of mode to major for the first time in the song, the designation of the star as the metaphor for love; the call for newly

Example 2, Fanny Hensel, "Schwanenlied," Op. 1, no. 1, mm. 5-9. Reproduced from *Fanny Hensel, Lieder Op. 1. Op, 7 für Singstimme und Klavier* (Boosey & Hawkes/Bote & Bock, n.d.).

softer dynamics demarcates it as such even more. In this passage, the E-flat B-flat harmonies are wonderfully troubled by C-sharp and G-sharp, dissonant neighbors to D and A, as we go through D minor to the cadence on D major. Cross-relations abound in this song, in which nothing is truly simple, not love, not language, not music.

As the apple blossoms and leaves fall in mm. 11-14, the bass inches up the length of an ascending chromatic tetrachord until we arrive at tonic G minor on the downbeat of m. 14 (D / E-flat / E-natural / F / F-sharp / G), heightening F major and G minor harmonies along the sequential way (see Ex. 3).

Ascending versions of a chromatic tetrachord or chromatic scale are usually drenched in tension; as the apple blossoms fall, we hear premonitions of death to come. When this same music recurs at the beginning of the final stanza ("Es ist so still und dunkel, *verweht ist Blatt und Blüth*'"), it fulfills the prophecy of dissolution and vanishment we have already heard in the song's first half and paves the way for the two final manifestations of the descending bass.

Hensel repeats the ostinato G in the bass for two-and-a-half bars (mm. 14-16) before leaping up to a higher register for the pitch F that turns the chromatic motion downwards (G in the lower bass / F / E-natural / E-flat underpinning an augmented sixth chord / D) (see Ex. 4).

Example 3, Fanny Hensel, "Schwanenlied," Op. 1, no. 1, mm. 11-14. Reproduced from *Fanny Hensel, Lieder Op. 1. Op, 7 für Singstimme und Klavier* (Boosey & Hawkes/Bote & Bock, n.d.)

Example 4, Fanny Hensel, "Schwanenlied," Op. 1, no. 1, mm. 16-18. Reproduced from *Fanny Hensel, Lieder Op. 1. Op, 7 für Singstimme und Klavier* (Boosey & Hawkes/Bote & Bock, n.d.)

Comprehending Heine in Fanny Hensel's "Schwanenlied"

Example 5, Fanny Hensel, "Schwanenlied," Op. 1, no. 1, mm. 20-24. Reproduced from *Fanny Hensel, Lieder Op. 1. Op, 7 für Singstimme und Klavier* (Boosey & Hawkes/Bote & Bock, n.d.)

Here, the alternating pitches F-natural and F-sharp we have noticed before actually clash in m. 16; for such a wistful, mellifluous song, it is shot through with subtle dissonance and disturbance. Finally, the last manifestation of the lamento tetrachord is a fully-fledged chromatic version in the *inner* voices of mm. 21-23 (G / F-sharp / F-natural / E-natural / E-flat / D) as Hensel repeats the last two lines of stanza two and stanza four in a manner that transgresses her previous tidy four-bar phrases (Ex. 5).

Not only is the chromatic descent placed on weak beats until the very end but the two implicit levels—one on the stronger downbeat and mid-measure beats, the other higher and chromatic—are drawn closer and closer throughout the phrase until finally they merge on D.

Notice the increasing intensity as we go from one statement to another of the tetrachord: the closer we come to the statement of dissolution and loss, the more chromaticized the figure becomes. That the last most intense statement is couched in the inner voices and echoed between them (but not completely), with echoes between the left and right hands for the pitches F-sharp and F-natural—again, those two pitches—paves the way for the surprise at the end, which is another antique gesture: the Baroque Picardy third close of each musical strophe on a wonderfully blurred G *major*, blurred by means of the minor mode's flatted sixth sounding with and over the tonic pedal tone (Ex. 6).

175

Example 6, Fanny Hensel, "Schwanenlied," Op. 1, no. 1, mm. 24-27. Reproduced from *Fanny Hensel, Lieder Op. 1. Op, 7 für Singstimme und Klavier* (Boosey & Hawkes/Bote & Bock, n.d.)

At first, we think that the Picardy third cadence in mm. 24-27—and it is a completed cadence that divides the song into two halves—is a response, via this unexpected lightening and brightening of the music, to the winds' play, but we are forced to rethink the matter at song's end, in the wake not only of recurrence but of variation. The last half is reserved for the swan and for the summation of all these disappearances: the heavens, Nature, and the symbolic swan. The heightening of the E-flat major harmony from mm. 6-7 is now even softer, *pianissimo* rather than *piano*, as the swan goes on its way to watery death—and the "Fluthengrab" is unforgettable. One of Hensel's signature maneuvers in song is to stop at some point near the end, here at the close of Heine's third stanza, by way of an arpeggiated chord that wafts upwards and is then arrested on a fermata. The D minor harmony in m. 34 becomes D major in mm. 35-36, with the C-sharp neighbor-note/leading tone to D lending its slight dissonant tincture, defining the crucial pitch C more sharply at the peak of the ascent (Ex. 7).

Example 7, Fanny Hensel, "Schwanenlied," Op. 1, no. 1, mm. 34-35. Reproduced from *Fanny Hensel, Lieder Op. 1. Op, 7 für Singstimme und Klavier* (Boosey & Hawkes/Bote & Bock, n.d.)

Try to imagine this evanescent wafting upwards—not a descent into a musical grave, but something that vanishes into the empyrean—without the C-sharps and you will realize how essential they are. At its peak on the single dominant pitch D in m. 36, the song falls momentarily silent, and we wait, our breaths held, for what will follow.

In both halves of the song, Hensel only gives us the words of stanza one and stanza three once, but she repeats the last two lines of stanzas two and four ("Es kommen die neckenden Lüfte / und treiben damit ihr Spiel," "der Stern ist knisternd zerstoben, / verklungen das Schwanenlied") in an extraordinary elongation each time; seven-bar phrases are hardly the norm. The octave leap to high G in the vocal line for the "Lüfte" in stanza two becomes the more tragic emphasis on the verb "zer-*sto*-ben" (note the word-music sizzle of "knisternd zerstoben") in stanza four: this is the climax of each half of the song. The breezes in the extended cadence in mm. 20-24 are repetitive (equivalent puffs of wind); in stanza 4, the song dies away by the same stages, "verklungen" prolonged and attenuated en route to its end.

It matters that these are antique gestures, these *lamento* tetrachords and Picardy thirds, and that they are couched within a Romantic chromatic vocabulary, complete with Fanny's signature clouding of the tonic key. What Heine gives us are metaphors he ostensibly tries to kill so that they may not be resurrected by the "Mondscheinpoeten" he derided, but he encloses them in a poem both beautiful and powerful: the metaphors paradoxically live on in the same poem in which they supposedly die. In Hensel's imaginative rendering, we hear the beauty of a mellifluous lament in minor *and* the singer's metamorphosis into song as it disappears in major mode. The flatted sixth tincture of minor in the interlude/postlude means that neither G minor nor G major is "pure"—and how appropriate that is for Heine, for whom nothing was monotonal. This conclusion always reminds me of "Auf dem Wasser zu singen," whose every musical strophe culminates in the hard-won victory of parallel major mode, when we have glided and swayed and danced our way through music mostly in A-flat minor en route to reconciliation with the thought of death in A-flat major at the close—but Schubert and Stolberg are more optimistic, more rooted, than Heine and Hensel. She postpones that last brief instant of *lieto fine*, of the Baroque ending, until the final moment and even then retains a wisp of cloud to darken the close.[32]

In other words, Fanny made of this song the perfect crossroads at which her fondness for barcarolles, her love of Bach, and her idiosyncratic treatment of tonality could come together in a swan song that rebels against death and disappearance, makes of it something beautiful. I remember this song each time I think of her early death and what we might have had if she had been granted a longer period in which to claim her rights as a composer—but the riches we have from her are considerable. To borrow from Schubert's "Das Lied im Grünen," D. 917 (it too can be considered a swan song), she made ample use of her "green season" while it lasted. If there is something unbearably poignant about the fact that her Op. 1, no. 1 is a swan song, it is also, so I choose to think, a statement that her first foray into print was worthy of immortality."

1. Adolf Bartels, from "Heine der Dichter und Macher seines Ruhms" in *Heinrich Heine. Auch ein Denkmal* (Dresden: C. A. Koch, 1906), 135-136. "'Du bist wie eine Blume' kommt uns Deutschen orientalisch-sentimental vor, wir haben der jugendlichen Schönheit gegenüber die unmittelbarere Empfindung, daß ihre Reinheit gar nicht beschmutzt werden kann, aber das Gedicht ist dennoch einfach-schön." In another example of utter misprision, Bartels declares that "Sie liebten sich beide, doch keiner" is "endlich einmal ein gelungenes schlichtes Gedicht" (135).
2. See the author's "Song, sex, society, and 'Du bist wie eine Blume'" in *Heinrich Heine and the Lied* (Cambridge: Cambridge University Press, 2007), 266-316.
3. R. Larry Todd, *Fanny Hensel: The Other Mendelssohn* (Oxford & New York: Oxford University Press, 2010), 109.
4. Sebastian Hensel, *The Mendelssohn Family (1729-1847)*, vol. 1 (London: 1882), 197. "Heine ist hier und gefällt mir garnicht; er ziert sich. Wenn er sich gehn liesse, müsste er der liebenswürdigste ungezogene Mensch sein, der je über die Schnur hieb, wenn er sich im Ernst zusammennähme, würde ihm der Ernst auch wohl anstehen, denn er hat ihn, aber er ziert sich sentimental, er ziert sich geziert, spricht ewig von sich und sieht dabei die Menschen an, ob sie ihn ansehn."
5. Ibid., 197, following directly from the words above. "Sind Ihnen aber Heine's Reisebilder aus Italien vorgekommen? Darin sind wieder prächtige Sachen. Wenn man ihn auch zehnmal verachten möchte, so zwingt er einen doch zum elften Mal zu bekennen, er sei ein Dichter, ein Dichter! Wie klingen ihm die Worte, wie spricht ihn die Natur an, wie sie es nur den Dichter thut."
6. See Fanny Hensel, *Briefe aus Paris an ihre Familie 1835*, ed. Hans-Günter Klein (Wiesbaden: Reichert Verlag, 2007), 56. In a letter to Rebecka Dirichlet of 17 August 1835, she wrote, "Heyne ist hier, den suchen wir aber zu vermeiden." When she refers to Rebecka in the next sentence as "Jedes Pfund ein Engel," she is referring to a letter Heine wrote 6 September 1829 to Gustav Droysen in which he says that he has at "den Palazzo Bartholdi; der Stadträtin [Lea Mendelssohn Bartholdy] lasse ich mich ehrfurchtsvoll empfehlen, mit etwas weniger Ehrfurcht grüße ich Fräulein Fannys schöne Augen, die zu den schönsten gehören, die ich jemals gesehen. Die dicke Rebekkla, ja, grüßen Sie mir auch diese dicke Person, das liebe Kind, so lieb, so hübsch, so gut, jedes Pfund ein Engel." See ibid., 89.
7. Marcia Citron, trans. and ed., *The Letters of Fanny Hensel to Felix Mendelssohn* (New York: Pendragon Press, 1987), 128.
8. R. Larry Todd, *Fanny Hensel*, 221.
9. Ibid., 198. Heine entitled the poem "Wahrhaftig," no. XX in the *Romanzen*. See *Säkularausgabe*, vol. 1: *Gedichte 1812-1827* (Berlin: Akademie-Verlag and Paris: Editions du CNRS, 1979), 56.
10. Eberhard Galley, *Heinrich Heines Werk im Urteil seiner Zeitgenossen, vol. 1: Rezensionen und Notizen zu Heines Werken von 1821 bis 1831* (Hamburg: Hoffman und Campe, Heinrich Heine Verlag, 1981), 170-171.
11. Anonymous, "Briefe einer Dame über die Almanachsliteratur des Jahres 1825. 3 Brief" in the Leipzig *Literarisches Conversations-Blatt*, no. 280 (6 December 1824): 1,118-1,119, in Eberhard Galley, ibid., 172. See Die Heimkehr XXXV, "Ich rief den Teufel und er kam" in *Säkularausgabe*, vol. 1: *Gedichte 1812-1827* (Berlin: Akademie-Verlag and Paris: Editions du CNRS, 1979), 109.
12. Adolf Peters, "Rezension zu Gedichte und Tragodien, nebst einem lyrischen Intermezzo" in *Der Gesellschafter*, cited in Eberhard Galley, ibid., 174-175.
13. Heinrich Heine, *Lyrisches Intermezzo LIX*: "Es fällt ein Stern herunter" in *Säkularausgabe*, vol. 1: *Gedichte 1812-1827*, 87-88.
14. Susan Gritton, soprano, and Eugene Asti, piano, *Fanny Mendssohn: Lieder* on Hyperion CDA67110 (1999), notes, 17.
15. Laura Hofrichter, *Heinrich Heine, Biographie seiner Dichtung* (Göttingen: Vandenhoeck und Ruprecht, 1966), 33-4.
16. Klaus Briegleb, ed., *Heinrich Heine. Sämtliche Schriften*, vol. 1 (Munich: Hanser, 1968), 713, 676-7.
17. Michael Perraudin, *Heinrich Heine. Poetry in Context: A Study of the Buch der Lieder* (Oxford, New York, Munich: Berg, 1989), 48.

18 Anthony Phelan, *Reading Heinrich Heine* (Cambridge: Cambridge University Press, 2007), 68-71.
19 Ibid., 69.
20 Ibid., 71.
21 "It is no ordinary flimsy wing which will bear me/Half-bard, half-bird, through the liquid air, / Nor shall I longer remain on the earth, /But, grown too large for envy, I shall leave/ / its cities. I, who am of the blood of poor parents, /I, who come at your command, /my beloved Maecenas, shall not die, /nor be confined by the Stygian wave. / / Already, even now, rough skin is forming/ on my legs, my upper part is changing / into a white bird and smooth feathers/are sprouting along my fingers and shoulders./ /Soon more famous than Icarus, son of Daedalus, /I shall be a harmonious bird and visit the shores/of the moaning Bosphorus, the Gaetulian Syrtes,/and the Hyperborean plains. / /The Colchian will know me, and the Dacian who / pretends not to fear a cohort of Marsians, the / Geloni at the ends of the earth, the cultured/Iberian and the Rhone-swigger will learn me by heart. / /Let there be no dirges or squalid mourning / or lamentation at my corpseless funeral / Check your cries of grief and do not trouble / with the empty honor of a tomb." See Horace (Quintus Horatius Flaccus), *Odes II: Vatis amici*, trans. David West (Oxford: Oxford University Press, 1998): 142-45.
22 William Butler Yeats, *The Collected Poems* (New York: Macmillan, 1956): 196.
23 Edmund Spenser "The Ruines of Time" in *Complaints*, ed. W.L. Renwick (London: Scholartis, 1928): 22-3. "Upon that famous Riuers further shore, / There stood a snowie Swan of heauenly hiew, / And gentle kinde, as euer Fowle afore; / A fairer one in all the goodlie criew/ Of white Strimonian brood might no man view: / There he most sweetly sung the prophecie / Of his owne death in dolefull Elegie. / At last, when all his mourning melodie / He ended ha, that both the shores resounded, / Feeling the fit that him forewarnd to die, / With loftie flight aboue the earth he bounded, / And out of sight to highest heauuen mounted: / Where now he is become an heauenly signe / There now the ioy is his, here sorrow mine." See also Friedrich Hölderlin, *Poems and Fragments*, trans. Michael Hamburger (Cambridge: Cambridge University Press, 1980): 340. Some of the most beautiful swans in all of poetry reside in the first stanza of "Hälfte des Lebens:" "Mit gelben Birnen hänget/Und voll mit wilden Rosen/Das Land in den See,/Ihr holden Schwäne,/Und trunken von Küssen/Tunkt ihr das Haupt/Ins heilignüchterne Wasser" (ibid., 370). See Michael Jakob, *Schwanengefahr: Das lyrische Ich im Zeichen des Schwans* (Munich: Hanser Verlag, 2000) for more on this subject.
24 Todd, *Fanny Hensel*, 237. See also Sebastian Hensel, *Die Familie Mendelssohn 1729-1847. Nach Briefen und Tagebüchern*, vol. 2 (Berlin: B. Behr's Verlag, 1907), 70. "An der Rückseite des Berges, der die Burg trägt, liegt ein prächtiger schwarz-grüner Alpensee, mit Schwänen, die sich auf dem dunkeln Wasser wie schwimmende Sternchen ausnehmen, dahinter mehrere Schichten hoher und höchster Berge (nicht Herrschaften)."
25 Fanny to Rebecka, November 11, 1839 in Hensel, *Briefe aus Venedig und Neapel an ihre Familie in Berlin 1839/40*, ed. Hans-Günter Klein (Wiesbaden: Reichert, 2004), 43.
26 Charles Burney, *The Present State of Music in France and Italy* (London: T. Becket and Co. Strand, 1773), 144.
27 Hermann Mendel, continued by August Reissmann, *Musikalisches Conversations-Lexikon. Eine Ecyklopädie der gesammten musikalischen Wissenschaften für Gebildete aller Stände*, vol. 1 (Berlin: Robert Oppenheim, 1880), 451.
28 See the author's "Swan Songs: Schubert's 'Auf dem Wasser zu singen'" in *Nineteenth-Century Music Review*, vol. 5, no. 2 (2008): 1-42.
29 Sethus Calvisius, *Melopoiia sive melodiae condendae ratio* (Erfurt, 1592).
30 See Peter Williams, *The Chromatic Fourth during Four Centuries of Music* (Oxford: Clarendon Press, 1997) for a vast array of examples. See also Ellen Rosand, "The Descending Tetrachord: An Emblem of Lament" in *The Musical Quarterly*, vol. 65, no. 3 (1979): 346-359.
31 See the author's "Reentering Mozart's Hell: Schubert's 'Gruppe aus dem Tartarus', D. 583" in *Drama in the Music of Franz Schubert*, ed. by Joe Davies and James William Sobaskie (Woodbridge, Suffolk: The Boydell Press, 2019), 171-201.

32 I sometimes wonder what Hensel would have thought of the after-life of the lamento tetrachord she deploys to such melancholy effect in this song. Only today, I read in *The New Yorker* a review by Alex Ross of Kate Soper's opera *The Romance of the Rose*: "We hear troubadour and madrigal strains, Baroque arias, modernistic sound labyrinths, punk-rock squalls, and torch songs fit for a Lynchian lounge. To execute the latter, Soper brings in Pleasure and Idleness, who vamp their way through an insinuating showstopper *that rests on a four-note descending bass, in the tradition of the Baroque lament* [italics mine]." See Alex Ross, "Medieval Romances by Kate Soper and Richard Wagner" in *The New Yorker* (March 6, 2023): 72.

13. "OTHER" MENDELSSOHNS: THE *LIED OHNE WORTE* OP. 19[B] NO. 2

Angela R. Mace

There's no reason to believe that Felix Mendelssohn Bartholdy was not the composer of the *Lied ohne Worte* op. 19[b] no. 2. However, murky autograph sources and a particularly Henselian musical marker do merit further exploration. This essay will present the context and documented facts surrounding the composition of op. 19[b] no. 2, identify a Henselian musical marker, and position this analysis within the broader discussion of the siblings' co-created style.

A GIFT FOR REBECKA

The earliest version of op. 19[b] no. 2 was a Christmas gift that Mendelssohn sent to his younger sister, Rebecka, in 1830. We have evidence that it was a gift for her via a letter he wrote to his mother, Fanny, and Rebecka from Rome, Italy on December 14.

> To you, dearest Beckchen,
> I'm sending you just the little song from London, which you probably remember from when we were sick with the measles; ... which was the only thing that went through my head when I was sick in England, and you praised it and no one else liked it (although no one else had heard it) so I wrote it down for you yesterday, and here it is.[1]

Even though this work was clearly written down in December 1830, this letter indicates that it had been in Mendelssohn's ear for about a year. Mendelssohn had been laid up in London after a carriage accident in the Fall of 1829, which caused him to miss Fanny's wedding. He had returned home in time for Christmas in 1829, but then remained in Berlin for the remainder of the Spring. In March, Rebecka contracted the measles, and even though she was quarantined, Felix caught it as well.[2] Presumably, they would have been isolated together at that point, and the two must have shared the tune then. This detail explains why Mendelssohn refers to it as "the little song from London" even though Mendelssohn did not travel to London in 1830. Thus, a year after his carriage accident, and in a nod to the misery he had shared with Rebecka earlier that year, Mendelssohn wrote down the work as Christmas gift for his sister and sent it along with several other gifts to his family from Rome.

DATES AND SOURCES

In the letter cited above, Mendelssohn stated he'd written down the *Lied* the day before, which would imply December 13, since the letter is dated December 14. However, the work is generally dated to December 11, as evidenced in a note from Mendelssohn's pocket calendar on that day, as cited by R. Larry Todd,[3] and codified in the definitive catalog of Mendelssohn's works by Ralf Wehner, excerpted and translated below.

U 80 Song without Words in A minor, op. 19[b] no. 2
Date of Composition: 11 December 1830

Sources
Autographs: (a) *Lied,* Andante, 11 December 1830; Location unknown ("Standort unbekannt"). (b) Andante espressivo, Proofs for Novello, [June 1832]; US-SM.
Copy: *Lied,* Andante, 78 bars, in an unknown hand (often mistaken as the autograph) copied from Autograph of 11 December 1830; US-NH, Misc. Ms. 423.[4]

Here, Wehner asserts that the 78-bar version in possession of the Yale University Music Library (US-NH, Misc. Ms. 423) is copied from Autograph (a) in an unknown hand. No evidence is offered for how we can be sure that the Yale source, if it is in fact a copy, accurately transmits Autograph (a). The second half of the Yale source bears no resemblance to the 91-bar final version of the *Lied* that Mendelssohn published in 1832, which means we don't know if the ending we recognize from the published version existed in Autograph (a), or if it was composed between 1830 and 1832.[5] Todd differs from Wehner in his analysis, saying that "A few articulation and dynamics markings, and the date at the end of the manuscript, are in a second, unidentified hand" rather than identifying the entire Yale source as a copy in an unknown hand.[6] Further complicating matters is that the Yale source is unsigned, which I've demonstrated elsewhere is telltale evidence that a manuscript is not Felix Mendelssohn's.[7] Without being able to compare Autograph (a) to the Yale source, these and many other questions must remain unanswered for now; notably, Wehner does not identify Autograph (a) as "verschollen" ("lost") but rather "Standort unbekannt" ("Location unknown") which means it could still exist. Hopefully it will come to light in the future to enable a more complete analysis.

"Other" Mendelssohns: the *Lied ohne Worte* op. 19[b] no. 2

HENSELIAN MUSICAL MARKER

Hensel's style, at risk of grossly over-simplifying the matter, is generally recognized as more dissonant than Mendelssohn's. This is not to say that Mendelssohn avoided dissonance, but rather that Hensel foregrounded dissonance. She was especially fond of Major and minor second intervals, whether voiced open or closed, and often wound them around a pedal tone. Hensel's Piano Sonata in G minor (1843) offers a useful example; the example shown here (Ex. 1) is taken from the final cadence in the first movement (there is no double bar present, as the first movement transitions directly into the second).

Example 1, Fanny Hensel, Sonata in G minor (1843), bars 129–34, all a's marked with arrows.

Hensel tended to close her minor works in the major mode and this movement continues that pattern.[8] Crunchy diminished seventh chords (vii°7/I – I) invert sequentially down the keyboard. She avoids the third in all but one of the diminished chords until she reaches the lowest instance. Only then does she prominently plant the A, growling tenaciously in the bass directly next to the G before releasing it to the exuberance of the major-mode tonic cadence.

Mendelssohn employs similar dissonance handling in the coda to his *Lied ohne Worte,* op. 19[b] no. 2, where fully diminished seventh chords are activated over an extended plagal cadence. The pedal tone on A rumbles in the bass as it clashes with fully diminished seventh chords spaced widely—up to four octaves—above it. These strikingly open, grating harmonies create a bleak sense of dislocation as the tritones and half steps waver in the empty space, both physically and tonally; the diminished seventh chord in bar 80 (Ex. 2a) is missing its root and third (vii°4/3/iv). "Bleak" and "grating" are not words one typically uses to describe Mendelssohn's music, which is one reason this moment strikes my ear as more typical of his sister's style.[9]

Mendelssohn, *Lied ohne Worte,* op. 19[b] no. 2

Example 2a, bars 80–81, vii°4/3/iv, spaced four octaves above pedal tone A, missing root (c#) and third (e), the b-flat falls to the a.

Example 2b, bars 84–90, vii°6/5 /i, the g-sharp rises eventually to the a in response to the b-flat in bars 80–81; by bar 88, the tendency tones have stopped ringing, leaving the cadence, i, sounding hollow.

While Hensel probably would have chosen to end this work in the major mode—as she does her "Easter Sonata" (1828), also in a minor—Mendelssohn closes it in the minor mode.

CO-CREATED STYLE

The coda analyzed here from op. 19[b] no. 2 is, of course, in the second half of the work. That is, in the half for which we do not have a known autograph source since the Yale source has a different ending. This is where doubt may creep in to fuel ideas that perhaps Hensel wrote this part of the work. It doesn't help dispel this notion that the next work in the Wehner catalogue, U 81, is an *Andante maestoso* in F Major, which Wehner subtitled "Gemeinschaftskomposition mit Fanny Hensel" ("Collaborative composition with Fanny Hensel"). Mendelssohn included a short sketch of the *Andante Maestoso* in his letter to his father on December 11, 1830 (yes, the same date as the presumed autograph manuscript of op. 19[b] no. 2) and added "Fanny would like to do the second part" ("Fanny mag den zweithen Theil dazu machen").[10] There is no evidence that the same applied to the second half of op. 19[b] no. 2, as the "unknown" hand in the Yale source is not Hensel's. There is also no evidence to support the idea that Hensel contributed the second half between 1830 and 1832.

The larger context around this question comes from the long-standing debate concerning to whom we owe credit for the creation of the Mendelssohnian style. This question was framed early on—even during the composers' lifetimes[11]—by debating whether or not some of Mendelssohn's works were written by Hensel, beyond the few instances that were authorized by the composers themselves: Mendelssohn's op. 8 (1826–27) and op. 9 (1830). I've shown elsewhere that the Mendelssohnian style belonged to both composers, and that neither composer would have existed without the other.¹² At the same time, Hensel and Mendelssohn did develop unique approaches to their shared style, especially as they went down separate paths after 1829. Mendelssohn embarked on his *Bildungsreise* and an international performing career, while Hensel committed herself to marriage, motherhood, and concert organizing. The siblings surprised even themselves at how close they remained as composers despite these challenges. Some allusions extended even to the melody, texture, and structure of a work, as Todd points out:

> On Felix's wedding day, March 28, 1837, Fanny composed an Andante […] in B-flat major, with striking similarities to Felix's prelude [in B-flat major, op. 35 no. 6]. In June, Felix was writing Fanny about the coincidental similarities between the two and thanking her for "your Prelude No. 6 in B-flat major to my Fugue in B-flat, for it really is the same inside and out, and delights me by the neat coincidence. Is it not strange that sometimes musical ideas seem to fly around in the air and come to earth here and there?"¹³

I, for one, do not think it strange at all to find moments of similarity in the works of Hensel and Mendelssohn given the intensity of their engagement as emerging composers. However, the true similarities between the two works Todd cites here are definitely uncanny, given that there was no knowledge of the other's work at the time of composition. As the two composers drifted further apart, both geographically and emotionally, these moments of resonance kept them close as creative kindred spirits. Now that we have the advantage of knowing the entire *oeuvre* of both composers, we can set their scores side-by-side on our music stands, study them closely, and play them repeatedly. Thus it happens that we are able to identify these moments when the inflection of one Mendelssohn crystalizes for a moment in the work of the other Mendelssohn, whether the "other Mendelssohn" is Fanny or Felix.

---

1   Felix Mendelssohn Bartholdy, *Sämtliche Briefe, Bd. 2,* ed. and comm. Anja Morgenstern and Uta Wald (Kassel: Bärenreiter, 2009), 170. All translations by the author unless otherwise noted. "Dir, [lieb]stes Beckchen, schicke ich nur das kleine Lied aus London, dessen Du Dich wohl noch aus der Masernzeit erinnerst; … Ende, als das einzige, was mir bei meiner Krankenzeit in England durch den Kopf gegangen ist, und Du lobtest es und es … keinem Andern gefallen hat, (es hat es auch noch kein Andrer gehört) so schrieb ich es Dir gestern auf, und da ist es."
2   R. Larry Todd, *Felix Mendelssohn: A Life in Music* (Oxford: Oxford University Press, 2003), 226.
3   Felix Mendelssohn Bartholdy, *Lieder ohne Worte,* ed. R. Larry Todd (Kassel: Bärenreiter, 2009), 189.
4   Ralf Wehner, *Felix Mendelssohn Bartholdy: Thematisches-systematisches Verzeichnis der musikalischen Werke* (Leipzig: Breitkopf und Härtel, 2009). 317.
5   To compare this early 1830 version to the final published version of 1832, see Todd's edition cited in fn. 3, where Todd provides a first publication of the full 78-bar version of op. 19[b] no. 2 (155–57).
6   Todd includes scans of the first two pages of the source in the front matter to his 2009 edition (XIV-XV), but one can access all four pages here: Richard Bousey, Yale University Library On-

line Exhibitions, "Boundaries of Romanticism." https://onlineexhibits.library.yale.edu/s/boundaries-of-romanticism/item/4412#?c=&m=&s=&cv=&xywh=-321%2C-85%2C2641%2C1686, accessed 29 February 2024.
7   Angela Mace Christian, "The Easter Sonata of Fanny Mendelssohn (1828)," *Journal of Musicological Research*, 41/3 (2022): 182–209.
8   See also the Finale of Hensel's *Ostersonate* ("Easter Sonata") written in 1828 just 1-2 years before Mendelssohn's op. 19[b] no. 2, for a more near-contemporary example. The parallels are a little less cleanly cut there, but her dissonance handling in that work is remarkably prescient of her Sonata in G minor. For more see Mace Christian, "The Easter Sonata" (2022).
9   There are, of course, notable exceptions such as the curse that prefaces the Overture to Mendelssohn's oratorio *Elijah,* op. 70 (1846).
10 Mendelssohn Bartholdy, *Sämtliche Briefe, Bd. 2* (2009), 161–62.
11 Hensel wrote to Mendelssohn on February 1, 1847 to share that she'd received a letter from Vienna asking if some of Mendelssohn's works were by Hensel. Quoted in Cornelia Bartsch, *Fanny Hensel geb. Mendelssohn Bartholdy: Musik als Korrespondenz* (Kassel: Furore, 2007), 78.
12 Angela R. Mace, "Fanny Hensel, Felix Mendelssohn Bartholdy, and the Formation of the Mendelssohnian Style" (PhD diss, Duke University, 2013).
13 Todd (2003), 333–34.

IV. MENDELSSOHN'S CIRCLE

14. "THE WOMAN FOR THE NEW ERA"?: JOHANNA KINKEL'S MUSICAL EXILE IN LONDON

Monika Hennemann

"So reich mit Talenten begabt und doch in keinem Fach ein Genie"
—Emanuel Geibel

Despite the recent upsurge in interest in 19th-century female musicians, the modest but multi-faceted achievements of the Bonn composer, pianist, conductor, teacher, and writer Johanna Mockel, married Matthieux, remarried Kinkel (1810–1858) have received relatively little attention in German scholarship, and even less in English.[1] The latter is all the more surprising in that she spent the last years of her life in London,[2] where she died in 1858 after a mysterious defenestration that might have formed the subject of a short story by Conan Doyle.[3]

Kinkel was, to quote Emanuel Geibel's somewhat acidic assessment, "so richly endowed with talent that she was a genius in no field."[4] She remains best known, in so far as she is known at all, for her contributions to the Lied. But her compositions are far from being confined to parlor pieces – they extend to two fairly ambitious *Liederspiele*, which still remain unpublished and unperformed. Her works were respectfully reviewed in the contemporary press, but they have so far resisted rehabilitation in the present day. I do not propose to offer a re-evaluation of her music here, although such an exercise would be well worth undertaking, but rather to concentrate on her activities in London, which form an illustrative example of what would now be called a "portfolio career." Her British pursuits were also of significance for the bourgeoning sphere of public music education, and of some tangential importance to the history of musical biography.

A brief biographical sketch of this unusual woman reveals that she was not only one of the century's best-connected female musicians, but also one of the most insistent and irritating musical "groupies" that clustered around the Mendelssohn family. Born in Bonn in 1810, Kinkel received a thorough pianistic and artistic education from childhood. In fact, her tuition had been much more extensive than usual for female pupils at the time. Her principal instructor was Beethoven's own teacher, the evidently almost immortal Franz Anton Ries (1755–1846), who significantly outlived his own son, the more celebrated Ferdinand. It was his musical circle that provided the members for a choir Kinkel directed in Bonn between 1829 and 1848, making her one of Germany's first female choral conductors. She even led private performances of operas (by Gluck, Mozart, Spohr, and Weber) and oratorios (by Handel, Mozart, and Pergolesi): a solid foundation for the numerous musical activities that would secure her family's financial survival later in her life. Her heavily chauvinistic critical position was also established early on. In her lecture "Friedrich Chopin als Komponist," she claimed that from her musically orthodox childhood onward "Beethoven reigned as musical god and Rossini as anti-Christ,"[5] a position she subsequently tried to soften in her posthumously published novel *Hans Ibeles in London*.

Her private life developed distinctly less smoothly. In 1832, her parents arranged, indeed forced, her marriage to a bookseller named Johann Paul Mathieux. Not entirely surprisingly, the marriage failed after just a few months, leaving her psychologically and physically shattered. The relationship took many years to disentangle because her estranged husband refused to agree to a divorce.

In the meantime, Kinkel took her fate into her own hands. Frustrated by the usual restrictions that women faced with regard to professional musical activities (including those actively enforced by her own parents), she looked for ways to escape her parochial environment. One promising possibility was to find the patronage of a famous composer. Based on what she regarded as a shared musical taste, she decided to turn to the young Felix Mendelssohn (roughly her coeval), whom she had long admired from afar. She was determined that she was going to make her already famous idol's acquaintance—whether he liked it or not—and her persistence brought its reward.

From her diaries and letters, the story of Kinkel's first personal encounter with Mendelssohn can be clearly reconstructed.[6] When she found out in the summer of 1836 that he was visiting relatives in a village near Frankfurt, she set off on a journey to meet him in person, despite the fact that she did not possess the necessary passport (and would have needed her estranged husband's permission to obtain one).[7] Eventually arriving at her destination after some difficulty, she contacted a number of Mendelssohn's acquaintances in order to obtain an introduction. It was most likely his aunt Dorothea Schlegel who finally initiated a meeting. Kinkel summarized the events in a letter of 5 July 1836, with only a hint of self-awareness: "I went through considerable trouble to meet Felix Mendelssohn in person. He is very reserved, loves solitude, dislikes playing in front of others, and avoids meeting new people as much as possible. But you can't really hold it against him because, as one knows, such a famous man is besieged everywhere by gawkers who steal his time and offer nothing in exchange." Mendelssohn no doubt wanted her to leave him alone. "Even though I had to be truly meddlesome," she added, "I must be excused by my pure enthusiasm for true art, for which I overcame so many obstacles."[8] Purity and truth, as usual, justifies anything.

When they finally met, Mendelssohn nevertheless turned out to be much more accommodating than the pushily intrusive Kinkel could ever have hoped for. He generously offered to play the piano for her. And in order to evaluate her own performance skills, he even agreed to a second meeting in a location with a less inadequate instrument. She managed to impress him with her rendition of Bach's Fugue in E-Flat major and Beethoven's Sonata No. 7, and he advised her to complete her musical education in Berlin, which offered a much wider range of opportunities than Bonn.

At a subsequent meeting, he introduced her to his friend Ferdinand Hiller, whom she described somewhat paradoxically as a "beautiful man of 24 years who was a bit too fat."[9] Hiller invited her into his parents' home, where she was allowed to play on a fine Erard piano. Because Kinkel was painfully aware of what she thought of as her own physical unattractiveness, she employed the strategy of taking along a "stunningly beautiful girl" to these meetings in order to please "the artists' eyes," despite the fact that this beauty was, again according to Kinkel "highly silly and stupifyingly dull."[10] The outcome of the whole episode was hardly an intimate, but nonetheless a long-lasting friendship with Mendelssohn.[11]

Following Mendelssohn's advice (and equipped with a letter of recommendation from him), Kinkel moved to Berlin in November 1836 to study composition and piano performance under Carl Böhmer und Wilhelm Taubert. She financed herself by giving piano lessons – among others, to the daughters of Bettina von Arnim, whom she had befriended. Inspired by the stimulating environment, Kinkel composed numerous songs (published as opp. 6-12)[12] and a few larger-scale works during her Berlin tenure. Some of them were included in Fanny Hensel's "Sonntagsmusiken," where Kinkel also frequently presented solo piano pieces, or performed duets with the hostess.

Although Kinkel was proud of the quality of her Lieder, she was branded a "lady composer" in almost every review, and classified as the creator of tender, emotional, but superficial songs. As a gesture of protest, she cheekily sent her most forthright work, labeled as a "wild drinking song for male choir" to the young Robert Schumann, disguising her first name by providing only the initial. "J. Matthieux" wittily argued in the accompanying letter that, as there were likely to be several contributions by ladies in the next *Musikalische Beilage*, this particular contributor had chosen a very different style in order to provide "some shadow for the moonlight."[13] Her hope thus to establish a presence in a male-dominated sphere had some success: the Berlin critic Ludwig Rellstab did indeed later assume that "J. Matthieux" was male and accordingly addressed her respectfully as "Herr Verfasser," writing: "the undersigned is more than pleased, if his individual opinion has any relevance in this matter, to say that he regards these songs as the most unique and beautiful he has recently become familiar with. He will publish a more specific motivation for his judgment in the music journal 'Iris,' which he edits."[14]

In 1839, Kinkel returned to Bonn, where she continued her musical activities and rewarded Fanny Hensel's support by performing her music in concert. Soon after, she met the theologian, politician, and art historian Gottfried Kinkel, whom she was only able to marry after her divorce was finalized in 1843, and after converting to Protestantism.

Her contact with Mendelssohn continued. They met again (by chance) in 1842 on a Rhine cruise, where the foundation for a collaboration on various opera projects, also involving her husband, was laid. A series of amicable letters was exchanged, but nothing concrete came of the plans. Although Kinkel composed little after the first of her four children had been born in 1844, she continued to provide for the family by teaching and editing. One notable exception in 1848 (after she had joined the "Democratic Party") was a "Demokratenlied" to her on text, which was premiered on 5 December of that year and appeared in print both in the *Bonner Zeitung* and by Sulzbach shortly after.[15] When her husband actively joined that year's revolutionary activities, she took on the role of editor of the democratic *Bonner Zeitung*, but turned down a request by Karl Marx, with whom the Kinkels were closely associated, to act as translator into German of his English texts. We can gather from this that Johanna Kinkel's English must already have been reasonably good, even before the family's move to Britain.

Gottfried fled to London exile in 1850 as a consequence of the uproar surrounding the 1848–49 revolution, in which he played a major role. He was joined by Johanna and the children in January 1851. Gottfried's departure from Germany was noted in Prussia, where for example the influential German diplomat, writer, and biographer Varnhagen von Ense wrote in his diary: "The government is completely beside itself because it is not more feared. For them, that man Kinkel is like a magic spell that renders them powerless; the King especially hates him."[16] Spies were sent to the British capital to collect information about the activities of Kinkel and Marx. The latter had also sought refuge in London with his family in August 1849.

Johanna was to spend the rest of her life in London as teacher, writer, and occasional lecturer, while her husband's own lecturing activities frequently took him away from their new home. He even traveled to America for some months to raise money for the democratic cause (the "German National Loan"), meeting with President Millard Fillmore during his journey. For her part, Johanna founded a children's singing school in London, gave piano lessons, and became especially interested in music history. She devoted much of her time studying in the new reading room of the British Museum, officially opened to the public on 2 May 1857.[17] It was at this point that she was invited to give a series of lectures on music and musicians, including one on Mendelssohn.[18] She wrote: "I have been engaged to give lectures on music, and it seems that I'll do so successfully. I find this satisfying, not mainly because it is more profitable than music lessons, but also because I have discovered my ability at an advanced age to turn to a completely new occupation."[19]

Particularly intriguing were Kinkel's ventures into the field of lecture-recitals, which she assayed in London educational institutions in the mid-1850s—around the same time as William Sterndale Bennett's better known, but not necessarily better, experiments of a similar type.[20] Despite Kinkel's predilection for lecturing extempore, five written examples fortunately have survived, probably because she had intended to publish them, as indeed did happen (albeit posthumously) with her previously mentioned lecture on Chopin.[21] The remaining four are on Mozart, "Beethoven's earliest Sonatas, incl. op. 10," on Mendelssohn, and a "second" lecture on harmony (the first being lost). These were supplemented by a treatise on piano playing, notes on music aesthetics, and (published) criticism on musical life in London. A projected *History of Music*, written in both English and German, remained fragmentary and unfinished, but it is probable that the lectures would have eventually found a place within that volume.

Kinkel's lecture series reflected the growing trend for public education and "self-improvement," and paralleled the development of music as academic discipline. Kinkel's more celebrated predecessors included William Crotch, Professor of Music at Oxford University, and the first speaker on the subject at the Royal Institution (from 1805). He had begun lecturing on music—including live illustrations both at the piano, and, more extravagantly, from an orchestra—at the university in 1798, with the aim of "raising the taste" of his audience. These improving homilies were published in revised form in 1831 with the ornate title *Substance of Several Courses of Lectures on Music*.[22] Kinkel's predecessors additionally included Samuel Wesley (denigrated by the less charitable of his contemporaries as "rambling"), Julius Benedict (not surprisingly on Mendelssohn; printed in 1850), and the aforementioned Sterndale Bennett (on the history of music in general, and also, from 1857, on individual composers such as Bach, Handel and Mozart).[23] It is not unlikely that Kinkel was present at some of these—she must at least have been aware of them. Her most immediate model, however, would likely have been her husband Gottfried Kinkel, who lectured on German language, literature, and cultural history at Hyde Park College in London, and later at Bedford College. And he gave lectures on "public speaking for women," a venture that would no doubt nowadays be characterized as "mansplaining."

Although the exact location of Johanna Kinkel's lectures is unknown, it seems probable that there was a direct connection between the institution that employed her husband and her own activities. And she spoke from a defiantly German standpoint. In her "Lecture on Mendelssohn," we read: "England, which has given a home to Händel, and where Haydn, Mozart, Weber and so many other of our German composers found a glorious reception, has also honoured Mendelssohn as a welcome guest. He spoke with terms of real gratitude of the kindness which he met with in this country, and of the stimulation which his genius received by the splendid performances of his oratorios."[24]

The last three words of her manuscript, "Schluss nach Belieben" (Close ad lib), supports the conjecture that she concluded with a musical performance, possibly even a four-hand rendering of Mendelssohn's *Midsummer Night's Dream* overture together with her son.

The unique and personal lecture on Mendelssohn is at least as noteworthy for its treatment of Fanny as of Felix. In fact, it is one of the first essays known to me that deals with both siblings' lives and artistic endeavors and includes representative musical examples. Of obvious importance for the history of Mendelssohn reception in Britain, and for the history of women in music, it also reveals much about Kinkel herself. A long-forgotten German translation was published in the *Deutsche Revue* of 1902/03, but I have myself made a transcription of the English original, currently in the Stadtbibliothek in Bonn, from which the quotes are taken.[25]

Although two biographies of Felix Mendelssohn had already been published at the time (Lampadius, 1848, and, more importantly for an English audience, Julius Benedict, 1850[26]), recollections of Fanny Hensel were scarce.[27] But nearly a quarter of Kinkel's supposed "Lecture on Felix Mendelssohn" is actually devoted to his sister. This would probably have come as a surprise to listeners, for Fanny's music was little known beyond Berlin, let alone England.

The lecture was given by invitation, and designed for a musically-inclined, upper-middle class London female audience, a clientele that Kinkel's earning power depended upon, but of which she was not, owing to her political bent, particularly fond. In an 1853 essay titled "Musical conditions and German musicians in London,"[28] published in the *Morgenblatt* für *gebildete Leute* in three installments, she bitterly complains about the declining fees offered for music lessons, the necessity of dressing expensively as an entry ticket to cultural events, the prevalence of worthless virtuoso music, and the downright corruption of some musical circles, where addresses of students were openly sold to the highest-bidding follow-on teacher, rather like consumer marketing information today.

Kinkel, of course, emphasized her personal connection with the Mendelssohns, which would no doubt have impressed her audience—they were getting a rare glimpse of the private family behind the public façade, as it were. Her main point of focus is the discussion of the symbiotic musical relationship between Felix and Fanny:

> Never there was between brother and sister a more ardent love, and a stronger influence of the artistical mind. Before Felix published a piece, he always sent it first to Fanny, in order that she might judge it. Any criticism that she might pronounce, would induce him to examine the passage in question, and even to alter it accordingly. She did the same with <u>her</u> compositions, which are very valuable. So great was her discretion however, that as long as she was in her younger years she never would publish a piece with her own name. There have appeared many songs of her in the first collections of her brother, who lent his name to them. [...] After her marriage with the painter <u>Hensel</u> she published several Pianoforte-Pieces with her own name. I will give you proof here of her "songs without words" in order to show you how nearly they are related in style to those of her brother, besides their being the creation of an independent spirit.[29]

For Kinkel, who never in her life found a musical confidante from whom she could draw inspiration, such a close artistic relationship must have seemed enviable—especially in her London exile. Perhaps Kinkel also felt increasingly estranged from her often-absent husband, whose lecturing and political activities demanded frequent travel.

Kinkel further underlined the close connections between the siblings through a fanciful description of their deaths:

> Fanny's death is so nearly connected again with the fate of her brother, and the circumstances are so poetical, that they might remind us of the old mythik [sic] tales, where heroes beloved by the gods were 1) killed by one flash of lightning from above, 2) taken from earth in a cloud, or 3) At the time when Mendelssohn wrote Elijah, Fanny resolved to venture also on a work of grand scale, and she chose one of the highest tasks, namely: to write the music to

Goethe's second part of Faust. It is well known how Felix overworked himself about a year before his death. It was, as if he had felt that a few days were only at his disposal, and like the silkworm who spins out of his own self the golden threads which must become his grave, so the Composer excited his brain to destruction.³⁰

Of course, Kinkel's chronology seems confused here: Hensel had composed and premiered her "Szene aus *Faust*"³¹ in 1843, long before her death, whereas Felix's *Elijah* did not see the light of day until 1846.³² By this casual act of historical revisionism—whether intentional or merely ill-informed—Kinkel prepares the climax of her lecture, moving in her last section to Fanny's celebrated "Sonntagsmusiken," which Kinkel occasionally participated in. Again, Fanny's fate is closely connected with Felix's:

> During Felix's stay in England where Elijah should be heard for the first time, Fanny was finishing her masterpiece, which was to be performed in one of her private morning-concerts. [...]
> One of these occasions was the day when Fanny's last composition, the before mentioned music to Göthe's [sic] F. (II p.) should be sung for the first time. Like her brother Felix, Fanny had overtasked her health in finishing the last work, but at last there she was sitting at her pianoforte in the old familiar saloon, the trees from the garden greeting with sunny leaves, and all her musical friends in a circle round her, full of expectation. It was the last rehearsal, and well might she pronounce the words of the dying Faust, which he speaks in the very Poem that lay before her: "Im Vorgefühle von solchem hohen Glück 'genieß' ich nun den höchsten Augenblick!" "Foreboding such a lofty happiness my highest moment I enjoy at last!" The Faust-Legend says that the hero must die at the instant, when he feels satisfied with life, and such was the fate of the composer. Fanny touched the first chord and fell down dead in the same moment.
> The other morning the assembly met as usual, because it had been impossible to spread the news of the composers [sic] sudden death so quickly. One of the friends undertook to announce in a few words the startling event, and around her pianoforte stood her Chorus in mourning, and sang a song of death. Many tears followed this noble woman, but none so bitter as those of her brother; they proved to be poisonous to him.³³

One may ask why Kinkel was so obsessed by Hensel. She obviously genuinely admired Fanny and must have been interested in promoting music by woman composers, not least for her own sake. In this case, however, Kinkel's personal acquaintance emphasized her critical authority. Clara Schumann is scarcely mentioned in Kinkel's lecture on Robert Schumann. We are therefore not only dealing here with a proto-feminist narrative, but also with someone wishing understandably to underline her "unique selling point."

It would be difficult to tell from Kinkel's comments that she and Fanny had never actually become close friends—Kinkel was much closer to Fanny's sister Rebecka. In fact, Kinkel seems sometimes to have been a figure of gentle fun in the correspondence between Felix and Fanny. When discussing Kinkel's recently published Lieder (Fanny found two of them "quite lovely," and Felix agreed), on 26 February 1839, Fanny added: "Mathieux will be passing through Leipzig any day. She wants to travel to Bonn to divorce her husband, but the foolish man doesn't want to do it. Have you ever heard of the like? Don't let this letter fall into the wastepaper basket, for then she might find it and read it."[34]

Another look at Kinkel's biography might provide more reasons for her promotion of Hensel: When the two women met in late 1836 or 1837, Kinkel was at a crossroads in her life. Her recollections must be evaluated with respect to the time of the initial encounter with Hensel, the Berlin of the 1830s, and the time of the lecture itself, London in the 1850s—the latter when Kinkel was struggling to be what her friend Malwida von Meysenburg referred to as "das Weib der neuen Zeit" under extremely adverse circumstances. Kinkel made not one, but two attempts to establish herself in the music profession, the first emulating the traditionally "male" model of a composer's career[35] (which was socially not permissible for Fanny Hensel). Obsessed with music and trained on the piano from a very early age, Johanna succeeded—despite the resistance of her parents and after her separation from her first husband—in integrating herself into Berlin's musical life due to persistent striving, youthful enthusiasm, and (this cannot be overlooked) the absence of a husband or children. She published, performed, taught, earned a living, and was a welcome guest in the city's most revered artistic households. Her second attempt, in London in the 1850s, was necessitated by economic considerations and was undertaken despite her triple vocation as "Gattin und Mutter und Weltbürgerin zugleich"—Kinkel now became a female "hero" to a few of her contemporaries, "eine der besten Frauen," as Fanny Lewald referred to her.[36] However, and this was something her literary friends could not quite comprehend, her activities did not now focus much on composing, which her daily chores and obligations made impossible, but on teaching, performing, and eventually writing about music. Perhaps less elevated activities, at least on the level engaged in by Kinkel, but they put food on the table.

In her lecture, Kinkel was fondly reminiscing about a period of her own life when she enjoyed freedom and success in an intellectually stimulating environment. She was perhaps idolizing the Fanny Hensel of the 1830s for what the exiled Kinkel herself lacked in the 1850s. She herself had met Hensel at a crucial time her life, namely when the latter began to contemplate publishing her compositions, thus turning into the "professional female musician" that she feared her family and other members of her class would strongly despise. Kinkel was under financial pressure to succeed as such a musician—she had already had the chance to establish herself in the professional musical world through a number of publications, mostly in the form of Lieder, and in this regard could even in turn have represented a role model for Hensel.[37]

Therefore, even though Fanny was more advanced as a pianist and composer in private, both women arrived almost simultaneously at the point when a "public career" started to become a pressing issue—in fact, Johanna was slightly ahead of Fanny. They had even appeared in print together in the 1839 song volume "Rhein-Sagen und Lieder," where Kinkel's contribution was reviewed more favorably than Fanny's by Schumann's "Lieder Minister" Oswald Lorenz—Kinkel's songs were described as "fresh," and "gracious," but "with an accompaniment revealing the tender female hand," whereas Hensel's Lied "Schloß Liebeneck," though regarded "as not without individual traits," was criticized for its "insecurities in declamation."[38]

Are there any other reasons why Hensel should have been such a prominent part of Kinkel's "Lecture on Mendelssohn," but not necessarily of her general history of music? There is one final issue that outweighs all the others already mentioned, but for this a little digression is necessary: Johanna's second husband, Gottfried, as one of the leaders of the revolutionary movement in the 1848 uprisings, was arrested and sentenced to death in 1849. Through the intervention of some of her influential Berlin friends (particularly Bettina von Arnim), the sentence was commuted to life imprisonment in the jail of Berlin-Spandau. With spectacular effort, he was able to escape from imprisonment in 1850 and immediately emigrated to London. His wife and children followed a few months later. What remained a well-kept secret is that it was likely Rebecka Dirichlet (née Mendelssohn) who provided Kinkel's friends with the financial means to organize the escape. Rebecka must surely have been the "gracious lady-friend of Kinkel, dressed in black, with a warm alto voice, a relative of the famous Mendelssohn" that Carl Schurz, the initiator of Kinkel's escape, mentions in his autobiography as having handed him a "large envelope" in order to "carry out plans that she was not familiar with, but that had to be good."[39] Kinkel, therefore, owed the Mendelssohns more than musical inspiration and artistic support—she owed them her husband's life.

Regrettably, despite her personal connection to Mendelssohn, Kinkel had little of much value to say about his music. Her evaluation chimed with what was already becoming the standard view, namely that Mendelssohn was a composer of prodigious talent, versatility and "good taste," but not of the very first rank. In fact, one of Kinkel's constant refrains is an appeal to decorum: a condemnation of what she regards as "vulgarity" in music, and indeed in personal behavior. She even mentions that Mendelssohn got decently dressed before rushing out of his bedroom to play something on the piano for a party of young women, lest we picture a naked composer outraging feminine propriety. And she partly attributes the success of his compositions to the calm and civilized atmosphere of the Biedermeier era in which he lived, in contrast to the political turmoil of a few years later. So, for all her revolutionary politics, and her proto-feminism, she remained conservative at heart. This was no exiled Wagner planning the "music of the future" in the wake of a failed political revolution, this was a woman staunchly defending the taste and social cohesion of the era in which she had felt most at home. "Bourgeois, all too bourgeois," as Nietzsche might ruefully have said.

*   Duke Carl Alexander of Weimar once said that Liszt was what a prince "ought to be." Larry Todd is what all musicologists should aspire to be: cultured, learned (but with a light touch), and unfailingly generous to younger colleagues. I was once one of these younger colleagues, to whom he gave selfless and supportive guidance. Larry and his work still remain a lodestar. Long may they both flourish!

1. Notable exceptions are Monica Klaus, *Liebe treue Johanna - Liebster Gottitt! Der Briefwechsel zwischen Gottfried und Johanna Kinkel 1840-1858*, 3 vols. (Bonn: Stadtarchiv, 2008) and Anja Bunzel, *The Songs of Johanna Kinkel: Genesis, Reception, Context* (New York: Routledge, 2020).
2. The Kinkels' household, first in St. John's Wood and later in Paddington, was regarded by democrat émigrés as their unofficial headquarters.
3. Rumors were flying high about the reasons for Kinkel's unexpected death. Karl Marx wrote in a letter to Joseph Weydemeyer on 1 February 1859: "What is really choice about Kinkel's exploitation of his wife's death is that the latter creature, who was suffering from heart disease, was outraged because our suave parson had seduced a Jewess by the name of Herz, and generally treated her 'coldly'. In Manchester the Jewish women swear that this is the reason why Johanna Mockel of blessed memory fell out of the window. Anyhow, this would show that, inane though Gottfried may be in other respects, he is cunning enough to exploit public credulity. But that's enough about this humbug." See Karl Marx and Friedrich Engels, *Collected Works*, vol. 40: *Letters 1856-59* (London: Lawrence Wishart, 1983), 374.
4. Emanuel Geibel's letter to his mother, 12 February 1838, in *Emanuel Geibels Jugendbriefe: Bonn—Berlin—Griechenland*, ed. E. J. Fehling (Berlin: Karl Curtius, 1909), 115.
5. Johanna Kinkel, "Friedrich Chopin als Komponist" [1855], in *Deutsche Revue* 27/1 (1902): 93.
6. See Adeline Rittershaus, "Felix Mendelssohn und Johanna Kinkel," *Morgenblatt der Neuen Freien Presse*, (Vienna, 19 April 1900): 1–4.
7. Adeline Rittershaus, "Felix Mendelssohn und Johanna Kinkel," 1.
8. Rittershaus, "Felix Mendelssohn und Johanna Kinkel," 1.
9. Ibid., 2.
10. Ibid.
11. Apparently, she remained in friendly contact with Mendelssohn until the latter's death, although the written correspondence seems to stop in 1843. His death marked the end of an important phase in the life of the Kinkels: "A symbol [for the end of an era in the aesthetic-literary world] was Mendelssohn's death and the strange step backwards in his *Elijah*. The current *Weltanschauung* sank into its grave in order to give way to the social period with its hotter heart-beat." Richard Sander (Hg.), *Gottfried Kinkels Selbstbiographie 1838-1848* (Bonn: Friedrich Cohen, 1931), 206.
12. Kinkel's op. 6 Lieder were published by Kistner in Leipzig and those in opp. 7-12 by Trautwein & Co. in Berlin. A hand-written inventory by Gottfried Kinkel of Johanna's works can be found D-BNu S 2409; it was printed in Sander, *Gottfried Kinkels Selbstbiographie 1838-1848* (Bonn: Friedrich Cohen, 1931), 220–223.
13. Johanna Kinkel's letter to Robert Schumann, 7 July 1838, Staats- und Universitätsbibliothek Dresden, Mus. Schu. 184a, quoted in Ann Willison Lemke, "'Alles Schaffen ist wohl eine Wechselwirkung von Inspiration von Willen' Johanna Kinkel als Komponistin," in Clara Mayer (ed.), *Annäherung an 7 Komponistinnen*, vol. 9 (Kassel: Furore 1998), 53–70, here 59: "Da Sie mir mittheilen, daß das nächste Heft mehre Beiträge von Damen erhalten und also vermuthlich das Sanfte, Zarte mehr darinnen vorherrschen wird, so habe ich ein andres Genre diesmal gewählt, weil ich glaubte, es würde Ihnen nicht unlieb seyn, wenn ein bischen Schatten auf diese Mondlichter fiele."
14. Ludwig Rellstab, "Sehr gern erklärt der Unterzeichnete, wenn seine individuelle Meinung dabei etwas gelten kann, dass er diese Lieder zu den eigenthümlichsten und schönsten zählt, die ihm neuerlich vorgekommen sind. Eine nähere Motivirung seines Urtheils wird er in der von ihm redigirten musikalischen Zeitschrift *Iris* geben." *Neue Zeitschrift für Musik* 8/9 (30 January 1838), "Musikalischer Anzeiger."

15 See Bunzel, *The Songs of Johanna Kinkel*, 14.
16 "Die Regierung ist ganz außer sich, daß man sie nicht besser fürchtet! Der Mann Kinkel ist ihnen wie ein Zauberspruch, bei dem sie ohnmächtig werden, der König besonders haßt ihn." Quoted in Klaus Schmidt, *Gerechtigkeit—das Brot des Volkes. Johanna und Gottfried Kinkel: Eine Biographie* (Stuttgart: Radius-Verlag, 1996), 124.
17 "Vor Beginn der Saison hatte ich Zeit, etwas eifriger als bisher meine Studien der Musikgeschichte wieder aufzunehmen. Ich arbeite zuweilen auf dem British Museum, wo mir die erforderlichen Bücher zu Gebote stehen. Mehrere des Preises wegen in Deutschland schwer zugängliche Werke sind da, die mir eine Menge neuer Aufschlüsse gegeben haben." Johanna Kinkel's letter to Auguste Heinrich, 4 December 1857, quoted in Adelheid von Asten-Kinkel, "Johanna Kinkel in England: Von ihrer Tochter," in *Deutsche Revue* 26/1 (January 1901, 67–80 and 178–192, here 188.
18 See Rittershaus, "Felix Mendelssohn und Johanna Kinkel," 4.
19 "Ich habe ein Engagement, über Musik Vorträge zu halten, und es scheint, daß mir dies gelingt. Das macht mir Freude, weniger deshalb, weil es ein besseres Geschäft als Stundengeben ist, sondern weil ich in mir die Fähigkeit entdeckt habe, im späteren Alter noch eine ganz neue Lebenstätigkeit zu ergreifen." Johanna Kinkel's letter to Auguste Heinrich, 4 December 1857, quoted in Asten Kinkel, "Johanna Kinkel in England: Von ihrer Tochter," 188.
20 Nicholas Temperley (ed.), *Lectures on Musical Life: William Sterndale Bennett* (Woodbridge: Boydell & Brewer, 2006).
21 Johanna Kinkel, "Friedrich Chopin als Komponist" [1855], in *Deutsche Revue* 27/1 (1902): 93–107, 209–223 and 338–360.
22 William Crotch, *Substance of Several Courses of Lectures on Music* (London: Longman, Rees, Orme, Brown, and Green, 1831).
23 At the "London Institution," founded in 1806 for the "Advancement of Literature and the Diffusion of Useful Knowledge," 120 lectures on music were given between 1819 and 1854, with the speakers including Crotch, Wesley, Henry J. Gauntlett, Vincent Novello, Edward Taylor, Henry Bishop, and William Monk. See Nicholas Temperley (ed.), *Lectures on Musical Life: William Sterndale Bennett* (Woodbridge: Boydell & Brewer, 2006), 3.
24 Johanna Kinkel, "Lecture on Mendelssohn" [ca. 1857], Universitäts- und Landesbibliothek Bonn Abteilung Handschriften und Rara S 2398, 35.
25 Ibid., 38.
26 W[ilhelm] A[dolf] Lampadius, *Felix Mendelssohn: Ein Denkmal für seine Freunde* (Leipzig: Hinrichs'sche Buchhandlung, 1848); English translation 1865 and Julius Benedict, *Sketch of the Life and Works of the Late Felix Mendelssohn Bartholdy* (1850).
27 Notably, John Thomson dedicates two paragraphs to Hensel's music in his "Notes of a Musical Tourist" in *Harmonicon* 8 (1830): 99; Sarah Austin, *Recollections of Felix Mendelssohn*, in *Frasier's Magazine for Town and Country* 37 (April 1848): 426–28; *Harmonicon*, Charles Gounod, *Memories d'un artiste* (Paris: Calmann Levy, 1896); see Marion Wilson Kimber "The 'Suppression' of Fanny Mendelssohn: Rethinking Feminist Biography," *19th Century Music* 26/2 (2002): 113-29, here 119.
28 Johanna Kinkel, "Musikalische Zustände und deutsche Musiker," *Morgenblatt für gebildete Leser* [Stuttgart and Tübingen] 47/11 (13 March 1853): 261–263; 47/13 (3 April 1853): 309–312; and 47/15 (10 April 1853): 359–360.
29 Kinkel, "Lecture on Mendelssohn," 21–22.
30 Ibid., 23–24.
31 (Part 2, Scene 1), based on Goethe, for 2 Sopranos, 2 Altos, 4-voiced women's choir and piano. The composition was begun on 23 March and completed no later than early July 1843; the premiere took place on 29 October 1843. ["Faust, auf blumigen Rasen gebettet, ermüdet, unruhig, schlafsuchend. Geisterkreis, schwebend bewegt, anmuthige kleine Gestalten", author unknown]. Fanny had copies of the parts, which are now considered lost, prepared for a performance; see Letter of Fanny Hensel to Wilhelm Hensel, in Renate Hellwig-Unruh, *Fanny Hensel, geb. Mendelssohn Bartholdy. Thematisches Verzeichnis der Kompositionen* (Adliswil: Kunzelmann, 2000),

321–322: " ... mein Elfenstück habe ich auf Felixens Rath umgearbeitet, u. es hat sehr gewonnen, jetzt ist es beim Notenschreiber u. nächste Woche werde ich es einmal probiren lassen, sobald Du zurückkommst, denke ich die Sonntagsmusiken wieder aufzunehmen, man muß sich in Athem halten, so lange man noch welchen hat."

32 The premiere took place in Birmingham in 1846; however, some musical parts had already been distributed as early as 1843.

33 Kinkel, "Lecture on Mendelssohn," 24–29.

34 "In diesen Tagen geht die Mathieux bei Dir durch. Sie will nach Bonn, um sich von ihrem Mann scheiden zu lassen, u. der närrische Mann will nicht. Ist Dir so etwas schon vorgekommen? Laß den Brief nicht in den Papierkorb fallen, damit sie ihn nicht findet u. liest. So diese ganze 4te Seite ist ein postscript. Weiblicher Pferdefuß." Fanny Hensel's letter to Felix Mendelssohn, 26 February 1839, in Marcia Citron, ed., *The Letters of Fanny Hensel to Felix Mendelssohn* (Hillsdale, NY: Pendragon Press, 1987), 556.

35 For a more detailed discussion of the 19th-century professional context, see Wilson Kimber, "The 'Suppression' of Fanny Mendelssohn: Rethinking Feminist Biography."

36 Fanny Lewald, "Johanna Kinkel," in *Zwölf Bilder nach dem Leben: Erinnerungen* (Berlin: Jahnke, 1888), 1.

37 Kinkel, however, came from considerably lower and less wealthy social circles, and much worse, was a separated woman in her mid-twenties who had left her husband for the sake of a musical career. She had to earn her living while Hensel didn't and was additionally "on the market."

38 Oswald Lorenz, "*Rhein-Sagen und Lieder* (1840)," *Neue Zeitschrift für Musik* (7 February 1840): 47.

39 Carl Schurz, *Lebenserinnerungen* (Berlin, 1906), 302.

15. HEARING FORWARD AND BACKWARD: CLARA SCHUMANN'S ROMANCE IN B MINOR *ALS DENKMAL UND RUINE*

Emily Shyr

"a monument is a ruin facing forward (the ruin a monument facing backward)"
— Robert Schumann

We know little about Clara Schumann's Romance in B Minor: she did not give the work an opus number, for it remained unpublished during her lifetime.[1] Composed in 1856, it was Schumann's penultimate composition after her husband committed himself to an asylum in Endenich in 1854 and passed away on 29 July 1856.[2] Dated to Christmas of that year and inscribed with the words "liebe Gedanken" (loving memories), the Romance, as Nancy Reich and John Daverio postulate, may have been presented as a gift to Brahms.[3] Schumann's Romance in B Minor submits to us a greater puzzle: How should we as historians and listeners contextualize this work, especially given the dearth of detail surrounding the composition and its place in Schumann's oeuvre as one of her final works?

That Schumann returned to the romance in 1856 after her last spate of compositions for the genre in 1853 speaks to the wider importance of the *Romanze* to her, especially when considered in light of her closest musical companions and the music that they performed and composed.[4] While further information regarding the Romance in B Minor has been lost, the work alludes to a constellation of answers found in her earlier music, that of her husband Robert Schumann, and that of Johannes Brahms, which are complemented by her identity as a concert pianist and musical partnership with Joseph Joachim. Thus, R. Larry Todd's assertion that "to explicate [Robert] Schumann's music is inevitably to consider the possibility of external references, of the rich intertextuality between his music and external musical-literary ideas" applies equally in endeavors to understand the music of Clara Schumann.[5]

The question of historical contextualization then gains specificity and becomes one of how to interpret the musical nexus of allusions within Clara Schumann's Romance in B Minor, even as they may present themselves "illusively" and "elusively," as Todd observes.[6] To that end, we may turn to Robert Schumann's musical prose concerning ruins and monuments for a framework through which we can understand the biographical context surrounding Schumann's musical allusions to Robert, Brahms, and Joachim. While the dearth of available historical evidence entails that aspects of the following historical contextualization must necessarily be speculative, as an informed act of scholarly and musical interpretation, an intertextual reading of Clara Schumann's Romance in B Minor reveals how musical memory, performance, and composition are intertwined with one another. The Romance in B Minor brings together Schumann's musical past and historical present, for it acts as both a monument and a ruin to the musical relationships it references.

"A monument is a ruin facing forward (the ruin a monument facing backward)."[7] Robert Schumann penned this famous phrase in his essay "Monument für Beethoven," written in 1836 to help raise funds for a memorial erected to the composer in his native Bonn. Robert's understanding of the monument, not unlike Johann Georg Sulzer's, possesses a public dimension. Defined in Sulzer's *Allgemeine Theorie der schönen Künste* (1771) as "a work of art located in public sites that is meant to perpetually sustain, and disseminate to posterity, the memory of noteworthy persons or objects," the monument immortalizes someone or something with collective significance.[8] Similarly, German historian of cultural memory Aleida Assmann conceives of the monument as an object "determined to outlast the present and to speak in this distant horizon of cultural communication."[9] The monument preserves a historical moment or person in a culturally visible manner or location; by extending a fragment of the past into the present and the future, a monument binds three temporalities within a single figure.

Robert's essay stakes clearly the duality between the past and the present that inheres in a commemorative work, for the temporal orientation of a monument both connects it to and differentiates it from another closely related object: the ruin.[10] While a ruin "facing forward" constitutes a monument, a monument directed towards the past is a ruin. The monument and the ruin appear as mirror images of each other: both are artifacts, but their difference lies in their direction. As phrased by John Daverio, the ruin "is after all a synonym for the dialectical image ... [of] the monument."[11] Robert's vision of the Janus-faced work of art as both a monument and a ruin is perhaps best exemplified in his Op. 17 *Fantasie*, which claims origins as both.

Although partly conceived as a musical monument for Beethoven, Robert's *Fantasie* was not explicitly published as such.[12] Scholars have documented the process by which he modified what became the Op. 17 *Fantasie* in ways that mediated between the composition as a monument and as a ruin. Nicholas Marston has assiduously demonstrated that the earliest germs of the work can be traced to September 1836, when Robert recorded "an idea for a contribution for Beethoven."[13] This idea – a "*Sonate für Beethoven*" – was purportedly sketched in detail by December of that year, the same month that Robert approached the publisher Kistner with his proposal. Yet, at the same time that Robert conceived of his personal monument to Beethoven, it was bound up with the image of ruins. In a letter to Kistner, Robert titled the first movement "*Ruine*."[14] He retained this title for the first movement almost until the publication of the work, for as late as April 1838, he wrote to Clara Wieck that "the next thing to appear in print are Fantasies, which I have called 'Ruins, Triumphal Arch and Constellation' and 'Poems.'"[15]

Not only did the genesis of the *Fantasie* take shape as a ruin, but so, too, did its content. Original features of the work were effaced during the compositional process to obscure overt memorialization to Beethoven; in this sense, Robert transformed the work from a monument to a ruin. By suppressing the explicit Beethovenian references in the *Fantasie*, Robert shifted the public function and meaning of this work to the private sphere with intimate significance.[16] Scholarship has discussed in detail Robert's allusions to Beethoven's music in the *Fantasie*. Evidence of one explicit reference can be found in the same letter to Kistner in which Robert proposed the idea of a Beethoven sonata. Robert specifies that in "Palms," the third movement, "there is a quotation from the Adagio of the A Major Symphony."[17] While some believe the quotation was completely expunged before the work's publication, others have linked the dactylic rhythm in the measures directly preceding the "Etwas bewegter section" of the third movement of the *Fantasie* to the slow movement of Beethoven's Seventh Symphony.[18] If one does take the distinctive rhythmic pattern as an allusion to Beethoven, then it has been suppressed — literally — in its transferal to the bass.

Robert also embeds within the Op. 17 *Fantasie* a romance, masked as the section "Im Legendenton," which combines the work's public-facing intent with matters of personal significance. As Marston has ascertained, the section now bearing the subtitle "Im Legendenton" was initially titled a "Romanza" in the autograph score, but Robert rechristened it in the *Stichvorlage* with the name that it bears today.[19] Robert's invocation of the romance genre, described by Rousseau as a song "whose subject is generally some amorous, and often tragic history," and moreover, the theme's similarity to Clara's Op. 3 *Romance variée*, musically supports Robert's confession to Clara that the first movement of the *Fantasie* was inextricably associated with her.[20] In 1838, he confided to her in a letter: "The first movement of it [the *Fantasie*] is possibly the most passionate I have ever written – a deep lament for you," and the following year, he maintained, "you can only understand the *Fantasie* if you imagine yourself back in that unhappy summer of 1836, when I was separated from you."[21]

While Robert undoubtedly kept Clara in mind as he composed the Op. 17 *Fantasie*, a definitive answer to the question of whether he musically referred to his beloved through a citation of Beethoven's *An die ferne Geliebte* remains more elusive. Although the conclusiveness of the quotation remains debatable, Nicholas Marston, Charles Rosen, and Berthold Hoeckner have presented compelling cases for hearing motives in the *Fantasie* as, at the very least, allusions to and transformations of the final song of the cycle, "Nimm sie hin denn, diese Lieder (Ex. 1)."[22]

Example 1, Beethoven, *An die ferne Geliebte,* mm. 266-7 (transposed to C major)

Musicologists have concentrated on the final bars of the first movement of the *Fantasie* (Ex. 2), where the purported allusion most strikingly resembles Beethoven's song.

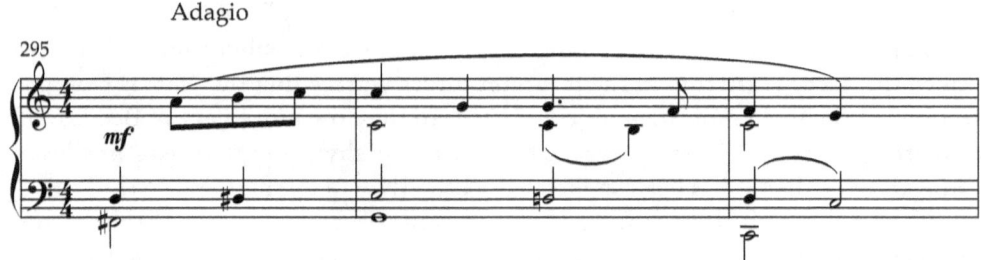

Example 2, Robert Schumann, *Fantasie* Op. 17, mm. 295–7

However, the reference first occurs in mm. 15-17 of the *Fantasie* (Ex. 3) with the phrase's characteristic contour of a descending fourth followed by a stepwise descending third.

Example 3, Robert Schumann, *Fantasie* Op. 17, mm. 14–17

Robert's progressive transformation and unmasking of the allusion over the course of the movement bespeaks his admission to Clara, "If I steal, I begin much more subtly, as you know from your own experience – namely with your heart." Furthermore, Robert's development of the musical figure demonstrates the process by which Charles Rosen notes that in the *Fantasie*, "the reference becomes self-reference ... one cannot take the full measure of [Robert] Schumann's accomplishment ... without observing that the quotation from *An die ferne Geliebte* sounds as if [Robert] Schumann had written it.²³ Keeping in mind the aesthetics of masking and unveiling in Robert's intertextual compositional process, the same techniques of concealment operate in Schumann's Romance in B Minor.

If the genesis and evolution of Robert's Op. 17 *Fantasie* blurs the distinction between a monument and a ruin and the boundaries separating the public and private spheres, then so, too, does Clara Schumann's Romance in B Minor, for by alluding to the music composed and played by herself and those in her intimate social circle, she memorializes the past in her historical present. At the same time, the nature of these allusions – fragmented, concealed, and oriented towards the past – also impart upon the work the quality of ruins.

HEARING BACKWARD: ALLUSIONS TO ROBERT'S OP. 17 *FANTASIE* AND BRAHMS'S OP. 5 PIANO SONATA IN THE ROMANCE IN B MINOR

Clara Schumann's Romance in B Minor contains subtle and fleeting allusions to music by Brahms and her husband. While their inherent ambiguity precludes a conclusive assertion of the Romance's relationship to the works alluded to, the date of Christmas 1856 on the autograph score and occasion of Robert's recent passing makes it tempting to read these allusions as a tribute by Schumann to her recently deceased husband and as a musical memory of the difficult period from 1854–56.

Beginning her composition with the lament topos, Schumann suggests hearing her Romance in B Minor as a private memorial. As if mourning the new, eternal distance between the couple, Schumann weaves the chromatically descending tetrachord throughout the A section and its reprise four times each, overlapping the second and third iterations through imitation. The introduction of the lament bass delays the establishment of the key of B minor until the cadence on the tonic in m. 5. Coupled with pervasive syncopation and melodic fragments, the opening measures suggest the aesthetic of ruins.

The realization of the permanent distance from her husband – both spatial and temporal – must have weighed heavily on Schumann's mind, for as she remarked, Robert's departure to Endenich in 1854 marked the first time in fourteen years that the couple had been separated; the last occurrence was in 1836–37, when Clara's father attempted to sever ties between the lovers.²⁴ In the period immediately following Robert's suicide attempt, Brahms provided Schumann with an invaluable source of comfort and strength. As she later recalled to her children, Brahms "came, like a true friend, to share all my sorrow; he strengthened the heart that threatened to break, he uplifted my mind, he cheered my spirits when- and where- ever he could, in short he was my friend in the fullest sense of the word."²⁵

Brahms's musical presence also consoled Schumann, especially when he could not accompany her as she resumed touring in the autumn of 1854 to financially support her large family. During her concert on 23 October in Leipzig, Schumann played the Andante and Scherzo from his Piano Sonata No. 3 in F Minor, which the younger composer introduced to the Schumanns almost exactly a year earlier in Düsseldorf.[26] As Uhde, Todd, and Daverio postulate, if Schumann did indeed compose the Romance as a Christmas present for Brahms, then it is possible that the chain of descending thirds (*Terzenkette*) that follows the lament bass in the Romance alludes to Brahms's Sonata.[27] Uhde's and Todd's hypothesis is strengthened by musical detail: The *Terzenketten* (mm. 3-4, Ex. 4) beginning Schumann's Romance and the Andante from Brahms's Sonata (Ex. 5) are accompanied by broken thirds in the left hand.[28]

Example 4, Clara Schumann, Romance in B Minor, mm. 1–5

Example 5, Johannes Brahms, Piano Sonata in F Minor, Op. 5 No. 3, mm. 1–2

Schumann's intimate knowledge of Brahms's Sonata through her performances thereof, her reminiscences on this happy period between the three, and Brahms's consoling presence throughout her husband's decline and after his passing suggests that her allusion to the F Minor Sonata can be heard as what her husband would have described as a musical ruin – "a monument looking backward."

If Schumann's allusion to Brahms reflects a shared period of their lives, then an allusion to Robert's Op. 17 *Fantasie* recalls the beginning of her life with him. After another chain of descending thirds, in mm. 15-16 of the Romance (Ex. 6), she expands the motive to a fourth, resulting in a leap of a descending fourth followed by a stepwise descending third: D-A-G-F-sharp, and B-F-sharp-E-D.

Clara Schumann's Romance in B Minor *als Denkmal* und *Ruine*

Example 6, Clara Schumann, Romance in B Minor, pickup to mm. 14–17

This particular configuration of intervals is identical to that in mm. 15-17 of the *Fantasie*, which by the end of the work becomes the alleged quotation from *An die ferne Geliebe* (Cf. Ex. 1-3).

Moreover, the process through which Schumann reveals the allusion to the Op. 17 *Fantasie* progressively unfolds like the putative reference to *An die Ferne Geliebte* in Robert's composition. The descending fourth and stepwise descending third in mm. 15-17 of Schumann's Romance originates from the Brahmsian *Terzenkette* that first appeared in mm. 3-4. Retroactively, one hears mm. 15-17 as a variant of mm. 3-5. This is similar to the way in which the melody from mm. 295-7 derives from mm. 15-17 of the Op. 17 *Fantasie*.

The ambiguity yet suggestiveness of Schumann's allusions to Brahms's F Minor Piano Sonata and Robert's Op. 17 *Fantasie* invokes the aesthetic of ruins through memory, for if as Charles Rosen asserts, "a quotation is, of course, a memory made public," then one could complement his statement by positing that an allusion is a memory recalled privately.[29] Just as Robert's references to Beethoven and Schumann in the Op. 17 bring together the public and private realms of musical memory, so, too, do Schumann's allusions recall past musical lives, both intimate and public. These allusions, "felt as both alien and intimate," become fragments "when we are aware that [they are] as much a sign of the present as of the past."[30] The investment of past and present in these fragments remind us, as Robert wrote, of the Janus-faced nature of monuments and ruins.

HEARING FORWARD:
SELF-REFERENCE IN SCHUMANN'S ROMANCE IN B MINOR

If we examine Schumann's Romance in its historical present, then in the years immediately preceding its genesis, Schumann was often on tour with her favorite violinist, Joseph Joachim. The frequency of their collaborations increased during the period of 1854–56; Ute Bär notes that after Robert's committal to the Endenich asylum, Joachim played with Schumann in about a quarter of her concerts.[31] At the end of 1855, the two performed in Berlin, Potsdam, and Leipzig, and Brahms joined them in Danzig.[32] This period also saw the duo's first public concert performance of Schumann's Op. 22 Romances for Violin and Piano. She composed these in the summer of 1853 and presented them to Joachim, the dedicatee, the following October. The Op. 22 heard its first audience on 28 January 1854 in a private gathering in Hanover, and Schumann and Joachim performed the romances at least twice while on tour in 1855: on 8 March in Danzig and 20 November in Berlin.[33] While only some of Schumann's recital programs survive, her request to Breitkopf & Härtel of "a speedy publication, particularly of the Violin Romances, which Joachim is fond of playing with me" suggests that they likely played the Op. 22 Romances on more than the three documented occasions.[34]

As in the case of many of Schumann's other compositions, the Op. 22 Romances attest to the relationship between performance and composition and the musical exchange between her and her husband. Op. 22, No. 1 alludes to Robert's Violin Sonata in A minor (1851), while the melody of Op. 22, No. 3 references the F major theme from the last of Robert's Op. 94 Romances for Oboe and Piano (1849).[35] Both of Robert's compositions were part of Joachim's and Schumann's repertoire (a version of the Op. 94 for violin and piano was also published in 1849). The quotations of Robert's music in Schumann's *Romanzen* testify to the significance of the genre as a site where "musical exchanges and allusions 'among friends' account for layers of meanings central for the understanding of works predominantly composed for and performed in intimate circles."[36] Given her concertizing with Joachim in 1854–56 and her circle's penchant for intertextual musical dialogues, it should not come as a surprise that Schumann alludes to the Op. 22 Romances in her B Minor Romance.

In the middle section of the B Minor Romance, Schumann modulates to G major, the same key as the B section of the Op. 22, No. 2. The main motive of this section (Ex. 7), a pair of interlocking rising sixths (D-B-G-E) followed by a descending chain of thirds that steps down to the dominant (D-B-G-E-D), is shortened in mm. 32 of her B Minor Romance (Ex. 8) so that the first rising sixth, D-B is followed by a descending *Terzenkette* and downward step (B-G-E-D).

Example 7, Clara Schumann, Romance for Violin and Piano Op. 22, No. 2, mm. 39–44

Clara Schumann's Romance in B Minor *als Denkmal* und *Ruine*

Example 8, Clara Schumann, Romance in B Minor, pickup to mm. 31–2

In mm. 41-3 of Op. 22, No. 2, the piano imitates the solo violin with C-sharp as a lower neighbor to the descending *Terzenkette* starting on D. Compared to mm. 32 of the B Minor Romance, Schumann retains C-sharp as a lower neighbor to D, but inserts G between the C-sharps and brings the chain of thirds up an octave starting on B.

In a wonderfully cyclic reminder of the ambiguities of allusion, Schumann's citation of her Op. 22, No. 2 in the B minor Romance emphasizes and develops upon the *Terzenkette* common to those works and Brahms's F Minor Piano Sonata. The question of whether Schumann cites herself (and consequently alludes to Joachim, the dedicatee, in her citation of the Op. 22), references Brahms, or both, brings the three figures into a musical constellation that illuminates the idyllic years of their shared music-making in the period preceding Robert's decline, illustrates how the young men supported Schumann during the most difficult period of her life, and attests to their shared music-making from 1854–6.

The comingling of musical past and present and performance and composition in Schumann's Romance in B Minor, and moreover, the way in which she blurs the distinction between the two temporalities and public and private spheres resonates with the riddle-like character of her late husband's music and musical prose. By invoking musical memory through allusions to Brahms's Piano Sonata in F Minor, Robert's Op. 17 *Fantasie*, and Schumann's own Violin Romances, the Romance in B Minor evokes the aesthetic of ruins and acts as a private memorial, not just to her husband, but moreover, to the happiest and most musically rewarding period of their lives with Brahms and Joachim.

---

1 The Romance in B Minor was first published in the 1970s. Nancy Reich, *Clara Schumann: The Artist and the Woman* (Ithaca: Cornell University Press, 1985), 250. John Daverio, *Crossing Paths: Schubert, Schumann, and Brahms* (Oxford: Oxford University Press, 2002), 279; Marian Wilson Kimber, "From the Concert Hall to the Salon: The Piano Music of Clara Wieck Schumann and Fanny Mendelssohn Hensel," in *Nineteenth-Century Piano Music*, ed. R. Larry Todd (New York: Routledge, 2004), 332.

2 John Daverio, *Crossing Paths*, 279; Reich, *Clara Schumann* (first ed.), 250; Wilson Kimber, "From the Concert Hall to the Salon," 332. Because the focus of this chapter is Clara Schumann's Romance in B Minor, I refer to her as "Schumann" and distinguish her from her husband by referring to him as Robert.

3 Reich, *Clara Schumann* (first ed.), 301; Daverio, *Crossing Paths*, 279.

4 Clara Schumann's last instrumental compositions in 1853 all belonged to the genre of the romance. Although Schumann's Op. 20 consists of variations on a theme by Robert Schumann, the last variation incorporates the theme from her Op. 3 *Romance variée* and speaks to a greater nexus of musical conversations that spans her and her husband's oeuvre. See Katharina Uhde and R. Larry Todd, "Contextualizing Clara Schumann's *Romanzen*," in *Clara Schumann Studies*, ed. Joe Davies (Cambridge: Cambridge University Press, 2021), 165–7.

5 R. Larry Todd, "On Quotation in Schumann's Music," in *Robert Schumann and His World*, ed. R. Larry Todd (Princeton: Princeton University Press, 1994), 92.

6 I borrow this play on words and framing of intertextuality in Clara Schumann's music from R. Larry Todd, "The Elusive Clara Schumann: Quotations and References, Allusive and Illusive," forthcoming in *The Schumanns in Context*, ed. Joe Davies and Roe-Min Kok (Cambridge: Cambridge University Press, 2024). Christopher Reynolds, *Motives for Allusion: Context and Content in Nineteenth-Century Music* (Cambridge, MA and London: Harvard University Press, 2003), 2. Ch. 1, "Definitions," provides some parameters for what Reynolds describes as "the question of audibility."

7 Robert Schumann, "A Monument to Beethoven: Four Views," in *The Musical World of Robert Schumann: A Selection from His Own Writings*, trans., ed., Henry Pleasants (New York: St. Martin's Press, 1965), 93.

8 "Ein an öffentlichen Plätzen stehendes Werk der Kunst, das al sein Zeichen das Andenken merkwürdiger Personen oder Sachen, beständig unterhalten und auf die Nachwelt fortpflanzen soll." Johann Georg Sulzer, *Allgemeine Theorie der schönen Künste*, Vol. 1 (Hildesheim: Georg Olms Verlagsbuchhandling, 1970), 596, also in Alexander Rehding, *Music and Monumentality: Commemoration and Wonderment in Nineteenth Century Germany* (Oxford: Oxford University Press, 2009), 21.

9 Aleida Assmann, "Kultur als Lebenswelt und Monument," in Aleida Assmann and Dietrich Harth, eds., *Kultur als Lebenswelt und Monument* (Frankfurt am Main: Fischer, 1991), 14, in Rehding, *Music and* Monumentality, 33.

10 John Daverio, *Nineteenth-Century Music and the German Romantic Ideology* (New York: Schirmer, 2003), 20.

11 Ibid., 47.

12 Although conceived of as a Sonata for Beethoven, the Op. 17 was ultimately dedicated to Liszt.

13 Nicholas Marston, *Schumann: Fantasie, Op. 17* (Cambridge: Cambridge University Press, 1992), 3.

14 Ibid., 3, 7. The autograph score of the first movement shows that the original title was *Ruines. Fantasie pour le pianoforte*.

15 Robert Schumann, letter to Clara Wieck, 16 April, 1838, in Ibid., 6. Although Schumann gave the work various titles between 1836–38, he did not decide on the ultimate title of the work that we now call the *Fantasie*, Op. 17, until December 1838, when he wrote to Breitkopf & Härtel to request the piece's publication under that title. Ibid., 8; Daverio, *Nineteenth-Century Music*, 47.

16 As a backward facing monument, Schumann's "*Ruine*" (what became the first movement of the *Fantasie*) pays homage to what he considered a musical "Golden Age" in which Beethoven stood at its pinnacle. After Beethoven, Schumann considered "the entire classical canon…in a state of decay" due to the philistinism of empty virtuosity and derivative compositions against which the *Davidsbündler* railed. Daverio, *Nineteenth-Century Music*, 21–34.

17 Marston, *Fantasie*, 36; Charles Rosen, *The Romantic Generation* (Harvard: Harvard University Press, 1995), 102.

18 Marston, *Fantasie*, 36.

19 Nicholas Marston, "'Im Legendenton': Schumann's 'Unsung Voice,'" *19th-Century Music*, Vol. 16, No. 3 (1993): 230–6.
20 Jean-Jacques, Rousseau, *A Complete Dictionary of Music Consisting of a Copious Explanation of all Words Necessary to a True Knowledge and Understanding of Music*, second ed., trans. William Waring (London: J. Murray, 1779), 347; Berthold Hoeckner, "Schumann and Romantic Distance," *Journal of the American Musicological Society*, Vol. 50, No. 1 (1997): 121–23.
21 Hoeckner, "Schumann and Romantic Distance," 110, fn. 128.
22 Ibid., 109-2; Rosen, *The Romantic Generation*, 100-12; Marston, *Fantasie*, 34–8. Transposed to C major in Example 1.
23 Marston, *Fantasie*, 35; Rosen, *The Romantic Generation*, 103.
24 Berthold Litzmann, *Clara Schumann: An Artist's Life Based on Material Found in Diaries and Letters*, Vol. II, trans. Grace E. Hadow (New York: Vienna House, 1972), 80.
25 Ibid., 83–4.
26 Ibid., 45–6; 89–91. Brahms played the F Minor Sonata on 30 October 1853, "as a farewell" to the Schumanns. Schumann played the same movements at other concerts in Frankfurt am Main and Berlin of that year. Robert Eshbach, "Joseph Joachim's Concerts," *Joseph Joachim: Biography and Research*, 2 December 2021, https://josephjoachim.com/category/concerts/.
27 Uhde and Todd, "Contextualizing Clara Schumann's *Romanzen*," 185.
28 While Daverio suggests affinities between the chain of thirds in Schumann's Romance and the Intermezzo movement of Brahms's Sonata, I propose that Schuman's Romance looks back to the Andante movement for two reasons: First, there exist more documented instances of Schumann performing the Andante rather than the Intermezzo in the period 1854–56; the musical texture of the Andante bears more similarity to the Romance than it does to the Intermezzo. Daverio, *Crossing Paths*, 279.
29 Rosen, *The Romantic Generation*, 111.
30 Ibid., 112.
31 Ute Bär, "Zur gemeinsamen Konzerttätigkeit Clara Schumanns und Joseph Joachims," in *Clara Schumann: Komponistin, Interpretin, Unternehmerin, Ikone* (Hildesheim: Georg Olms Verlag, 1999), 55; Ute Scholz, "Zur Gemeinsamen Konzerttätigkeit Clara Schumanns und Joseph Joachims," in *On Tour: Clara Schumann als Konzertvirtuosin auf europas Bühnen*, ed. Ingrid Bodsch (Bonn: Verlag StadtMuseum Bonn, 2019), 293–5.
32 Alexander Stefaniak, *Becoming Clara Schumann: Performance Strategies and Aesthetics in the Culture of the Musical Canon* (Bloomington: Indiana University Press, 2021), 195–6.
33 Reich, *Clara Schumann* (revised ed.), 315; Stefaniak, *Becoming Clara Schumann*, 195–6.
34 Schumann, letter to Breitkopf und Härtel, 7 October 1855, in Reich, *Clara Schumann*, 315.
35 Uhde and Todd, "Contextualizing Clara Schumann's *Romanzen*," 182; Ute Scholz, "Zur Gemeinsamen Konzerttätigkeit," 302.
36 Uhde and Todd, "Contextualizing Clara Schumann's *Romanzen*," 166; Todd, "The Elusive Clara Schumann," 9; Reich, *Clara Schumann*, first ed., 267.

16. SCHUMANN FANTASIES: SCENE AND STYLE IN ROBIN HOLLOWAY'S MUSIC

Philip Rupprecht

> In my twenties (1963–1973) I composed myself into an impasse and then, with the help of Schumann, composed myself out of it.
> Robin Holloway (recording liner note, 1998)

> The very type of an author without a style is Gide, whose craftsmanlike approach exploits the pleasure the moderns derive from a certain classical ethos, just as Saint-Saëns has composed in Bach's idiom, or Poulenc in Schubert's.
> Roland Barthes, *Writing Degree Zero* (1953), 12

That the British composer Robin Holloway's first major breakthrough with audiences and critics came with *Scenes from Schumann* (1970)—subtitled "seven paraphrases for orchestra"—is more than a belated instance of twentieth-century musical neoclassicism, or a reminder of a Sixties fashion for musical borrowings. Holloway's notion of *paraphrase* is to be distinguished from quotation, either as passing intertextual reference, or arising through collage-like juxtaposition of disparate "historical" items, as in, say, the scherzo of Luciano Berio's *Sinfonia* (1968–69). Holloway's elaborate reworkings of famous Schumann *Lieder* were made, he noted, in "affectionate homage to the spirit and style" of German Romanticism.[1] The closest precedent for this kind of "re-composition," he suggests, was Stravinsky's 1928 ballet *Le Baiser de la Fée*, a score incorporating both orchestrations of Tchaikovsky piano works and other, original passages, composed by the younger Russian to closely match the idiom of his nineteenth-century forebear. The historical distance between Holloway and Schumann, however, clearly exceeds that between the two Russians, and the British composer's choice of a German source only intensifies the questions of voice, tradition, and style that lie close to the heart of the enterprise.

Premiered in July 1970 as *Souvenirs de Schumann*, the piece was eventually published under the title *Scenes from Schumann*. Holloway's evolving title choice opens intriguing questions of technique and emotional referent, regarding the "contents" of a wordless instrumental score. The French wording of his original title alluded directly to a nineteenth-century tradition of "Wagner send-ups."[2] The definitive English title, on the other hand, invokes Schumann's *Kinderszenen*,[3] so leading beyond the surface romantic-erotic concerns of the *lieder*. Memories become scenes, and searching for the conscious adult self, one returns, instinctively, to real or imagined childhood memories. The central preoccupation in *Scenes from Schumann*, perhaps unsurprisingly, will also be with dreams and nocturnal visions; we may expect that the images to be encountered in the score will, in Freud's sense, offer manifest representations of latent psychological content.

To paraphrase Schumann was to emulate a composer well versed in references, explicit or esoteric—alter egos or masks in a carnival of richly intertextual meanings. Schumann's listeners, as R. Larry Todd brilliantly shows, will find only "thin lines separating quotation, allusion, and mere thematic resemblances," throughout his oeuvre.[4] Besides quoting contemporaries and his own music, Schumann embraced a third, historically explicit practice: his return to Bachian counterpoint was both an act of "musical memory" and, by the 1830s and 40s, a gesture of national canon formation.[5] The music's play of meanings and cross-references enacts a kind of polyphonic utterance particularly suited to the relatively non-denotative medium of untexted instrumental music. By offering listeners moments of recognition—typically, of familiar thematic items—Schumann claimed membership in an emergent national tradition, while asserting artistic independence of precursors. Whether quoting or alluding, we may savor the rhetoric of Schumann's practices at the most local, gestural level. As Todd shows, it is the whimsical moment of recognition that Schumann creates, interpolating his own earlier music into *Carnaval*'s "Florestan," and labeling the notes on the page with a teasing verbal question—"(Papillon?)"—addressed to the performer. The composer tips his hand to the fleeting or literally parenthetical aspect of the allusion, what Schumann calls a *Gedankenflug*, a flight of musical thought.[6]

Holloway, like Schumann, was drawn to passing intertextual asides. His First Concerto for Orchestra (1967–69) quotes at two climactic points from Brahms's song "O Tod" (*Vier Ernste Gesänge*).[7] In *Scenes from Schumann*, the following year, such fragmentary reference is superseded by full-scale paraphrase of complete songs, publicly identified by title. In Holloway's re-compositions of Schumann, as Michael Oliver observed, the original songs are "analytically rewritten": they become "raw material for a wholly original work."[8] Holloway followed up, in 1971, with a kind of sequel: the *Fantasy-Pieces* on Schumann's Heine "Liederkreis." This later score, on closer inspection, no longer pursues the earlier technique of paraphrasing single songs. Rather, Holloway emphasized, his aim was to create "abstract forms out of song-material, to align borrowed and original composition."[9] Looking back on the two scores of 1970–71, Holloway later concluded that it was "with Schumann's help" that he had negotiated a protracted artistic "impasse."[10]

The impasse, in 1969–70, was in essence one of musical style. It was the first Schumann derived score, *Scenes*, that most British critics noticed as a significant "breakthrough" from the atonal-modernist realm of Holloway's 1960s productions to, in Bayan Northcott's words, the "golden warmth, flow, and directness of feeling" of German romanticism.[11] For Northcott, writing in the early 1970s as an eyewitness, Holloway's endeavor appeared "entirely un-parodistic."[12] Holloway himself also stressed his attraction to a music of face-value feeling—"clearly lyrical and full of deep emotion"—as a nineteenth-century norm to be reclaimed.[13] The wider self-consciousness of many twentieth-century borrowings from earlier music appeared remote from Holloway's own temperament, David Matthews noted.[14] Yet he also recognized the complexity of tone in Holloway's Schumann-centered works: "a tension between identification and detachment."[15] As Julian Anderson later remarked, Holloway's paraphrase techniques (one approach among many "borrowings" from the past) lack the irony of the collage techniques of Berio or Schnittke, or the "destructiveness" of B. A. Zimmermann.[16]

Amid so much critical comment on the appropriation of pre-existent "material," one might at this stage query insistence on some *original*, in Schumann's Biedermeier Germany or Holloway's post-austerity Britain. True, the very gesture of quotation or paraphrase foregrounds the precursor; yet the intelligence that chooses to revisit, quote, or allude to an antecedent remains intact—a subject defining an object. Rather than fetishizing origins, the paraphrases in *Scenes* may invite our attention as Schumannesque "flights of thought," of personal, emotional significance. Holloway's engagement with historical sources need not connote a postmodern attitude to the past, dominated by skepticism (what Umberto Eco called "an age of lost innocence").[17] His interest in Schumann, he has often affirmed, sprang from an emotional need—to engage musically with "everything most loved and yet prohibited by the *Zeitgeist*."[18] The return to a proscribed German Romanticism, for the twenty-something Englishman, was even to yield a third Schumann-themed piece—the tone poem *Domination of Black* (1974)—drawing on another song collection, the Op. 35 *Kerner-Lieder*. Proclaiming his desire to embrace a lyricism "running against the current compositional tide," Holloway at the time spoke of having sought "To build an oasis in the desert rather than burying my head in the sand."[19] Apart from his artistic work, Holloway has, in musicological-critical writings, charted an entire tradition of musical back-reference. The engagement with eighteenth-century models among German composers from Beethoven to Brahms, for example, "has to be called 'neo-classicism.'"[20] This is not, however, to deny a panoply of twentieth-century practices—an "explosion of allusion, pastiche, quotation, parody, stylistic game-playing"—flowing out of the inter-war neoclassicism of Stravinsky and others.[21]

Holloway has never shied away from foregrounding the challenges of a "drastic break in continuity" posed by musical modernism.[22] Nor does he downplay the situation of his own artistic generation: "I remember, as a dissatisfied child of the 1950s–60s avant-garde, how difficult psychologically as well as technically it was to break away."[23] The affinities between Holloway's capacious reading of musical history and his personal artistic stance in *Scenes from Schumann* appear all too clear, even as one acknowledges the particularity of any one artist's angle on tradition. In what follows, I will limit discussion to the psychological and technical apparatus of the central triptych within Holloway's return to Schumann—recognizing that this return is itself haunted by others.

Philip Rupprecht

"FREE-ASSOCIATION": THE NOCTURNAL FORM OF *SCENES FROM SCHUMANN*

A fantastical and mostly night-time locale is communicated to listeners from Holloway's titles for the seven numbered movements of *Scenes*. The first published score prints only Schumann's German titles; in the revised edition, Holloway adds English language titles, with parenthetical references to the German songs and source collections. The complete scheme, including a listing of Schumann's chosen poets, is thus:

1 Dedication (*Widmung* Op. 25 No. 1) — Friedrich Rückert
2 Flowering Lotus (*Die Lotosblume* Op. 25 No. 7) — Heinrich Heine
3 Dream Vision (*Allnächtlich im Traume I* Op. 48 No. 14) — Heine
4 Enchanted Forest (*Auf einer Burg* Op. 39 No. 7) — Joseph von Eichendorff
5 Dream Visitation (*Allnächtlich im Traume II* Op. 48 No. 14) — Heine
6 Moonlit Night (*Die Mainacht* Op. 39 No. 5) — Eichendorff
7 Spring-Night-Rounds (*Frühlingsnacht*, Op. 39, No. 12) — Eichendorff

Holloway's decision to credit Schumann (including exact opus numbers), while excluding poets' names from the printed score, foregrounds the musical side of his paraphrase. At the same time, the "Composer's Note" clearly observes that specifically literary, as well as musical meanings, are in play: "Images and feelings from the poems as well as from the music have been allowed to ramify in free-association." Holloway's declared purpose is bounded by affective states, without necessarily aiming for critique of original meanings: "I have attempted to get 'inside' the songs and from inside to send them in different directions. Though there is hardly a bar left that could have been written by Schumann, the intention is not to distort but rather to amplify and intensify the originals." One notes the productive tension between talk of "different directions" and the avowed intention "not to distort." The salient passing reference, surely, is to "free-association"—for the Freudian psychoanalytic technique is pertinent to the nocturnal world of *Scenes*. Here is a cycle whose emotional territory is defined by a fusion of the poetry's erotic, passionate effusions with the disturbing domains of dream imagery. Holloway's artistic openness to an unguarded or impromptu play of meaning—as well as his emphasis on an almost physical notion of interiority—opens the door to unconscious modes of signification. Feelings have "been allowed" to ramify: to branch out and become more complex. We may expect *Scenes* to treat Schumann's songs (and their source poems) in ways comparable to the mechanisms of dream representation identified by Freud—in Holloway's score, we will encounter, as it were, condensation, displacement, and transformations of latent verbal thoughts into manifest images.[24]

Within the shadow-cum-dream milieu of *Scenes*, the opening "dedication" is an apparent exception, for Rückert's passionate address ("Widmung") offers no signs of anything but waking consciousness.[25] Passions unleashed, *Scenes* moves—like Mahler, like Britten in the *Serenade* and the *Nocturne*—into "night music." Without the direct, denotative force of the poetic texts, title images sketch the landscape. Heine's lotus opens its blossoms to moonlight. A recurring dream recounted in one Schumann song ("Allnächtlich im Traume") generates *two* Holloway amplifications of radically contrasting perspective—the first, "Dream Vision," is fleet and playful; the second, "Visitation," is halting and weighty. These two frame the "Enchanted Forest" of the fourth movement as the core of a central triptych. The moss-covered stone knight in Eichendorff's "Auf einer Burg" is speckled in sunlight, but he too sleeps. The mood sequence brightens with the final Eichendorff lyrics: the poet surveys a peaceful moonlit May night ("Die Mainacht") and hears the nightingale's reassurance ("Frühlingsnacht") that his passion will soon be consummated: "Sie ist Dein!"

One might chart this loose narrative progression of poetic images through the distinctive manipulations of timbre Holloway draws from conventional orchestral forces. The addition of a piano, at one level, alludes to the originary sonic terms of the *Lied* tradition; *martellato* attacks lend "Widmung" a certain sonic aggression.[26] The sense of exuberance is intensified, as the composer noted, by "well-loved tunes coming on solo trumpets."[27] The lotus flower's delicacy floats on a surface of woodwind shadings (flutes and alto flute, bass clarinet, double bassoon), muted violins, and liquid harp harmonies. In "Dream Vision" (see Ex. 1), the lower drone-fifth (double basses, harp) and the upper-register melody (flutes, solo violin) do not fuse, sonically, in the way that Schumann's original piano texture does (see Ex. 2). Scoring the single pitch E for muted French horn (*sfp*, then swelling, "hairpin" fashion), Holloway pointillistically sets Schumann's original syncopated inner voice (m. 4) apart from a supporting chord that no longer arrives. What follows is a rapid cutting from mischievously scurrying clarinets and bassoon to a nervous English horn line, descanting over some well-known chords (mm. 9–10), scored for muted strings.

Moving on to Holloway's "Auf einer Burg" paraphrase, the display of poetic song, remade for wordless instruments, is still more overt. A solo French horn intones the original vocal line, to aethereal piano-harp filigree, as if to map sonically the geographical and historical distance between the old castle "up there" (*da oben*) and the wedding party on the Rhein far below (*da unten*). As the critic Nicholas Kenyon put it, Schumann's song is "magically half-heard," but in the yearning English horn solo that follows, references are quite clear: "Act Three of *Tristan* drifts into view."[28] A still more famous "chunk" of Wagner's opera—the opening of the Act I Prelude—has, of course, drifted into view earlier: few listeners will miss the identity of the string chords in Example 1. Holloway defamiliarizes them slightly by the muted string scoring; his English horn descant, meanwhile, is an unmistakable timbral allusion to the later action of Wagner's music drama.[29] So while the paraphrase technique in *Scenes* often works on thematic and rhythmic levels by faithfully retracing Schumann's original ideas, it is in orchestrational and coloristic domains that Holloway articulates other channels of intertextual reference.

With Wagner's arrival on the scene, Holloway defines the central triptych of his Schumann cycle dialectically—to hear Schumann's *Lieder*, effectively, we must engage with another imposing presence and a more public genre, music drama. The musical images, as Holloway says, will gain in complexity and intensity. The claim is best explored in a closer reading of the three central songs of *Scenes from Schumann*.

"DREAM VISION"

Holloway brings the central triptych of *Scenes*—"Dream Vision," "Enchanted Forest," and "Dream Visitation"—into focus as a drama of overtly Wagnerian profile, with the medieval ruins of "Auf einer Burg" standing at the center (the double of Tristan's castle in Brittany). The English horn, alter ego for the shepherd's melancholic piping in *Tristan,* will take center-stage in the "Enchanted Forest." But it is the opera's famous opening phrases, the so-called desire (Sehnsucht) motive, that appear earlier in *Scenes*, intruding momentously on the first "Allnächtlich" paraphrase (see again Ex. 1). These fragments are interpolated into the body of the song, or else one might speak of a figure against a ground. Sustained paraphrase is expanded by brief quotation; Schumann is paired with Wagner. What was an opening, unmoored from its original operatic setting, is now an interruption.

We may wonder at Holloway's historical, dramatic, or psychological point—recalling that Schumann himself died tragically, a year before Wagner's first sketches for *Tristan*. Should we brush off the quotations as a mere flourish—something any audience will "get"—perhaps akin to the *Tristan* quotations in Debussy's *Children's Corner* (1908)? Underlining the opera's incongruity with American ragtime dance steps, Debussy's score specifies that the pianist play "avec une grande émotion." Yet such a gesture engages: as Holloway himself cautions, "it is none the less serious for being so frivolous."[30] The kaleidoscopic color shifts of Holloway's first two Schumann paraphrases remain astonishing. But as Wagner's ancient legend expands *Scenes* to a fully intertextual register, Holloway's score begins to make its most serious points.

Holloway's double paraphrase—two contrasting views of one Schumann song—dramatizes the idea reported by Heine's poetic speaker, of a dream vision that returns "each night" (*Allnächtlich*). Musically, it is as if *Tristan* itself here represents the central dream-image, framed by a surrounding Schumannesque reality. The three breezy quatrains of Heine's poem move in a string of quick images—the beloved, tears, a "soft word," a cypress-wreath—before the poet awakens in the abrupt final couplet, having forgotten the word:

> Allnächtlich im Traume seh' ich dich
> Und sehe dich freundlich grüssen,
> Und laut aufweinend stürz' ich mich
> Zu deinen süssen Füssen.
>
> Du siehest mich an wehmüthiglich
> Und schüttelst das blonde Köpfchen;
> Aus deinen Augen schleichen sich
> Die Perlen Tränentröpfchen.

Du sagst mir heimlich ein leises Wort
Und gibst mir den Strauss von Cypressen.
Ich wache auf, und der Strauss ist fort,
Und's Wort hab' ich vergessen.

In Holloway's hands, the buoyant, quirky features of Schumann's original first strophe are intensified, initially with modest nudges to the rhythms (Exx. 1–2). Holloway's B-F# drone is a beat "early" in relation to the flutes; their second note is stretched; their C# (mm. 4–5) compressed. The horn's bizarrely unaccompanied E freezes harmonic rhythm and metric definition. Racing wind triplets in the continuation phrase match Schumann's chord progressions, decorating but retaining its breathy rising-falling shape.

Holloway is true to the syncopated motions of Schumann's original,[31] but what has been lost is the song's still recognizably classical phrase pattern. Where Schumann restates a four-bar basic idea (in a conventional sentence [*Satz*] schema), Holloway's first strophe omits the repeat entirely. In strophes 2 and 3, he reinstates the first-phrase repeat, but with a change of key (the drone-fifth dropping a wholestep, to A-E). A brief synopsis of these events is shown in Figure 1. It is within this larger reworking of Schumann's three-strophe ground plan that the famous *Tristan* opening is interpolated, at original pitch levels. Wagner's phrases (mm. 1–11 of the operatic Prelude), are essentially unmodified in pitch content. Their rescoring from woodwinds to muted strings gently signals a borrowing, but Holloway's technique involves far bolder adjustments. The first is a cropping of Wagner's expressive rising cello gestures. Their place is ostentatiously filled by Holloway's sinuous English horn line: a garrulous, anxious descant to the quoted Wagnerian progression. The English horn's entrance pitch D (m. 8) negates the bright major mode D# of the wind-triplet cadence just accomplished, before launching into its near-chromatic arabesque. Upstaging even *Tristan*, the English horn seems to intensify the hectic pattern of Schumann's piano interlude (Ex. 2, mm. 11–13). The gesture is redolent of Strauss's *Salome* or Schoenberg's Op. 16 Orchestral Pieces, but if this descant is itself a quotation—or a cipher-like encoding of dramatic presences—its provenance has remained hidden.[32] The larger function of this descant-laden *Tristan* quotation (apart from announcing a famous source) is formal: an autonomous phrase-logic runs parallel to the strophic frame of the host song. The circularity of Schumann's strophic design is overlaid by the restless teleology of Wagner's phrases.

Holloway's paraphrase embeds the *Tristan* progressions—chromatic, sequential, harmonically unstable—within the tonally conventional B-major frame of "Allnächtlich" (though he eschews a traditional key signature). The final arrival of the third *Tristan* phrase is to "Schumann's" B major, destabilized, however, as a "yearning" dominant seventh, rather than a stable B-major home tonic. In this third phrase, meanwhile, the earlier descant solos (English horn, oboe) are restated as a loosely imitative duet—a two-part invention that splinters the coherent flow of musical/narrative time. The woodwind returns, a kind of mechanical backward glance, work

mm.		
1–8	**Strophe 1**	
	(Schumann/Heine):B-F# drone	
8–10		*Tristan* first phrase chords /English horn "Descant"
10–21	**Strophe 2**	
	phrase repeat, transposed A-E	
21–24		*Tristan*, second phrase / Oboe Descant
25–39	**Strophe 3**	
	phrase repeat, transposed A-E	
40–43		*Tristan*, third phrase / English horn+Oboe (duet)
43–		French horn signal (E to F)…
44–45	Schumann V-I cadence (B major)	
–46		… (E to F)

Figure 1, Holloway, "Dream Vision": synopsis

against the forward momentum of the strings' *Tristan* phrase below.[33] While Heine's poem ends with the speaker's sudden awakening—the dreamer's present tense replaced by a quotidian past-tense "forgetting"—the musical closure of Holloway's "Vision" is compromised. Schumann's jokingly flippant cadence gesture arrives over the original B-F# tonic fifth (mm. 44–45), yet it is dynamically muted (*pp*), and occluded by the foreground brilliance of the French horn's tonally disruptive E-to-F vacillation. The music presses on to the fourth movement's "Enchanted Forest," where the horn's E is finally established as home tonic. The horn soloist has, as it were, ignored Schumann's triadic syntax, and the new song arrives as an epiphany.[34]

"ENCHANTED FOREST" AND "DREAM VISITATION"

The "Enchanted Forest" movement, paraphrasing "Auf einer Burg," works less as an autonomous episode than as a continuation of the Wagner-infused scene of the preceding "Dream Vision." The Heine song traces a dream explicitly in brief motifs (tears, cypress-wreath, and so on); in turning to Wagner's well-known *Tristan* prelude, Holloway could appropriate a musical manifest image as a sign of psychically latent referents, erotic longing and death. Wagner's medieval romance, returning in the "Forest" scene, brings the listener to the opening of *Tristan*'s Act III, through an artfully arranged allusion to the English horn's piping (see Ex. 3). Before this happens—before the Wagnerian saga resumes—Holloway's "Auf einer Burg" paraphrase flows through its first strophe with the vocal line intoned by the French horn at pitch. The melody fuses elements of Schumann's neo-Baroque melody with Wagner's "alte Weise"—two "old" tunes condensed into a single image. In Schumann's Eichendorff scene, the old knight watches the Rhein from castle ruins; in Wagner, the Shepherd watches from Tristan's castle, above the Brittany cliffs. Isolde's ship has not yet been sighted: "Oed' und leer das Meer," he sings, moments before the dying Tristan is roused by his piping.

Holloway's English horn is a ghostly revenant who appears as Schumann's cadence ("in der stillen Klause") fades away. The falling fifths (F# to B) echo Schumann's head-motive, though his stolid trochees are superseded by rhapsodizing triplets reminiscent of Wagner's folk-like "alte Weise."[35] The melody's rising-sixth yearning (F# sliding up to G, then G#) echoes both Schumann and Wagner, while the somber tritone (G–C#) leans closer towards Wagner's original melody.[36] And we return, leitmotif-style, to the English horn's anxious chromatic descant of the earlier "Dream Vision."

Further Wagnerian quotations haunt the dense undergrowth of the central panel, within the "Enchanted Forest." As if to match the birdsong in Eichendorff's second strophe ("Waldesvögel einsam singen"), Holloway's French horn repeatedly quotes the Woodbird whose words Siegfried suddenly understands (from the so-called "Waldweben" episode in Act II, Scene 3 of *Siegfried*).[37] From Schumann's texted articulations of passion, Holloway has moved to Wagnerian instrumental motives, orchestral songs without words, layered with accumulated meanings. The growth in this "Forest" densifies the central panel, as derivatives of the Descant-shape rustle between muted string and woodwinds. It is a hushed yet intricate tangle of lines: woodwind miniature-fanfares assert a vestigial E Phrygian tonic in delicate modal opposition to the E-major (with added sixth) that ties Holloway's scene to *Siegfried*.

From the "Enchanted Forest," *Scenes* flows on, shockingly, into the fifth movement return of Schumann's "Allnächtlich" song (Ex. 4). This second paraphrase, a "Dream Visitation," is everything that the earlier "Dream Vision" was not—a fierce *tutti* rather than kaleidoscopic weave of orchestral colors; an earnest *maestoso* chorale, rather than a scherzo. The "Visitation" also restricts itself to a single strophic utterance, as if to banish (or resist) the earlier Wagnerian interpolations. This belated, alternative scene reaches an overblown climax, one that smacks of artificiality and exaggeration. The steady crescendo from a diffident *mezzo piano* or *mezzo forte* to the deafening *fff* of the final phrase is underpinned by the tam-tam's metallic edge (among the composer's few coloristic additions in the 1986 revision). Tonally, there is a stolid and static tonic, for the Db-Ab pedal is maintained throughout.[38] Yet the triadic harmonies in the middle register are caught between a noisy low-bass cluster (piano, *sempre con pedale*) and tintinnabulating ghost pitches. The triumphant tonal cadence that sweeps away the atonal clouds of the "Enchanted Forest" is itself hollow. Holloway's third-movement "Vision" might still have attempted to forget the beloved's mourning wreath, but in the fifth movement "Visitation," nightmare images cannot be dismissed so easily.

SCENES FROM SCHUMANN AND WAGNER: MODERNISM AS STYLE

"Instead of narrative method, we may now use the mythical method," T. S. Eliot observed, in an early appreciation of James Joyce's *Ulysses*.[39] In "a continuous parallel between contemporaneity and antiquity,"[40] the novelist had mapped Bloom's travels around twentieth-century Dublin to those of Homer's hero. For Eliot, Joyce's technique represented a genuinely modern approach to narrative, at a time when the realist novel genre appeared exhausted. A half century later, Robin Holloway was sensing a comparable style-historical impasse in his own artistic realm. That he sought to navigate the obstacle by explicit "borrowing" from precursors might not surprise students of mid-twentieth century European-American art music. For Holloway, the crisis looked like a challenge to personal conditions of possibility in the realm of artistic technique and style: "I hated the *Zeitgeist* both in general and in music… Things were absolutely forbidden, and it was basically everything that I loved most."[41] The claims of a post-1945 hegemony of atonal or twelve-tone serial techniques, led by a dogmatic and prestigious avant-garde, are familiar. But we may wonder, with further hindsight, if Holloway's move in the Schumann-inspired works was as singular a solution as it appeared to critics of the time. As Holloway's own documentation of a historical line of musical "cross-pollination" confirms, in quoting, paraphrasing, or stealing from the past, he was composing within a venerable counter tradition in concert music.

Nor was Holloway's practice necessarily a strictly musical affair. We may note, in closing, the affinities of his quotation-cum-paraphrase techniques with non-musical models. The *Tristan* quotations, beyond their function as some meme-like signifier of "eros," tie Holloway's Wagnerism to a *literary* modernist lineage of some specificity. Through "sudden memory or premonition," Alex Ross recounts, Joyce had produced a narrative consciousness steeped in familiarity with Wagner's operatic canon.[42] In Eliot's *The Waste Land*, meanwhile, the Wagnerian references are quotational, and the opera quoted is *Tristan und Isolde*. Eliot interpolates the Sailor's "*Frisch weht der Wind*" quatrain, then the Shepherd's single line "*Öd und leer das Meer*" (both set off in italic font) into the poem's first two pages. Wagner's *Öd* directly echoes Eliot's titular image, and he publicly identifies these quotations—and a later snippet of *Götterdämmerung*—in "notes" printed with the poem, first published in 1922.

Holloway's move in *Scenes*, from the first to the third act of Wagner's *Tristan*, loosely parallels Eliot's poetic scheme. Still more intriguing, though, is his artistic decision to do so decades after his literary modernist colleague. Getting at Holloway's relations to his own historical conjuncture—his position in some purported *Zeitgeist*—would ultimately require a fuller historical contextualization than space allows. What that scene encompasses, synoptically, stands somewhere between Holloway's personal sense of things "absolutely forbidden" and a wider critical consensus, perhaps only recently emergent in the mid-1960s, that the abstractionist ideology of the post-1945 avant-garde had already run its course. Leonard B. Meyer's identification, in music, of a "fluctuating stasis" argued a new status quo and a reigning pluralism within which "no style is necessarily superfluous."[43] From that perspective, Holloway's *Scenes from Schumann* was nothing if not timely. In a sense, he was attempting the kind of modern "writing" posited by Roland Barthes, a stylistic position derived overtly by back-reference to "a certain classical ethos."[44]

Does Holloway's large-scale paraphrase in *Scenes* respond actively to the near-contemporary example of Berio's Mahler-derived *Sinfonia,* or to a British canon of trans-historical works, from Vaughan Williams's *Fantasia on a theme of Thomas Tallis* (1912) through Peter Maxwell Davies's two *Taverner Fantasias* (1962, 1965)? The latter pair both thematize imagined community, yet Holloway's turn to Schumann, of course, positions the nation dialectically—a closer model, in that sense, might have been Michael Tippett's *Fantasia Concertante on a Theme of Corelli* (1953). Other blunt questions—why choose Schumann, and why bring in Wagner too?—to the extent definitive conclusions are imaginable, lead the critical discussion back to Holloway's skillful play of genre codes. Paraphrasing German *Lieder* in full-orchestral garb, he expands and *stages* the domestic voice-and-piano miniature, while conversely miniaturizing the vast temporal-mythic expanse of Wagnerian music-drama. In the resulting interference pattern, one discerns a second order play with conventions, operating at the level of formal dimensions. The "Dream Vision" of the first "Allnächtlich" moves almost too quickly to take in (as if *Tristan* has been reheard as cartoon music); in "Visitation," the vehemence is threatening but again, out of correct scale—something lies beyond the scene.

Lastly, there is Schumann "himself," the composer of the 1840 *Lieder* that populate Holloway's scenario. That the score does not treat him in isolation—as do Vaughan Williams or Maxwell Davies with named Renaissance forebears—but partnered by Wagner, is troublesome. Holloway's provocative casting choices foreground his own act of historical selection, while broadening the terms of reference from single character to wider cultural field. Still, we may accept Holloway's affirmation that in *Scenes* he was after "images and feelings," not irony or some creative working out of Oedipal anxiety. The belated return to Schumann is sincere, admiring, and the approach is surely apt. Schumann's music was never emotionally innocent, and precisely when confining himself to small-scale forms, he reached, as Charles Rosen wrote, a "hypnotic intensity," voicing "a new complexity and a new uneasiness."[45] In Holloway's attraction to Schumann's flights of musical thought, we may acknowledge fidelity to these expressive qualities. We may also discover a composer's separation of superficial categories of style from questions of character or personality. For in Holloway's *Scenes from Schumann* the regard for the other is always an assertion of self.

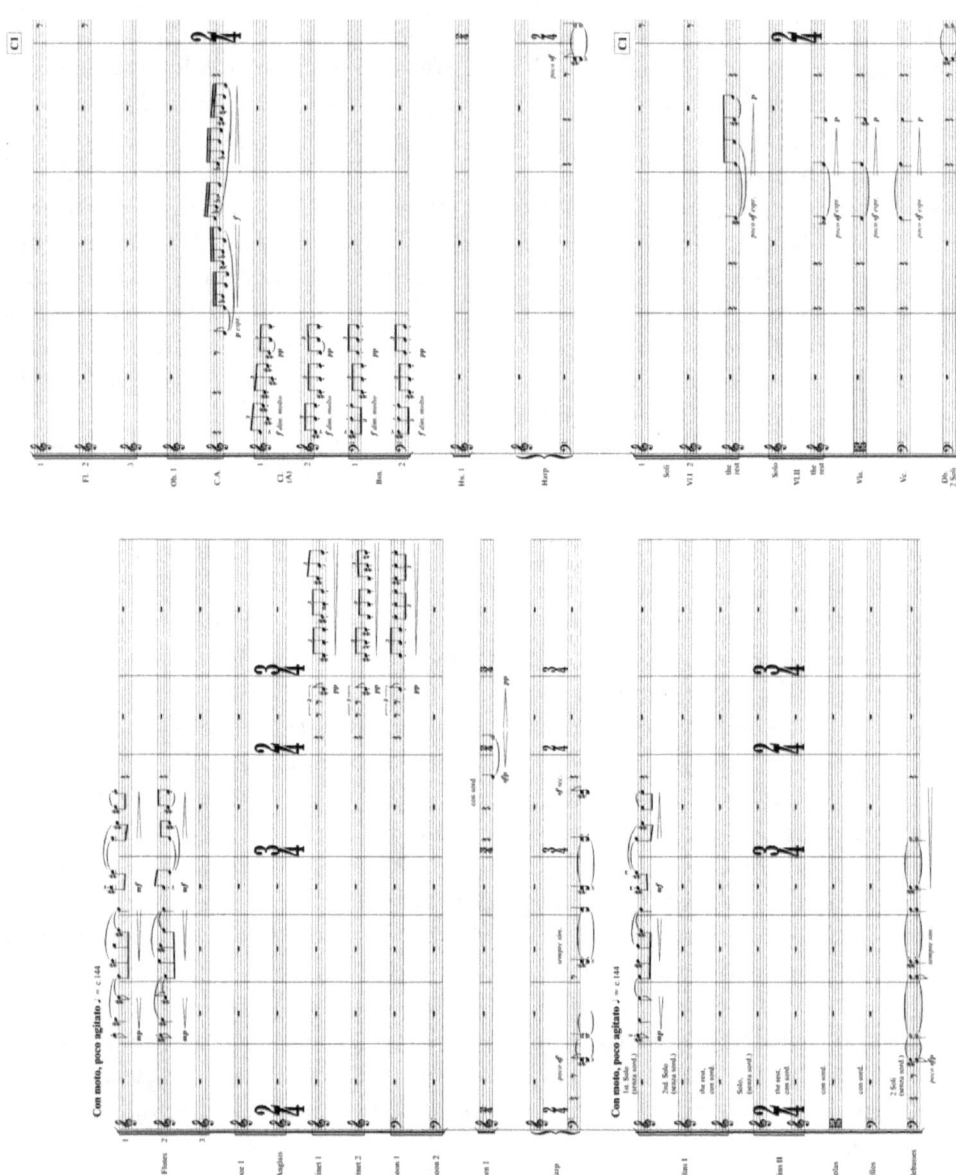

Example 1, Holloway, *Scenes from Schumann*, III, "Dream Vision," opening

Example 2, Schumann, "Allnächtlich im Traume," *Dichterliebe*, Op. 48, xiv, first verse

Example 3, "Enchanted Forest," English horn solo

Scene and Style in Robin Holloway's Music

Example 4, "Dream Visitation": opening

1. Robin Holloway, "Composer's Note" (May 1977), in *Scenes from Schumann: Seven Paraphrases for Orchestra*, op. 13 (London: Boosey and Hawkes, 1978); also reprinted in the 1992 revised score.
2. Robin Holloway, "Notes by the Composer," Holloway, *The Lovers' Well,* Delphian DCD 34216 (2018). Following two-piano scores by Fauré, Messager, and Chabrier, Holloway's *Souvenirs de Montsalvat* (1984) is a waltz-synthesis of themes from *Parsifal*.
3. Not to mention a suggestion of Schumann's *Szenen aus Goethes Faust*.
4. R. Larry Todd, "On quotation in Schumann's music," in *Schumann and his World*, ed. R. Larry Todd (Princeton: Princeton University Press, 1994), 83.
5. Todd, "On quotation," 96, 108.
6. Ibid., 80.
7. Holloway himself describes the Brahms quotations in Bayan Northcott, "A composer ... and his concerto," *Music and Musicians* 20/3 (Nov. 1971): 18, 20; see also Northcott, "Robin Holloway," *Musical Times* 115 (Aug. 1974): 644–46 (644).
8. Michael Oliver, "Miscellany," *British Music Now*, ed. Lewis Foreman (London: Paul Elek, 1975), 176.
9. "Composer's Note" (June 1979), in Holloway, *Fantasy-Pieces*, op. 16 (London: Boosey and Hawkes, 1979), [ii]. This work, too, originally premiered under a different, non-English title, *Liederkreis*.
10. Holloway, Liner note to Holloway, *Fantasy-Pieces,* recording Hyperion CDA 66930 (1998): see also the first epigraph quotation.
11. Northcott, "Holloway," 645.
12. Ibid.
13. Robin Holloway, "Why I write music," *Tempo* 129 (Jan. 1979): 3–8 (7).
14. David Matthews, "Music for Chamber ensemble (and *Scenes from Schumann*)," *Tempo* 129 (June 1979): 20–26 (23).
15. Ibid., 23.
16. Julian Anderson: "Robin Holloway: in medias res," *Tempo* 187 (Dec. 1993): 1–6 (2).
17. Postscript to *The Name of the Rose,* cited in Kenneth Gloag, *Postmodernism in Music* (Cambridge, 2012), 53.
18. Holloway, in Paul Griffiths, *New Sounds, New Personalities: British Composers of the 1980s* (London: Faber, 1985), 119.
19. Alan Blyth, "Composer inspired by Schumann," *The Times* (9 August 1974), 9; on *Domination of Black*, see also Bayan Northcott, "Robin Holloway," *Tempo* 117 (June 1976):15–17.
20. Robin Holloway, "Models of invention: old music with a new ear" (1993); repr. in Holloway, *Essays and Diversions* (Brinkworth: Claridge Press, 2003), 393–400 (393).
21. Holloway, "Models of invention," 397.
22. Robin Holloway, "Modernism and after in music." *Cambridge Review* 110 (June 1989): 60–66 (66).
23. Ibid., 65. Long prior to these essays, Holloway began critical study of music-historical borrowings in a Ph.D. thesis (completed 1971), later published as *Debussy and Wagner* (London: Eulenburg, 1979).
24. For Freud's classic exposition of "The Dream-Work," see *The Interpretation of Dreams*, trans. and ed. James Strachey (New York: Avon Books, 1965), chapter VI.
25. Holloway, like Schumann, places this song at the head of his collection.
26. On scoring shifts in Holloway's "Widmung," see Angela R. Mace, "'An affectionate homage': Robin Holloway's adaptations of Robert Schumann" (seminar paper, Duke University, 2008), 9–12.
27. Holloway, in Griffiths, *New Sounds, New Personalities*, 118.
28. Nicholas Kenyon, "Philharmonia/Knussen," *The Times* (25 June 1983): 7.
29. Sealing the *Tristan* presence in *Scenes*, the oboe's response to the English horn descant (later in "Dream Vision") will later make a fleeting, last-second return at the conclusion of Holloway's seventh movement.

30 Holloway, *Debussy and Wagner*, 142.
31 For Eric Sams, Schumann perhaps responds to the speaker's "confused dream state" by a halting text delivery: *The Songs of Robert Schumann*, rev. edition (Bloomington: Indiana University Press, 1993), 121.
32 Students of cipher will recognize the English horn opening <D S C H> as a potential "Schumann" (or Shostakovich) motto, though Holloway's succeeding phrase lacks comparable tetrachordal groupings.
33 Holloway's *Tristan* phrases 1 and 2 are faithful to Wagner, but his third *Tristan* phrase includes a stray additional pitch (viola, G#, m. 43).
34 In this narrative shift between movements, one might catch Holloway's admiration for a modernist precursor such as Berg's *Kammerkonzert*.
35 To Wagnerian listeners, the "Auf einer Burg" head-motive (falling fifth, stepwise rising third) may recall the motive opening *Tristan*'s Act II Prelude, and Wagner's leitmotivic underlining of the lovers' nocturnal defiance "treacherous" daylight in Scene 2 (Tristan: "Dem Tage! dem tückischen Tage"). On comparable pun-like melodic associations in later scores, see John Fallas, "Into the new century: recent Holloway and the poetics of quotation," *Tempo* 61 (2007): 2–10.
36 In the 1978 score, Holloway writes an additional phrase preceding the *agitato*.
37 The *Siegfried* reference is briefly noted in Matthews, "Music for chamber ensemble," 22.
38 A point noted in Gloag, *Postmodernism*, 68.
39 T. S. Eliot, "Ulysses, Order, and Myth," *The Dial* (Nov. 1923): 480–83 (483).
40 Ibid.
41 Holloway, in Griffiths, *New Sounds*, 118, 119.
42 Alex Ross, *Wagnerism: Art and Politics in the Shadow of Music* (New York: Farrar, Straus and Giroux, 2020), 474. The Act III *Tristan* scene figures explicitly in Virginia Woolf's novel *Jacob's Room* (1922), Ross notes (503–4).
43 Leonard B. Meyer, *Music, the Arts, and Ideas* (Chicago: University of Chicago Press, 1967), 171. Meyer's well-stocked survey of visual and literary paraphrase—from Picasso's Velazquez studies to John Barth's novels—complements his account of musical techniques from Ives and Stravinsky forward.
44 Roland Barthes, *Writing Degree Zero* (1953), trans. Annette Lavers and Colin Smith (New York: Hill and Wang, 2012), 12; Barthes's comment is given above as an epigraph.
45 Charles Rosen, *The Romantic Generation* (Cambridge: Harvard University Press, 1995), 694, 698.

17. "MY LAST HOPE IN THIS RESPECT": THE SAGA OF THE SWEDISH COMPOSER WILHELM BAUCK'S CORRESPONDENCE WITH FELIX MENDELSSOHN

KIRSTEN SANTOS RUTSCHMAN

In late 1841, the Swedish composer and music critic Wilhelm Bauck (1808–77) was frustrated by the lack of opportunities for advancement on the northern periphery of Europe. Though he would go on to become a well-respected teacher of the history and aesthetics of music at the Conservatory of the Royal Academy of Music in Stockholm, as well as a renowned music critic for daily newspapers and specialized music journals, these achievements lay as yet in the future.

The early 1840s, when Bauck's career had been launched but not yet established, can be viewed as a time of in-between. In terms of musical prominence, the golden age of Swedish opera had long since passed with the assassination of King Gustav III during a masked ball in his own Royal Opera House in 1792, while in 1840, soprano Jenny Lind was still at the very beginning of a career that would put her country (back) on the map. To be sure, throughout the nineteenth century, musically minded citizens of Stockholm could enjoy not only performances by resident musicians, but also traveling virtuosi who stopped en route to St. Petersburg. But with a population barely a quarter that of Berlin, Stockholm could not support the high level of musical activity to which residents of the Prussian capital were accustomed, a situation with which Felix Mendelssohn's mother, Lea, was well aware, thanks to reports from her niece, Josephine ("Peppi") Benedicks, who resided in the Swedish capital for two decades.[1] Wilhelm Bauck—in his early thirties, working primarily as a piano teacher and would-be composer struggling to attract a following—felt constrained by the limits of musical life in Sweden.

Bauck's first attempt to seek larger audiences in German-speaking regions was as calculated as it was unsuccessful. He sent a songbook to Breitkopf & Härtel, offering to forego any compensation in order to increase the publisher's potential returns, but to no avail. He then decided to make one more try. As if testing the limits of degrees of separation, he wrote a letter to the first cousin of the mother of the sister-in-law of his brother-in-law: Felix Mendelssohn.[2] The two had never met, nor would they meet in future, and there is no reason to believe that Mendelssohn knew of Bauck's existence prior to receiving the letter. But Mendelssohn's positive response would have a more enduring effect than either could have envisioned. Thus opens a saga in two acts.

ACT I: THE CORRESPONDENCE

Writing in November 1841, Bauck opens with an appeal to Mendelssohn's nature as a "true composer who might not withhold from a foreign and less noteworthy fellow artist a word of recognition and support, if he should find him not to be unworthy of this."[3] Bauck explains that, although he has dedicated his life to composing, the current situation in Sweden is such that

> no composition written here can find a way outside of the country; it can only reach a small and not very receptive audience, and from a purely artistic point of view finds extremely limited recognition. In reality, a composer writes only for a very few friends and in order to satisfy his own urge.[4]

Forced to earn a living by what he describes as the "spirit-killing" [*geistertödtende*] teaching of lessons, supplemented by the even more lowly duties of copying notation and tuning pianos, he mentions his failed attempt to interest Breitkopf & Härtel in his songs. His "last hope" [*letzte Hoffnung*] now is that Mendelssohn will be moved to consider his "little pieces" [*Werkchen*] and, if he finds them worthy, write a short evaluation that Bauck can then send on to a more receptive publisher, if Mendelssohn would be so kind as to suggest any names.

As proof of his good character, he suggests near the letter's end that Mendelssohn consult with Madame Åkerman, née Henriette Benedicks, daughter of the aforementioned Peppi Benedicks. Benedicks had taken up residence in Stockholm in the 1810s, remaining close to Felix's branch of the Mendelssohn family via letters and occasional visits to Berlin. Bauck offers the assurance that Madame Åkerman "will certainly bear witness to the fact that I am not an unworthy object of your attention."[5] There is no indication that Mendelssohn and Åkerman ever saw each other after 1824—when he was 15 and she scarcely half his age—and no correspondence between Mendelssohn and Åkerman survives, as it was Åkerman's mother who filled the role of correspondent with Lea. Nevertheless, writing eight years after Peppi Benedick's death in 1834, Bauck either knows first-hand that the channels of communication remained open, or assumes that communication was at the least a real possibility.

In his closing sentence, Bauck places himself on the same moral level as Mendelssohn even as he humbly insists on his own inferiority as a composer: "Once more, I implore you from the depth of my soul not to interpret my deed as being intrusive; I have done this in the confidence that a good person can offer a friendly hand even to a stranger, when both have dedicated their lives to the same goal, albeit with differing powers."[6]

Mendelssohn's lukewarm initial reaction can be inferred from a brief annotation he made, "Ja Ja so geht es." Nevertheless, he examined the enclosed songs, found them of interest, and penned a letter (now lost) recommending the compositions. His positive words can be inferred from the letter of thanks that Bauck sends three months later, in February 1842. Having secured Mendelssohn's approval of the songs, he takes care once more to differentiate his mission from that of an unworthy opportunist seeking to exploit the famous composer's goodwill:

> Without a doubt, there is no shortage of soldiers of fortune who overrun and torment a man of good reputation, and they become all the more intrusive, the more mediocre their achievements are. I was really afraid that you would count me as one of these people, and now I feel sincere joy that you have done the opposite.[7]

With this brief note, direct contact between the two composers comes to a close; Mendelssohn fulfills Bauck's request, but makes no effort to develop a closer acquaintance or extend the correspondence.

Upon receiving Mendelssohn's favorable report on the songs, Bauck wrote to the publisher Carl Friedrich Kistner (1797–1844) in Leipzig to offer the songs for publication.[8] Eager to avoid the appearance of exploiting Mendelssohn's approval for commercial gain, Bauck informs him that he also enclosed the written recommendation "with express instructions not to publish it."[9] With winter conditions preventing the shipment of a copy of the songs themselves from Stockholm, Bauck attempted to hasten the publication process by engaging a courier, Mr. Wittich, to pick up the manuscripts from Mendelssohn and deliver them to Kistner in Leipzig. But Mendelssohn was away in Leipzig when Bauck's letter arrived. This circumstance leads to Mendelssohn's final direct action in this matter, in the form of a letter the following month to Ludwig Heinrich Wittich;[10] he sends the scores, along with a short note explaining the delay. Presumably, Bauck's songs did eventually arrive in Leipzig. While it is not clear whether Kistner published them, Bauck's efforts were ultimately rewarded, as Schlesinger in Berlin did publish at least one set of his songs.

ACT II: THE DEFENSE

More than three years after this brief correspondence, Bauck found himself once more in need of Mendelssohn's recommendation. As a music critic for the newspaper *Aftonbladet* [Evening Page], Bauck typically reviewed the work of other composers, but occasionally his own music was addressed by fellow critics in the daily press. The present chain of criticism begins innocently enough with the mention of a well-received performance of Bauck's "Elfdrottningen" [The Elf-Queen] by tenor Julius Günther (1818–1904) at a soirée in Stockholm. The writer praises the song by calling attention to its counterparts on the program: "that [Bauck's "Elfdrottningen"] was placed alongside such heroes as Mendelssohn and Meyerbeer is truly an honor that not many have shared."[11] In closing, the reviewer promotes Bauck's fledgling career, noting that Bauck teaches piano and has been writing music criticism for the *Aftonbladet* for the past two years.

At the end of the 1844–45 concert season, "Elfdrottningen" was reprised, together with Bauck's song "Romance"; the unsigned critic briefly notes in a concert review in April that these "two recently published beautiful songs... were excellently sung" by Günther, to whom the published edition was dedicated, and he follows up with a more detailed review in July—coincidentally, alongside a review of a set of Mendelssohn's *Lieder ohne Worte*.[12] Confirming Bauck's characterization of Swedish musical life as narrow, the July review mentions the existence of Schlesinger's edition in German translation "as proof that [Bauck's] songs are valuable and popular," foreign opinion being necessary to validate his worth as a composer.[13] Bauck's style of melody and accompaniment win great praise, although the reviewer takes the opportunity to offer a few small suggestions for improvement; on the whole, the tone expresses genuine approval of the songs at hand and promising expectations for future works to come.

Two months later, however, a savage review signed by the critic —w— at the rival paper *Dagligt Allehanda* [Daily Variety] attacks these same two songs on all grounds, pronouncing them to be below average, bereft of inspiration, and with melodies that "lack all inner originality and original spirit; they are lacking in strength, leaving the heart cold and the mind empty."[14] Bauck is not to be condemned for his lack of musicality, the critic concedes; how is he to blame if he simply does not have the God-given gift of genius? Rather, his grievous fault lies in that he continues to write and publish music "that he himself ought to recognize is entirely lacking in inspiration."[15] The article then proceeds to a lengthy discussion of musically unsatisfying writing, including specific errors such a false relation "that catches the eye immediately, and moreover is so torturous to the ear, that even an ordinary pupil at our Royal Swedish Academy of Music knows enough to watch out for the same."[16] Only one other composer is mentioned by name in this tirade: speaking of Bauck's "Elfdrottningen," the author cautiously holds Mendelssohn up as having "not without success" achieved an appropriately "light and airy" style in many of his larger compositions. In contrast, Bauck's compositional skills are simply not up to the task.

Four days later, *Aftonbladet* publicly comes to Bauck's defense, acknowledging that Bauck often writes reviews (signed —u—) for *Aftonbladet* and arguing that not only the songs, but also his reputation, have unjustly suffered because of the negative review in *Dagligt Allehanda*.[17] With what can only be Bauck's blessing, the article makes it known that Bauck had previously sought and received Mendelssohn's opinion on several songs in manuscript, including "Elfdrottningen." The author then systematically brings Mendelssohn to Bauck's rescue by citing richly from both the negative review and from Mendelssohn's letter, showing how the latter contradicts the former point by point. For example, where —w— dismisses Bauck's melodies as "*unmusical prose*, or a *highly prosaic music*," Mendelssohn praises the "pleasant, naturally flowing, and yet not familiar or common melodies."[18] With tongue in cheek, the reviewer finishes up by asking, "What should one conclude from all of this, where two musicians as great as *Dagligt Allehanda's* —w— on the one hand and Mendelssohn-Bartholdy on the other, are standing here in glaring opposition to each other?,"[19] knowing full well that no Swedish musician, least of all —w—, could be construed as having approached parity with Mendelssohn. Closing the argument with incontrovertable proof, the author invokes Mendelssohn's authority by inviting interested readers to review the original letter in person at the editorial office.[20]

Not to be outdone, the anonymous —w— responded two days later on October 9, reiterating his views. He says that he had learned of the existence of Mendelssohn's letter five years earlier (an impressive feat, considering that at the time, just shy of four years had passed since the letter was written); per —w—, only the fact that he had been told in confidence by one of Bauck's friends prevented him from mentioning the letter in his initial October 7 review. The critic goes on to say that Mendelssohn's words ring empty, saying "less than nothing" [*mindre än intet*]; and even if they did, they referred to older songs of Bauck, which the author "doesn't deny have a certain value" [*ha vi ju ej heller förnekat dem ett visst värde*] and which seem to have been written under "a luckier star" [*en lyckligare stjerna*] than the one now leading Bauck astray in more recent compositions. The letter is a sign of Mendelssohn's politeness, he argues, nothing more.

Nevertheless, in the court of critical opinion, Mendelssohn's words won out. On October 7, *Morgonen* [*The Morning*] printed a friendly review of Bauck's latest song collection; the critical attack is not mentioned, but the author takes care to point out that recent performances of "Elfdrottningen" have received thunderous applause and also underscores the all-important international connection, that several of Bauck's songs were recently published by Schlesinger in Berlin.[21] The following day, the *Post- och Inrikes Tidningar* [Post and Domestic Times]—the source of the friendly review from July mentioned earlier—printed a brief summary of the October 3 attack in the *Dagligt Allehanda* together with the October 7 response in *Aftonbladet*, using italics to emphasize the key piece of evidence: "*a letter from Mendelssohn that praised Mr. Bauck's compositions quite profusely.*"[22] As the official communications organ tasked by the government to gather and disseminate news countrywide, the *Post- och Inrikes Tidningar* had a wide reach, spreading news quickly.

On October 10, *Den Konstitutionelle* [The Constitutional] printed a longer column that quickly pivots from praise for Bauck to a withering attack on —w—:

> We had intended to offer Mr. Bauck our condolences in our last issue, because of the crushing review that ran last week in the *Dagligt Allehanda*; but when we remembered that everything that *Allehanda's* music reviewer condemns is praised by all other newspapers and vice versa, we have every reason to congratulate Mr. Bauck instead. But from the bottom of our hearts we pity the *Allehanda*, in whose music articles we have now lost all trust.[23]

In addition to Mendelssohn's positive words, this author also places importance on the fact that Bauck's songs have been published "in Berlin itself" [*i sjelva Berlin*], and notes that Bauck now finds himself elevated to the ranks of more established Scandinavian figures like Adolf Fredrik Lindblad, Ole Bull, and Franz Berwald, all of whom have found themselves at the sharp end of —w—'s pen.[24]

On October 28, three weeks to the day after the *Aftonbladet* article printed Mendelssohn's words in support of Bauck, the German composer was elected a foreign member of the Royal Swedish Academy of Music in an otherwise opera-oriented class comprised of Rossini, Meyerbeer, and Auber.[25] In the second and final election of that same year, held on December 16, Bauck himself was elected a first-class member of the Academy, securing him a place in official musical life and preparing the way for his eventual position as a popular lecturer in the history and aesthetics of music in the educational institute of the Royal Academy in the years before and after its restructuring as the Royal Conservatory in 1866.[26]

APPENDIX: HISTORICAL NEWSPAPER ARTICLES CITED[27]

Several articles referenced above either lack titles or have nearly identical titles. Articles referenced are listed below, in chronological order.

A. "Musik: Herrar Steins, d'Auberts, och Sacks första subskriberade Soirée i Hr De la Croix's nya local sistl. Fredag," *Den Konstitutionelle* (December 20, 1844): 3.

B. "Inrikes: Stockholm: Hrr Steins, d'Auberts och Sacks femte (sista) musikaliska Soirée sistl. Tisdag," *Post- och Inrikes Tidningar* (April 10, 1845): 1.

C. "Musik: Sånger vid Piano, komponerade och tillegnade Julius Günter; af Wilhelm Bauck," *Post- och Inrikes Tidningar* (July 24, 1845): 1.

D. —w—, "Musik: Sånger vid Piano, komponerade och tillegnade Julius Günter af hans vän Wilhelm Bauck," *Dagligt Allehanda* (October 3, 1845): 2-3.

E. "Revy af Tidningarna… Ibland smärre saker," *Aftonbladet* (October 7, 1845): 2.

F. "Musik: Sånger vid Piano, komponerade och tillegnade Julius Günther af Wilhelm Bauck," *Morgonen* (October 7, 1845): 2.

G. "Tidnings-öfversigt," *Post- och Inrikes Tidningar* (October 8, 1845): 3.

H. —w—, "Stockholm: I anledning af en uppsats i gårdagens A.B." *Dagligt Allehanda* (October 9, 1845): 3.

I. "Ett och annat: Vi hade ämnat att i vår sista nummer," *Den Konstitutionelle* (October 10, 1845): 4.

"My Last Hope in this Respect"

1. See, for example, the letter from Lea Mendelssohn to her cousin Henriette von Pereira-Arnstein, November 26, 1821, *Ewig die deine: Briefe von Lea Mendelssohn-Bartholdy an Henriette von Pereira-Arnstein*, ed. Wolfgang Dinglinger and Rudolf Elvers (Hannover: Wehrhahn-Verlag, 2010), 1:57. In 1840, the official population of Stockholm was 84,161, as opposed to 322,626 in Berlin. *Historisk statistik för Sverige, Del 1, Befolkning 1720–1967*, 2nd ed. (Stockholm: Statistiska Centralbyrån, 1969), 62; *Statistisches Jahrbuch der Stadt Berlin*, vol. 34 (Berlin: P. Stankiewicz, 1920), 4.
2. Bauck's sister Jeanna Elisabeth married Fredrik Åkerman (1800–77). Fredrik's brother Anders Helmich Åkerman (1791–1869) married Henriette Benedicks (1816–73). Henriette was the daughter of Josephine "Peppi" Benedicks née Seligmann, who was Felix's first cousin—her mother, Rebecka Seligmann née Salomon, was sister to Felix's mother, Lea.
3. Bauck grounds his request in the hope that "ein wahrer Künstler auch dem fremden und weniger bedeutenden Kunstgenossen ein Wort der Anerkennung und des Beistandes nicht versagen werde, wenn er ihm dessen nicht unwerth befinden sollte." Wilhelm Bauck to Felix Mendelssohn Bartholdy, November 19, 1841, Green Books reel 14, no. 177, M. Deneke Mendelssohn Collection (Oxford: Bodleian Library). All English translations are my own.
4. The situation in Sweden is such that "kein einheimisches Tonprodukt ausser dem Lande gehen kann, sondern nur ein kleines und wenig empfängliches Publikum, und auch in rein künstlerischer Hinsicht eine äusserst beschränkte Anerkennung findet." Bauck to Mendelssohn, November 19, 1841.
5. "Sie wird gewiss bezeugen, dass ich als Mensch kein unwürdiger Gegenstand Ihrer Beachtung bin." Bauck to Mendelssohn, November 19, 1841.
6. "Nochmals bitte ich Sie aus voller Seele, diesen meinen Schritt nicht als Zudringlichkeit aufzunehmen; er ist aus der Zuversicht hervorgegangen, dass ein guter Mensch auch dem Fremden eine freundliche Hand bieten kann, wenn zum Beide ihr Leben demselben Ziel, wenn auch mit verschiedenen Kräften, gewe[iht] haben." Bauck to Mendelssohn, November 19, 1841.
7. "Es ist wohl kein Zweifel, daß es nicht an Glücksrittern fehlt, welche einen Mann von Ruf überlaufen und quälen, und desto zudringlicher sind, je mittelmäßiger ihre Leistungen. Mir war wirklich bange, daß Sie mich in Eine Reihe mit diesen Personen setzen möchten, und ich empfinde jetzt eine herzliche Freude darüber, daß Sie das Gegentheil thaten." Bauck to Mendelssohn, February 15, 1842, Green Books reel 15, no. 92.
8. Letter presumably lost; see Bauck to Mendelssohn, February 15, 1842.
9. "... mit der ausdrücklichen Vorschrift sie durchaus nicht zu publizieren." Emphasis original. Bauck to Mendelssohn, February 15, 1842.
10. Bauck informs Mendelssohn that L. W. Wittich, who delivered Bauck's letter, will return to pick up the manuscripts; however, Mendelssohn addresses his letter to Ludwig Heinrich Wittich (1816–87), the son of the deceased publisher Ludwig Wilhelm Wittich (1773–1832). See Mendelssohn to Ludwig Heinrich Wittich, March 10, 1842 in *Sämtliche Briefe*, ed. Juliette Laurence Appold et al. (Kassel: Bärenreiter, 2008–17), 8:351.
11. "Att den sistnämnde blef bemärkt vid sidan af sådana hjältar som Mendelssohn och Meyerbeer, är i sanning en ära, som icke många delat." See Appendix, Article A.
12. "Tvenne nyligen utgifna vackra sånger... sjöngos utmärkt väl"; for the brief report published immediately after the concert in April, see Appendix, Article B. For the longer review of Bauck's songs in July, see Appendix, Article C.
13. "Såsom ett bevis derpå att hans sånger äga både värde och äro omtyckta..." See Appendix, Article C.
14. "Hr B:s melodier... sakna nemligen all inre ursprunglighet och egen anda; de stå der kraft- och saftlösa, lemna hjertat kallt och förståndet tomt." See Appendix, Article D. The songs being reviewed are "Elfdrottningen" and "Fogelns sång mig gläder mer" [The bird's song delights me more]. The latter is presumably the same as the "Romance" reviewed earlier, as the two songs had been performed together in Stockholm the previous April and subsequently published as a pair by Abraham Hirsch in Stockholm; see Appendix, Article C.
15. "...hvad han likväl sjelf borde inse, sakna all inspiration." See Appendix, Article D.

16 Detta fel är så genast i ögonen fallande och är dessutom så plågande för gehöret, att troligen till och med en vanlig elev af vår Svenska Kongl. Musikaliska Akademi förstått att akta sig för detsamma." See Appendix, Article D.
17 See Appendix, Article E.
18 Where the critic decries "… en *omusikalisk prosa*, eller en *högst prosaisk music*," Mendelssohn proclaims that the songs "zeichnen sich vor vielen durch ihre angenehme, natürlich fliessende, und doch *nicht bekanntgewöhnliche* Melodie aus." Emphasis original. In this article, many of Mendelssohn's quotations are given in the original German as well as in Swedish translation. See Appendix, Article E.
19 "Hvad skall man nu sluta af det föregående, då tvänne så stora musici, som Dagl. Allehandas —w— å den ena och Mendelssohn-Bartholdy å den andra sidan, här stå i uppenbar motsägelse till hvarandra?" See Appendix, Article E.
20 Bauck told Mendelssohn in his letter from February 15, 1842 that he had enclosed the recommendation ["Ihre gütige Empfehlung beigefügt"] in his letter to Kistner, yet the newspaper promises the "original German letter" ["tyska originalbrefvet"]. Unless Kistner returned the original review, one of these must refer to a copy.
21 See Appendix, Article F.
22 "… ett *bref från Mendelssohn, som deri ganska ampelt lofordade Hr Baucks kompositioner*." See Appendix, Article G.
23 "Vi hade ämnat att i vår sista nummer uppvakta herr Bauck med en Condoleance, i anledning af den *dräpande recension* som stod att läsa en dag sistl. vecka i Dagl. Allehanda; men då vi ihågkommo att allt hvad Allehandas musikrecensent fördömmer, berömmes af alla andra tidningar och tvärtom, så hafva vi alla skäl att i stället lyckönska hr Bauck. Men vi beklaga deremot af allt hjerta Allehanda, hvars music artiklar numera förlorat allt förtroende." See Appendix, Article I.
24 For more on Adolf Fredrik Lindblad's friendship and correspondence with Mendelssohn, see Kirsten Rutschman, "Midsummer Dreams: Felix Mendelssohn's Swedish Connections," *Nineteenth-Century Music Review* 17, no. 1 (April 2020): 3-33.
25 For a complete list of foreign members of the Royal Swedish Academy of Music through 1995, see Pia Nyström and Anne Marie Elmquist, *Kungl. Musikaliska akademien matrikel, 1771-1995* (Stockholm: Kungl. Musikaliska akademien, 1996), 161–214.
26 A list of Swedish members of the Academy is printed in Nyström and Elmquist, *Kungl. Musikaliska akademien matrikel*, 29–159. As a first-class member of the Academy, Bauck was recognized in the category of theoretician/composer/poet, rather than a second-class membership honoring performers and connoisseurs.
27 At the time of writing, all historical newspaper articles quoted in this chapter are accessible at "Sök Bland Svenska Dagstidningar," Sök bland svenska dagstidningar (Kungliga biblioteket), accessed February 15, 2023, https://tidningar.kb.se/.

18. JOSEPH JOACHIM IN OXFORD

Susan Wollenberg

Last Sunday we had the most brilliant Sunday-music ... twenty-two carriages in the court, and Liszt and eight princesses in the room ... quintet by Hummel, duet from *Fidelio*, variations by David, played by that capital little Joachim, who is no infant prodigy, but a most praiseworthy child.

Thus, Fanny Hensel reported in 1844 on her concert at the family home.[1] "Little Joachim," that "praiseworthy child," would gain lasting fame as a violinist of exquisite abilities. He also achieved the status of a quasi-"English gentleman," providing reassurance for Donald Tovey's father, the Reverend Tovey, who, on perceiving in Joachim impeccable gentlemanly qualities, was persuaded that music might after all be a suitable profession for his son.

While Joachim's presence in England was primarily London-based, he toured not only as soloist, but also in the chamber group with Clara Schumann and Alfredo Piatti, among other ventures. Joachim's visits belonged to the influx of musicians coming from Germany to visit or take up residence in England at the time, a topic inviting fuller consideration than can be given to it here, and that, to my knowledge, still awaits the book-length treatment it deserves.[2] It was only later that a negative attitude surfaced among the host population in time of war. Even then, German performers and repertoire continued to feature in British musical culture.

Less well embedded in the general consciousness than Joachim's legendary status is that his long and prolific concert career included a series of appearances in the world-famous university city of Oxford.[3] Among the highlights discussed further below, in 1852 "Herr Joachim" on violin, alongside "Signor Bottesini" on double bass, with the Professor of Music, Henry Bishop, conducting, contributed to the University's Commemoration Festival in the Sheldonian Theatre, the University's meeting room.[4] In the open concert of the University Musical Club at the Sheldonian in 1889, marking the jubilee (fiftieth) year of his public career, Joachim was presented with a laurel wreath by Mendelssohn's grandson, Paul Victor Mendelssohn Benecke.[5]

Also hosting Joachim in Oxford were the Balliol Musical Society's concerts, established in 1885 amid the burgeoning cultivation of music in individual colleges of the University.[6] Joachim's nephew, Harold Henry Joachim (1868–1938), keen violinist, studied as an undergraduate at Balliol (1886–1890) under the tutelage of Lewis Nettleship, Classics Fellow and supporter of music in the college. (Harold Henry Joachim became Wykeham Professor of Logic and Fellow of Merton College.) In another family link, Joachim's great-nieces, Jelly d'Arányi and her sister Adila Fachiri, enjoyed considerable popularity as part of the Oxford concert scene. At their debut in 1910, in a performance for the Oxford Ladies' Musical Society (OLMS, founded in

1898), "Jelly was under 15 years old, and this was the first of many concerts she gave for the society;" later that year, "Adila and Jelly were accompanied on the piano by their younger sister Hortense."[7]

Joachim's involvement in the Balliol Concerts belonged to the earliest decades of their history. The list of performers during those formative years was beginning to reach beyond local talent; it included in the 1890s, among piano soloists, Leonard Borwick and Fanny Davies; and among vocalists, Marie Fillunger. Of the memorable concert at Balliol in 1896, when "Dr. Joachim" played (with Ernest Walker's skilful accompaniment) the Brahms G-major Sonata, and three Hungarian Dances, the *Oxford Magazine*'s critic noted how Joachim was "at his best," and his spirit "seemed to be contagious, for his fellow performers fairly surpassed themselves."[8] Also accompanying Joachim on that occasion, in Mozart's E-minor Sonata, was the young Donald Tovey, Nettleship music scholar at the college.

In 1899, Joachim accepted the invitation to serve as Hon. President of the newly formed Oxford & Cambridge Musical Club, based in London and providing opportunity for graduates of the two ancient universities to continue the enthusiasm for music they acquired as students.[9] While its membership was primarily associated with the musical clubs of the two universities, it stretched to others desiring to cultivate their musical interests further via the club's activities.

For Oxford's concert entrepreneurs, and the performers involved in the events they promoted, the local press was a vital conduit, carrying advertisements for concerts, and evaluative reports following the performances. *Jackson's Oxford Journal* was by Joachim's time a long-established source of such information. Circulating within the University, the *Oxford Magazine* (hereafter *OM*) carried notices of musical events in its calendar for the week, as well as critical evaluations of performances in its "Music of the Week" column.

Mentions of Joachim in the local press, progressing from the title "Herr," referred to him as "Professor," presumably apropos his conservatoire role, or as "Dr" Joachim. The latter reflected the University of Oxford's bestowal of the Honorary degree of D. Mus. on Joachim in 1888, granting him a position in a lineage that (perhaps most famously) featured Joseph Haydn. Honorands in the late-nineteenth and early-twentieth century tended to be influential scholars or leading composers, occasionally conductors, as with Hans Richter (1885) and later August Manns (1903). The award of the Hon. D. Mus. to instrumentalists became common only in the later twentieth century: Joachim's honorary Oxford doctorate appears a special case in its time.

"FOREIGN-BORN VIOLINISTS" IN BRITAIN: SCHOLES'S LIST

Percy Scholes, in the anthology with commentary that he produced in connection with the centenary of the *Musical Times*, compiled a list of violinists of foreign origin who contributed to concert life in Britain during the period. They included the "prolific and popular violin composer, redoubtable violinist, and incessant traveller," Henri Vieuxtemps (1820–1881),[10] Lady Hallé (1839–1911), of whom Joachim exclaimed: "When people have heard her they will think less of me,"[11] Wieniawski (1835–1880), and Marie Soldat (b. 1864). The last-named Scholes described as having built up "a reputation here as a player of refinement and taste." To Joachim, Scholes referred particularly warmly: "His position in the estimation of the British musical public was rightly unique and has become a tradition so widely accepted that it is hardly necessary to dwell upon the mastery of his playing." Scholes added that "his programmes in the later part of his career were of the very best and by them he exercised a strong influence upon public taste."[12]

Scholes's belief that Joachim held a special place in the pantheon of violinists is confirmed by the double-page spread he devoted to the musician as part of a four-page illustrative section inserted between pages 344 and 345 of his text. These pages contain plates featuring photographic or artistic portraits of performers from his list. Each of the outer pages shows pictures of six violinists arranged in rows in a gallery.[13] Scholes dedicated the two inner pages exclusively to Joachim (Plates 44–45). The items in Plate 44 range from Wilhelm Gurtner's crayon drawing of Joachim aged thirteen, "much as he was" (as Scholes described it) "when he first appeared in this country in 1844, as 'The Celebrated Hungarian Boy'," to "[what] may be considered the culmination of Joachim's British career, the Queen's Hall occasion of June 1904," marking the Diamond Jubilee.

Plate 45 offers a reproduction of the program of Joachim's British debut with the Philharmonic Society on 27 May 1844 (when he had made a sensation with his rendering of the Beethoven Violin Concerto), signed and dated by him on 1 June 1899 with the words: "The little fellow." As Scholes explained, apropos of the fifty-fifth anniversary concert (in 1899), when Joachim again played that concerto at the Philharmonic Society, in "what was to be his last appearance" there:

> MT [*Musical Times*]'s then Editor, F.G. Edwards, was present on this latter occasion, and had brought with him, from his collection … a copy of that first programme [27 May 1844]. This he put before the violinist asking him to autograph it. In doing this the violinist recalled the epithet of a London journal on that long-past occasion and added it below his signature.[14]

Scholes, in his second volume, found an opportunity to feature Joachim, and in particular his debut at the Philharmonic Society, at further length, quoting from reports in the *Musical Times*, and from J.W. Davison in the *Musical World*, in a section headed "The Procession of Prodigies."[15]

Susan Wollenberg

JOACHIM IN OXFORD – GRAND OCCASIONS

From the opening in 1748 of the Holywell Music Room, considered the earliest purpose-built concert room in Europe, Oxford attracted "foreign-born" musicians, joining the orchestral band, or visiting as soloists, booked to enhance the subscription concert series established from around the mid-century.[16] Leading performers of international provenance also regularly contributed to the more formal occasions at the University's Sheldonian Theatre, which had housed music and ceremony since its inception in the late seventeenth century.[17]

Among the attractions afforded by the presence of a great university, the Oxford commemoration festivals held a special place in the calendar. Already in a period housing the beginnings of modern marketing, these had developed during the eighteenth century to include some impressive musical offerings.[18] In the nineteenth century, they expanded further. During commemoration week in the summer, the city and its venues were crowded with visitors and residents, strolling around and attending ceremonies, concerts, garden parties, and balls.

For the "Oxford Grand Commemoration Musical Festival" of 1852, amid a series of evening balls (also bearing the epithet "grand"), the repertoire programmed over four days from Monday 21 June onwards included Mendelssohn's *St. Paul*, scheduled, together with "a miscellaneous selection of sacred music," for performance in the Sheldonian Theatre on the Tuesday afternoon.[19] Guest soloists and extra orchestral and chorus members were imported to reinforce local stalwarts: among the vocal soloists were Clara Novello and Sims Reeves, together with "Mademoiselle S. Cruvelli," and "Herr Staudigl." Conducting the proceedings was "Sir Henry R. Bishop, Prof. Mus. Oxon." Below the festival notice, an advertisement for the "Civet Cat Emporium," housed centrally in the city, informed visitors (and "those about to leave the University for the vacation") that it supplied, among an "immense variety of Fancy Goods suitable for their uses," items "for making presents commemorative of Oxford." The Great Western Railway put on "extra trains" to and from Oxford for the festival.

It was in this splendid context that "Herr Joachim (Violin)" and "Signor Bottesini (Contra-Basso)" were booked as solo instrumentalists for the "Grand Miscellaneous Concert," also in the Theatre, on the Wednesday afternoon. The *Journal*, reporting in detail on the week's proceedings, noted the presence of the Queen and Prince Albert at the Encaenia ("commemoration of the founders and benefactors" of the University), held in the "densely crowded" Theatre on the Wednesday morning, together with numerous others of special note, including "Mr. Gladstone," and "Mr. Disraeli." From 4 pm, in a concert lasting 4 hours, an audience of some 1,200 at the Theatre heard, among the miscellany making up the program, vocal items involving the much-admired soloists from the previous day, and a fantasia played by "Mdlle. Clauss, the celebrated Bohemian pianiste." Bottesini's double bass solo "excited wonder and delight," while "the fantasia on the violin by Herr Joachim displayed his perfect mastery over an instrument which, in his hands, appeared capable of imparting any tone or expression."[20]

UNIVERSITY CLUBS

The University Musical Club (founded in 1872) regularly hosted Joseph Joachim and his quartet colleagues, as well as his nephew, Harold Henry Joachim, who also played in string quartets.[21] The *OM*, 1889, carried in its regular notices under the heading of "Clubs and Societies," the "Programme of the Open Concert held in the Sheldonian on Friday, March 8" (an OUMC event), as follows:

> String Quartet in A major, Op. 41, No. 3 ... *Schumann*
>   Professor Joachim, Herr L. Ries, Mr. A. Gibson, Mr. C. Ould
> Songs, Op. 91 (1) "Gestillte Sehnsucht" ... *Brahms*
>   (2) "Geistliches Wiegenlied"
>   Miss R. Price   Viola obbligato – Mr. A. Gibson
> Sonata for Pianoforte and Violin in A major, Op. 47
> ("Kreutzer") ... *Beethoven*
>   Mr. J. Taylor, Professor Joachim
> Violin Solo, Sarabande and Bourrée ... *Bach*
>   Professor Joachim
> String Quartet in C major, Op. 76, No. 3
> ("Emperor") ... *Haydn*
>   Professor Joachim, Herr L. Ries, Mr. A. Gibson, Mr. C. Ould

A note at the end of the program recorded: "At the last meeting of the Musical Club Professor Joachim was elected an honorary member."[22]

The reviewer for "Music of the Week," in the same issue of *OM*, devoting the column to an account of the concert, noted that it was the "third successive year that he [Professor Joachim] has honoured the Musical Club by playing for them." The penultimate paragraph began:

> We must say, finally, that Dr. Joachim had a very hard time. He only arrived from a six hours' railway journey just in time for a very long and trying programme; yet, except for his appearance and a morsel of careless intonation, it was hardly possible to detect how tired he was.

The concert "was a grand success, and the audience almost filled the Sheldonian."[23]

The comments on the performance included reference to "Dr. Joachim's innumerable delicacies of shading, combined with the overwhelmingly broad effects which give the flavour of grand art to his conceptions," seeing something of this reflected in the playing of Herr Ries (2nd violin). Joachim's solo item, consisting of the two unaccompanied Bach movements, demonstrated, in the columnist's view, "the extreme purity and nobility of his rendering."[24] As the *Journal* reported, before the Bach item, "Sir John Stainer, with Mr. Benecke, President of the Club, brought onto the platform a laurel wreath, decorated with a long streamer of the Oxford dark blue ribbon, and presented it to Herr Joachim," who received it "very graciously" and shook hands with them. Stainer ended his speech (quoted further in the *Journal*) by wishing Joachim "a long life and happy days."[25]

The "Music of the Week" column in the *OM*, 1892, commented apropos OUMC's fifth Public Classical Concert [PCC] at the Sheldonian on 1 March: "As his solo, Dr. Joachim selected a somewhat uninteresting Romance in A minor by Max Bruch, adding, for the inevitable encore, one of his favourite Bach pieces for violin alone." The reviewer thought him at his best in the quartets (Haydn's Op. 77 no. 1, and Beethoven's Op. 59 no. 3), especially the slow movements, and concluded:

> Though it is impossible now altogether to avoid recognising the effect of time on Dr. Joachim's playing, he will always remain the supreme example of single-minded and uncompromising devotion to all that is strong and noble in art, and for depth of true feeling and breadth of interpretation he still more than holds his own among violinists.[26]

In the third series of the PCC (1893–94), Joachim formed a piano trio with Fanny Davies and William Whitehouse, who had studied with Piatti, in performances of works by Dvořák and Beethoven; their chamber music programme on 6 February 1894 (for the fourth concert, in the Sheldonian) also included the Brahms–Joachim Hungarian Dances, with Fanny Davies accompanying Joachim. For the orchestral concert that followed in the series, on 6 March, Joachim was billed as playing the Beethoven concerto.[27]

The chamber concert in the fifth series at the Sheldonian on Shrove Tuesday, 26 February 1895, featured Joachim, with his colleagues in a Haydn Quartet (Op. 17 No. 6), and Beethoven's "Harp" Quartet, as well as playing Tartini's "Devil's Trill" Sonata. The instrumental items were programmed alongside Schubert Lieder, and folksongs arranged by Brahms, performed by Marie Fillunger, whose rendering of Schubert's "Die Junge Nonne" drew particular critical acclaim, in an altogether enthusiastic review in the press.[28] The event attracted "a good and attentive audience," although, with its "being a spring day and a football match being advertised in the Parks," there was "not such a crowded gallery as hoped for." The *Journal*'s critic believed that the Tartini sonata was "one of Dr. Joachim's favourite concert pieces," deeming it "hardly necessary to add that he played it as only he can," and adding that Joachim received a standing ovation.[29]

Under Joachim's Presidency, the OCMC (uniting alumni of the two universities, as mentioned earlier) in its first few years flourished in every respect, attracting a growing number of members and widening the scope of its activity. The Club's report for 1901, published the following year, showed its financial position as "again very satisfactory."[30] Membership had risen steadily. The year had been busy with music meetings, including twenty-three Thursday concerts and visits to the OUMC, OUMU, Cambridge University Musical Club and Rugby Musical Union. Eighty-eight members had taken part in the year's programme; the "informal meetings on Sunday nights and other times" had been well attended, and it had carried out the previous year's resolution to set apart one of the regular meetings "for Lady Visitors," in a concert that proved "an unqualified success." (This became an annual event, later increased to two such occasions per annum.)

The "Joachim dinner" in honour of their "distinguished President" was 'one of the most important events of the year":

> Dr. Joachim was good enough on that occasion to inaugurate his first introduction to the Club by playing a quartette with his colleagues from Berlin, and expressed both then and subsequently his great interest in the Club and its prosperity.

The OCMC report for 1902 declared: "It is impossible to value too highly the friendly support this Club has received from the Chamber Music Clubs at both Universities." Sir Walter Parratt and "Dr. Elgar," newly elected, joined Joachim and his fellow honorary members of the OCMC. Income had increased steadily. Ninety-nine members had taken part in the programmes: "the meetings were [again] well attended," and "the two to which Ladies were admitted as guests proved as popular as ever." Satisfactory proceedings were recorded for 1903: the "principal event" was the Club dinner, enhanced by "the visit ... of our President, Dr. Joachim and his Quartet," who performed "delightful music" after dinner, together with "Mr. Leonard Borwick, Mr. Shakespeare and others." Chairing the proceedings at the dinner, attended by some 140 members, was Sir Hubert Parry. In 1904 and 1905 there were continuing successes for the Club on the concert scene; in 1904 a record number of members (100) took part in the music meetings during the year, and the Club celebrated its 150th music meeting in May 1905.

The report for 1906 conveyed sad news, under the heading of "The Late President":

> It is sad to have to record the death of our distinguished President, Dr. Joachim. The whole world deplores the loss of his attractive personality and splendid genius, and lovers of Chamber Music can never forget him.

In January 1908 a remarkable concert took place in the Queen's Hall, "in memory of Dr. Joseph Joachim, in which [Hugh] Allen conducted the combined forces of the London, Oxford and Cambridge choirs in a performance of the Brahms Requiem." This occasion prompted the *Times* critic, admiring the technical and expressive qualities it evinced, to comment that "no finer performance" of the Requiem had been heard in London.[31]

CONCLUSION

Joachim's involvement in Oxford concerts, and in the activities of the Oxford and Cambridge Club, evidently engendered a particularly admiring and affectionate response to his person and his performance, together with a deep respect for the sensitivity of his interpretation, as a performer. He established roots in the city and University as a well-loved figure in the musical life of "town and gown." Joachim's

Oxford visits, and his involvement in the OCMC, enabled his audiences, and the performers with whom he appeared, to encounter a person of great qualities and to hear musical performances of a rare distinction.

1 Sebastian Hensel, *The Mendelssohn Family (1729–1847): From Letters and Journals*, transl. Carl Klingemann [Jr], 2 vols (London: Sampson Low, Marston, Searle and Rivington, 1881), vol. 2, 260: letter of Fanny Hensel to her sister Rebecka. For Joachim's performance at Hensel's Sunday concerts in February and March 1844, see R. Larry Todd, *Fanny Hensel: The Other Mendelssohn* (Oxford: Oxford University Press, 2009), 302–3.
2 General coverage of the German presence is found in Rosemary Ashton, *Little Germany: Exile and Asylum in Victorian England* (Oxford: Oxford University Press, 1986).
3 For bibliography on Oxford see Susan Wollenberg [hereafter 'SW'], "Oxford." in *GMO*. On music in Oxford during Joachim's lifetime see particularly Chapter 18, "Music," in Michael Brock and Mark Curthoys (eds), *History of the University of Oxford*, vol. 7, *The Nineteenth Century, Part 2* (Oxford: Oxford University Press, 2000), 428–42, and Robin Darwall-Smith and SW (eds), *Music in Twentieth-Century Oxford: New Directions* (Woodbridge: Boydell and Brewer, 2023), hereafter *MTCO*.
4 On the commemoration festivals see SW, "The Oxford Commemorations and Nineteenth-Century British Festival Culture," in Peter Horton and Bennett Zon (eds), *Nineteenth-Century British Music Studies*, 3 (Aldershot: Ashgate, 2003), 225–49; and, for a broader contextual study, Pippa Drummond, *The Provincial Music Festival in England, 1784–1914* (Farnham: Ashgate, 2011).
5 SW, *Music at Oxford in the Eighteenth and Nineteenth Centuries* [*MO*] (Oxford: Oxford University Press, 2001), 176. On Benecke see Margaret Deneke, *Paul Victor Mendelssohn Benecke, 1868–1944* ([Oxford]: Printed privately [by A.T. Broome & Son], [1954]), and SW, "Three Oxford Pianistic Careers: Donald Francis Tovey, Paul Victor Mendelssohn Benecke, and Ernest Walker," in Therese Ellsworth and SW (eds), *The Piano in Nineteenth-Century British Culture: Instruments, Performers and Repertoire* (Aldershot: Ashgate, 2007), 239–61.
6 See Arthur Burns and Robin Wilson, *The Balliol Concerts: A Centenary History* (Oxford: Balliol College Music Society, 1985); and SW, "The Balliol Concerts," in *MTCO*, 119–35.
7 G. K. Woodgate, *The Oxford Chamber Music Society: A Brief History* (Oxford: Oxford Chamber Music Society, 1997), 9. The OLMS changed its name to the Oxford Chamber Music Society in 1968.
8 Quoted in *MTCO*, 120, n. 8. This was concert 1001, on 8 March 1896.
9 On the history of the Oxford and Cambridge Club [hereafter OCMC], see Graham Thorne (ed.), *The Oxford & Cambridge Musical Club: An 80th Anniversary History* (Oxford: Oxford and Cambridge Musical Club, 1979). See also Ian Maxwell, "'For the purpose of encouraging the practice and knowledge of chamber music': The Oxford & Cambridge Musical Club 1899–1940," in *MTCO*, 213–32.
10 Percy A. Scholes, *The Mirror of Music 1844–1944: A Century of Musical Life in Britain as reflected in the pages of the Musical Times*, vol. 1, 345.
11 Quoted in Scholes, *Mirror of Music*, vol. 1, 346, from her obituary in the *Musical Times*.
12 Scholes, *Mirror of Music*, vol. 1, 345. On the 'Joachim-kultus' (the Joachim cult) in Germany see Beatrix Borchard, *Stimme und Geige: Amalie und Joseph Joachim* (Wien: Böhlau, 2005), 578–9. Borchard refers to Joachim's '*Monumentalisierung*' (Monumentalisation) amid German culture.
13 Scholes, *Mirror of Music*, vol. 1, Plates 43 and 46.
14 Ibid., Plate 45.
15 Scholes, *Mirror of Music*, vol. 2, 833–4.

16 The classic source for the history of the Holywell Room is J.H. Mee, *The Oldest Music Room in Europe: A Record of Eighteenth-Century Enterprise at Oxford* (London: John Lane, 1911).
17 On the history of the Sheldonian Theatre see Christopher Hibbert with Edward Hibbert (eds), *The Encyclopædia of Oxford* (London: Macmillan, 1988), 430.
18 On eighteenth-century advertising stratagems see Rosamond McGuinness, "Gigs, Roadies and Promoters: Marketing Eighteenth-Century Concerts," in SW and Simon McVeigh (eds), *Concert Life in Eighteenth-Century Britain* (Aldershot: Ashgate, 2004), 261–71.
19 *Jackson's Oxford Journal* [hereafter 'the *Journal*' in text, *JOJ* in notes], (19 June 1852): 2, from which further extracts quoted in this paragraph are derived.
20 *JOJ* (26 June 1852): 3.
21 The Oxford University Musical Club [hereafter OUMC] joined with the Oxford University Musical Union [OUMU, founded 1884] to form the OUMCU, from 1916. On individual college societies in the period, see SW, *MO*, Chapter 10. On the wider concert scene see ibid., Chapter 9. (The University clubs attracted membership from across the colleges.)
22 *OM*, VII/16 (13 March 1889): 270.
23 Ibid., 267.
24 Ibid.
25 *JOJ* (16 March 1889): 5.
26 *OM*, X/13 (Wednesday 9 March 1892): 226.
27 *JOJ* (3 February 1894): 5.
28 *JOJ* (2 March 1895): 8.
29 Ibid. As encore, Joachim again chose unaccompanied Bach.
30 Oxford, Bodleian Library, Per. 17402 c. 19 (n.p.). Quotations in this and the following paragraph are from that source.
31 Cyril Bailey, *Hugh Percy Allen* (London and New York: Oxford University Press, 1948), 91–2.

19. "I FELT AS IF I HAD FOUND A DIAMOND": THE MOZART-ENTHUSIAST SIR WILLIAM STERNDALE BENNETT IN THE CONTEXT OF HIS MULTIFACETED MOZART REVIVAL

WALTER KURT KREYSZIG

In more recent times, the well documented cross-cultural exchange between England and the Continent has focused on aspects of compositional practice, particularly those shared among Continental composers and their British counterparts. R. Larry Todd has identified Sir William Sterndale Bennett[1] and Felix Mendelssohn Bartholdy, the latter who enjoyed a canonical status in England,[2] as staunch advocates of the cultural axis between the British Isles and the Continent,[3] which was responsible for heralding in the nineteenth-century musical renaissance in England,[4] an endeavour supported by the Society for British Musicians[5] and the Royal Philharmonic Society.[6]

Mendelssohn travelled to England ten times between 1829 and 1847.[7] These sojourns allowed him to be present at the British premiere of several of his compositions by the Royal Philharmonic Orchestra, including two overtures preserved in the Library of the Royal Philharmonic Society:[8] the Concert Overture Nr. 1 to the *Midsummer Night's Dream* in E-Major, op. 21 in 1829, the Concert Overture Nr. 2 *Die Hebriden* in b-minor, op. 26 in 1832 and the Symphony No. 4 in A-Major, op. 30 in May of 1833.[9] Bennett conducted the latter work on several occasions in the Subscription Concerts of the Royal Philharmonic Society of London between 1857 and 1860.[10]

While in England, Mendelssohn's personal encounter with Bennett in London, and his invitation to Bennett to visit Germany, paved the way for Bennett's four sojourns in Germany between 1836 and 1842 – travels which took him to Düsseldorf in 1836 for the premiere of Mendelssohn's oratorio *St. Paul* on May 26,[11] to Leipzig in 1837 and 1839 for several appearances with Mendelssohn at the Gewandhaus in Leipzig,[12] and to Berlin in January 1842 to attend the premiere of Mendelssohn's Symphony No. 3 in a-minor ("Scottish"), op. 56.[13] Bennett's trips to Germany helped solidify his friendship with Mendelssohn,[14] to whom Bennett dedicated his Piano Sonata in f-minor, op. 13.[15] These trips also enabled Bennett to form a closer association with the Schumanns, in particular Robert Schumann, the dedicatee of Bennett's *Fantaisie in A-Major* op. 16.[16]

In the lengthy 1842 review of Bennett's compositions for solo piano for the *Neue Zeitschrift für Musik*, Schumann, who had met Bennett on several occasions that year,[17] expressed considerable interest in the Englishman's musical contributions. He placed Bennett's piano oeuvre,[18] beginning with the *Suite de pièces*, op. 24,[19] within the broader context of eighteenth- and nineteenth-century music, thereby acknowledging Bennett as a composer in his own right.[20] In this review, Schumann alluded to compositional similarities between Bennett and Mendelssohn, though without reference to specific compositional practices shared between these composers. R. Larry Todd has substantiated Schumann's general observation by convincingly tracing specific allusions to Mendelssohn's *Lieder ohne Worte* (op. 19, No. 5; op. 30, No. 2 and No. 3; op. 85, No. 4), *Duetto ohne Worte* (op. 38. No. 6)[21] and chamber music (String Quartet No. 2, op. 13) in Bennett's early keyboard compositions (i.e. Bennett's Piano Sonata in f-minor, op. 13).[22] In these works, Bennett draws on inspiration from Viennese classicism, an influence directly tied to his life-long interest in the works of Wolfgang Amadeus Mozart, which guided his career as performer, lecturer, composer, and collector. Todd also elaborates on two additional facets of this cultural exchange, which proved to be exceptionally beneficial for Bennett. Spearheaded by advice from Mendelssohn, who had considerable experience with publishers,[23] Bennett secured a publishing contract[24] with two prominent Leipzig publishing firms—the Kistner brothers[25] and Breitkopf & Härtel[26]—for a number of his early piano compositions, including the two aforementioned piano sonatas and fantasia in addition to the *Three Romances*, op. 14.[27] Beyond the allusions to Mendelssohn's piano works[28] in Bennett's *Impromptu*, op. 12, No. 2,[29] and *Romanza*, op. 14, No. 2,[30] Bennett's four-movement Piano Sonata in f-minor, op. 13 also reveals the influence of Viennese classicism, especially the sonata form, with its three-part division in the finale and the four-part division (with coda) in the opening movement, and in both forms the support of the tonic-mediant dichotomy, the traditional tonal frame of minor-key pieces.[31] With regard to his approach to sonata form, Bennett, whose contribution attracted attention and praise on the Continent, as for example in the writings of François Fétis,[32] may have been inspired by Mendelssohn.[33]

★ ★ ★

The British music scene, encompassing the years 1790 to 1875, also played a decisive role in the reception of Viennese Classicism. The practice of importing to England Viennese repertories, as advanced by Johann Peter Salomon with his founding of the so-called Salomon concerts,[34] was met with great enthusiasm by Bennett, the noted concert impresario, whom Mendelssohn in 1836 extolled as "the most promising young musician I know"[35] and about whom Robert Schumann prophetically remarked that "if there were only many more artists who composed like Bennett, no one would be afraid of the future of our art."[36]

During his lengthy trips to Germany (October 1836 – June 1837; October – March 1839, January – March 1842),[37] Bennett kept a detailed diary of important events.[38] His close association with Mendelssohn dates back to 26 June 1833.[39] On 4 November 1833, Bennett received a ticket from Mendelssohn for a performance of Mozart's Symphony in E-flat Major, KV 543 at the Gewandhaus. In a review of 13 November 1836, Bennett pointed to the slow movement of Mozart's String Quartet in B-flat-Major, KV 589 as "very much out of time,"[40] presumably in reference to the permanent displacement of the accentuation within the *tactus* stemming from the multifaceted formation of syncopated figures, which in turn contribute to an unusual texture.[41] Schumann refers to the common bond between Bennett and Mendelssohn and describes their relationship not as teacher-disciple, but rather in their sharing of a common heritage.[42] To reflect on the brotherly affinity between Bennett and Mendelssohn, Schumann used the term *Brüderähnlichkeit*, which became evident in Bennett's performance of an all-Mendelssohn pianoforte recital on 15 February 1848[43] and in his collecting of music by Mendelssohn, as, for example, the autograph of Mendelssohn's String Quartet No. 3 in D-Major, op. 44, No. 1, which Bennett had received from the composer in 1842.[44] This was a work dear to Mendelssohn's heart. On 30 July 1838 he wrote to Ferdinand David: "I have finished my third quartet in D Major and I love it very much. ... it is more fiery and ... more satisfactory than the others."[45]

Bennett's close relationship with the Schumann family becomes evident from Bennett's documentation in his diary of Clara Schumann's performance of her own *Premier Concerto pour le pianoforte avec accompagnement d'orchestre (ou de quintuor)*, op. 7 at the Gewandhaus under Mendelssohn's baton on 9 November 1835.[46] Beyond that, Clara Schumann's arrangements of some of Bennett's instrumental works, such as the Three Diversions for the Pianoforte, à quatre mains, op. 17, attests to her interest in the Englishman's compositions.[47] Notwithstanding his bond with Mendelssohn, Bennett displayed an even closer spiritual affinity to Mozart, whose compositional legacy accompanied Bennett throughout his life.

Here, it seems most fitting to consider the bond between Bennett and Mozart, not alluded to by Schumann or any other contributor to the *Neue Zeitschrift* für *Musik*, but most forcefully articulated by Bennett himself in his discovery of Mozart's legacy as a composer, which he likened to the unearthing of a diamond, here recalling his "discovery" of Mozart's Piano Sonata in F-Major,[48] "in the library of a country-house."[49] Bennett's son, John R. Sterndale Bennett, substantiates his father's bold claim at the beginning of his biography, with comments on the importance of choosing a model of emulation for one's own engagement in music, be it in composition or other activities such as listening and performance.[50]

★ ★ ★

By the time Bennett had become known as a Mozart enthusiast, England had already developed into a cultural stronghold of Mozart, thanks in part to Salomon's aforementioned initiative and in part to Mendelssohn's enthusiastic promotion of Mozart's legacy, both in his own compositions[51] and in his performances as pianist and conductor.[52] These multifaceted activities provided Robert Schumann with ample reason to refer to Mendelssohn as "the Mozart of the nineteenth century."[53]

Beyond that, many Englishmen had also cultivated an interest in Mozart. A prominent group of musicians, the so-called "British Mozartians,"[54] gave performances of Mozart's works at meetings of the Anacreontic Society.[55] Among these enthusiasts were Thomas Attwood, Muzio Clementi, and Johann Baptist Cramer, the latter whose performance of Mozart's Piano Concerto in A-Major, KV 414 (= 386a) on 18 January 1786 attracted the attention of an anonymous reviewer,[56] who referred to this performance as proof of the composer's "knowledge of science," perhaps inadvertently alluding to the notion of an all-embracing *Kompositionswissenschaft* ("profound knowledge of composition")—a term that Franz Joseph Haydn had coined with regard to Mozart's skills and achievements as a composer, specifically in reference to his six string quartets dedicated to Haydn.[57] Obviously, Haydn's praiseworthy comments in his oral communication with Mozart's father Leopold must have enthused him to such an extent that he, in turn, related Haydn's term of the *Kompositionswissenschaft* in a letter to his daughter Anna Maria, dated Vienna, 16 February 1785.[58] Like Haydn, Bennett also assigns a position of pre-eminence to Mozart.

Bennett was an exquisite performer of his own compositions, many of which display compositional practices of the London Pianoforte School[59] and the Austro-German tradition.[60] On 26 June 1833, he performed his own Piano Concerto No. 3 in c-minor, op. 9 (dated 14 July 1834)[61] at Windsor Castle before the presence of the King and the Queen. He performed the same work on 18 January 1837 at the Gewandhaus[62] in the presence of Mendelssohn.[63] This work was inspired by Mozart according to an analysis prepared by James William Davison (1813–1885).[64] Bennett also appeared in solo performances and chamber music settings with a predilection for Mozart on numerous occasions in his Classical Chamber Concerts (1843–1856) in London.[65]

Of special interest was Bennett's performance of Mozart's Concerto in Eb-Major, KV 449 on the opening night of a new musical organization, the Vocal Concerts. This performance was made possible thanks to Bennett's copying the full score from the band parts.[66] On 15 May 1848, Bennett performed Mozart's Concerto in d-minor. KV 466[67] at the Royal Philharmonic Society (founded in 1813, with Attwood as one of the co-founders)[68]—marking Bennett's final appearance at the Philharmonic[69] and as such a memorable event, as Bennett added necessary ornamentation in addition to his supplying of his own cadenzas.

In his lectures at the University of Cambridge, Bennett displayed a special penchant for g-minor compositions of Mozart, such as the Symphony in g-minor, KV 550, "as an example of marvellous power and pathos displayed with sparing use of instruments"[70]—a work that stands out amongst the oeuvre of Mozart for its preservation in various versions, including one for septet, arranged by the London publisher, composer and violinist Giovanni Battista Cimador. Upon hearing this arrangement, Clementi remarked that "Mozart has reached the boundary gate of music and he has leapt over it, leaving behind the old masters, the moderns and posterity itself."[71] This observation provided ample reason for Clementi's own arrangement. In his lectures Bennett also examined one of his favorite works, Mozart's Quintet in g-minor for two violins, two violas and violoncello, KV 516.[72]

"I felt as if I had found a diamond"

* * *

Beyond his interaction with Mendelssohn, Bennett's interest in Mozart was kindled as a result of his engagement with other musicians, all of whom held Mozart in the highest regards, including Thomas Attwood, W.A. Mozart's student in Vienna in 1785,[73] and Cipriano Potter, a professor of piano at the Royal Academy of Music in London,[74] to whom Bennett had dedicated his Piano Concerto No. 2 in Eb-Major, op. 4,[75] and who, as a second-generation student of Leopold Mozart, had published a volume of piano arrangements of W.A. Mozart's pianoforte works.[76] Included in this volume of piano arrangements was Mozart's Rondo for Piano and Orchestra in A-Major, KV 386, the autograph comprising fourteen leaves which is dated Vienna, 19 October 1782—the year of Mozart's marriage to Constanze Mozart. After Mozart's death in December 1791, the autograph of KV 386 came into the possession of Constanze.[77] The publisher Johann Anton André,[78] who played an important role in the dissemination of Mozart's legacy, acquired the autograph of KV 386 on 3 May 1800.[79] In the spring of 1803, André's son Gustav transferred to London several autographs of Mozart, J.S. Bach, Haydn, and Carl Maria von Weber, including the Mozart autograph of KV 386, which Bennett purchased.[80]

Bennett had a habit of giving away the autographs of his own works once a work had appeared in print.[81] This practice of dissemination regrettably extended to Mozart's KV 386, as we readily glean from the distribution of the autograph, beginning in 1846, with the individual leaves finding separate homes in the United States, Germany and England.[82] Owing to the already fragmentary preservation of this autograph when Bennett purchased it, he saw no wrongdoing in continuing with the further dispersal of individual leaves of KV 386. He also divided some of the leaves, such as leaf 6, into smaller segments and distributing them among friends. Curiously, Dr. Ritter Ludwig von Köchel, in his preparation of the first edition of his thematic catalogue,[83] was completely unaware of Bennett's dealings; the sole source of his information on KV 386 was André's Manuscript Catalogue of 1833.[84] Even the arrangements of Mozart's works for pianoforte released in England by Potter in 1838 and Robert Barnett in 1856,[85] incidentally the only editions to preserve Mozart's KV 386 as a complete piece, were totally unknown to Köchel. In England, Thomas B. Odling, who had acquired many manuscripts of Bennett's own compositions,[86] became the initial owner of four leaves from Mozart's KV 386, each of which later joined parts of other collections. However, with regard to KV 386, Bennett went one step further, for on 26 February 1846, he handed over portions of leaf 6 of Mozart's autograph, specifically measures 101-104 of the recto of folio 6 and measures 110-115 of the verso of the same folio,[87] to an unidentified person, as we glean from the anonymous note appended to this fragment: "Mozart's autograph given to me by Mr. Sterndale Bennett Sunday, February 26, 1846 in 4 Wigmore Street in London."[88] Perhaps it was Bennett himself, who extracted these aforementioned measures from Leaf 6 of Mozart's autograph—measures that formed part of Episode I (measures 40-124) of the Rondo comprising three statements of the Refrain with two interspersed episodes.[89]

For Bennett the aforementioned incident does not represent an isolated occurrence in the 1840's. Even in the case of his own overture to *Lord Byron's Poem of Parisina*, op. 3, with the autograph of the first version dated 20 March 1835,[90] Bennett acted accordingly, as disclosed in a testimony of his son, James R. Sterndale Bennett.

> ... In a fit of despondency, he tore the score of Parisina into fragments, this destroying his final edition of the work. Now, too, it may have been that he registered a vow that he would compose no more; for later in life he hinted that he had come to such determination, adding the words: – I gave them nothing for ten years. ...[91]

While James R. Sterndale Bennett does not provide a reason for his father's draconic actions, Peter Horton sees a plausible connection between Bennett's irresponsible behavior regarding his *Parisina*, and four setbacks that Bennett experienced in the late 1840s, namely, his withdrawal from the Philharmonic Society, the failure to complete the oratorio *Zion*,[92] difficulties with the Sixth Piano Concerto, and the passing of Mendelssohn.[93]

Some ten years prior to the dissection of the Mozart autograph for KV 386—a practice that had been initiated by Constanze Mozart in connection with Mozart's autograph of the Twelve Piano Variations in C-Major "Ah vous dirai-je Maman," KV 265 (=300e)[94] and the Sonata in D-Major for four hands, KV 381[95] — Bennett had encouraged his teacher Cipriano Potter, a second-generation student of Leopold Mozart,[96] to publish the aforementioned one-volume edition of piano arrangements of Mozart's compositions, including the arrangement of KV 386.[97] Potter was eminently qualified as an editor of Mozart's works, for he had given the English premiers of several Mozart piano concertos in 1831 (G-Major, KV 453), 1837 (A-Major, KV 488), 1840 (B-flat-Major, KV 456), and 1841 (D-Major, KV 451).

Notwithstanding the deplorable mutilation of the sixth leaf of Mozart's autograph of KV 386, the aforementioned fragment, once in the possession of Bennett, and since January 1984 preserved as the so-called "Jeffery-Fragment" at the Gustav Mahler / Alfred Rosé Archive of the Music Library of Western University (olim University of Western Ontario) in London, Canada,[98] provides a vivid testimony to the *stile galante* as the preeminent style of composition employed by Mozart and also resorted to by Bennett in many of his own compositions, such as the Theme and Variations on Mozart's "Là ci darem la mano" (from *Don Giovanni*, KV 527),[99] the Sextet for piano and strings in f-sharp minor, op. 8,[100] the Piano Concerto in d-minor, op. 1,[101] and the Piano Concerto in Eb-Major, op. 4, dedicated to Potter[102]—in emulation of Mozart's ritornello and sonata forms.[103] Obviously, Bennett, in his cutting of Mozart's autograph of KV 386, regarded this particular manuscript not as a seminal source for the preparation of a modern edition, but merely as a composer's souvenir, and as such a potential object for dispersion amongst admirers of Mozart—a view clearly in line with the carefree dissemination of autographs of some of his own works.

In light of the emulation of Mozart in his own oeuvre, Bennett may be regarded as a conservative composer, one who displays a decisively retrospective perspective, not at all uncommon in the nineteenth century.[104] In a somewhat similar manner, Bennett derives many of his ideas from Mozart's oeuvre, with special attention to Mozart as a master of "broad rhythm, which so few could manage,"[105] presumably in reference to an overall regularity of harmonic rhythm, a hallmark of the *stile galant*. Notwithstanding Bennett's overall conservative approach to composition in his own oeuvre, his works enjoyed a rather wide dissemination, with performances in the United States of America and Australia.[106]

★ ★ ★

The affinity between Bennett and Mendelssohn may have further directed Bennett's attention to the oeuvre of Mozart. Already in a letter of 7 June 1822, Heinrich Heine identified Mendelssohn as "a musical miracle and can become a second Mozart."[107] An anonymous Leipzig reviewer concretised the relationship between Mendelssohn and Mozart while referring to Mendelssohn's Piano Quartet in c-minor, op. 1,[108] a work that openly displayed Mendelssohn's indebtedness to Mozart.[109] On 3 February 1824, Carl Friedrich Zelter identified Mendelssohn in the brotherhood of Bach, Mozart, and Haydn.[110] In 1840, Robert Schumann praised Mendelssohn as the Mozart of the nineteenth century.[111] In a similar vein, more than a century later, Sir Donald Francis Tovey acknowledged the influence of Mendelssohn upon Bennett when he observed that Ravel would become "no more distinguishable from an echo [of Debussy] than Sterndale Bennett is from the echo of Mendelssohn."[112]

Already on 14 February 1831, Johann Wolfgang von Goethe, who had cherished an amicable relationship with Mendelssohn[113] and Zelter,[114] and had heard the seven-year old Mozart in a live performance in Frankfurt am Main in August 1763,[115] remarked that "an appearance like Mozart always remains a wonder, which cannot be explained any further."[116] This may account for Bennett's longstanding preoccupation with Mozart. In light of Bennett's seminal importance with regard to the nineteenth-century dissemination of Mozart's oeuvre and the resultant reception of his legacy as a composer, the failure to acknowledge Bennett as a decisive link in Mozart reception history becomes abundantly apparent in the most recent encyclopedias, including the *Mozart Handbuch*,[117] the *Mozart-Lexikon*,[118] and the more recent *Mozarts Welt und Nachwelt*.[119] Thus, the present examination serves to fill an important lacuna in the secondary literature, one which will allow for a re-evaluation of Bennett's manifold contribution as performer, lecturer, collector, and composer, all within the context of his multifaceted Mozart revival, thereby acknowledging Mozart as one of the great masters, all of whom "constitute the links of an inseparable chain."[120]

When Sir William Sterndale Bennett compares the "discovery" of a Mozart manuscript, as in the case of KV 386, to the discovery of a diamond, he could have realistically contemplated this comparison as such only in a metaphorical sense. For the cutting of diamonds in different sizes and configurations for various purposes cannot be compared with the dissection of KV 386. Obviously unaware of the impact of his action for posterity regarding KV 386, Bennett tried to preserve Mozart's legacy, at least in the case of this rondo, in an attempt to distribute this particular composition among various unknown people and thus increase the awareness and familiarity of mankind with the oeuvre of Mozart. Unlike a diamond, which can be enjoyed as a whole or in smaller pieces separated from each other, a composition can only be fully appreciated when its dissemination pertains to the entire piece, and that in defence of the *Werkkonzept*, integral to Robert Schumann's aesthetics and compositional practice.[121]

---

1. Arthur O'Leary, "Sir Wiliam Sterndale Bennett: A Brief Review of His Life and Works," *Proceedings of the Musical Association* 8 (1881–1882): 123–146; J[ames] R[obert] Sterndale Bennett, *The Life of William Sterndale Bennett* (Cambridge: Cambridge University Press, 1907) [thereafter: Bennett]; Charles Villiers Stanford, "William Sterndale Bennett: 1816–1875," *The Musical Quarterly* 2 (1916): 628–657; Barry Sterndale-Bennett, "Sir William Sterndale Bennett (1816–1875)," *British Music Society Journal* 1 (1979): 41–46; Nicholas Temperley, ed., *Lectures on Musical Life: William Sterndale Bennett* (Woodbridge: Boydell & Brewer, 2006); see also Barry Sterndale-Bennett, "The Bicentenary of William Sterndale Bennett," *Brio: Journal of the United Kingdom Branch of the International Association of Music Libraries, Archives and Documentation Centres* 53 (2016): 3–18.
2. Robert Bledsoe, "Mendelssohn's Canonical Status in England, the Revolution of 1848, and H.F. Chorley's 'Retrogressive' Ideology of Artistic Genius," *Nineteenth-Century British Music Studies*, Vol. 2, ed. Jeremy Dibble and Bennett Zon (Aldershot: Ashgate, 2012), 139–153.
3. R. Larry Todd, "Mendelssohnian Allusions in the Early Piano Works of William Sterndale Bennett," *The Piano in Nineteenth-Century British Culture: Instruments, Performers and Repertoire*, ed. Therese Marie Ellsworth and Susan Wollenberg (Aldershot: Ashgate, 2007) [thereafter: Todd 2007], 101–118; see also Nicholas Temperley, "William Sterndale Bennett: Imitator or Original?," *Nineteenth-Century Music Review* 13/2 (2016): 173–193.
4. Meirion Hughes and Robert Stradling, *The English Musical Renaissance, 1840-1940: Constructing a National Music* (Manchester: Manchester University Press, 2001).
5. Simon McVeigh, "The Society of British Musicians (1834–1865) and the Campaign for Native Talent," *Music and British Culture, 1785-1914: Essays in Honor of Cyril Ehrlich*, ed. Leanne Langly (Oxford: Oxford University Press, 2000), 145–168.
6. Therese Marie Ellsworth, "The Piano Concerto in London Concert Life Between 1801 and 1850" (Ph.D. Dissertation, University of Cincinnati, 1991); Niall O'Loughlin, "The Philharmonic Society of London and Its Nineteenth-Century Contribution to the Rehabilitation of British Composers," *Galsbena društva v dolgem 19. stoletju: Med ljubiteljsko in profesionalno kulturo / Music Societies in the Long Nineteenth Century: Between Amateur and Professional Culture.* (Portorož, Slovenia: Založba Univerze na Primorskem, 2023), 175–192.
7. On Mendelssohn's sojourns in England, see R. Larry Todd, "Constructions of Mendelssohn and British-ness," idem, *Mendelssohn Essays* (New York: Routledge, 2008), 23–48.
8. Peter Ward Jones, "Mendelssohn's Scores in the Library of the Royal Philharmonic Society," *Felix Mendelssohn Bartholdy*, ed. Christian Martin Schmidt (Wiesbaden: Breitkopf & Härtel, 1997), 64–75.
9. For an overview of Mendelssohn's participation in public and semi-public performances during his ten sojourns in England, see Colin Timothy Eatock, *Mendelssohn and Victorian England* (Farnham: Ashgate, 2009), 161–171.
10. According to Bennett's entry in *Manuscript London, British Library MS Loan 4.290*; John Michael Cooper, *Mendelssohn's "Italian" Symphony* (Oxford: Oxford University Press. 2003), 51.
11. Bennett, 40; Frederick George Edwards, "First Performances I – Mendelssohn's St. Paul," *The Mendelssohn Companion*, ed. Douglas Seaton (Westport, CT: Greenwood, 2001), 383–386.

12 Bennett, 49.
13 Ibid., 123–124.
14 Bettina S. Muehlenbeck, "Felix Mendelssohn Bartholdy and William Sterndale Bennett: Undiscovered Letters of Friendship and Admiration," *Ad Parnassum* 18/35 (2020): 69–86.
15 Bennett, 61; Rosemary Williamson, *William Sterndale Bennett: A Descriptive Thematic Catalogue* (Oxford: Clarendon Press and New York: Oxford University Press, 1995) [thereafter: Williamson], 52–57.
16 Williamson, 70–75; Yun-Chung Yang, "William Sterndale Bennett's Fantasia in Its Historical Context" (AMusD, University of Illinois at Urbana-Champaign, 2002).
17 Wolfgang Boetticher, *Robert Schumann: Leben und Werk – Quellen, Daten, Dokumente* (Wilhelmshaven: Noetzel, 2004), 247.
18 For an overview see Geoffrey Bush, "Sterndale Bennett: The Solo Piano Works," *Proceedings of the Royal Musical Association* 91 (1964–1965): 85–98.
19 Williamson, 120–126.
20 Robert Schumann, "Pianofortemusik," *Neue Zeitschrift für Musik* 17/43 (25 November 1842): 175–177. A freer, slightly abridged version in English is included in Bennett, 130; see also Aaron C. Keebaugh, "Sterndale Bennett's Piano Music," *The Musical Times* 149/1904 (2008): 61–68.
21 For details, see Todd 2007, 108–113.
22 R. Larry Todd, "Mendelssohn's *Lieder ohne Worte* and the Limits of Musical Expression," *Mendelssohn Perspectives*, ed. Nicole Grimes and Angela Mace (Farnham: Ashgate, 2012), 197–222; see also R. Larry Todd, "'*Gerade das Lied wie es dasteht'*: On Text and Meaning in Mendelssohn's *Lieder ohne Worte*," *Musical Humanism and Its Legacy: Essays in Honor of Claude V. Palisca*, ed. Nancy Kovaleff Baker and Barbara Russano Hanning (Stuyvesant, New York: Pendragon Press, 1992), 355–379.
23 Peter Ward Jones, "Mendelssohn and His English Publishers," *Mendelssohn Studies*, ed. R. Larry Todd (Cambridge: Cambridge University Press, 1992), 240–255.
24 Bennett, 52; Rosemary Jane Williamson, "William Sterndale Bennett (1816–75) and His Publishers: Some Aspects of the Production of Music in Mid-Nineteenth-Century England" (Ph.D. Dissertation, University of Nottingham, 1995).
25 Joseph A. Kruse, "Ein schöner Stern geht auf in meiner Nacht: Das Album aus dem Musikverlag Kistner in Leipzig," *Schumanniana nova: Festschrift Gerd Neuhaus zum 60. Geburtstag*, ed. Bernhard R. Appel et al. (Sinzig: Studio, 2004), 387–399.
26 For a letter from Hermann Härtel of Breitkopf & Härtel to Sir William Sterndale Bennett, concerning the publication of Mendelssohn's Overture in C-Major, op. 24, see *Homage to Felix Mendelssohn Bartholdy (1809-1847): A Collection of Manuscripts and Autographs Presented on the Occasion of the 150th Anniversary of Mendelssohn's Death* (Basel: Erasmushaus, 1997).
27 Williamson, 58–61.
28 On the importance of Mendelssohn's piano oeuvre for Bennett's compositional practice, see R. Larry Todd, "Piano Music Reformed: The Case of Felix Mendelssohn Bartholdy," *Nineteenth-Century Piano Music*, ed. *idem* (New York: Routledge, 2004), 178–220, at 192–199.
29 Williamson, 48–51. For details, see Todd 2007, 102–104.
30 Williamson, 58–61. For details, see Todd 2007, 104–108.
31 For an overview of the formal layout and underlying tonality, see Todd 2007, 108.
32 Entry "Bennett, Sir William Sterndale," in: François Fétis, *Biographie universelle des musiciens [...]*, 8 vols. (Paris: Firmin-Didot, 1860–1865); reprint (Brussels: Culture et Civilisation, 1963), Vol. 1, 346–347.
33 Paul Wingfield and Julian Horton, "Norm and Deformation in Mendelssohn's Sonata Forms," *Mendelssohn Perspectives*, 83–112.
34 David Wyn Jones, "Haydn, Hoffmeister, Beethoven and Mozart: Salomon's 1801 Concert Series," *Festschrift Otto Biba zum 60. Geburtstag*, ed. Ingrid Fuchs (Tutzing: Schneider, 2006), 29–37.
35 Mendelssohn's letter dated 28 May 1836 to Thomas Attwood; as reproduced in: Bennett, 41.

36 "... Ja, gäb' es nur noch viele Künstler, die in dem Sinne, wie W. Bennett wirkten—und Niemandem dürfte mehr vor der Zukunft unsrer Kunst bange sein—," as reproduced in: Robert Schumann, *Gesammelte Schriften über Musik und Musiker* (Leipzig: Wigand, 1854), Vol. 2, 159–162: 162; Nicholas Temperley, "Schumann and Sterndale Bennett," *Nineteenth-Century Music* 12/3 (1989): 207–220.
37 Williamson, xxii.
38 William Sterndale Bennett, *Von fernen Ländern und Menschen: Reisetagebücher 1836 bis 1842*, ed. Bettina S. Mühlenbeck (Hannover: Wehrhahn, 2016); see also Bettina S. Mühlenbeck, "On Musical Journeys: William Sterndale Bennett's Diaries, 1836–1842," *Nineteenth-Century Music Review* 13/2 (2016): 221–232.
39 Bennett, 29–30.
40 Ibid., 51.
41 Nicole Schmidt, "Die Kammermusik," *Mozart-Handbuch*, ed. Silke Leopold (Kassel: Bärenreiter and Stuttgart: Metzler, 2005), 384–480: at 443.
42 Schumann, "Wm. Sterndale Bennett," *Neue Zeitschrift für Musik* 6/1 (3 January 1837): 3.
43 For a facsimile reproduction of the front cover of this concert program, see Rohan H. Stewart-MacDonald, "The Recital in England: Sir William Sterndale Bennett's Classical Chamber Concerts, 1843–1856," *Ad Parnassum* 13/25 (2015) [thereafter Stewart-MacDonald]: 115–175: at 138.
44 *D-B, N.Mus. ms. 9*; see Ralf Wehner, *Felix Mendelssohn-Bartholdy: Thematisch-systematisches Verzeichnis der musikalischen Werke* (Wiesbaden: Breitkopf & Härtel, 2009), 279–280.
45 "Ich habe mein drittes Quartett in D dur fertig und habe es sehr lieb ... es ist feuriger und ... dankbarer als die anderen," as cited in: Friedhelm Krummacher, *Mendelssohn, der Komponist: Studien zur Kammermusik für Streicher* (Munich: Fink, 1978), 92; English translation by W. Kreyszig.
46 Bennett, 122, 124, 125; see also Nancy B. Reich, *Clara Schumann: The Artist and the Woman* (Ithaca, New York: Cornell University Press, 1985), 240.
47 Williamson, 75–79; Jonathan Krieger, ed., *Arrangements for Solo Piano* (Middleton, CT: A-R Editions, 2012).
48 Bennett does not identify the specific sonata by Mozart; who had written several piano sonatas in F-Major, including KV 280 (= 189e); KV 332 (= 300k); KV 533; KV 547a (=Anh. 135); as well as KV 497, a sonata for piano four hands.
49 Bennett, 93.
50 Ibid, 23.
51 See Martin Wehnert, "Mendelssohns Traditionsbewußtsein und dessen Widerschein im Werk," *Deutsches Jahrbuch für Musikwissenschaft* 16 (1974): 5–45.
52 R. Larry Todd, "The Second Mozart," *idem*, *Mendelssohn: A Life in Music* (Oxford: Oxford University Press, 2003), 79–108; *idem*, "The 'Second Mozart': Mendelssohn and Precosity Revisited," *Musical Prodigies: Interpretations from Psychology, Education, Musicology and Ethnomusicology*, ed. Gary E. McPherson (Oxford: Oxford University Press, 2016), 603–620.
53 Schumann, *Gesammelte Schriften*, Vol. 3, 266–274: at 273.
54 Percy M. Young, *A History of British Music* (London: Benn, 1967), 393–400.
55 Simon McVeigh, "Trial by Dining Club: The Instrumental Music of Haydn, Clementi and Mozart at London's Anacreontic Society," *Music and Performance Culture in Nineteenth-Century Britain: Essay in Honour of Nicholas Temperley*, ed. Bennett Zon (Farnham: Ashgate, 2012) [thereafter McVeigh], 105–138: at 132–133 (Table 6.5).
56 *Morning Chronicle* 21.1.86; as cited in: McVeigh, 131, 134.
57 John Irving, "'Er hat Geschmack, und über das die größte Compositionswissenschaft': Geschmack, Fertigkeit und Kreativität in Mozarts 'Haydn'-Streichquartetten," *Die Musikforschung* 57/1 (2004): 2–17.
58 Emily Anderson, translated, *The Letters of Mozart and His Family*, 3 vols. (London: Macmillan, 1958), Vol. 3, 1320–1322: at 1321.

59 Nicholas Temperley, ed. *Works for Pianoforte Solo by William Sterndale Bennett: From 1834 to 1840*, 2 vols, (New York: Garland, 1984–1987); see also *idem*, "London and the Piano, 1760–1860," *The Musical Times* 129/1744 (1988): 289–293; Peter Horton, "William Sterndale Bennett, Composer and Pianist," *The Piano in Nineteenth-Century British Culture*, 119–148.
60 Nicholas Temperley, "William Sterndale Bennett," *Nineteenth-Century Music Review* 13/2 (2016): 173–193; Stephen D. Lindeman, "Continental Composers and Their English Influence, as Manifested in the Piano Concertos of William Sterndale Bennett," *Ad Parnassum* 5/10 (2007): 103–141.
61 Williamson, 29–35; see also Rohan H. Stewart-MacDonald, "Locating the Early-Romantic British Piano Concerto: William Sterndale Bennett and His Contemporaries," *Muzio Clementi and British Musical Culture: Sources, Performance Practice and Style*, ed. *idem* (Abingdon: Routledge, 2019), 200–219.
62 Bennett, 55.
63 Ibid., 29.
64 Richard Kitson, "James William Davison, Critic, Crank and Chronicler: A Re-Evaluation," *Nineteenth-Century British Music Studies*, Vol. 1, ed. Bennett Zon (Aldershot: Ashgate, 1999), 303–310.
65 Stewart-MacDonald, 115–175; 154–175.
66 Bennett, 69.
67 Ibid., 187.
68 Thomas Attwood served as director of this Society in 1814, 1816–1820 and in 1824–1832; see Daniel Heartz, "Attwood, Thomas," *Die Musik in Geschichte und Gegenwart: Allgemeine Enzyklopädie der Musik*, 29 vols., ed. Ludwig Finscher (Kassel: Bärenreiter and Stuttgart: Metzler, 1994–2008), Vol. 1 (Personenteil, 1999), cols. 1126–1129: at 1126.
69 Therese Marie Ellsworth, "The Piano Concertos of Mozart and Beethoven: Early Performances in Nineteenth-Century London," *British Music Studies*, Vol. 2 (Aldershot: Ashgate, 2002), 169–181, at 176.
70 Bennett, 120.
71 Muzio Clementi, as cited in: Alec Hyatt King, *Mozart in Retrospect: Studies in Criticism and Bibliography* (London: Oxford University Press, 1955), 1–54, at 18.
72 Bennett, 125.
73 Daniel Heartz, "Thomas Attwood's Lessons in Composition with Mozart," *Proceedings of the Royal Musical Association* 100 (1973–1974): 175–183; Walter Kurt Kreyszig, "Humanistische Tendenzen im *Versuch einer gründlichen Violinschule* (1756) von Leopold Mozart, im *Versuch einer Anweisung die Flöte traversiere zu spielen* (1752) von Johann Joachim Quantz und im Notenbuch (1785) von Thomas Attwood," *Leopold Mozart: Chronist und Wegbereiter*, ed. Thomas Hochradner and Michaela Schwarzbauer (Vienna: Hollitzer, 2022), 119–153, at 143–150.
74 Philip H. Peter, "The Life and Work of Cipriani Potter (1792–1871)" (Ph.D. Dissertation, Northwestern University, 1972).
75 Williamson, 19.
76 Cecil B. Oldman "Cipriano Potter's Edition of Mozart's Pianoforte Works," *Festschrift Otto Erich Deutsch zum 80. Geburtstag*, ed. Jan LaRue and Wolfgang Rehm (Kassel: Bärenreiter, 1963), 120–127.
77 Holger M. Stüwe, "Constanze Mozart und Johann Anton André: Der Erwerb der Mozartschen Autographen," *Johann Anton André (1775-1842) und der Mozart-Nachlass: Ein Notenschatz in Offenbach am Main*, ed. Jürgen Eichenauer (Weimar: Verlag und Datenbank für Geisteswissenschaften, 2006), 33–50.
78 Britta Constapel, *Der Musikverlag Johann André in Offenbach am Main: Studien zur Verlagstätigkeit von Johann Anton André und Verzeichnis der Musikalien von 1800 bis 1840* (Tutzing: Schneider, 1998); see also Wolfgang Matthäus, *Johann André Musikverlag zu Offenbach am Main: Verlagsgeschichte und Bibliographie, 1772-1800* (Tutzing: Schneider, 1973).

79 On the dissemination of Mozart's oeuvre after his death, see Birgit Grün, "Zur Geschichte der Andréschen Mozart-Sammlung nach 1842," *Johann Anton André (1775-1842)*, 115–125.
80 Alfred Einstein, ed., *W.A. Mozart: Rondo für Klavier und Orchester KV 386* (Vienna: Universal Edition, 1936) [score], Vorbemerkung [preliminary remark]; see also Alfred Einstein, ed., *W.A. Mozart: Rondo für Klavier und Orchester KV 386 für 2 Klaviere zu vier Händen* (Vienna: Universal Edition, 1936), Vorbemerkung.
81 Williamson, xv.
82 For a chronology of Mozart's autograph for KV 386 and its gradual dissection, see Walter Kurt Kreyszig, "Das Jeffery-Fragment der University of Western Ontario in London, Kanada: Zur Wiederauffindung eines Teiles des Autographs von Wolfgang Amadeus Mozarts Rondo für Klavier und Orchester in A-Dur, KV 386," *Mozart-Jahrbuch 1986*, 142–171, at 156–157 [thereafter Kreyszig]; see also Alan Tyson, "The Rondo for Piano and Orchestra, K. 386," idem, *Mozart: Studies of the Autograph Scores* (Cambridge, MA: Harvard University, 1987), 262-289.
83 Ludwig Ritter von Köchel, *Chronologisch-thematisches Verzeichnis sämtlicher Tonwerke Wolfgang Amadé Mozarts [...]* (Leipzig: Breitkopf & Härtel, 1862), 500.
84 A[nton] André, *Thematisches Verzeichnis W.A. Mozartscher Manuskripte, chronologisch geordnet von 1764 – 1784* [manuscript].
85 Robert Barnett, selected and ed., *Mozart's Piano Forte Works* (London: Hutchings & Roper, 1856).
86 Williamson, xiv.
87 For facsimile reproduction of this fragment, see Kreyszig, 159.
88 For a facsimile reproduction of Bennett's handwritten note, see Kreyszig, 160.
89 For a detailed discussion of this fragment, see Kreyszig, 148–158.
90 Williamson, 11–18.
91 Bennett, 194.
92 Williamson, 454–465.
93 Peter Horton, "An Obsession with Perfection: William Sterndale Bennett and Composer's Block," *Nineteenth-Century Music Review* 13/2 (2016): 257–287. For the letter of Ferdinand David to William Sterndale Bennett on the death of Mendelssohn, see Robert Sterndale Bennett, "The Death of Mendelssohn," *Music and Letters* 86 (1955): 374–376.
94 Ulrich Konrad, ed., *Wolfgang Amadeus Mozart: Zwölf Variationen in C für Klavier über das französische Lied "Ah, vous dirai-je Maman", KV 265 (300e)* (Augsburg: Deutsche Mozart-Gesellschaft, 2001).
95 Ernst Fritz Schmid, "Schicksale einer Mozart-Handschrift: Ein unbekanntes Streichquartett-Menuett und zwei unveröffentlichte Kadenzen," *Mozart-Jahrbuch 1957*, 43–56.
96 G[eorge] A[lexander] Macfarren, "Cipriani Potter: His Life and Work," *Proceedings of the Musical Association* 10 (1883–1884): 41–56: at 42.
97 Cipriano Potter, ed. *Rondo (Posthumous) by W.A. Mozart Arranged from the Original (in the Author's Own Hand Writing) by the Editor*, Chefs d'Oeuvre de Mozart: A New Grand Edition of the Piano Forte Works of the Celebrated Composer (London: Coventry & Hollier, 1936), No. 14, p. 5.
98 *Music and Continental Books, Autograph Letters and Manuscripts* (London: Sotheby's, 1983) [Auction Catalogue], Item 142. The manuscript was donated by the late President of the *Aeolian Town Hall Society* in London, Canada, Gordon D. Jeffery, who had acquired the fragment, incidentally the sole Mozart autograph on Canadian soil, from the Sotheby's Auction in London, England, on 17 November 1983.
99 Williamson, 447–448.
100 Ibid., 23–28.
101 Ibid., 3–8.
102 Ibid., 18–22.
103 Jeremy Dibble, "Context, Form and Style in Sterndale Bennett's Piano Concertos," *Nineteenth-Century Music Review* 13/2 (2016): 195–219.
104 Georg von Dadelsen, "Alter Stil und alte Techniken in der Musik des 19. Jahrhunderts" (Ph.D. Dissertation, Universität Berlin, 1951).

105 Bennett, 25.
106 Therese-Marie Ellsworth, "The British Isles and Beyond: The Performance of Instrumental Music by William Sterndale Bennett During the Long Nineteenth Century," *Nineteenth-Century Music Review* 13/2 (2016): 233–256.
107 Klaus Briegleb, ed., *Heinrich Heine: Sämtliche Werke* (Munich: Hanser, 1959), II, 59.
108 Wehner, 254–255.
109 *Allgemeine Musikalische Zeitung* 1 (1824): 181–184.
110 R. Larry Todd, "A Mendelssohn Miscellany," *Music and Letters* 71 (1990): 52–63, at 52.
111 Schumann in the *Neue Zeitschrift für Musik* 13 (1840): 198.
112 Sir Donald Francis Tovey, *Musical Articles from the Encyclopaedia Britannica* (London: Oxford University Press, 1944), 139.
113 Lorraine Byrne Bodley, "'An old man young or a young man old?': On Goethe's Friendship with Felix Mendelssohn," *Musicologie sans frontières / Muzikologija bez granica: Svečani zbornik za Stanislava Tuksara / Musicology Without Frontiers: Essays in Honour of Stanislav Tuksar*, ed. Ivano Cavallini and Harry White (Zagreb: Hrvatsko Muzikološko Društvo, 2010), 387–404.
114 Friedrich Wilhelm Riemer, ed., *Briefwechsel zwischen Goethe und Zelter in den Jahren 1796 bis 1832*, 5 vols. (Berlin: Duncker & Humblot, 1833–1834).
115 Ute Jung-Kaiser, "Als Kind und verschuldeter Künstler in Frankfurt," *Österreichische Musikzeitschrift* 61 (Sonderband, 2006): 96–99.
116 "Eine Erscheinung wie Mozart bleibt immer ein Wunder, das nicht weiter zu erklären ist."; as cited in: Joseph Müller-Blattau, *Goethe und die Meister der Musik: Bach – Händel – Mozart – Beethoven – Schubert* (Stuttgart: Klett, 1969), 34; see also Robert Spaethling, *Music and Mozart in the Life of Goethe* (Columbia, SC: Camden House, 1987), 85–94.
117 *Mozart-Handbuch*, ed. Leopold.
118 Gernot Gruber, ed., *Mozart-Lexikon* (Laaber: Laaber, 2005).
119 Claudia Maria Knispel and Gernot Gruber, ed., *Mozarts Welt und Nachwelt* (Laaber: Laaber, 2009).
120 Bennett, 23.
121 Edward A. Lippman, "Theory and Practice in Schumann's Aesthetics," *Journal of the American Musicological Society* 17 (1964): 310–345; Thomas Alan Brown, *The Aesthetics of Robert Schumann* (New York: Philosophical Library, 1968); see also Siegfried Oechsele, "Forminterne Eigenzeiten und narrative Strukturen: Zum Werkkonzept der d-moll Symphonie op. 120 von Robert Schumann," *Robert Schumann und die große Form*, ed. Bernd Sponheuer and Wolfram Steinbeck (Frankfurt am Main: Lang, 2009), 29–51.

20. FERDINAND HILLER AND FRANZ LISZT: A FRIENDSHIP BUILT AT THE KEYBOARD, THEN SUNDERED AND NEVER HEALED*

Jürgen Thym and Ralph P. Locke

Ferdinand Hiller and Franz Liszt were almost exact contemporaries. Born in 1811 just two days apart, they died in two successive years: Hiller in 1885 and Liszt in 1886, at ages 74 and 75, respectively. They also were similar in their range of activities, having started out as virtuoso pianists, then gradually becoming known also as composers, conductors, and essayists. Each reigned for years over a substantial musical establishment: Hiller as director of the Cologne Conservatory (Rheinische Musikschule) from its founding in 1850 until 1884, the year before his death; Liszt, from 1848 onward, as the adulated central figure at the court in Weimar. Even after Liszt resigned as music director there in 1861, he remained the undisputed leader of what was sometimes called (half-jokingly) the École de Weymar through masterclasses that he held there every summer until a year before his death. Both remained devoted to piano composition and piano performance and instruction throughout their lives. Nonetheless, conducting for large-scale forces (orchestra, chorus, even to some extent opera) became a major, parallel outlet for each of them, no doubt because it gave them an opportunity to bring a much wider repertory of older and newer works to the awareness of their respective audiences. Strangely, it would be the issue of conducting that, on the surface, would play a major role in the dissolution of their friendship. But the real issue (and no doubt related to conducting) was their divergent approaches to musical composition and, on a larger scale, the split between two musical camps after 1850 (crudely put: the conservatives and the progressives) that prevailed in the German-speaking lands throughout the rest of the century.

Previous writers have described the downward curve of the Hiller-Liszt relationship largely from the viewpoint of Liszt's disciples. In this paper, we make full use, for the first time, of Hiller's three extensive published writings on Liszt (two reviews and an Open Letter). We also use numerous private letters between the two, most of which have been available in printed form since 1958 yet were not used by scholars interested in this matter. We have structured the present essay in roughly chronological sequence, for clarity. The final section—after the break-up of their friendship—is presented more briefly than the rest, because that is the part that has already been most extensively discussed and debated.

Jürgen Thym and Ralph P. Locke

EARLY-CAREER YEARS: PARIS, MILAN, LEIPZIG

Hiller and Liszt had, at least initially, what Goethe might have called a "Wahlverwandtschaft"—an "elective affinity," spurred by various similarities in their gifts and life goals. The two met as young, budding pianists in Paris. Liszt had arrived in the French capital with his parents in 1823, at age 12, and soon raised a stir as a child prodigy, playing in the salons of elegant society and in large concert halls. Several piano manufacturers had their headquarters in Paris (Érard, Pleyel) and realized that they could advertise their wares by promoting this or that young pianist who enchanted audiences not only through his (or sometimes her) pianistic prowess but also through a manifestly attractive manner and physical appearance. Young François Liszt became known after 1825 as "le petit Litz" and, though only a teenager, became the favorite piano teacher of the Parisian aristocracy.

Hiller made it to Paris in the fall of 1828 after several years of study with Hummel, in Weimar, where he also met, and played for, Goethe. Ludwig Spohr had admonished the 17-year-old Hiller in a letter to avoid the "temptations" that he and others often associated with the French capital.[1] As far as we know, Hiller did. For seven years (aside from some trips home to Frankfurt), he was one of the main representatives of the colony of German artists and journalists drawn to Paris (a group that included, among others, the poet Heinrich Heine, the left-leaning political commentator Ludwig Börne, and, during a visit of several months' duration, Felix Mendelssohn). Hiller became known as a performer of Beethoven's music, notably giving the Paris premiere of the "Emperor" Concerto in 1829, when he was just 18 years old. The orchestra was conducted by the highly respected François Habeneck. In one-on-one gatherings, Hiller nurtured Berlioz's love for Beethoven's piano sonatas. For a few years, he taught organ at Choron's reputable music school.

Paris around 1830 was a place that drew piano virtuosos as if by a magic force of gravitation: "Dozens of steel-fingered, chromium-plated virtuosos played there."[2] Cramer, Dreyschock, Herz, Hünten, Kalkbrenner, Pixis, and Thalberg need to be mentioned in addition to Liszt, Hiller, and (soon to arrive from Poland) Chopin – all perfecting their pianistic techniques and competing for the attention of audiences in the salons and concert halls.

Soon after his arrival in Paris, Hiller tried to make the acquaintance of Liszt (who already was a celebrity) and, with the help of the aforementioned Johann Peter Pixis, a fellow German pianist residing in the French capital, succeeded in meeting the reclusive Liszt. Hiller described Liszt as rather shy at the time. Liszt's father had died in 1826, and the teenager himself had just come through an unhappy love affair with Caroline de Saint-Cricq (her father, the French minister of commerce, simply put a stop to it). Liszt withdrew for a time from public life and even contemplated becoming a priest. When Hiller and Liszt met, after the obligatory small talk, Liszt sat down at the piano and played Schubert's "Wanderer" Fantasy, not so much playing it as seeming to create it himself from scratch. As Hiller put it in an Open Letter to Liszt nearly fifty years later:

> You did not really play it, you improvised it, as if you were creating it for the second time. I will never forget the impression! It has stayed in my memory like a splendid blazing fire at night.[3]

The pianists drawn to Paris also dazzled audiences by playing together, two or more at one or more pianos. We know of Liszt and Hiller being joined by Pixis and Paër to play Beethoven's *Fidelio* Overture in a version for eight hands in the Salons Pape.[4] Chopin, Hiller, and Liszt (an early manifestation of the "Three Tenors" syndrome of our own time) appeared together performing J. S. Bach's Triple Concerto (or at least one movement from it) at the Conservatoire in December 1833, and, at the same concert, Liszt and Hiller played a piano duet by Hiller.[5] A few weeks later, the two repeated the duet at the Salons Pleyel.[6] A benefit concert for Polish refugees in 1835 brought all three pianists together again in the Théâtre Italien.[7] They were joined in their music making by other artists, including the distinguished tenor Adolphe Nourrit. Hiller in his Open Letter to Liszt of 1877 described the "three pianists" event as follows:

> You and Chopin were very kind to perform with me, in one of my concerts, a triple concerto by Bach. It was not a rewarding task. At the time, Bach was not yet popular in Paris. [Hiller then adds somewhat sarcastically:] Gounod had not yet written his [wildly beloved] *Méditation* on the first prelude from the *Well-Tempered Clavier*.[8]

The camaraderie established during those years was not limited to the concert halls and the salons of Paris but manifested itself also in other ways. There is a letter to Hiller, written jointly by Liszt and Chopin, when Hiller had left Paris for a few weeks to see his dying father. Hiller later wrote about the document:

> The two of you joined up in an even more charming collaboration that likewise involved me. I was spending some time in my hometown, and you wrote letters to me, in which you and Chopin alternated, line by line, and gave free reign to your pen and humor. When looking at these letters, one can imagine your octaves leaping out from your handwriting and hearing Chopin's embellishments [*Fiorituren*] in his.[9]

Here is the letter in excerpts (Liszt's contributions are printed in roman font, Chopin's in italics):

> This must be the twentieth time at least that we have met here or at my place with the intention of writing to you. ... I do not know whether Chopin will be able to apologize to you: but as far as I am concerned, I believe we have taken incivility and insolence so far that excuses are now neither permissible nor possible. ...
>
> *I am writing without knowing what my pen is scribbling, because at this moment Liszt is playing my Études and putting honest thoughts out of my head. I should like to steal*

> *from him his way of interpreting my Études. ... The whole Plater family was most upset when you left and has enjoined me to extend their condolences to you.*
>
> Do you know Chopin's marvelous Études? *They are admirable pieces! ... and they will last until your own appear,* a little modesty from the composer! *A little rudeness on the part of the teacher—I must explain that it is he who is correcting my spelling mistakes. ...*
>
> You'll return to us in *September,* won't you? *Try* (and let us know the day in good time, because we intend to offer you a serenade or [maybe] a [noisy] charivari).¹⁰

Friendship, and an informal conversational tone in communication, was also forged in many social gatherings in the Parisian salons where artists mingled with countesses and other members of the aristocracy. (Countess Marie d'Agoult was born in Frankfurt, before she married into the Parisian aristocracy; Hiller may thus have known her long before she and Liszt began a decade-long affair and quasi-marriage that brought forth three children: Blandine, Cosima, and Daniel.) In his open letter to Liszt, Hiller recalled the flirtatious tone prevailing in the exchanges of these gatherings.

> Do you remember what one nervy old society-lady said to Chopin on one occasion? (I present it ["I" is Hiller speaking here] in the original French wording; in German it might sound too salacious.) "Si j'étais jeune et jolie, mon petit Chopin," she said, "je te prendrais pour mari, Hiller pour ami et Liszt pour amant." ["If I were young and pretty, my dear little Chopin, I would take you as a husband, Hiller as a friend, and Liszt as a lover." And Hiller continues in his open letter to Liszt:] You will hardly be astonished by that statement. But perhaps by the next. There was an evening when you had brought together at your home the aristocracy of French literati. (George Sand was not to be missing in this group.) On the way home, Chopin said to me: "What an antipathetic person, this Sand; is she really a woman? I doubt it." ... Dark are the intertwinements of fate, especially when it reveals itself in female form.¹¹

The irony in Chopin's remark, of course, is that he and George Sand (to use her pen name) would end up living together during much of the 1840s.

In the mid-1830s, Hiller and Liszt both left the French capital, the former to live in Milan and other Italian cities for a few years and connect with artists and musical institutions there, the latter to take temporary residence with his mistress, Countess Marie d'Agoult, in the lake district of northern Italy (when he was not touring European musical centers). Even so, the bonds of friendship established during their Paris years continued. Hiller's Open Letter to Liszt recalls frequent meetings during the winter of 1837–38 in Milan, having morning coffee with Liszt, as well as the *furore* that Liszt caused in Milan's social world, both as a pianist and a ladies' man.

The *furore* caused by Liszt the pianist is captured in Hiller's alternately laudatory and dismissive description, from, again, his Open Letter of 1877:

> In your concerts at the time, you had begun to request topics [from the audience] upon which you would improvise. They were jotted down on paper, folded, and placed in a big vase. And what treasures were pulled out of the vase! Dante, Tasso, the Milan cathedral, a last love—the most fantastical things and the most stupid. And how it amused you to witness all the rumblings around you![12]

As for the *furore* that the ladies' man Liszt caused, this reverberates in a story discreetly hinted at by Hiller: namely, that letters with salacious information about some Milanese women became public, resulting in Liszt's being invited to life-challenging duels with Italian *nobili*. Reportedly, another person of nobility[13] called a halt to such silly practices of asserting one's manhood. (Liszt, we know, lived into old age, unharmed.)

Hiller and Liszt met again in Leipzig in the spring of 1840. Hiller was there to prepare the premiere of his important, indeed (in Schumann's view) pathbreaking, oratorio *Die Zerstörung Jerusalems* (*The Destruction of Jerusalem*, performed there on April 2). Liszt was in Leipzig during the second half of March to give concerts. Playing for Leipzig audiences, however, evoked unpleasant memories for Liszt. The city's musical taste was rather conservative, and Friedrich Wieck, who was feeling snubbed because he had not received free press tickets for a concert Liszt gave in Dresden a few days earlier, turned the local press in Leipzig against the keyboard lion and his student and assistant Hermann Cohen. Moreover, Liszt fell ill before one of his recitals and had to postpone it, an act that was interpreted as a "diplomatic withdrawal" to signal Liszt's irritation about the cool reception he had received. Alan Walker sees in the events surrounding Liszt's Leipzig visit of 1840 the seeds for the later division of musical life into two camps: Leipzig vs. Weimar, conservative vs. progressive, music of the past vs. [the self-styled] Music of the Future.[14] Ultimately, however, Liszt's concerts were a great success, with Robert Schumann writing quite favorably about them in the *Neue Zeitschrift für Musik*.[15]

TWO COMPOSERS IN FULL FLOW, EACH NOW ALSO CONDUCTING

And now we must fast forward to the 1850s. Revolutions shook up many European countries in 1848 (among the prominent exceptions: the Scandinavian lands, Great Britain, and Russia), but the hopeful expectations for a better political and social order were thwarted a year later, with conservative and reactionary forces gaining the upper hand. (In France, another Napoleon soon became emperor.) The caesura in European political history can be felt to some extent also in music history. Mendelssohn died in 1847, Chopin in 1849, and Schumann's creativity peaked in 1848–49 to be followed by a steady decline after 1850. Wagner, who had participated in the revolutionary uprisings in Dresden in 1849, was forced into exile, and Liszt gave up his career as a traveling keyboard virtuoso to take up residence in Weimar and establish that small town as a center for a very different kind of music and music-making than decades earlier when Herder, Goethe, and Schiller were at the center of Weimar's cultural life.

The new approach to music, later encapsulated in the binary opposites just mentioned, was aided by the musical journal, the *Neue Zeitschrift für Musik*, that Schumann (a close ally of the ultimate conservative, Mendelssohn) had founded in 1834 and edited until 1844. The new editor, Franz Brendel, gradually turned the journal into a mouthpiece of the Wagner-Liszt camp. The political revolution may have failed, but the musical revolution could be brought forth, advancing history and progress, through powerful artistic figures such as Wagner (composing the *Ring of the Nibelungen* tetralogy in his Swiss exile), Liszt (gathering his forces in Weimar), and Berlioz, who had already anticipated the new approach in numerous revolutionary large-scale compositions, such as the genre-defying dramatic symphony *Roméo et Juliette*. And it was Brendel, in 1859, who, in an act of journalistic simplification and hubris, declared these three highly disparate composers (one of them French, another one a sort of Hungarian) as leaders of the New *German* School (the *neudeutsche Schule*).

What we have just sketched is crucial background for understanding the tension that arose, indeed exploded, between Hiller and Liszt in the mid-1850s. Much of this is captured in letters written by the two composers or by others with whom they were in contact, notably Berlioz. Liszt's and Hiller's letters to each other are mostly in French and a few in German (sometimes using the familiar "Du," especially when writing in German). Since almost none of these letters were mentioned by Alan Walker in his monumental three-volume Liszt biography or by Beverly Jerold in two important recent articles on Hiller and the Liszt circle, we may be allowed to dwell on them in some detail. The letters offer no evidence of Walker's thesis that a "rivalry" existed between the two artists, with Hiller resorting to "intrigues" to undermine his friend. By contrast, the letters support Jerold's argument vindicating Hiller's honesty and forthrightness.[16] Indeed, despite the growing rift—mentioned earlier—about the direction that music should be following (and Liszt and Hiller were indeed in opposing camps), their friendship continued at a time when front lines were being drawn (in matters of musical aesthetics, style, form, and genre, e.g., Wagnerian "music drama" and Lisztian "symphonic poem" vs. the continuation of the four-movement string quartet and symphony in the works of Mendelssohn, Schumann, Hiller, and, eventually, Brahms).

In the fall of 1851, Liszt was making plans to conduct Hiller's Symphony in E minor ("Es muss doch Frühling werden"—in short, his "Spring" Symphony) in Weimar, and Hiller, who, at the time, was conducting operas in Paris at the Théâtre-Italien, sent him a manuscript score and parts as well as his recently published and highly innovative *Rhythmische Studien* or Rhythmic Etudes, which freely alternate 3/4 and 4/4 meter. He dedicated the latter to Liszt, referring to them in the letter as "the piano pieces that I have embellished with your name" ("les morceaux de piano que j'ai ornés de votre nom").[17]

Shortly after the performance of Hiller's "Spring" Symphony in Weimar, Liszt wrote to its composer (14 January 1852), critiquing some details of orchestration. He dutifully returned manuscript score and parts to Hiller, recommending that Hiller perform the symphony in Paris. Liszt expressed unreserved admiration for the *Rhythmic Etudes*—"very timely" (or, in modern parlance, "cutting-edge") and called them "perfectly worked out"—and he encouraged Hiller to compose more along those lines (which Hiller promptly did).[18] Liszt invited Hiller to come to Weimar (conveying also regards from Dr. Eckermann, Goethe's amanuensis whom Hiller had gotten to know when he was studying with Hummel in Weimar). It would take three years until Hiller could find enough free time to follow up on this invitation.

In 1853, a year after that exchange of letters about Hiller's "Spring" Symphony and his metrically experimental piano etudes, a review of a music festival in Karlsruhe was published that took issue with Liszt's conducting. It appeared in the *Niederrheinische Musikzeitung* and was signed "H." It summed up Liszt's conducting style as follows:

> After the Karlsruhe Festival it is universally agreed that Liszt is not qualified to wield a baton, at least not in front of large forces. It's not just that he generally gives no beat ..., his strange vivacity constantly causes the most severe vacillation in the orchestra. On the podium he does nothing but shift the baton from his right hand to his left, sometimes putting it down altogether, ..., giving signals in the air in accordance with his earlier instruction to the players 'not to take too much notice of [my] beat' (these were Liszt's very words at rehearsal).[19]

Given the place of publication (Cologne), the editor of the newspaper (Hiller's friend Ludwig Bischoff), and the letter H, it was widely assumed that Hiller had penned the review. But Hiller was not, so far as any scholar has established, in Karlsruhe at the time, and there is no correspondence preceding the Karlsruhe Festival that suggests that the two artists made plans to meet there, as they surely would have if a meeting had been contemplated. Liszt never suspected Hiller to be the author of the review (and there is evidence in their correspondence, to be revealed shortly, that Hiller was indeed not the author). Nonetheless, Liszt's acolytes hastened to spread a report that Hiller was behind the H of the review (and this was still taken as fact over a century later in Alan Walker's three-volume biography).[20] We can now safely state that the H=Hiller issue was an invention of some unknown Liszt acolyte looking for a way to smear Hiller. Alas, it succeeded, and we are glad, finally, to be able to put the matter to rest.

Liszt responded quickly to the allegations of his inadequacy as a conductor. In an Open Letter to Richard Pohl dated 5 November, he addressed the issue, differentiating between conductors who were merely time-beaters [*Taktschläger*] and meter accountants [*Takt-Profosses*] who functioned much like a windmill, and conductors—like himself—who were able to convey the spirit of a work, its essence and expressive core, by way of frequent tempo modifications. As a piano virtuoso, Liszt had been demonstrably successful with this approach, and he considered it applicable also for directing large orchestral and vocal forces. Simply maintaining "the beat and each individual part of the beat *1, 2, 3, 4* | *1, 2, 3, 4* very much runs counter to a meaningful and intelligible form of expression," he said; and he emphatically insisted that "here and elsewhere, the letter kills the spirit." A little later, he professed that the conductor's task was to make himself superfluous, adding, with typographical emphasis: "*We are pilots, not crew members.*"[21]

Behind the controversy concerning Liszt's conducting lurks the issue about the future direction of music that had gained momentum around 1850. The works going back to the last period of Beethoven's creativity—besides Beethoven, Liszt mentioned Berlioz but not Wagner's or his own compositions—require a different style of performance that was not practiced everywhere (certainly not in Karlsruhe). What Liszt may have been able to accomplish at his own musical "court," in Weimar, with a group of extraordinary instrumentalists and singers (and his record in premiering new works there is indeed admirable) was not transferrable—hook, line, and sinker—to music festivals with their tight rehearsal schedules, with large instrumental forces gathered for a few days from various orchestras in the region, and with amateurs singing in the choir.

Liszt was to repeat his approach to conducting four years later in Aachen—this time with a few "ringers" hired from his Weimar ensemble—but the results were as disastrous as in Karlsruhe, and this time the reviewer of the event was not an anonymous "H" but a well-known and fully written-out H: Ferdinand Hiller, his friend from the days when both were budding pianists in Paris. Aachen would tear their friendship asunder.

At the end of 1854 (that is, a year after the review by the unknown "H"), the Hiller-Liszt correspondence moved into high gear, as the long-delayed visit to Weimar became reality. Liszt hosted his friend at the Ettersburg near Weimar for nearly an entire week in late January/early February 1855. Hiller could have come earlier, but he wanted to see a Cologne production on January 23 of Wagner's *Lohengrin*, a work whose world premiere Liszt had personally conducted in Weimar in 1850 and about which Hiller felt lukewarm. He seems to have wanted Liszt to know that he was not refusing, on principle, to get to know the music of the self-styled avant-garde or "futurists"; quite the contrary, he was even willing to delay his arrival in Weimar to gain familiarity with one of that movement's most notable recent products.

The visit in the Ettersburg, the country residence of the Grand Duke of Weimar, was filled with social gatherings, music making, whist playing, discussions, and lavish meals. Liszt and Hiller performed Hummel's Sonata for Piano 4 Hands at a soirée of the Grand Duchess Maria Pavlovna, to whom that very sonata had been dedicated.[22] (More than twenty-five years earlier, Hiller had performed the piece in the same rooms for her when she was still a princess.) Hiller was introduced to Liszt's students, whom he referred to as the "Neu-Weimar-Club," and their compositions. Liszt was also eager to show off what he had wrought lately: daring and ear-challenging new compositions. Hiller admitted that his eyes "started flickering" at Mazeppa's wild ride, and what he called the Mephisto symphony "frightened and scared" him, even made him think of sulfurous odors. (In other words, Liszt played for Hiller, at the piano, his symphonic poem *Mazeppa* and the *Faust* symphony.)[23] There were frank exchanges about both composers' different approaches to music, but, overall, the days at the Ettersburg were an unclouded celebration of a friendship going back nearly thirty years.[24]

Hiller then went on to Leipzig to perform one of his three piano concertos. (Other works of his were also on the program, possibly with him conducting.) In a letter from Leipzig (12 February 1855), thanking Liszt for the "unforgettable days" in Weimar, he mentioned that his piano concerto received a somewhat chilly reception there (whereas he did better with his *Phèdre* overture and some songs). Liszt immediately responded (14 February), consoling Hiller by pointing to the fickleness of audiences in Leipzig (perhaps remembering his own experiences there in 1840) and praised the piano concerto as a work "excellently put together" and "containing numerous moments that are sure to make an effect." He continued: "Perhaps (please pardon this supposition) you allowed yourself to play it a bit in a composerly manner, with that philosophical objectivity [literally: disinterest] which long ago became habitual with you." And he offered to have his small orchestra in Weimar (he called them his "chamber virtuosos") work their way through the concerto, once it was published, adding "they surely will pull it off." In a letter from Dresden (four days later), Hiller brushed off Liszt's characterization of him in a somewhat jovial tone: "Your remark about my philosophical objectivity made me laugh a lot. My own explanation is that the grapes hang too high [meaning perhaps that he simply could not please the audience. And he concluded:]. Nonetheless, I willingly accept your critical-philosophical explanation."[25]

The letters exchanged by Hiller and Liszt in the years 1851–55 are full of mutual admiration mixed with frankness. Hiller, for example, wrote in 1852: "I do not completely share your admiration for certain things" (perhaps an allusion to recent works of Wagner) but he admired Liszt's "courageous" way of carrying out his convictions.[26]

THE COLLISION: AACHEN, 1857

All this came to a sudden halt in 1857, when the organizational committee of the Lower Rhine Music Festival invited Liszt to direct the festival that year (in late May and early June), to take place in Aachen: that is to say, Liszt was to choose most of the repertory and be the main conductor. (The Festival was held once a year in either Aachen, Cologne, or Düsseldorf.) Liszt apparently started hearing reports from Aachen that suggested that Hiller, who had co-directed the festival in 1853 and had directed it on his own in 1855, was uncomfortable with Liszt's having been chosen and might refuse to attend. Liszt wrote to Hiller, echoing Hiller's 1852 letter about their disparate aesthetic aims: "We are by now rather old friends, and even the disparity between our [respective] intellectual temperaments in no way prevents us from becoming even older and possibly better friends." Liszt's phrase for "intellectual temperaments" is "geistige Temperatur"—suggesting differences not just in intellectual approach but also spirit and feeling, including Liszt's greater tendency toward warmth (emotional intensity and spontaneity) and Hiller's toward coolness (emotional self-control and steadiness). In the letter, Liszt begged Hiller to greet him in Aachen, not as the festival's conductor nor as a "musician of the future" (*Zukunftsmusiker*) but as a faithful old friend.[27]

Hiller replied that Liszt should not pay attention to rumors and gossip from Aachen. What is considered worth saying in Aachen, he wrote, is not necessarily worthy of anybody else's attention. (This is a play on words: what is *aachenswerth* may not be *achtungswerth*.) And he closed with the expressed desire to experience, finally, Liszt as conductor, after having heard so much in this regard from Liszt's supporters and detractors.[28] This is the evidence to which we referred earlier about the authorship of the damning review of Liszt's conducting in Karlsruhe. Hiller would not likely have lied outright to Liszt in 1857 that he had not yet seen him conduct. In short, Hiller was not that "H" who wrote so damningly, and truthfully, about Liszt's shortcomings as a conductor.

What happened in Aachen was, by all accounts, a series of disasters. Liszt had agreed to conduct some works that he preferred not to, including Handel's *Messiah*. Liszt also tried to perform all of Berlioz's oratorio *L'enfance du Christ*, but it proved too tricky on the short rehearsal time available, and, in the end, he only performed its Part 2: "La fuite en Égypte" (which is mainly orchestral, with a small part for chorus). Other pieces needed a steady, clear beat to keep the vast festival forces together, and this (as we mentioned before) was something that Liszt generally avoided doing and probably felt was beneath his dignity as an interpretive artist who relied on the inspiration of the moment.

Hiller, an experienced professional at conducting an orchestra and chorus in public situations, and very attentive to the challenges of keeping an ensemble "tight," must have been aghast.[29] Indeed, we know he was because he, foolishly, accepted an offer from the *Cölnische Zeitung* (whose regular music critic, Hiller's friend Ludwig Bischoff, was out of town) to write up a series of reviews of the open rehearsals and public performances. What he wrote was frank and devastating. Here is the last paragraph:

> Incidentally, I had not [previously] had an occasion to see Liszt conduct, but I had heard so many contradictory things about it that, I admit, my curiosity was piqued to the utmost. Now, after seeing and hearing him direct the most diverse compositions in five full-length rehearsals and three entire concerts, I am convinced that Liszt is *not* a conductor, at least not a conductor who is up to the challenges he faces or the expectations that one justifiably places in such a man.[30]

This passage provides further proof that Hiller had not seen Liszt conduct before. He would hardly have lied publicly about never having seen Liszt conduct. Among other things, he was a well-known and easily noticeable figure by this point in his career. Clearly, Hiller was not the "H" who had blasted his friend's conducting in Karlsruhe in 1853. But blast it he did in 1857. Hiller was clearly horrified, and perhaps deeply embarrassed, at what he saw during those eight rehearsals and concerts over the nearly week-long 1857 festival. The evidence is twofold.

First of all, on the festival's final day, Hiller wrote a letter to Liszt saying that he was glad that their paths had barely crossed during that time—perhaps they had at most gestured at each other across a room at some point—because Hiller would have not been able to refrain from alluding to his intense disappointment (while others stood nearby, eager to overhear). The letter is worth quoting in its entirety. Though it was published in facsimile in the first edition of *Die Musik in Geschichte und Gegenwart*, it has rarely if ever been cited by scholars interested in the Hiller/Liszt relationship and has never been published in translation.

> Dear Liszt,
> During the days [you have just spent] here [in Aachen], I have scarcely seen you. For one thing, you were overwhelmed with [professional] activities; but, for another, I would have been unable to say many friendly things without engaging in play-acting and even less, under these circumstances, would I have wanted to meet you with criticism. If I now can say with the greatest of sincerity that the sympathy that you engendered in me from the very beginning will always be the same, I must add that it is completely different with certain of your musical strivings: I not only do not agree with you about them, but, on the contrary, consider it my duty to oppose you in this respect with all my powers, even though my opposition may attack your position and your influence. From the bottom of my heart, I wish that our old friendship not be endangered too much during these skirmishes, and I want to see to it that, at least from my side, the [kinds of] boundaries are not be crossed that artistic passion can violate so easily.
> In the hope, "in spite of everything," of seeing you at my place in Cologne, I give you my hand as your sincere
> Ferd. Hiller.
> Aachen, 5 May [i.e., June] [18]57 [31]

Second, there is Hiller's aforementioned blow-by-blow report—in the widely read Cologne newspaper—of the series of misfires and instances of bad judgment that had just occurred during a festival with which he was closely associated. The festival involved, every year, dozens or even hundreds of musicians (including members of the choruses) with whom Hiller had been and would remain involved, and he had co-directed it in 1853 and been sole director in 1855. His report makes clear that some of the musicians had complained to him about Liszt's casual or inept (as it seemed to them) conducting of the festival's massive forces, to which he added his own judgment about some of Liszt's basic decisions about what works to put on the programs. Hiller, in "taking a critical position" against Liszt in print, must have known that he was now risking the wrath of the proponents of the New German School.[32]

THE AFTERMATH

For years thereafter, Hiller and Liszt seem—unsurprisingly—not to have met nor corresponded. But Liszt's disciples took matters into their own hands, launching diatribes and rumors against Hiller, one of which was particularly mean-spirited and patently false: that Hiller, during one of those 1857 dress-rehearsals, had blown into his housekey as a signal to other enemies of Liszt to start launching audible protests (hooting, etc.) against the music coming from the stage. This rumor finally reached the public twenty-five years after the fact, when the chief supposed witness was no longer alive. Hiller took the current rumor-spreader to court, and won, forcing the man to retract the charge in a newspaper.[33] As mentioned at the outset, the supposed housekey-whistle event was, unfortunately, reported as fact in Alan Walker's Liszt biography, but it has been definitively discredited by Beverly Jerold in two articles published in 2016 and 2017.[34] More generally, private letters of the Weimarians (such as Hans von Bülow and Hans Bronsart von Schellendorf), over the course of many years, make clear—as Beverly Jerold has convincingly demonstrated—that their animus against Hiller was rooted in a deep-seated prejudice against the supposedly excessive influence of Jews in the musical world.[35] Hiller, for his part, took a public stand against the Liszt-Wagner circle in 1860, signing (along with Brahms, Joachim, and some two dozen others) what would quickly become one of the most renowned petitions in music history: a manifesto declaring "the so-called Music of the Future" to be "contrary to the innermost spirit of music."[36] And, in 1868, he republished his review of the Aachen festival in one of his many compilation volumes of his reviews and essays.[37]

In 1877, Hiller tried to apologize to Liszt for his part in turning the often-messy performances during the 1857 festival at Aachen into a public attack on Liszt's limitations as a conductor. In an Open Letter, he wrote: "I only know this: it was wrong for you to conduct *Messiah*, because musical artists of such pronounced individuality as yours can only direct works for which they feel sympathy. And it would have been better and wiser for me to let someone else say this."[38]

The two actually met, one year before the Open Letter, in Düsseldorf. Hiller was attending, with Clara Schumann, one or more concerts Liszt gave there in the spring of 1876 and wrote that he was astounded anew by Liszt's personality and musicianship: "But to you I could shout from the bottom of my heart: 'It's you, yes, it's you entirely as you were thirty years ago.' The same élan, the same power, the same passion and grace. To have maintained such proud artistic youthfulness for half a century—that is spiritual heroism of the rarest kind."[39]

This gesture of reconciliation was apparently rejected.

Liszt must have been even more upset by Hiller's final published comment about him: a review of the revised (November 1881) edition of Liszt's book *The Gypsies and Their Music*. This publication had been stuffed full of antisemitic diatribes by Liszt's mistress Princess Carolyne von Sayn-Wittgenstein. Alas, Liszt felt obliged—was it some perverse sort of chivalry?—to maintain silence on the matter, allowing the public to wonder how this famously generous and open-minded person had become so prejudiced against one particular religious/ethnic group. Hiller (like Hanslick and a few others) hinted broadly that the Liszt he knew could not have written these pages.

> Saddening news recently came from a living master, who in his way is great and brilliant. In a booklet about the music of the Gypsies, Franz Liszt has added a postscript that is sure to be incomprehensible to anybody who knows him. I have hardly encountered another artist who received anybody approaching him with as gracious a manner; he was someone who knew how to show kindness to even the most insignificant person. A rare talent for recognition seems to be natural for him; indeed, one never could doubt that true and real warmth of the heart was characteristic of him. And now, he suddenly surpasses the most fanatical loudmouths with an anti-Semitic manifesto of the nastiest kind. And this comes from him: an artist who is more upright than any other, who is a pious priest of the God of love. To be clear: I do not believe that he penned this writ of excommunication [*Bannbulle*]; I do not believe that it originated with him. Why he let himself be associated with it and thus must bear the unavoidable consequences—that cannot be explained. It is incomprehensible.[40]

Again, there seems to have been no reply from Liszt. His loyalty to the Princess outweighed any sense of justice toward fellow musicians who also happened to be of Jewish origin, such as Hiller, the late Giacomo Meyerbeer (whose operas had inspired major keyboard works by Liszt: the *Robert le diable* Fantasy and the organ fantasy on "Ad nos, ad salutarem undam," from *Le Prophète*), and the late Felix Mendelssohn.

★ ★ ★

Thus, a friendship that had sprung effortlessly in the soil of Parisian musical life in the late 1820s, in the comparatively tolerant cultural atmosphere that reigned in post-Napoleonic France—when works of Bach could alternate on a concert with the most superficial display pieces—and that had survived, though just barely, the tensions between the traditionalists in the conservatories, on the one hand, and the Liszt/Wagner circle, on the other, was shattered because Hiller, perhaps naïvely or in a spirit of determined honesty, picked up the pen and wrote some hard truths about the limitations of one the most famous musicians of the age.

It is time that Hiller be appreciated for his own strengths, which included the courage to say things that some people wished not to hear. Furthermore, it is time that Hiller be appreciated for his own compositions, some of which are truly marvelous— and that were, as Robert Schumann wrote at the time, quite forward-looking.[41]

Figure 1, Ferdinand Hiller. *Carte de visite* photograph. Leopold Haase (probably Cologne, in or after 1865).

Figure 2, Franz Liszt. *Carte de visite* photograph. Fratelli D'Alessandri (Rome, 1862 or 1863).

* We wish to thank Gunther Braam for helpful comments, and for kindly providing the two photographs, both of which are in his personal collection and have apparently never been published before.
1 Letter from Ludwig Spohr to FH, 20 September 1828, in *Aus Ferdinand Hillers Briefwechsel*, 7 vols., ed. Reinhold Sietz (Cologne: Arno Volk Verlag, 1958–70) 1:6–7: "dem Verlockenden in Kunst und Leben."
2 Alan Walker, *Franz Liszt*, 3 vols., 1: *The Virtuoso Years, 1811-1847*, rev. edn. (Ithaca, NY: Cornell University Press, 1988), 161.
3 Ferdinand Hiller, "Offener Brief an Franz Liszt," in *Künstlerleben* (Cologne: Dumont-Schauberg, 1880), 204: "Du spieltest sie eigentlich nicht. Du improvisirtest sie. Du schufst sie zum zweiten Mal. Nie habe ich den Eindruck vergessen! Einer prachtvollen, nächtlichen Feuersbrunst gleich, ist er mir in der inneren Anschauung geblieben."
4 22 January 1830. See Malou Haine, "Les concerts communs de Ferdinand Hiller et Franz Liszt à Paris," in *Ferdinand Hiller: Komponist, Interpret, Musikvermittler*, ed. Peter Ackermann, Arnold Jacobshagen, Roberto Scoccimarro, and Wolfram Steinbeck (Kassel: Merseburger, 2014), 309–27, esp. 324.
5 There are two triple concertos by Bach beginning with an Allegro (in D minor, BWV 1063—the one probably programmed in Paris—and in C major, BWV 1064). The "three pianists" performed it twice: on Saturday, 23 March 1833, and on Sunday, 15 December 1833, in the Salle du Wauxhall and at the Conservatoire, respectively. See Haine, "Les concerts communs," 325–26.
6 19 January 1834 (Haine, "Les concerts communs," 326).
7 4 April 1835 (Haine, "Les concerts communs," 327).
8 Hiller, "Offener Brief," *Künstlerleben*, 206: "Freundlich war es von Dir und Chopin, in einem meiner Concerte ein Tripel-Concert von Bach mit mir zu spielen—es war keine dankbare Aufgabe. Bach war damals noch nicht populär in Paris—noch hatte Gounod seine Méditation über das erste Präludium des wohltemperirten Claviers nicht geschrieben."
9 Hiller, "Offener Brief," *Künstlerleben*, 206–07: "Zu einem noch liebenswürdigeren Zusammenwirken, mir gegenüber, hattet Ihr beiden Euch aber vereinigt, als ich einige Zeit in meiner Vaterstadt zubrachte—Ihr schriebt mir ein paar Wechselbriefe [*gesperrt*]—indem zeilenweise bald der Eine, bald der Andere seiner Feder und seinem Humor freien Lauf ließ. Wenn man sich diese Briefe ansieht, glaubt man aus Deinen Zügen Deine Oktaven—aus denen Chopin's seine Fioriituren herausspringend zu erblicken."
10 Quoted from Ernst Burger, *Franz Liszt: A Chronicle of His Life in Pictures and Documents*, trans. by Stewart Spencer (Princeton: Princeton University Press, 1989), 73. The translation has been slightly adjusted and American spelling has been given preference.
11 Hiller, "Offener Brief," *Künstlerleben*, 205–6: "Weißt Du, was eine alte übermüthige Dame aus diesem Kreise einst zu Chopin sagte? (ich gebe es in der französischen Orginalausgabe, auf Deutsch würde es zu unmoralisch klingen) 'Si j'étais jeune et jolie, mon petit Chopin,' sagte sie, 'je te prendrais pour mari, Hiller pour ami et Liszt pour amant.' In Verwunderung wird Dich diese Äußerung schwerlich setzen. Aber vielleicht folgende Chopin's. Du hattest eines Abends die Aristokratie der französischen Schriftstellerwelt bei Dir versammelt—Georges [sic] Sand durfte hier nicht fehlen. Beim Nachhausegehen sagte Chopin zu mir: 'Welch eine antipathetische Frau, diese Sand! Ist's denn wirklich eine Frau? Ich möchte es bezweifeln.' … Dunkel sind die Verschlingungen des Schicksals—vollends, wenn es sich in weiblicher Gestalt birgt."
12 Hiller, "Offener Brief," *Künstlerleben*, 207: "In Deinen Concerten begannst Du damals, Dir Motive zur Improvisation geben zu lassen—man legte sie, geschrieben und gefaltet, in eine große Vase. Was wurde da alles herausgezogen! Dante, Tasso, der Dom von Mailand, eine letzte Liebe, das Tollste und das Dümmste. Und wie es Dich amüsirte, wenn so alles um Dich herum rumorte."
13 Wilhelm Albert of Neipperg (1819–95) was the (illegitimate) son of Count Adam Albert of Neipperg (1775–1819) and Marie Louise (1791–1847), Duchess of Parma and Napoleon's second wife

(and thus Empress of France). His parents married in 1821 after the death of their respective spouses.
14 Walker, *Franz Liszt* 1:345–51.
15 *Neue Zeitschrift für Musik*, no. 12 (1840): 118–20.
16 Walker, *Franz Liszt* 1:188 and *Franz Liszt* 2: *The Weimar Years, 1848-1861* (1988; reprint: Cornell University Press, 1993), 296–97, 338–40, 348–51, 416–22; Beverly Jerold, "*Zukunftsmusik*/Music of the Future: A Moral Question," *Journal of Musicological Research* 36, no. 4 (2017): 311–35 and "A Vindication of Ferdinand Hiller," *Journal of Musicological Research* 37, no. 2 (2018): 141–65.
17 Hiller to Liszt, 4 January 1852, in Sietz, *Briefwechsel* 1:93.
18 Hiller to Liszt, 8 March 1852, in Sietz, *Briefwechsel* 1:94.
19 Quoted from Hugh Macdonald, *Music in 1853: The Biography of a Year* (Woodbridge: Boydell, 2012), 118.
20 Walker still stated, in 1989, that "the general view today is that this ['H.'] was Hiller"—*Franz Liszt* 2:281n.
21 Burger, *Franz Liszt*, 191, transl. in Appendix (341); we have also consulted the English translation in Macdonald, *Music in 1853*, 118–19, which quotes the emphasized phrase in French rather than German: "nous sommes pilotes, et non manoeuvres." The original French text of the letter (5 November 1853) is in *Franz Liszt's Briefe*, ed. La Mara [Ida Marie Lipsius] vol. 1 (Leipzig: Breitkopf und Härtel, 1893), 144.
22 Maria Pavlovna (1786–1859), daughter of the Russian tsar Paul I, married Karl Friedrich, the grand duke of Saxony-Weimar-Eisenach in 1804.
23 Liszt had conducted the premiere of the *Mazeppa* symphonic poem (based ultimately on his Transcendental Etude No. 4 of 1851) in 1854. "Eine Faust-Symphonie in drei Charakter-Bildern" was first completed in 1854; revised and with a brief finale for tenor solo and men's chorus, it would receive its world premiere in Weimar in 1857.
24 The information in this and surrounding paragraphs comes mainly from Hiller's aforementioned "Open Letter" to Liszt (1877).
25 An allusion to Aesop's fable about the fox and the grapes. They look sweet and juicy, but when he jumps and cannot reach them, he goes away, saying, "Oh, they were probably sour anyway." So Hiller is shrugging off his failure to please the listeners and simultaneously mocking his pretense at not being upset. The quotations in this paragraph and the previous one are from letters first published in Sietz, *Aus Ferdinand Hillers Briefwechsel* 1:104–7.
26 "Vous faites de grandes et de belles choses à Weimar, mon cher Liszt, et je vous suis avec tout l'intérêt possible, ce qui ne veut pas dire que je partage complètement *toutes* vos admirations—mais ceci est un chapitre beaucoup trop long pour une lettre. Vous avez de[s] convictions sérieuses, vous les poursuivez courageusement—c'est la seule bonne manière de vivre." Hiller to Liszt, 8 March 1852 (written in Paris), in Sietz, *Aus Ferdinand Hillers Briefwechsel* 1:94. (Sietz prints the word "toutes" *gesperrt*, thereby somewhat Germanizing it. Also, he, or the typesetter, gives "avec" for what Hiller surely wrote as "avez.")
27 "Wir sind bereits ziemlich alte Freunde, und selbst die Verschiedenheit unserer geistigen Temperatur verhindert keineswegs, dass wir noch ältere, und wo möglich bessere, werden. Gieb mir den Beweis, dass diese *Gefühls*meinung auch die Deine ist und besuche mich in Aachen, nicht als Dirigent oder Zukunftsmusiker sondern einfach als Deinen alten, sich selbst und seinen Freunden getreu bleibenden [signed:] F. Liszt." Liszt to Hiller, 22 May 1857, in Sietz, *Aus Ferdinand Hillers Briefwechsel* 7:122–23.
28 "Möglich dass ich mich irre, möglich dass allerlei ungewaschenes Gewäsch Dich dazu veranlasst (denn es ist manches von Seiten einiger Aachener gedacht und ausgesprochen worden, was vielleicht aachenswerth aber nicht achtungswerth war). . . . Dass ich nie einen Augenblick Willens war, *nicht* nach Aachen zu kommen, versteht sich von selbst. . . . Und wenn ich mich sehr darauf freue Dich zu sehen und zu sprechen, so bist Du mir hoffentlich nicht böse, wenn ich Dir sage, dass es mich auch

sehr interessirt, Dich als Dirigenten kennen zu lernen, nachdem ich Dich in dieser Hinsicht seit Jahren auf die mannichfachste Weise von Freund und Feind geschildert bekommen habe. Adieu, Lieber Liszt, und à bientôt. Stets Dein unveränderter (und auch dicker gewordener) [signed:] Ferd. Hiller." Hiller to Liszt, 26 May 1857, in Sietz, *Aus Ferdinand Hillers Briefwechsel* 7:123.

29 One can sense Hiller's awareness of the challenges involved in conducting an ensemble from his critique of Berlioz's conducting technique, which was, to his mind, nervous and fussy, irritating the players instead of making them feel confident ("Hector Berlioz," in *Künstlerleben*, 98–99).

30 Hiller, "Das Musikfest in Aachen 1857," *Aus dem Tonleben unserer Zeit*, 2 vols. (Leipzig: Hermann Mendelssohn, 1868), 1:138–40: "Ich hatte zufälligerweise keine Gelegenheit gehabt, Liszt dirigieren zu sehen, und hatte so viel sich Widersprechendes darüber gehört, daß meine—Neugierde, nun ja, aufs höchste gespannt war. Jetzt, nachdem ich ihn in fünf großen Proben und drei großen Concerten die verschiedensten Tonwerke habe einstudiren und aufführen hören, bin ich zur Überzeugung gelangt, daß Liszt kein [*gesperrt*] Dirigent ist—keiner wenigstens im Verhältnisse zu der Aufgabe, die er sich stellt, zu den Ansprüchen, die man an einen solchen Mann zu machen berechtigt ist."

31 Hiller to Liszt, 5 May [recte: June] 1875, facsimile in *Die Musik in Geschichte und Gegenwart*, ed., Friedrich Blume, et al., 14 vols. and supplements (Kassel: Bärenreiter, 1949–68), 6 (1957): 405–6 (in Reinhold Sietz's entry on Hiller: 6:399–410). "Lieber Liszt, Ich habe Dich die Tage hier wenig gesehen – Du warst einestheils mit Geschäften überhäuft, andrentheils hätte ich Dir mit dem besten Willen nicht viel Freundliches sagen können ohne Komödie zu spielen und noch viel weniger wollte ich Dir unter diesen Umständen kritisch gegenüber treten. Wenn ich es nun mit der größten Aufrichtigkeit aussprechen darf, daß die Sympathie die Du von jeher in mir zu erwecken gewußt immer die gleiche ist, so muß ich doch hinzufügen, daß es sich mit einem Theil Deiner musikalischen Bestrebungen ganz anders verhält, daß ich nicht allein in denselben nicht mit Dir übereinstimme sondern es nachgerade für [meine] Pflicht halte, Dir darin mit allen Kräften entgegenzutreten, so sehr Dich dieselben auch Deiner Stellung und Deinem Einfluß gegenüber angreifen mögen. Von Herzen wünsche ich daß bei diesen kleinen Kämpfen unsere alte Freundschaft nicht in allzu große Gefahr kommen möge und werde wenigstens von meiner Seite alles aufbieten um die Grenzen nicht zu überspringen welche künstlerische Leidenschaft so leicht verletzen kann. In der Hoffnung, Dich 'trotz alledem und alledem' in Köln bei mir zu sehen drücke ich Dir die Hand als Dein Altergebener Ferd. Hiller. Aachen, 5. Mai [recte Juni] [18]57.—" Liszt reported in a letter that, at a banquet in his honor at the end of the festival, he had to walk through a room that Hiller was in, and moved a little to the left "to avoid passing too near the large person of my former friend!" (Walker, *Franz Liszt* 2:421). "Trotz alledem und alledem" is an allusion to a poem of 1843 by Ferdinand Freiligrath that was widely sung by German proponents of social revolution in the years 1848–49. Hiller, by alluding to it, is inviting Liszt to remember their spirited youthful years together in Paris.

32 Including Wagner, with whom Hiller had been friendly in the 1840s, but who repeatedly attacked Hiller in later years. See Giselher Schubert, "Wagners Hiller-Polemik," in Ackermann, et al., *Ferdinand Hiller*, 501–11.

33 A full account is given in Jerold, "Vindication." The accusation was, among other things, wildly belated, referring to events 25 years earlier.

34 Walker, *Franz Liszt* 1:416–21; Jerold, "*Zukunftsmusik*/Music of the Future" and "Vindication."

35 Further, see Jerold, "Zukunftsmusik/Music of the Future" and "Vindication."

36 Walker, *Franz Liszt* 2:349–50.

37 *Aus dem Tonleben unserer Zeit*; see n. 30.

38 Hiller, "Offener Brief," in *Künstlerleben*, 212: "Dir aber konnte ich aus voller Seele zurufen: 'Du bist's ja, Du, ganz und gar, wie vor dreißig Jahren.' Derselbe Schwung, dieselbe Kraft, dieselbe Leidenschaft und Anmuth. Solch eine stolze künstlerische Jugendlichkeit, sich durch ein halbes Jahrhundert zu bewahren – es ist sicherlich ein geistiges Heldenthum der allerseltensten Art."

39 Hiller, "Offener Brief," in *Künstlerleben*, 212: "Einstweilen weiß ich nur soviel: Du thatest nicht wohl daran, die Leitung des Messias zu übernehmen – denn Tonkünstler von so ausgeprägter Individualität wie Du können nur leiten, was ihnen sympathisch – ich aber hätte besser und klüger gehandelt, es einem Anderen zu überlassen, dies auszusprechen."

40 Hiller in *Hamburgische Nachrichten* (February 1882?), republished as "Briefe an einen Hamburger Verleger," in *Erinnerungsblätter* (Cologne: Dumont-Schauberg, 1884), 51: "Von einem lebenden, in seiner Weise großen und glänzenden Meister hat die letzte Zeit Betrübendes gebracht. Franz Liszt hat bekanntlich seiner Broschüre über die Musik der Zigeuner ein Postskriptum angehängt, das Jedem, der ihn kennt, unbegreiflich erscheinen muß. Kaum habe ich einen Künstler gekannt, der in gleich liebenswürdiger Weise Jeden empfing, der sich ihm näherte—sich gleich ihm dem Unbedeutendsten verbindlich erzeigen wußte. Ein seltenes Anerkennungstalent [*gesperrt*] scheint ihm angeboren—ja, man konnte nie daran zweifeln, daß ihm die wahre, wirkliche Herzensgüte zu eigen. Und nun überbietet er plötzlich die fanatischsten Schreihälse durch einen antisemitischen Aufruf, er, der fromme Priester des Gottes der Liebe. Die Wahrheit zu sagen—ich glaube nicht, daß er diese Bannbulle geschrieben—glaube auch nicht, daß sie von ihm herrührt. Warum er sie über sich ergehen ließ, die unvermeidlichen Folgen zu tragen sich entschloß, das ist freilich nicht erklärlich—nicht begreiflich."

41 Schumann review of *Die Zerstörung Jerusalems*, quoted at length in Reiner Heyink, "'Es neigt sich mehr nach der Zukunft hin'—Das Oratorienschaffen von Ferdinand Hiller," in Ackermann, et al., *Ferdinand Hiller*, 237–62.

21. "BECOMING" JOSEPH JOACHIM, OR, "BECOMING" JOHANNES BRAHMS, THE COMPOSER OF VIOLIN CONCERTO OP. 77 (1878)

Katharina Uhde

This chapter inquires how Brahms's process of "becoming" the composer of Violin Concerto Op. 77 was impacted by being in Joseph Joachim's surroundings and in close interaction with him between 1853 and 1878, and later (notwithstanding the rift in the 1880s when Brahms defended Amalie Joachim in Joachim's divorce case). There were early days the two spent together in Göttingen; there were several visits by Brahms to Hannover, where Joachim lived between 1853 and 1869; there was the famous counterpoint exchange that started in 1856; and there were lots of shared concerts. And there were many exchanges about each other's compositions (See Table 1).

Table 1, Johannes Brahms and Joseph Joachim's Exchange about Joachim's Compositions[1]

Joachim's Music	Comments	Reference to Compositions, Arrangements, Revisions
Andantino and Allegro scherzoso Op. 1	V, 89.	
Violin Concerto Op. 3	V, 26.	Revision of piano score
Overture to Hamlet Op. 4	V, 10ff.	Arrangement
Three Pieces Op. 5	V, 47, 80	Quoted in "Hymne zur Verherrlichung …."
Overture to Demetrius Op. 6	V, 57-58.	Arrangement
Overture to Heinrich Op. 7	V, 102-104.	Arrangement
Overture to Gozzi Op. 8	V, 92, 218.	
Hebrew Melodies Op. 9	V, 89.	
Var. Op. 10	V, 89.	
Hungarian Concerto Op. 11	V, 251–254.	
Kleist Overture Op. 14	V, 173–175ff.	
String Quartet	V, 218.	

"Becoming" Johannes Brahms the composer of the Violin Concerto was inspired by seeing, hearing, and being with Joachim, which included commenting on Joachim's music.

I am also using the term "becoming" in a second way. In recent literatures, performer-scholars including Elisabeth Le Guin, Pheaross Graham, and Samantha Ege have written or reflected on what it means to radically identify with a composer to the extent of "becoming" this composer in the act of embodying their music.

The understanding of "becoming" as "radically identifying with" allows a performer such as myself to explore what the violin part of Brahms's concerto consists of in a corporeal, embodied sense. This understanding of "becoming," which never reaches the state of being because it is always in flux, is evoked in Nietzsche's *Philosophy in the Tragic Age of the Greeks* (1873), where the character Heraclitus, based on the ancient Greek philosopher of that name, says: "I see nothing other than becoming. Be not deceived, even the stream into which you step a second time is not the one you stepped into before."[2]

Le Guin, in showing how radical composer-performer identification challenges the work concept and the nature of music's existence as text, writes:

> ... In a very reasonable voice, you cannot have a physically reciprocal relationship with someone no longer living. Yet I do claim it as reciprocal. My role constitutes itself as follows: as living performer of Boccherini's sonata ... I am aware of acting the connection between parts of someone who cannot be here in the flesh. ... As this composer's agent in performance, I do in this way become him, in much the same manner as I become myself. And my experience of becoming him is grounded in, and expressed through the medium of the tactile.[3]

I am applying performative methodologies—including Elisabeth LeGuin's carnal musicology and Arnie Cox's ideas of listening, the latter tied to the "bodily actions" of performance which compel the listener to imitate the act of performance overtly or covertly when listening—via questions such as: What's it like to do that?[4] For example, when Brahms was composing his violin part, was he "listening" to Joachim in his mind, conjuring up the actions of Joachim's body and imagining them as he was writing? I am also including autoethnographic methodologies, including interview excerpts of people in my network. Autoethnography, or "the use of personal experience to explore cultural practices"[5] is etymologically constructed of three concepts: "auto" refers to the first-person reports that this chapter encompasses; "ethno" refers to the "cultural texts, experiences, beliefs, and practices" in which I am grounded, and "graphy" refers to "describing and interpreting" these texts, experiences, beliefs, and practices.[6]

In presenting explorations into Brahms's concerto and attempting a radical identification with his violin part, I am responding to those descriptions and analyses in the literature where passagework, playability, and idiomacy are part of some hierarchical view that privileges themes and non-virtuosic or non-idiomatic contents as a composer's actual language. Such views keep Joachim's share in the process firmly limited to the violinistic domain, allowing scholars to write that "Brahms's language is entirely his own" in this work.[7]

With my autoethnography I aim to challenge the idea that "Brahms's language is entirely his own," and I respond as follows: In my lived experience as a violinist and Joseph Joachim scholar, Brahms's approach to the violin idiom in the violin part—which is part of his "language" in the violin concerto—occurs for me as deeply enmeshed with the kinesthetic and haptic world of the music of Joseph Joachim. *The Music of Joseph Joachim* is the title of my 2018 monograph, the first to discuss all of

Joachim's compositions. As a violinist-musicologist who writes about, performs, and records Joachim's music, I've been an advocate for Joseph Joachim's works since 2011.

The danger of an autoethnographic methodology, as Carolyn Ellis and others have pointed out, consists of just "telling [my story]" without looking at experience analytically.[8] One way for me to frame "story-telling", or those first-person narratives about how I hear certain passages of Brahms's violin concerto, which I will get to, is to embed my discussion in the existing Brahms literature; to feature brief interview excerpts with other performing scholars from my cultural network on issues of idiomacy, and to reflect on my subjective stance in the end.

THE GENESIS OF BRAHMS'S VIOLIN CONCERTO

As Styra Avins tells us, "the first indication Brahms had something wonderful in the making was the arrival of two short letters in quick succession, discreet heralds of the Violin Concerto. They reached Joachim at his summer villa near Salzburg."[9] This happened in August 1878. Brahms writes: "Dear friend, I wish I knew how long you'll be there and would like to send you a number of violin passages!"[10] The second letter, written soon after the first, requests Joachim to write in a few "difficult, uncomfortable, impossible" markings. Joachim was delighted by the developments, impressed by its then four-movement structure, and commented on the work:

> To me it's a great, genuine joy that you're writing a violin concerto ... Most of it is manageable, some of it even very original, violinistically. But whether it can all be played comfortably in a hot concert-hall I cannot say, before I've played it straight through. Any chance that one might get together for a couple of days?[11]

The two friends did come together several times on behalf of this concerto, allowing the kind of knowledge transfer to happen that recent scholarship on distributed creativity has described. Is it surprising that Brahms in the end admitted: "You will be careful to ask for another concerto? Something justifies that the concerto carries your name, that is, that you are this way a little bit responsible for the violin part."[12]

SHARED PROCESS, OR, LISTENING TO JOACHIM'S "IDIOM"

Questions of shared process emerge in all the arts. According to Shakespeare scholar Emma Smith, discussions of who did what, and who contributed to whom, are subject to fashions. In some periods, everything that was good in Shakespeare was done without any collaborations; in other periods writers or musicians were praised for certain collaborative efforts.[13] How did Joachim contribute to Brahms in "becoming" the composer of this concerto, and how do scholars view Joachim's presence in it? For Karen Leistra-Jones, Joachim's role in this concerto is revealed through Joachim's "carefully crafted persona as a performer and the cultural meanings that this persona activated."[14] With the exception of an early critic of 1879, who tore the concerto into pieces for many reasons, including the participation of a violinist in the compositional process,[15] several writers posit that Brahms was mainly interested in Joachim helping him by suggesting alternatives for Brahms to consider.[16]

Karl Geiringer has argued that "the Violin Concerto ... is governed by the same principles as Brahms's first Pianoforte Concerto,"[17] elaborating that despite the "exceptional" showcase of "technique on the part of the soloist, virtuosity for its own sake is entirely excluded"; and, to be sure, for "Brahms the artistic idea was always of supreme importance [while] ... the sound of the instruments inspired him only in a minor degree."[18]

Ossip Schnirlin, Linda Correll Roesner,[19] and Boris Schwarz have discussed the colored holograph score at the Library of Congress and commented on the Abschrift of the violin part (hereinafter "Copy 3"), also held at the Library of Congress, and on the autograph fragment of the violin part held in Berlin (hereinafter "Solo-part No. 1").[20] The Abschrift contains comments by Joseph Joachim. Most scholars agree that Joachim improved idiomacy. As Michael Musgrave writes: "Brahms's [had an] intimate acquaintance with Joachim's idiom," but wherein exactly the passages in question show Joachimian idiomacy is left unclear.

Though Schwarz acknowledges that the work was composed for a "particular interpreter,"[21] the implications of Joachimianness—which could be investigated by looking at Joachim's works side-by-side—have not been iterated in detail. Thus, the manner in which "personal idiosyncrasies of the instrumentalist [Joseph Joachim] were reflected in the emerging work"[22] leaves open the nature of these idiosyncrasies. Furthermore, studies of Op. 77 involving performative methodologies within the framework of Joachim's music have not been undertaken.

Let's move onto Brahms's "intimate acquaintance with Joachim's idiom" (Musgrave). There are, for example, "too hard" comments and ossia markings in the margins of the Abschrift of the violin part. Brahms had ordered these ossia markings explicitly from Joachim in the letter of 21 January 1879.[23] These markings are refreshingly pragmatic, thus clashing with early biographers' and analysts' claims that where Joachim is technical, that technicality was produced "unconsciously," as Donald Francis Tovey insists.[24] Similarly, Leistra-Jones's article on Joachim's choreographed performance persona or his "presence" in Brahms's Violin Concerto has revealed that what critics viewed as an entirely enraptured way of performing was, in fact, to no small extent a conscious effort of choreography on Joachim's part, an active crafting of a performance persona.[25] Brahmsians seem conscious of Joachim's ability to contribute to the "[removal of] excessive difficulties from the solo part" and to turn "difficult" into "violinistic."[26]

The Composer of Violin Concerto Op. 77 (1878)

JOACHIM'S CONTRIBUTIONS TO IDIOMACY AND PLAYABILITY

The following discussion elaborates on a few discrepancies between earlier manuscripts and the holograph of the Brahms Concerto used for the premiere on January 1879 and later revised again for the first edition.[27]

By pointing to these discrepancies, we can trace some of Joachim's contributions to the violin part. The most revealing discrepancies emerge when looking at the Berlin fragmental autograph of movements 1 and 3 ("Solo-part No. 1") and the Abschrift Joachim had made for a tour to England which contained his annotations and fingerings ("Copy No. 3"); Joachim's markings were eventually transferred into the color-printed Holograph Score used for the premiere,[28] which formed the basis for the first edition.

To briefly describe some of those discrepancies: First, in measures 102–104 of the first movement, shortly after the first solo entrance, a descending arpeggio pattern emerges, which begins on what is the highest pitch to this point, A6. This descending arpeggio passage went through iterations as the manuscripts show. The fragmental autograph ("Solo-part No. 1") shows an arpeggio pattern whereby the violinist would have to lift fingers during the arpeggio pattern twice, which is cumbersome. The way the passage was corrected, which is visible in Copy No. 3 and in the holograph, allowed smoother string crossings because lifting fingers was eliminated within each slur (lifting fingers would still occur between slurs, where it is less cumbersome). Playability was greatly improved by Joachim's suggestion of replacing the A at the end of each slur with a D (m. 102–104).

Another discrepancy occurs in the animato near the end of the first movement (m. 559). As can be seen in the fragmental solo part ("Solo-part No. 1"), Brahms initially notated rapid repeated triplet figures before coming up with an alternate version of broken chords of two repetitions, with slurs connecting notes 2 and 3 as well as 4 and 1 (xy, yx). That alternate version went through additional changes whereby 3-note chords were reduced to double-stops, thereby allowing the bow to remain on one plane versus having to be curved in order to catch three strings at once. According to Schwarz, Joachim "certainly had a hand in" the improved alternate version.[29]

Some of Joachim's advice to Brahms is passed down through *ossia* markings, which Brahms had explicitly ordered from Joachim. These *ossia* markings were only notated in the violin part, not the score. Schwarz commented on an *ossia* passage in the first movement in m. 483, which was suggested by Joachim to help violinists with small hands who couldn't stretch the left hand to the interval of a tenth.[30]

Joachim's suggestions for improving the violin part sometimes concerned the tiniest details, some of which seem so minor that they make sense only to a violinist. In the first movement, m. 509, Joachim gave feedback on a descending 15-note run. He suggested changing the durations from three sixteenth-note quintuplets to an eighth, two sixteenths, and two sextuplets, keeping the number of notes in the run the same. In addition, Joachim suggested changing the slurring so that the first note would be alone on a bow. This suggestion allows the violinist to use a full bow on that note, which has an immense effect on the kinesthetic level—the violinist's bow arm would be unfolded in a large gesture—and thus, the volume of the note.

THE WAY I "LISTEN" TO BRAHMS: RADICAL IDENTIFICATION AND THE MUSIC OF JOSEPH JOACHIM IN BRAHMS'S OP. 77

The autoethnographic methodology of this essay allows me to explore now how I listen to Brahms, having performed many of Joachim's works. Such a perspective might complement the allusions to Beethoven, Bach, and Viotti's violin concertos that others have heard in Brahms's Op. 77.

In what ways do I participate mimetically with what I see on the page in Brahms's music? How do the patterns and figurations in Brahms's music feature an approach to "idiom", which in my own lived experience shows up as Brahms's intimate acquaintance with Joachim's idiom? To provide a brief overview, Table 2 shows my interaction with Joseph Joachim's compositions over the years.

Table 2, Selected violin works by Joachim, my performance histories, my publications & recordings

Joachim's Music for Violin	When I began learning this piece	Recording on CD or Youtube / projected professional recording session	Publication where this work is discussed
Fantasy on Hungarian Themes; Fantasy on Irish Themes, WoO	2016	"Two Fantasies Rediscovered" (2021)	Uhde, 2017; Uhde, 2018a; Uhde 2018b
Fantasy on Irish Melodies [collaboration with Otto Goldschmidt]	2019	Projected for 2025 with RTE Orchestra Dublin	Uhde, 2018a
Andantino and Allegro scherzoso Op. 1	2020		Uhde, 2018a
Violin Concerto Op. 3			Uhde, 2018a
Three Pieces Op. 2	2018	Romance [Op. 2 No. 2] 'Two Fantasies Rediscovered' (2021)	Uhde, 2018a; Uhde, 2023a Uhde, 2023b
Three Pieces Op. 5	2011		Uhde, 2015 Uhde, 2018a
Variations Op. 10	2019		Uhde, 2018a Uhde & Todd,
"Hungarian" Violin Concerto Op. 11	2020	Recorded professionally in 2021 (Prague)	Uhde, 2018a
Notturno Op. 12	2013	"Two Fantasies Rediscovered" (2021)	Uhde, 2018a
Variations for Violin and Orchestra in E minor	2022		Uhde, 2018a
Violin Concerto No. 3 WoO	2022	Recorded in Dec. 2023 with Radio Orchestra Belgrade	Uhde, 2018a

The Composer of Violin Concerto Op. 77 (1878)

I shall begin my discussion of how I listen to Brahms with a comparison between a passage in the Brahms Concerto and a passage from Joseph Joachim's Hungarian Concerto, this one pertaining to the topic of idiomatic slurs. Brahms conducted Joachim's concerto when Joachim performed it in Hamburg on 16 April 1861.[31]

Idiomatic Slurs:

This version of the animato passage in Brahms [Example 1a] feels rich and brilliant, fit for an idiomatic closing of a movement. How do I look at this passage from the inside? I am noticing that I can sink into the string with a heavy legato stroke, enjoy what my fingers and soft knuckles knead out of this passage; in these final bars the music almost plays itself in my hands; notwithstanding my fear of the sixth-to-last measure: tenth intervals for which there is no ossia alternative. My feeling of this passage, the way I catalogue it in my internal database, has to do with the slurring pattern, with the ascending sequence, and with the double-stop activity in the left hand. I notice less of the harmonic development and more about the athletic nature. This passage feels so meaty! But what does it remind me of … Of course [Example 1b]!

Example 1a, Johannes Brahms, Violin Concerto Op. 77 (mm. 557–571)

Example 1b, Joseph Joachim, Violin Concerto Op. 11 (mm. 475–482)

Three-voice chord preceding main chord unusually rapidly
(like a grace-note to a main note):

I proceed to a reflection on a passage from Brahms's Concerto Op. 77, which involves thick chords and unusually rapid upbow-downbow gestures.

> I am looking at Brahms [Example 2a]. As I reflect on "what's it like to do that?"– I am stunned by the unique demand of this passage. I am eager to stay at the bow's heel, where I have most control; I'm feeling the pressure of time being too short for this much action. My body has experienced this tightness before. I am recalling inadvertently the way I know Joachim to be when he is most fiery, such as in this Hungarian Concerto passage [Example 2b]. In my mind I see quotes I have looked at a thousand times, about what Joachim writes disparagingly about the Hanover musicians who lacked rhythm according to him, as Robert Eshbach has discussed in detail. Joachim's sharp eye for rhythmic fire is everywhere. It reveals who he is as a composer; far removed from that stately old gentleman he would later become. In my imagination I see him play this, his high wrist, how he would have attacked the two chords in such rapid succession. Was Brahms "listening" to Joachim or a violin-playing body when composing this? Would he have remembered Joachim executing this passage of the Hungarian Concerto?

The Composer of Violin Concerto Op. 77 (1878)

Example 2a, Johannes Brahms, Violin Concerto Op. 77 (mm. 487–491)

Example 2b, Joseph Joachim, Violin Concerto Op. 11 (mm. 140–147)

Separate Bows in a Cascading Climactic Run, from a High-position E-string Note:

Moving on to a downward run on the E-string in Brahms's concerto near the end of the recapitulation, which both in the holograph (US-Wc) and in the Abschrift (copy 3) reveals a separation of the slurring discussed above. What is my lived experience when I play this run in the way Joachim suggested – with a full bow on the first note E?

> The slurring of the run near the end of the recapitulation that was suggested by Joachim reminds me of a passage in the Hungarian Concerto. I can hear in my head Brahms's version of the passage that Joachim corrected – with the E alone on a bow. What Brahms had notated first is frustrating because he seems to have wanted a climax and wanted me to make it happen without enough bow, which equals not enough oxygen, equals frustration.
> To think that it is thanks to Joachim's intervention that I can play that E on an independent bow before starting the run ... it allows my arm to fully stretch out before getting on my way. I am noticing an attachment to the manner I have learned to hear this concerto; I am also noticing an attachment to Joachim, both to this particular annotation in Op. 77 and to his slur in the Hungarian Concerto. I am noticing that I don't care what notes come after the E; but the E I care about, because it wants to be climactic.

The Circling Figure:

Joachim sent a copy of his Overture to Gozzi (1854) to Brahms for feedback shortly after the piece was composed. Brahms remained interested in Carlo Gozzi's play *The King Stag* (1762)—the basis of Joachim's overture—and Brahms played with the idea of using this play as a libretto.[32] A passage in the Gozzi Overture near the beginning of the recapitulation (mm. 204–215) attracted me due to its circular figures, which repeat incessantly in a manner Joachim was known for.[33] These incessantly repeating three-note figures reminded me of the secondary theme in Brahms's solo exposition (mm. 179–195), where the violin plays figurations that implement register (B5-B4-G5 etc.) to create a sense of circularity. Comparing these passages brought to mind the following reflection:

> I begin my sensation-to-concept translation with Brahms's figurative passage derived from the secondary theme. The slurs that Brahms is asking me to play here are not terribly long but need to be legatissimo. With my right index finger, I guide the bow to smoothly move through the triplets with one note on the E string, two on the A. The dolce is particularly uncomfortable to execute—I knead the fingerboard and my fingertips sink into the string, connecting me with this pattern to the point of getting dizzy. The sensation for me, as I repeat these transforming 3-note motives, translates into a distinct experience of circularity. It reminds me of something ... I play the first and second violin parts from the orchestral score of Joachim's Overture to Gozzi. I am wondering what Brahms saw in the Gozzi Overture when he studied this score in the early 1850s. I am overwhelmed by the matching kinesthetic, tactile feel between the two passages, despite all the differences, indeed, from a theoretical perspective the resemblance is rather minor. But for me, as a Joachimian, I know that what I witness here is Joachim at his most idiosyncratic. He excelled at inventive rhythmic patterns, "trapped" motives that repeat over and over. The passage in the Gozzi Overture brings together an improvisatory feel with minor shifts in note values and shifting metric accents as well as an obsessive repetition familiar to me from Joachim's *Abendglocken* Op. 5. I know that Joachim stole this combination of repetitive circular motives plus perdendosi from Beethoven's Violin Concerto Op. 61. I am noticing how difficult it is to memorize Joachim's passage here. My brain is resisting these patterns because of how similar many of the three-note groups are.

The Bariolage Pattern:

In my journey with Brahms's Concerto, I next realize that yet another measure in the first movement feels to me identical to something I am familiar with, that I would like to dive into this resemblance.

> These barriolage patterns in Brahms's first movement (mm. 168–174) creates this stunning momentum like no other texture I know, whereby a seesaw-

ing-pattern felt in the right arm lets the bow take me for a ride as I pivot between a lower string and the E-string. The passage I inadvertently recall from Joachim's body of violin compositions is a passage from Joachim's Variations in E minor (mm. 541–564). "First mentioned on 21 August 1878, the ... [Variations in E minor for violin and orchestra] were completed in a first draft in December 1878. In January 1879 Joachim sent the work to Brahms."[34] I am struck by the interaction between Brahms and Joachim. I know that they exchanged most of their works with each other. But to think about what this interaction could have changed in their listening and perception—and in their composing—is again and again an inspiration for me.

Any other violinist would unpack idiom in any other way. What I tried to show is that those passages that were made more idiomatic by Joachim being in the room, belong to "the language" of this concerto; they are "actual content" and not secondary elements. In the interviews I conducted within my network—with Ning Hui See, Karin Hellqvist, Camilla Köhnken, and Anna Scott, I was able to gain insights into what performing scholars in my own network have to say about the question of approaching idiomatic passagework versus "themes" or other less virtuosic contents of a concerto.[35]

Clara Schumann scholar Ning Hui See, whom I interviewed on 8 November 2022, says:

> The act of formal analysis on paper versus performing a passage for deeper understanding are two different things because it is physical work that produces sound and evokes emotional responses [and that] ... what looks most interesting on paper is not the most interesting part when it becomes sound. ... In some instances, passage work may actually be more moving than the phrases with the themes.

Furthermore, Ning Hui See argued that for her passage work looks "visually impressive" on the page. This is a point anyone can understand who remembers tackling a virtuoso piece or concerto at a younger age and being afraid of all the black notes. Lastly, Ning Hui See writes that due to the performer's active physical involvement in display episodes of Romantic concertos, they can offer a window into "perceive[d] structure or drama based on the 'movement' behind the sound." This "movement" behind the sound is performative and embodied and corporeal, offering an audiovisual drama that is distinct from the rational knowledge that comes with listening without the instrument in hand or on one's mind.

The interview with Karin Hellqvist was fascinating. As a violinist and artistic researcher, Karin conducts research on shared compositional processes between performers and composers. When I shared with her my ideas about Joachim's contributions to the creation of Brahms's Violin Concerto—the differences between interpreting and performing Brahms's Violin Concerto thematically versus idiomatically—she had this to say:

> There are so many levels that one wants to think about in this. First of all there is this view of musicians just contributing to the craft and not the art of the composition. ... I mean just having Joseph Joachim in the room and speaking to him [would have] already contributed so much to the whole process of creating this work. There are so many studies nowadays that highlight how this contributes to the process. And this thing about idiomacy—I have to say I've been thinking a lot about it, especially in my own collaboration with [contemporary Swedish composer] Henrik Strindberg. What is idiomatic on one's instrument? What is personal, and what is idiomatic? I guess I am always trying to figure out if something is idiomatic, and if I have the mindset to understand what a composer wants it to sound like. Henrik and I have been trying so many different sketches, techniques, and drafts. Sometimes with contemporary music, and classical music too, you have to work for many months before you can play a passage, and it's difficult to know if something is idiomatic if you just read from the page or practice a day or two. This is something that has been circling in my mind. How do we as musicians decide what is idiomatic, what works and what doesn't?[36]

Camilla Köhnken, pianist and Liszt scholar, offers another revealing perspective on idiom. Like Joachim, Liszt focused on virtuosic passages when creating concertos that satisfied his own standards and his enjoyment of virtuosic passagework.

> From the historical recordings on which I base my performance practice research, i.e. especially of Liszt students, it emerges that really fast, virtuosic passagework might not present too much room for individuality, but it is often interesting for observing stylistic means like general/"long-term" tempo fluctuations, like rushing when emotions rise, slowing down when complex harmonic turning points or sequences demand it, etc. However, slower (often transitory) passagework encapsulates a lot of the particular "taste" of a performance and the players temperament and personality; for example the (from a modern perspective) "premature" sliding into the next phrase, which is so typical for Eugen d'Albert or Frederic Lamond and other 19th-century interpreters in the polyphonic treatment of continuous note values.[37]

Anna Scott also commented on my question on hierarchical views of idiom versus thematic contents:

> Histories and analyses of music tend to privilege thematic materials. ... As you probably know, my work is undertaken with as anti-score a perspective as is possible in this kind of music, which is to say that I try not to do anything or make any decisions based primarily on the notated topography of scores. I'm sure, if one looks hard enough, that the resulting performances reveal interesting things about my treatment of idiomatic versus thematic materials in Brahms's music, but this is not the result of some conscious decision on my part.[38]

The Composer of Violin Concerto Op. 77 (1878)

The way I've been "becoming" Joseph Joachim has been greatly impacted by my turn towards Artistic Research within the last few years. The four individuals I interviewed—See, Hellqvist, Köhnken, and Scott—have in varying degrees been involved in my YouTube Channel on Artistic Research, titled "BEING in Artistic Research."[39] They are my community. Being a member of this community has allowed me to keep pursuing Artistic Research, which is a reconciliation between my violinistic and musicological activity. Performer-scholars among my readers will understand that a journey of "becoming" a composer through performative-scholarly activity is still something many performers and many musicologists do not fully understand. To "become" anything, one needs a context in which this becoming can take place; a mirror in which one sees who one is becoming. The individuals I interviewed have provided this context and mirror, for which I am deeply grateful.

From Anna Scott's comment I got that my research does rely on music-as-text. How else would I have been able to identify how Joachim feels in how I listen to Brahms. Anna Scott's focus in Brahms research is influenced by her "anti-score" approach, her efforts to draw insights from recorded sound. She inspired me to think about where I may take my Joachim research next. From Camilla Köhnken's comments I got that "virtuosic passagework might not present too much room for individuality." Is this perhaps one of the things that has led to the hierarchical view I have detected in the Brahms literature on the concerto? Köhnken's comments on broader tempo issues in thematic areas invites further reflection and encourages me to explore this idea in a future research project on Brahms's concerto. From Karin Hellqvist I learned that idiomacy is, indeed, a rather individual thing. This made me realize that calling something "idiomatic" might be a subjective choice; what one performer calls "idiomatic" could theoretically occur as "thematic" in the lived experience of another performer. I asked myself whether I am perhaps attributing "thematic" importance to Joachim's idiom, because of how much I love Joachim's music. From Ning Hui See I discovered that there is an interesting question to ask with idiomacy: Does "idiomacy" reside equally in the music-as-text realm and the "music-as-sound" realm? Is it easier to "see" or "hear" idiomacy? In this essay I have approached idiomacy through the haptic and sensory realms, that is, I've called things "idiomatic" that felt technical or difficult in my hands. And I am noticing that I have approached idiomacy as residing, at least in part, on the notation level of the works at issue. This begs the question: How could I have made the points I made *without* my musical examples?

I have explored some of the passages in Brahms's Violin Concerto that Joachim gave feedback on; I have entered a subjective search for how I listen to Brahms. Evidently, I detach passages from their surrounding context, forgetting everything else while I do so, diving into the world of sensation and experience, often focused on a single note or a glimpse of familiarity that brings to my mind *The Music of Joseph Joachim*. I acknowledge the limitation of my own sense-making and my fixation on the violin part. I see my own bias when it comes to being attached to virtuoso music. I see my own enjoyment of playing music that feels rhythmic, mechanical, textural, and granular. All of this has shaped my choice of what to discuss in this essay. As a performer, I evidently "listen" to Brahms with an attraction to Joachim that makes me search for him.

In my effort to identify with Brahms and his Concerto Op. 77 in a way of embodying it – along the lines of what Elisbathe LeGuin has proposed about her relationship with Boccherini and his sonatas[40] – I notice that I resisted the Brahms I thought I knew. I have portrayed another Brahms, one whose playable and idiomatic textures and violinistic idiosyncracies are also part of his "language" and in sympathy with Joachim's idiom, pointing to their distributed creativity and shared compositional process. The Brahms emerging from this experiment is a conglomerate of Joachimian and Brahmsian things, throwing light on both the one who "became" Brahms the composer of the Violin Concerto Op. 77 and the body that provided the vessel for this grounded lived experience of enmeshed subjectivities to interact with each other.

1. This table contains information from the letters published in Andreas Moser, ed., *Johannes Brahms im Briefwechsel mit Joseph Joachim*, 3rd edn, 2 vols [vol. 5 and 6] (Tutzing: Hans Schneider, 1974)
2. Friedrich Nietzsche, *Philosophy in the Tragic Age of the Greeks* (Washington, DC: Regency Gateway, 1962 [1873]), 51–52. In Nietzsche's book, the character Heraclitus proclaims: "I see nothing other than becoming. Be not deceived. It is the fault of your short-sightedness, not of the essence of things, if you believe you see land somewhere in the ocean of becoming and passing-away. You use names for things as though they rigidly, persistently endured; yet even the stream into which you step a second time is not the one you stepped into before." Christoph Cox, *Nietzsche: Naturalism and Interpretation* (Berkeley, Los Angeles, London: University of California Press, 1999), 186.
3. Elisabeth LeGuin, *Boccherini's Body. An Essay in Carnal Musicology* (Berkeley, Los Angeles, and London: University of California Press, 2006), 24.
4. Arnie Cox, *Music and Embodied Cognition: Listening, Moving, Feeling, and Thinking (Musical Meaning and Interpretation)* (Bloomington and Indianapolis: Indiana University Press, 2016), 12. As Cox describes: "Part of how we comprehend music is by imitating, covertly or overtly, the observed sound-producing actions of performers … This occurs through the process of mimetic motor action (MMA) in which physical actions are performed in imitation, and mimetic motor imagery (MMI) in which imitation occurs through mental representation." Cox distinguishes between three forms that MMI and MMA can take: "Intramodal, or direct-matching (e.g. finger imitation of finger movements); Intermodal, or cross-modal (e.g., subvocal imitation of musical sounds generally); Amodal (abdominal exertions that underlie limb movements and vocalizations)." Cox's theory is based on these key principles: "Sounds are produced by physical events; sounds indicate (signify) the physicality of their source … Any and all acoustic features can or will be mimetically represented: pitch, duration, timbre, strength (acoustic intensity, or "volume"), and location … MMI (mimetic motor imagery) and MMA (mimetic motor action) can be stronger in live performance than in recorded performance … Mimetic participation results in a sense of belonging and shared achievement."
5. Ronald J. Pelias, *Writing Performance, Identity, and Everyday Life* (New York, NY: Taylor & Francis, 2018), 5.
6. Tony E. Adams, Carolyn Ellis, and Stacy Holman Jones, "Autoethnography", in *The International Encyclopedia of Communication Research Methods*, edited by Jörg Matthes, Christine S. Davis and Robert F. Potter (Hoboken, NJ: John Wiley & Sons, 2017).

7 Michael Musgrave, *The Music of Johannes Brahms* (London: Routledge & Kegan Paul, 1985), 210.
8 Carolyn Ellis, Tony E. Adams, and Arthur P. Bochner, "Autoethnography: an overview," *Historical Social Research*, 36 (4): 273–290.
9 Styra Avins, *Johannes Brahms: Life and Letters,* translated by Josef Eisinger and Styra Avins (Oxford and New York: Oxford University Press, 1997), 540.
10 Ibid., 540. Letter from Brahms to Joachim of 21 August 1878.
11 Ibid., 541. Avins cites a letter from Joachim to Brahms of [24 August 1878], Moser, ed., *Johannes Brahms im Briefwechsel mit Joseph Joachim*, 3rd edn, 2 vols [vol. 5 and 6] (Tutzing: Hans Schneider, 1974), VI:141.
12 Moser, ed., *Johannes Brahms im Briefwechsel mit Joseph Joachim*, VI:140, 170 ff.
13 Emma Smith, *This is Shakespeare* (New York, NY: Pantheon, 2020), Ch. 17.
14 Karen Leistra-Jones, "Improvisational Idyll," *19th-Century Music* 38/3 (Spring 2015): 243–271.
15 Adolf Weissmann, "Die Musik der Weltstadt," *Die Musik: Verzeichnis der Kunstbeilagen* 10/3, 3–76, here 13. Review of an 1879 performance of Brahms's Violin Concerto. "The Violin Concerto by Brahms seems to belong in its outer form and in its inner values to that category of works where three people, one composer, one publisher, and one performing artist (Joachim is meant) quasi participated. These three [people] interfere with each other, meaning, that in the end there is hardly anything left for art." "Das Violinkonzert von Brahms scheint seiner äußeren Form wie seinem inneren Werte nach in jene Kategorie musikalischer Handelsunternehmungen zu gehören, bei welchem drei Personen, ein Komponist, ein Verleger und ein ausübender Künstler (gemeint ist Joachim) quasi beteiligt sind. Diese drei arbeiten einander in die Hände, und die Kunst geht so ziemlich leer aus."
16 Karl Geiringer, *Brahms His Life and Work* (Boston: Houghton Mifflin, 1936), 255: "It is characteristic of Brahms that he consciously asked his friend's advice on all technical questions—and then hardly ever followed it." In fact, Geiringer goes on to say, "the result of all the great violinist's suggestions, which were almost entirely directed to excluding excessive difficulties from the solo part, is comparatively small; for example, the addition of *ma non troppo* to the tempo-direction vivace of the Finale was made at Joachim's request."
17 Geiringer, *Brahms, His Life and Work*, 255.
18 Ibid.
19 Linda Correll Roesner, "Review: Johannes Brahms. Concerto for Violin, Op. 77: A Facsimile of the Holograph Score. Introduction by Yehudi Menuhin. Foreword by Jon Newsom. Washington, D.C.: Library of Congress, 1979," *Current Musicology* 30 (1980): 60–72.
20 To keep the different manuscripts apart, I use Boris Schwarz's abbreviations, see Boris Schwarz, "Joseph Joachim and the Genesis of Brahms's Violin Concerto," *The Musical Quarterly*, 69/4 (Autumn, 1983): 503–26, 512. Roesner, 62: "Sometime around 8 February Joachim sent the original copy of the part to Brahms, mentioning that he was taking another copy with him to England. This copy that Joachim had made for himself is, I believe, the solo part that eventually served as *Stichvorlage*." Roesner: "Four were eventually used as *Stichvorlage* for the first edition: the holograph score, the copy of the solo part made for Joachim in February 1879, the orchestral parts, and the piano arrangement."
21 Schwarz, "Joseph Joachim and the Genesis of Brahms's Violin Concerto," 503.
22 Ibid.
23 Ibid., 509. Also see Ibid, 514: "Aware of the 'unusual difficulties,' Joachim offered ossias for players with smaller hands. He also insisted on moderating the tempo of the Finale by reinstating 'ma non troppo vivace' with the explanation 'otherwise too difficult.'"
24 Donald Franics Tovey, *Essays in Musical Analysis, Vol. III: Concertos* (London: Oxford University Press, 1936), 164: "Joachim's works are full of technical difficulties produced with unconscious ease."
25 Karen Leistra-Jones, "Improvisational Idyll: Joachim's "Presence" and Brahms's Violin Concerto, op. 77," *19th-Century Music* 38/3 (2015): 243–271.

26 Geiringer, *Brahms, His Life and Work*, 255.
27 The holograph located at the Library of Congress (*Library of Congress, ML/31/.H43a/no. 43/Case*) was undoubtedly the score used by Brahms for the Leipzig premiere on 1 January 1879. The red-ink changes in the holograph's solo violin line were entered not by Joachim but by the music editor Robert Keller (1828–1891). He transferred the corrections from Joachim's personal copy of the solo violin part into said holograph. Schwarz, 512: "In several places there are discrepancies with the final printed version which indicates last-minute changes during the proofreading."
28 Call number: US-Wc, ML/31/.H43a/no. 43/Case.
29 Schwarz, "Joseph Joachim and the Genesis of Brahms's Violin Concerto," 518.
30 Ibid., 514.
31 Katharina Uhde, *The Music of Joseph Joachim* (Woodbridge, UK: The Boydell Press, 2018), 318.
32 Heather Platt, *Johannes Brahms. A Research and Information Guide*, 2nd edn (New York and London: Routledge, 2012), 354: "Gozzi's *Das laute Geheimnis* and *König Hirsch* are among the works he considered as sources for a libretto. Nevertheless, changes in public taste in opera and the influence of Wagner probably deterred him from writing the type of number opera he preferred."
33 I have previously referred to Joachim's obsessively repetitive three or four-note figures as "trapped motives," see Uhde, *The Music of Joseph Joachim*, 122.
34 Uhde, *The Music of Joseph Joachim*, 286–287.
35 Because the interviews were conducted to learn more about other's views on performing passage work, this falls under the category of "about what"-research and does not meet the criteria of "research with human subjects." Ethical clearance was nevertheless provided by Valparaiso University.
36 Karin Hellqvist Interview on November 7, 2022.
37 Camilla Köhnken email dated November 8, 2022.
38 Anna Scott email dated 4 November 2022.
39 *Being in Practice-Based Research*. https://www.youtube.com/channel/UCTalnpgtOnTv-urHcS-9HTw, accessed 1 March 2024.
40 LeGuin, *Boccherini's Body. An Essay in Carnal Musicology*, 14: "Anyone who performs old music or who has written about ist history can attest to identifying with composers. The identification can be … somehow reciprocal. I will contend two things here: first, that the sense of reciprocity in this process of identification is not entirely wistful or metaphorical, but functions as real relationship; and second, that this relationship is not fantastic, incidental, or inessential to musicology. … Because the performer's relationship to the work of art must have an extensively explored bodily element, a performing identification with a composer is based on a particular type of knowledge which could be called carnal."

INDEX

Page numbers in **bold**: detailed discussions
Page numbers in *Italics*: examples/Illustrations

A
Adorno, Theodor, 110
Agoult Marie d', 266
Åkerman, Henriette, 232
Albert, Prince of Saxe-Coburg and Gotha, 73, 77, 91, 103, 242
Alexander, Anne Joanna, 65
Alstyne, Egbert van, 127, 128
  "Darkies' Spring Song", 128, 130
Amati, Nicola, 45
Andersen, Hans Christian, 65
André, Johann Anton, 253
Apostel, Hans Erich, 102
Appy, Jean Henri (Henry), 55
Aranyi, Jelly d', 239, 240
Arendt, Hannah, 108, 111
Arling, Charles, 134
Aristophanes, 64
Arnim, Achim von, 106
Arnim, Bettine von, 191, 197
Arnstein, Fanny Itzig von, 141
Asti, Eugene, 168
Attwood, Thomas, 252, 253
Auber, Daniel, 235

B
Bach, Johann Sebastian, 32, 34, 37fn14, 46, 62, 69fn5, 97, 104, 141, 142, 144, 146, 151, 152, 153fn9, 154fn17, 162, 171, 177, 190, 193, 213, 214, 243, 244, 247fn29, 253, 255, 265, 275, 278fn5, 288
  Cantata, BWV 28, 171
  Cantata, BWV 139, 142
  Cantata, BWV 161, 143
  Cantata "Christ ist erstanden", BWV 276, **146**
  Chorale "Befiehl du deine Wege", BWV 270, **143**
  Fugue in C major, BWV 545, 32
  Fugue in E-flat major, BWV 552, 190
  Fugue in E major, BWV 878, 32
  Fugue in E-flat major, "St. Anne", BWV 552, 32
  Orgel-Büchlein, BWV 276, 146

Cello Suite (unspecified), 45
St. Matthew Passion, 46, 62, 143, 145, 154fn17
Triple Concerto (either D minor, BWV 1063 or C major, BWV 1064), 265, 278n5
Well-Tempered Clavier, BWV 846–893, 265
Bach, Carl Philipp Emanuel, 141, 143
Bach, Johann Christoph Friedrich, 141
Bach, Wilhelm Friedemann, 141
Ball, Ernest R., 131
Barnett, John, 69fn11
Barnett, Robert, 253
Barnum, P. T., 53
Bartels, Adolf, 165
Barthes, Roland, 222
  Writing Degree Zero, 229fn44
Bartholomew, William, 83, 84, 85, 86, 92fn12
Basevi, Giacobbe, *see* Giacobbe Cervetto
Bauck, Wilhelm, *231–237*
  Romance, *233*
Beethoven, Ludwig van, 31–35, 39, 52, 96, 100, 104, 120, 189, 190, 202, 203, 204, 207, 215, 244, 264, 265, 270
  Andante favori WoO 57
  An die ferne Geliebte, **203,** 204, 207
  Beethoven's last works, 32
  Beethoven trios (various), 42
  Cello Sonata No. 3 in A major, Op. 69, 43
  Fidelio, 239, 265
  Grosse Fuge, Op. 133, 32, 36fn11
  Piano Concerto No. 5 in E-flat major, Op. 73, "Emperor", 117, 264
  Piano Sonata No. 7 in D major, Op. 10 No. 3, 190, 192
  String Quartet No. 10 in E-flat major, Op. 74, "Harp", 34, 244
  String Quartet No. 13 in B-flat major, Op. 130, 32
  String Quartet No. 14 in C-sharp minor, Op. 131, *32–34*, 33, 34, 35, 36fn9
  Symphony No. 3 in E-flat major, Op. 55, "Eroica", 34, 115
  Trio in B-flat major, Op. 97, "Archduke", 46
  Triple Concerto in C major, Op. 56, 42
  Violin Concerto in D major, Op. 61, 49, 292
Bendemann, Eduard, 123
Benecke, Paul Victor Mendelssohn, 243
Benedict, Julius, 193

Index

Benedicks, Josephine, 231
Benedicks, Henriette, *see* Henriette Åkerman
Bennett, John. R. Sterndale
Bennett, William Sterndale, 65, 69fn11, 192, 249–259
   Fantasie in A major, Op. 16, 249
   Impromptu, Op. 12 No. 2, 250
   Lord Byron's Poem of Parisina, Op. 3, 254
   Piano Concerto No. 2 in E-flat major, Op. 4, 253
   Piano Concerto No. 3 in C minor, Op. 9, 252
   Piano Sonata in F minor, Op. 13, 249, 250
   Romanza, Op. 14 No. 2, 250
   Suite de pièces, Op. 24, 249
   Three Diversions for piano four hands, Op. 17, 251
   Three Romances, Op. 14, 250
   Zion oratorio, 254
Benny, Jack, 59fn51
Berg, Alban, 102
Berio, Luciano, 213, 215, 222
   Sinfonia, 222
Berlin, Irving, *127–137*
   A Pretty Girl is like a Melody, 133
   Ev'ry Little Movement, 132
   Herman, Let's Dance That Beautiful Waltz, 132
   I Wish I Had a Girl, 132
   I Wish I Had My Old Girl Back Again, 132
   Tell Her in the Springtime, 134
   That Mesmerizing Mendelssohn Tune ("The Mendelssohn Rag"), 127, 129, 130, 131, 132, 135, **136**
   The Arab's Dream, 132
Berlioz, Hector, 44, 264, 268, 272
   L'enfance du Christ, 272
   Symphony *Roméo et Juliette*, 268
Berwald, Franz, 235
Bishop, Henry, 119, 239, 242
Blocket, Karl Maria von, 117
Boccaccio, Giovanni, 65
Boccherini, Luigi, 284
Bottesini, Giovanni, 55, 239, 242
   Grande Allegro di Concerto in E minor, 55, 242
Böhm, Joseph, 58fn18
Böhm, Karl, 109
Böhmer, Carl, 191
Börne, Ludwig, 264
Brahms, Johannes, 43, 49, 97, 100, 105, 201, 205, 206, 207, 209, 211, 214, 215, 228fn7, 240, 243, 244, 245, 268, 274, *283–298*

Cello Sonata No. 2 in F major, Op. 99, 43
Double Concerto in A minor, Op. 102, 43
Piano Sonata No. 3 in F minor, Op. 5, 205, **206**, 209, 211fn26
Vier Ernste Gesänge, Op. 121, 214
Violin Concerto in D major, Op. 77, 49, 283, 285, 286, 287, **289**, 290, **291**, 293, 296
Brand, Max, 102
Brauenfels, Walter, 102
Braunfels, Walter, 110
Breitkopf & Härtel, 46, 50, 83, 87, 208, 231, 232, 250
Brendel, Franz, 268
Brentano, Clemens, 106
Bronsart von Schellendorf, Hans, 274
Bruch, Max, 49, 97, 100
   Violin Concerto in G minor, Op. 26, 49
Bruckner, Anton, 102, 107
Bull, Ole, 235
Bülow, Hans von, 274
Burns, Robert, 73, 88, 89
Burke, Joseph, 55
Burney, Charles, 170
Busch, Adolf, 97
Buxton, Edward, 52, 76, 79, 80, 83, 84, 85, 92fn9, 92fn10
Byron, Lord, 74, 76, 80, 81, 88, 93fn19

C

Calatin, Agnes von, 119
   Ewige Nähe, 119
Calvisius, Sethus, 171
Campbell, Maud, 131
Cervantes, Miguel de, 65
Cervetto, Giacobbe, 41
Chatelain, Clara de, 74, 84, 87, 91
Cherubini, Luigi, 52
Chopin, Frédéric, 42, 190, 264, 265, 266, 267, 278fn8, 278fn11
   Cello Sonata in G minor, Op. 65, 46
   Introduction and Polonaise brillante in C major, Op. 3, 42
Cimador, Giovanni Battista, 252
Cimarosa, Domenico, 52
Clementi, Muzio, 252
Clodius, Christian August Heinrich, 67
Collins, Arthur, 130
Collins, Viotti, 54
Comstock, Anthony, 129
Couperin, Francois, 28f2
   Ordres, 28fn1

Index

Cossman, Bernhard, 43
Cramer, Johann Baptist, 252
Cristiani, Lisa, 45
Crotch, William, 193

D

Dante (Dante Alighieri), 68
Daverio, John, 201, 202, 205, 210fn2
David, Ferdinand, 42, 44, 46, 50, 56, 59fn51, 239, 251
    Variations (unspecified), 239
Davidov, Karl, 44
Davies, Fanny, 240, 244
Davies, Peter Maxwell, 223
    Taverner Fantasias, 223
Davison, James William, 79, 242, 252
Debussy, Claude, 218, 255
    Children's Corner, 218
de la Motte-Fouqué, Friedrich, 167
Devrient, Eduard, 62
Dickens, Charles, 119
Dirichlet, Rebecka, 63, 65, 67, 68, 145, 178fn6, 181, 197
Disney, Walt, 135
    Fantasia, 135
    Silly Symphonies, 135
Donizetti, Gaetano, 45
    Romanze, 45
Douglass, Frederick, 128, 129
Dragonetti, Domenico, 41
Dreyschock, Alexander, 264
Dvořák, Antonin, 244
Dwight, John Sullivan 55

E

Eaton, Doris, 133
Eco, Umberto, 215
Eckermann, Johann Peter, 269
Edward VII, King of the United Kingdom and the British Dominions, and Emperor of India, 77
Edwards, Gus, 131
Egk, Werner, 109
Eichendorff, Joseph von, 81, 84, 85, 93fn27, 161, 216, 217, 220, 221
    Auf einer Burg, 216, 220
    Die Mainacht, 216
    Frühlingsnacht, 216
Eisler, Hanns, 102
Elgar, Sir Edward, 245
Eliot, T. S., 222
    The Waste Land, 222
Ellington, Duke, 134
    Rhapsody Jr., 134
Elvers, Rudolf, 157, 158
Ernst, Heinrich Wilhelm, 54
Eskeles, Cäcilie Itzig von, 141
Essler, Fanny, 119
Eutropius, 67
Ewer, J. J. (publisher), 50, 74, 76, 77, 79, 80, 81, 83, 84, 87, 88, 92

F

Fachiri, Adila, 239, 240
Fetis, F. J., 103, 250
Fillmore, Millard, 192
Fillunger, Marie, 240, 244
Fitzenhagen, Wilhelm, 43
Fleming, Paul, 82
    "Pilgerspruch", 82
Flesch, Carl, 104
Franchomme, Auguste 46
Frederick II, King of Prussia, 141
Frederick William III, King of Prussia, 141
Freud, Sigmund, 214, 216
    The Interpretation of Dreams, 228fn24
Furtwängler, Wilhelm, 103, 105, 107, 109

G

Gade, Niels, 46, 97
Gans, Eduard, 67
Ganz, Moritz, 44, 46
Geibel, Emanuel, 189
Geiringer, Karl, 286, 297fn16
Gerhardt, Paul, 145
Gershwin, George, 134
    Rhapsody in Blue, 134
Gieseking, Walter, 109
Gluck, Willibald, 171, 189
Goethe, Johann Wolfgang von, 74, 84, 86, 95, 97, 103, 149, 158, 195, 199fn30, 264, 268, 269
    Faust, 95, 149, **150**, 154fn30, 155fn31, 195, 199fn31, 228fn3
Goldschmidt, Otto, 55, 288
Gounod, Charles, 265
Grabau, Johann Andreas, 42, 43
Grenser, Friedrich Wilhelm, 42
Grove, Sir George, 45
Günther, Julius, 233, 236
    "Elfdrottningen", 233
Gurtner, Wilhelm, 241
Gustav III, King of Sweden, 231

Index

H

Hallé, Lady *see* Norman-Neruda, Wilma
Handel, George Frideric, 193
   Messiah, 274
Hanslick, Eduard, 275
Harlan, Byron, 130
Hartmann, Karl Amadeus, 110
Hassler, Hans Leo, 143
   Lustgarten, 143
Hauer, J. M., 102
Hausmann, Robert, 43
Haydn, Joseph, 34, 52, 53, 62, 69fn5, 240, 244, 252
   Piano Sonata in E-flat major, Hob. XVI:52, 34
   String Quartet, Op. 17 No. 6, 244
Heine, Heinrich, 150, 165, 167, 168, 171, 177, 216, 217, 220, 264
   Allnächtlich im Traume, 216
   Buch der Lieder, 166, 169
   Die Lotosblume, 216
   Lyrical Intermezzo No. 59, 168
Heinrich, Anthony Philip, *115–126*
   An Elegiac Impromptu Fantasia, 121
   Bohemia's Funeral Honours to Josef Jungman, 118
   compositions (various), 122
   General Taylor's Funeral March, 120
   La Promenade du Diable, 117
   The first Labour of Hercules, 117
   The Laurel and Cypress, 115, 118, 124
   "The Musician's Requiem", 115
   The Rübezahl Dance on the Schneekoppe, 115
   The Tomb of Genius, 115, 118, **119**, 121, 124
   To the Spirit of Beethoven, 118, 121
Hellmesberger, Georg (the elder), 51, 56, 57fn18
Hellmesberger, Joseph, 51, 56
Henschke, Eduard, 63
Hensel, Fanny (née Mendelssohn Bartholdy), 35, 37fn16, 44, 63, 64, 65, 73, 87, 90, 91, 102, *141–155*, *157–163*, *165–180*, *181–186*, 193, 194, 195, 196, 197, 199fn26, 199fn30, 239
   "Aglaë", 160
   Andante Maestoso (collaborative work with Fanny Hensel), 184
   "Bergeslust" H-U 466, 160
   Das Jahr, 142, 146, 149, 150, 152,
      "Februar", **149**
      "März", **147, 148**, 149, 152
   "Easter" Sonata, 184, 186fn8
   Italien H-U 157, 73

   Lieder für das Pianoforte, Op. 8 No. 3 ("Lenau"), 141, 162
   Lieder (research on), 157
   Lobgesang, 158
   Oratorium, 158
   Overture, 158
   Piano Sonata in G minor, **183**
   "Schloß Liebeneck", 197
   "Schwanenlied", Op. 1 No. 1, 168, 170, **172, 173, 174, 175, 176,** 177.
   Six German Songs by FMB and Fanny Hensel, 90
   String Quartet in E-flat major, 35, 37fn16
   Szene aus *Faust*, 195
Hensel, Wilhelm, 111, 123, 150, 199fn30
Herder, Gottfried, 268
Hill, Ureli Corelli, 127
Hiller, Ferdinand, 46, 51, 97, 107, 191, *263–281*, **276**, 278fn3
   Rhythmische Studien, 268–269
   "Spring" Symphony in E minor, 268–269
Hindemith, Paul, 95, 97, 102, 110
   one-act operas, 102
Hinrichs, Marie, 165
Hoffman, Gertrude, 129, 131
Hoffmann, Ernst Theodor Amadeus, 51
Hölderlin, Johann Christian Friedrich, 170, 179
Holloway, Robin, *213–226*
   Domination of Black, 215
   Scenes from Schumann, Op. 13, *213–226*
      "Dedication", 216
      "Dream Vision", **220,** 221, 223, **224**
      "Dream Visitation, 216, 217, 218, 220, 221, 226
      "Enchanted Forest", 220, 221, 226
      "Flowering Lotus", 216, 217
      "Moonlit Night", 216, 217
      "Spring-Night-Rounds", 216
Homer, 64, 68
Horace, 169, 170
Horkheimer, Max, 110
Horsley, Charles Edward, 52, 64, 65
Horton, John, 32
Hübner, Julius, 123
Humboldt, Alexander von, 116
Hummel, Johann Nepomuk, 239, 270

I

Immermann, Karl, 99, 112fn7

Index

J
Jacob, Heinrich Eduard, 49
Jaspers, Karl, 108
Jean Paul (Johann Paul Friedrich Richter), 69
Joachim, Amalie née Weiss, 327
Joachim, Harold Henry, 239, 242
Joachim, Joseph, *49–56*, 57fn13, 59fn33, 100, 105, 201, 207, 208, 209, *239–247*, 274, *283–298*
    Brahms/Joachim *Hungarian Dances*, 244
    Fantasie über irische [*schottische*] *Motive*, 288
    Fantasie über ungarische Motive, 288
    Hebräische Melodien, Op. 9, 283
    Hungarian Concerto in D minor, Op. 11, 289, **290, 291**
    overtures (various), 283
    Overture to Gozzi's *The King Stag*, 292
    variation works (various), 283
    violin pieces, 283, 288
    Violinschule, 51
    violin concertos (various), 283
Joyce, James, 221
    Ulysses, 221, 222
Jullien, Louis-Antoine, 53, 54, 56, 58fn29

K
Kalkbrenner, Friedrich, 264
Karajan, Herbert von, 109
Kaufmann, Philipp, 80, 88, 89
Keller, Hans, 32
Kessler, Harry Grad, 95, 96, 97, 99, 100
Kinkel, Gottfried, 191, 192, 193, 197
Kinkel, Johanna, née Mockel, married Matthieux, remarried Kinkel, *189-200*
    Hans Ibeles in London, 190
    Lieder, Op. 6, 198fn11
Kistner (publisher), 44, 202, 232, 233, 238fn20, 250
Klingemann, Carl (Karl), 92fn5, 166
Köchel, Ritter Ludwig von, 253
König, Marie, 119
Körner, Ludwig, 98
Krauss, Clemens, 109
Krenek, Ernst, 102
Kreutzer, Bernhard, 52, 58fn22
Kummer, Friedrich, 42, 45

L
Lang, Josephine, 119, 165
Lanjuinais, Victor, 67
Laemmle, Carl, 134, 135
    Mendelssohn's Spring Song, 134, 135
Laub, Ferdinand, 51
Le Hon (Lehon), Adolphe-Adrien, 54, 59fn36
Lenau, Nikolaus, 141
Léonard, Hubert, 59fn36
Lessing, Gotthold Ephraim, 65
Levy, Sara Itzig, 141
Lincoln, Henry J. (pianist), 52, 58fn23
Lind Goldschmidt, Jenny, 55, 59fn33, 118, 231
Lindblad, Adolf, 33, 36fn12, 235
Lindley, Robert, 41
Liszt, Blandine & Cosima & Daniel, 266
Liszt, Franz, 44, 210fn12, *263–281*, 264, 270, 277
    Fantasy and Fugue on the chorale "Ad nos, ad salutarem undam", 259, 275
    Faust Symphony, 271, 279fn23
    Mazeppa, 271, 279fn23
    Réminiscences de "Robert le diable", 413, 275
    The Gypsies and Their Music, 275
    Vallée d'Obermann, 156 / 5
Ludwig II, King of Bavaria ("Swan King"), 170
Lyser, Johann Peter, 27

M
Mahler, Gustav, 100, 105, 106, 108, 216
Mann, Heinrich, 95
    Der Untertan, 95
Manns, August, 54, 240
Marija Pawlowna Romanowa, Grand Duchess, 270, 279fn22
Marschner, Heinrich, 117, 120
Marx, Karl, 192, 198fn2
Mason, Daniel Gregory, 129
Mathieux, Johann Paul, 190
Maximilian II, King of Bavaria, 170
Mendelssohn, Felix, 19–27, 31, 32, 36, 45, 50, 52, 53, 54, 55, 56, 57fn13, 58fn18, *61–69*, *73–93*, *95–113*, *115–126*, *127–137*, *141–155*, 166, 181, 184, 190, 181, 192, 193, 194, 195, 197, 198fn10, *231–237*, *249–259*, 268
    "Ah! Tell Me Not", Op. 41, MWV SD 18, 73, 93fn21
    Andante Maestoso (collaborative work with Fanny Hensel), 184
    Antigone, incidental music, Op. 55, MWV M 12, 83, 84
    Assai tranquillo in b minor, 46
    "Befiehl du deine Wege", chorale

Index

adaptation, 142, 149
"By Celia's Arbour All the Night", MWV K 44, 74
Cantata *O Haupt voll Blut und Wunden*, 145
Capriccio R 23, 35, 36fn2
Cello Sonata No. 1 in B-flat major, Op. 45, 40, 42, 43, 44
Cello Sonata No. 2 in D major, Op. 58, 40, 43, 44, 45, 46, 47
Die beiden Neffen, 62
Die erste Walpurgisnacht, Op. 60, 87, 135
Duetto ohne Worte, Op. 38 No. 6, 250
Elijah, Op. 70, MWV A 25, 83, 87, 113fn22, 115, 141, 186fn9, 194, 198fn10
"Frühlingslied", MWV K 71 / Op. 19[a], no. 5
"Frühlingsglaube", Op. 9 No. 8, 75, 76, 87
Fugue in E-flat major, Op. 81 No. 4 R23, *31–35*, **31**, 32, **35**
"The Garland", MWV K 44, 74, 88
6 *Gesänge*, Op. 47, 83
The Hebrides Overture, "Fingals Cave", Op. 26, 41, 113fn22, 116, 135, 249
Lobgesang, 115
A Midsummer Night's Dream Overture, Op. 21, 42, 103, 104, 117, 135, 193, 249
A Midsummer Night's Dream incidental music, Op. 61, 87, 127, 135
3 Motets, Op. 69, 83
Octet in E-flat major, Op. 20, 40, 43, 44, 103
"Pagenlied", MWV K 75, 83
Piano Sonata in E major, Op. 6, 36fn2
Piano Trio in C minor, Op. 66, MWV Q 33, 83
Piano Quartet in C minor, Op. 1, 61, 255
4 Pieces for String Quartet, Op. 81, 31, 32, 35
"Pilgerspruch", Op. 8 No. 5, MWV K 31, 75, 76, 84, 87, 92fn3
Romance sans paroles, 45
Romances, two, on texts by Byron, MWV K 76 and K 85, 74
Rondo Capriccio, 135
Sechs Lieder, Op. 59, **79**, 87
Sieben Characterstücke, Op. 7, 19
Sinfonia VI, 142, 143, **144**
Six German Songs by FMB and Fanny Hensel, **90**
Song without words, Op. 19 No. 4, 19
Songs without words, Op. 19 No. 5, 250
Song without words, Op. 19b No. 1, MWV U 86, 21
Song without words, Op. 19[b] No. 2, MWV U 80, 21, 181, 182, **184**
Song without words, Op. 30, 19
Songs without words, Op. 30 No. 2, 250
Songs without words, Op. 30 No. 3, 250
Song without words, Op. 30 No. 5, MWA U 97, 21
Song without words, Op. 38 No. 1, 21
Song without words, Op. 53 No. 2, MWV U 109, *23–27*, **24**, **25**, **26**, **27**
Song without words, Op. 62 No. 6 ("Spring Song"), 127, 129, 132, 133, 134, 135
Song without words, MWV U 88, 22
Songs without words (unspecified), 56, 118, 141, 234
Songs, Op. 57, MWV SD 26, 77, **78**
Songs (various), 76, 77, 80, 81, 83
St. Paul, Op. 36, MWV A 14, 84, 99, 115, 127, 242, 249
String Quartet No. 1 in E-flat major, Op. 12, 34, **35**
String Quartet No. 2 in A minor, Op. 13, 31, 32, 34, 36fn2, 250
String Quartet No. 3 in D major, Op. 44 No. 1, 251
String Quartet in E-flat major, MWV R 18, 32
String Quartet in E major (unfinished), two movements R 34 and R 35, 35
Symphony No. 1 in C minor, Op. 11, 40
Symphony No. 3 in A minor, Op. 56 "Scottish", 103, 109, 249
Symphony No. 4 in A major, Op. 30, 249
Symphony No. 5 in D major/D minor, Op. 107 "Reformation", 32
Trauermarsch, Op. 62 No. 3, MWV U 177, 21, 28fn9
Variations concertantes, Op. 17, 40, 41, 43
Violin Concerto in E minor, Op. 64, *49–56*, 57fn18, 113fn22
Mendelssohn, Abraham, 141, 151, 152
Mendelssohn Benecke, Paul Victor, 239, 243
Mendelssohn, Henriette, 61
Mendelssohn, Lea (née Salomon), 43, 61, 141, 151, 231
Mendelssohn, Moses, 64, 98, 106, 141, 151
Mendelssohn, Paul, 40, 43, 44
Mendelssohn, Rebecka, *see* Rebecka Dirichlet
Mendelssohn, Sebastian, 61

Index

Mendel, Hermann, 170
Merk, Joseph, 42, 44
Meyerbeer, Giacomo, 96, 97, 98, 102, 107, 111, 233, 235, 275
Meysenburg, Malwida von, 196
Miller, Josephine von, 22, 27
Monteverdi, Claudio, 171
    "Lamento della Ninfa", 171
Moore, Thomas, 74, 88, 117, 120
Moscheles, Ignaz, 28fn7, 45
Moser, Hans Joachim, 105, 106
Mozart, Leopold, 253
Mozart, Wolfgang Amadeus, 32, 52, 57fn17, 62, 69fn5, 98, 100, 115, 120, 171, 189, 192, 193, 240, *249–256*, 260fn79, 260fn82
    Don Giovanni, 171, 254
    Piano Concerto in A major, K. 414 (386a), 252
    Piano Concerto in E-flat major, K. 449, 252
    Piano Concerto in G major, K. 453, 254
    Piano Concerto in D minor, K. 466, 252
    Piano Concerto in A major, K. 488, 254
    Piano Sonata in F major, 251
    Quintet in G minor, K. 516, 252
    Requiem, 115
    Rondo in A major, K. 386, 253
    String Quartet in B-flat major, K. 589, 250
    Symphony No. 39 in E-flat major, K. 543, 250
    Symphony No. 40 in G minor, K. 550, 252
    Symphony No. 41 in C major, K. 551 "Jupiter" 32
    Variations in C major, K. 265, 254
Müller, August, 43
Müller brothers, four siblings and quartet players employed at the duchy of Brunswick, 43
Müller, Wilhelm, 166

N
Nabokov, Nicolas, 95
Napoleon (Napoleon Bonaparte), 96, 201, 275
Nietzsche, Friedrich, 197, 284, 296fn2
    Philosophy in the Tragic Age of the Greeks, 284, 296fn2
Norman-Neruda, Wilma, 241

O
Offenbach, Jacques, 45, 107
    Adagio and Bolero, 45
Orff, Carl, 102, 109

Ovid, 67, 170

P
Paganini, Niccolò, 55, 56, 119
Parry, Sir Hubert, 245
Pfitzner, Hans, 100, 107,
Piatti, Carlo Alfredo, 45, 239, 244
Plato, 170
Pollitzer, Adolf, 58fn18
Purcell, Henry, 171
    Dido and Aeneas, 171

R
Radziwill, Anton Fürst, 61
Rameau, Jean-Philippe, 28fn2
Rapetti, Michele, 55
Reger, Max, 97
Reich, Nancy, 201, 209fn1
Reinicke, Carl, 97
Rellstab, Ludwig, 191
Rembrandt (Rembrandt Harmenszoon van Rijn), 68
Reményi, Edouard, 54
Richter, Hans, 240
Riehl, Wilhelm Heinrich, 102
Ries, Ferdinand, 189
Ries, Franz Anton, 189
Rietz, Eduard, 40, 46
Rietz, Julius, 40, 46, 47, 50, 54, 69fn11
    Cello Concerto in E major, Op. 16, 46
Riterman, Lewis, 128
Romberg, Bernard, 41, 46
Rosen, Charles, 203, 204, 207, 223, 229fn45
Rosier, F. W., 88, 89
Rossiter, Will, 128
Rossini, Gioachino, 170, 190, 235
    Otello, 170
Rückert, Friedrich, 216
    Widmung, 216

S
Saint-Cricq, Caroline de, 264
Sainton, Prosper, 52, 53, 54, 59fn31
Salomon, Bella Itzig, 141, 151
Sarasate, Pablo de, 59fn51
Schadow, Friedrich Wilhelm, 111
Schenker, Heinrich, 105, 106
Schiller, Friedrich, 64, 98, 103, 268
Schinkel, Karl Friedrich, 110
Schlegel, Dorothea, 190
Schlesinger, Adolph Martin, 61

Index

Schlesinger, Maurice (Moritz Adolf) (publisher), 61, 233
Schmidl, J. B. (conductor), 51
Schnittke, Alfred, 215
Schoenberg, Arnold, 100, 102, 107
Scholes, Percy, 241
Schreker, Franz, 100, 106
Schubert, Franz, 45, 170, 171, 177, 244, 264
   "Auf dem Wasser zu singen", 170
   Ave Maria, 45
   "Das Lied im Grünen", D. 917, 177
   "Die junge Nonne", 244
   "Gruppe aus dem Tartarus", 171
   Quartettsatz, 171
   Wanderer Fantasy in C major, Op. 15 D 760, 264
Schultze, Wilhelm, 55
Schumann, Clara, 7, 23, 42, 44, 54, 100, 165, 195, *201–211*, 239, 251, 274
   Concerto for piano and orchestra, Op. 7, 251
   Romance variée, Op. 3, 203, 210fn4
   Romance in B minor, Op. posth, *201–212*, **206, 207, 209**
   Romance on a Theme by Robert Schumann, Op. 20, 210fn4
   Three Romances for violin and piano, Op. 22, 208
      Romance, Op. 22 No. 2, **208**, 209
Schumann, Robert, *19–23*, 28fn2, 42, 44, 55, 97, 98, 100, 104, 162, 163, 191, 195, 197, *201–211*, *213–226*, 249, 250, 251, 252, 254, 267–268
   Auf einer Burg, Op. 39 No. 7
   Carnaval, Op. 9, 28fn2, 214
   Dichterliebe, Op. 48, 225
      "Allnächtlich im Traume", Op. 48 No. 14, 216, 217, **225**
   Die Lotosblume, Op. 25 No. 7, 216
   Die Mainacht, Op. 39 No. 5, 216
   Fantasy, Op. 17, *202–212*, **204**, 210fn12
   Five Pieces in Folk Style, Op. 102 (*Fünf Stücke im Volkston*), 42
   Frühlingsnacht, Op. 39 No. 12, 216
   Kerner-Lieder, Op. 35, 215
   Kinderszenen, Op. 15, 213
   Lieder (unspecified), 213, 217
   Liederkreis, Op. 39, 214
   Romance for oboe and piano, Op. 94, 208
   Widmung, Op. 25 No. 1, 216
Schurz, Carl, 197
Schwarzkopf, Elisabeth, 109

Scott, Sir Walter, 65, 66
Servais, Adrien-François, 46
   Souvenir de Spa, Op. 2, 46
Shakespeare, William, 64, 99, 245, 285
   A Midsummer Night's Dream, 95, 99
Sharon, Ula, 134
Shaw, George Bernard, 102
Shostakovich, Dmitri, 108, 229fn32
Sibelius, Jean, 55, 108
Simon, Adolf, 56, 57fn18
Sivori, Camillo, 52, 54, 55, 58fn21
Soldat, Marie, 241
Sophokles, 67
Souchay, Marc André, 20, 21, 27
Spohr, Louis, 55, 189, 278fn1
Stockhausen, Karlheinz, 110
Strauss, Richard, 100, 107, 108, 109
Stravinsky, Igor, 213
   Le Baiser de la Fée, 213
Sullivan, Arthur, 46
Sulzer, Georg, 202
   Allgemeine Theorie der schönen Künste, 202

T

Tartini, Giuseppe, 244
Taubert, Wilhelm, 191
Tennyson, Alfred, 68
Terence, 65
Thorwaldsen, Bertel, 111
Tippett, Michael, 223
   Fantasia Concertante on a Theme of Corelli, 223
Toch, Ernst, 107, 110
Tovey, Sir Donald Francis, 239, 255, 286
Tchaikovsky, Pyotr Ilyich, 55, 213
Türk, Daniel Gottlob, 68
Tyson, Grace, 130, 131

U

Uhland, Ludwig, 65, 98

V

Varnhagen, Rahel von, 166
Vaughan Williams, Ralph, 223
   Fantasia on a theme of Thomas Tallis, 223
Victoria, Queen of Great Britain and Ireland, Empress of India, 73, 77, 87, 91, 103
Vieuxtemps, Henri, 55, 241
Viotti, Giovanni Battista, 288
Virgil, 170
Vogelweide, Walther von, 98

Index

W

Wagner, Richard, 95, 97, 100, 103, 105, 107, 108, 111, 112fn2, 128, 197, 213, 218, 219, 220, 221, 222, 268, 270
   Das Judenthum in der Musik, 100
   Der Ring des Nibelung, 268
   Tristan und Isolde, 218, 222, 229fn33, 229fn35
   Siegried, 221
   Zukunftsmusik, 197
Walker, Ernest, 240
Weber, Carl Maria von, 53, 98, 99, 117, 189, 193, 253
   Konzertstück, 117
Webern, Anton, 102
Weill, Kurt, 95, 102, 106
Weist-Hill, Henry, 54
Wellesz, Egon, 110
Whitehouse, William, 244
Wieck, Friedrich, 42, 205
Wielhorsky, Count Mateusz, 44
Wieniawski, Henri, 54, 56, 241
Wittich, Ludwig Heinrich, 233
Wittmann, Carl Franz, 44

Y

Young, Cyrus "Cy", 135
   Mendelssohn's Spring Song, 135

Z

Zelter, Carl Friedrich, 62, 142, 255
Zemlinsky, Alexander, 100
Zimmermann, Bernd Alois, 110

www.ingramcontent.com/pod-product-compliance
Lightning Source LLC
Chambersburg PA
CBHW032002220426
43664CB00005B/108